Praise for *Bill Snyder: My Football Life and the Rest of the Story*

It is a great honor to share with you the impact that Coach Snyder continues to have on my life and so many others because of the opportunity that he gave Kansas kids many years ago. I didn't have a single Division I-A football scholarship offer when I graduated from nearby Riley County High School and I only had a scholarship offer from a couple of Division I-AA schools. However, it had been my lifelong dream to be a member of the Kansas State football program and to play for one of the greatest coaches in the history of college football.

I decided to walk on at Kansas State and see what happened.

When Coach Snyder arrived at Kansas State prior to the 1989 season, the process of beginning the greatest turnaround in college football history started with bringing young players into the program, giving them an opportunity, teaching them hard work and midwestern values, and helping them to enhance all aspects of their lives, including as a player. Coach Snyder gave Kansas kids a chance and he initiated a walk-on tradition that eventually spanned two generations. He built his program with overlooked, chip-on-the-shoulder players, who developed under a great coaching staff and helped to set the foundation.

As the Kansas State walk-on tradition flourished over the years, Coach Snyder gave Jon McGraw an opportunity. Jon arrived from our hometown as a walk-on player, developed into a great talent, and went on to enjoy a great NFL career. I aspired to be like Jon and live out my own dream of playing under Coach Snyder while dedicating myself to be the best student, person, and player possible. It's a process began the very first day I reported to the Vanier Football Complex.

Then one day, my life changed forever.

Joan Friederich, Coach Snyder's secretary, called me and said that Coach wanted to speak with me inside his office. I was a redshirt sophomore walk-on safety who hadn't played in a game—and Coach wanted to speak with me. My instant reaction: *What did I do over the last couple of weeks that must have angered Coach?* It turned out that my friend Marcus Watts, a redshirt sophomore wide receiver, had been invited to the same meeting. Once seated, Coach shared that upon watching us in practice, he wondered if it might benefit us both if Marcus switched to safety and I switched to wide receiver. Of course, I trusted Coach and I believed that he would put me into the proper situation to be successful for the good of the team.

I only had one concern. I had never played wide receiver in my life.

Coach Snyder deserves all of the credit possible, and I know that he always deflects the credit to everyone else, but what he built and maintained at Kansas State for nearly three decades was legendary. I'll never forget the time someone asked Coach, "How do you continue to coach the old-school way?" He replied, "Well, it's not the old-school way; it's just the only way I know how."

I have always been a major proponent of Coach's ideology. Coach's work ethic, the 16 Wildcat Goals for Success, and his simple request to become a little bit better every day served as the blueprint that elevated Kansas State to great heights—and to a No. 1 national ranking in two different stints as head coach. Nothing replaces hard work, doing things the right way, and possessing a strong value system. Those are traits that my wife Emily and I instill into our children Royal (11), Brooks (six), and Adda (four), as we get to watch them grow up in Riley. Today I find myself sharing many of the values that Coach Snyder taught me as I coach Royal's fifth-grade athletic teams.

Although Coach Snyder's greatness is well documented and his legacy as one of the all-time greatest coaches is set in stone, there is one fact that goes unmentioned far too often and that everyone reading this book should recognize: Coach Snyder was the first coach to fully implement the quarterback run game. Coach started the national trend. I heard the stories about Urban

Meyer visiting Coach Snyder and how Coach tutored him on the quarterback draw, the zone-read, and the option game. All of that began when Coach mapped out a plan upon witnessing the raw athletic talent of Michael Bishop and developed him into the most dangerous player in college football his senior year. Coach was a step ahead of everyone else, and it forced defenses into the unique position of having to prepare for Kansas State differently than any other team. It is important for everyone to always remember how Coach Snyder's innovation of the dual-threat quarterback changed the course of college football and bled into the NFL.

I'm so appreciative of Coach Snyder and the opportunity that he gave me and countless other Kansas kids over the course of his career. He made my lifelong dream of playing for him and being a part of his program come true. Eventually, I was blessed to fulfill another dream of playing professional football, which changed my life in ways I never thought possible.

Thank you, Coach, for your impact upon Kansas State University, Manhattan, the state of Kansas, and college football. Most of all, thank you for giving myself and so many other young people an opportunity to live out our dreams.

—*Jordy Nelson*
Kansas State, 2003–07
2007 Consensus All-American

The hole was immense. President Jon Wefald knew things must change, or a future competing in the Big 8 Conference was in jeopardy. After 93 years competing on the gridiron, Kansas State had a career record of 299–509–1. The ever-optimistic and fighting Wildcats were headed for the Missouri Valley Conference—or worse. In 1988 President Wefald charged athletic director Steve Miller with what seemed like an impossible task: find a football coach who could win in the Little Apple.

Nobody could have imagined the impact that Miller's choice would have on the football program, the university, the Manhattan community, the state of Kansas, and college football. From 1989 to 2005 and 2009 to 2018, coach Bill Snyder and his teams demonstrated that core values, a strong work ethic, and execution were key to success on and off the field.

As a native of Holton and a fourth-generation Kansan, I lived through Kansas State's worst losses and heard all of the jokes. When I learned that a soft-spoken offensive coordinator from the University of Iowa was taking over as head coach, I wasn't overly optimistic.

Then Kansas State beat North Texas State in 1989. Then Kansas State beat Kansas in 1991. Then Kansas State won the 1993 Copper Bowl. On the plane ride home from our first bowl victory in history, an elderly woman dressed in purple paused as she reached the middle of the plane. She shouted, "Anyone ever seen our boys play that way? God bless Bill Snyder! Everyone a Wildcat!" The rest of the passengers erupted in cheers.

The excitement surrounding Kansas State football spread across the entire campus. There was a renewed spirit among the students, faculty, and generations of alumni regarding the football team, the university, and the Manhattan community.

Little could we predict that Kansas State, the losingest football program in the history of college football, would earn a No. 1 national ranking in 1998 and again in 2012. Bill invited me into the locker room after games. Even after a big win, he always remained soft-spoken in addressing his players. He said, "Represent your teammates, your school, and yourself well. Respect our opponents. We've all been there." Then he would turn to me and say, "We have our assistant tight ends coach with us tonight, senator Pat Roberts. Coach Roberts, would you like to make any comments?"

For years I urged Bill to throw the football to the tight end, which was a rarity within his offensive system and a topic that remains a serious debate between us. In those moments when I addressed the team, I always took the opportunity to apologize to our tight ends because my duties in Washington, D.C., had prevented me from attending practice and I always assured them that I was collaborating with Bill and designing new plays to involve them in the passing game. Of course, the players always met my comments with laughter.

It was the privilege of a lifetime to witness the joy that one man and his teams could bring to thousands of people. Bill provided the blueprint for anyone to reach their potential. Through the virtues of hard work and dedication, that opportunity for success still exists today and shouldn't be taken lightly.

After Bill retired in 2018, I hoped to finally meet him for that steak dinner we had long discussed. But Bill was always busy—either speaking to a youth group in a small town in southwest Kansas, or attending a Chamber of Commerce meeting, or visiting a Boys & Girls Club. That hardly came as a surprise, though, as he had always dedicated his life to coaching and mentoring.

After my 40 years of public service and knowing Bill and his family for most of that time, I feel very privileged to call him a friend. To me, the real Bill Snyder is the kind of man we desperately need in our world today. Now Bill won't buy into all of that, but everyone that knows him will. After all of that, you know, I just wish he could've thrown it to the tight end a little bit more.

—Pat Roberts
Senator of Kansas, 1997–2021

Coach Bill Snyder is a Kansas treasure. I first knew him as the successful football coach of my husband's alma mater, Kansas State University, where he created a powerhouse team from what had been one of the worst programs in the country. My husband Gary and other alums were thrilled to see their beloved Wildcats recruit talented players and begin to win.

But Bill Snyder was different as a college coach. He was known as someone who really believed education was primary and, in addition to building great football skills, he wanted to help develop great people. And that's the program that he built at Kansas State University and the culture that he developed. Then Bill Snyder chose to retire in 2005.

At the time, I served as governor of Kansas and I knew that Coach Snyder was one of the most popular people in the state. I took a chance, reached out to him upon his retirement, and asked him if he would consider being involved in a new statewide effort I wanted to launch. Although communities across the state of Kansas possessed quality programs to help those kids who needed a caring adult in their lives, many of those programs needed more adult volunteers. We didn't create a new program, but we decided that we could play a role in mapping the volunteer opportunities in each town and then recruit volunteers to match the needs.

And who better to lead that effort than coach Bill Snyder?

When I approached Coach to ask if he would lend a hand to our effort to recruit more mentors for kids, he enthusiastically accepted my offer. He was amazing. I originally expected that he would issue an endorsement. Instead, he enthusiastically embraced the initiative and agreed to lead it. Coach helped to raise funds and establish an office with staff to catalog and organize the program resources. Coach Snyder was so effective not only because he was beloved throughout the state, but also because he was willing to share his own life experience. He told audiences about growing up in a single-parent household and shared stories about the mentors who made a difference in his life. Coach Snyder led the Kansas Mentors Program, raised money, recruited volunteers, gave speeches, and served as speaker for public service announcements that positively impacted thousands of kids throughout the state of Kansas.

I tried to convince Coach Snyder to consider an elected office because I believed that he would be so successful, but he decided to return to his passion and he rejoined the Kansas State football program. He continued to lead the Kansas Mentors program even while serving as head football coach.

Bill Snyder has been a good friend, a wonderful coach, and an amazing volunteer leader. He has made such a positive contribution to Kansas. We are proud to be his adopted state and know that there are legions of young people—football players he coached, coaches he trained, and children who were mentored— whose lives were greatly improved because of the work of coach Bill Snyder. On their behalf, we say thank you to a remarkable man.

—Kathleen Sebelius
Governor of Kansas, 2003–09

From 1936 to 1986, Kansas State University had seen 11 football coaches, nine athletic directors, and four presidents. None of them was able to transform our football program—not even close. The 12th hire for a new football coach came just before I became the new president of Kansas State in July of 1986. The new hire was Stan Parrish. In his three years as the head football coach from 1986 to 1988, Stan's record was two wins and 30 losses.

How bad was our football team over the decades? I accepted an invitation to speak to the Kansas City Rotary Club in October of 1986. I talked about the challenges of increasing enrollment, building a new library and art museum, raising more private funds, and increasing our research funding. At the end of my speech, I briefly mentioned that Kansas State had to create a successful and competitive football team. At the end of my speech, former All-American basketball player Rick Harman approached me and said: "Young man, don't ever talk about football again because it can't be turned around. It can't be done."

How bad was our football program in the eyes of the American sports media? On September 4, 1989, Doug Looney of

Sports Illustrated wrote an article about the Kansas State football program after we hired coach Bill Snyder in November of 1988. The title of the *Sports Illustrated* article was brutal: "FUTILITY U—KANSAS STATE, WINLESS SINCE 1986, HAS ONE CLAIM TO FAME: IT IS AMERICA'S MOST HAPLESS TEAM."

Looney's second paragraph was riveting: "When it comes to college football, *nobody does it worse than* Kansas State. After 93 years of trying to play the game, the Wildcats' record is 299–509–41—dead last among the 106 schools in Division I-A."

Indeed, the Kansas State football program had a horrible record. Equally important: our football facilities were arguably the worst facilities in Division I-A. Our football stadium was mediocre. The turf was in horrible shape. Our press box was without question the worst press box of all 106 Division I-A schools. Our parking lots were all gravel. Virtually the majority of high schools in Texas and the Kansas City metropolitan area had much better football facilities than Kansas State.

When we were looking for a new head football coach in the fall of 1988, we interviewed or at least talked to 18 different head coaches and assistants like Jack Bicknell of Boston College, John Fox of Pittsburgh, Bill Thornton of TCU, and Frank Solich of Nebraska. At least 18 different coaches told us they were not interested in our job. One day, our associate athletic director, Jim Epps, was looking though a Big Ten Conference media guide on each team's coaches. He spotted the name Bill Snyder. He was the offensive coordinator at the University of Iowa. Jim was quite impressed with the achievements of Coach Snyder and the number of excellent passers that he had developed over his time in the program.

We were lucky. Coach Snyder decided to visit Kansas State. Many of us talked with Coach Snyder. Personally, I talked to Bill for an hour. Like everyone else, I liked Coach Snyder immediately. I had a lot of questions, and Bill answered every one. Many K-Staters have asked me what I saw in him that would make him the perfect choice for our new football coach. Here is what I saw: I saw a person who had vision and a gameplan to turn around our football program. I saw a person who had an incredible work ethic. I saw a person who had both total dedication and a never-give-up attitude. I saw a person who was an optimist and who always had hope. I saw a person who would insist on hiring great assistant coaches, and that he and his nine assistant coaches would form a first-rate team of doers, recruiters, and coaches.

After we hired Coach Snyder, I never doubted that he would win games and transform the entire football program. I knew that we would soon have a very competitive football team. But I did not know that Kansas State would go to 11 straight bowl games between 1993 and 2003 and that we would beat KU and Missouri virtually every year in the 1990s. I certainly did not know that Kansas State would win 11 games in six out of seven years between 1997 and 2003 and, finally, I did not know that we would win the 2003 Big 12 Championship against undefeated and No. 1-ranked Oklahoma. Our Snyder-led football program accomplished so much by 1999 that former Oklahoma head coach Barry Switzer said, "Bill Snyder isn't the coach of the year and he is not the coach of the decade. He is the coach of the century."

Just think: Coach Snyder was one of very few coaches in 1988 who had any interest at all in our head football coaching job. But in his 27 years as our head coach, Bill compiled a fantastic record of 215 wins and 117 losses. My dear friend and great colleague, Bill Snyder, earned five national Coach of the Year honors, seven conference Coach of the Year honors, and was a member of the 2015 College Football Hall of Fame class.

Let me summarize the greatness of Bill Snyder. For any generation there are only a handful of iconic and legendary coaches. Indeed, there are only four or five coaches that you can call a "transformational head football coach" for each generation. Between the 1920s and 1960s, you can include Knute Rockne, Frank Leahy, Bud Wilkinson, Bob Devaney, Woody Hayes, and Paul "Bear" Bryant. From the 1970s to today, you have to include Barry

Switzer, Don James, Darrell Royal, Pete Carroll, Eddie Robinson, Nick Saban, Dabo Swinney, Bob Stoops, Urban Meyer, and, of course, Bill Snyder.

Bill Snyder will forever be remembered as a transformational head college football coach for the ages. And Bill will always be my dear friend and colleague for the ages.

—Dr. Jon Wefald
Kansas State University President, 1986–2009

The first time I met Bill Snyder was at Chins in Las Vegas, Nevada, after the 1991 football season. Ernie Barrett and Snyder were on a fund-raising trip on behalf of the Kansas State football program and athletic department. My old friend Ron Fogler and I owned a golf course management company called Jim Colbert Golf, and we had public and private golf courses from California to Florida. We agreed to meet with Barrett and Snyder to discuss a possible monetary gift over dinner. I grew up in Prairie Village, Kansas, and went to Kansas State on a football scholarship from 1959 to 1964. I also finished my collegiate golf career as the runner-up at the NCAA Championships before turning pro and finishing seventh all time in career earnings as a member of the Champions Tour. I hadn't paid attention to Kansas State football in forever. I just knew that they didn't win any games. Ernie said, "Coach Snyder won seven games this past season."

I sat across from Snyder and I said, "What? You won seven games? Heck, if you win seven games again, you can have any job in the country and you better take one of them. You can't keep winning seven games—not at this place. It just can't be done."

Snyder just looked at me. Dinner conversation was all about Kansas State football. Snyder didn't say a word.

On the morning of December 29, 1993, I took Ernie, Bob Krause, and Howard Sherwood to play a round of golf at Tucson National in

Arizona. That evening we were going to watch Kansas State play in the 1993 Copper Bowl. Kansas State was playing in just its second bowl game in history, and I wasn't going to miss it. Kansas State won eight games in the regular season, which marked its most wins in a season since 1931. After Barrett, Krause, Sherwood, and I finished golfing, we went back to the hotel. I walked through the front door carrying my golf bag across my shoulder and passed a crowd of Kansas State fans as I headed toward the hallway. Suddenly, the Kansas State football team appeared in the hallway and walked toward me. The fans stood on both sides of the hallway and began cheering. I moved out of the way of the players, who just stared straight ahead, and I backed up against the wall with my golf bag in front of me. Of course, my name was sewn onto the front of my golf bag.

Snyder came out last. He walked straight down the hallway with his head down. He wouldn't have known me from Adam except for the fact that I stood with my golf bag with my name sewn across it. Snyder never turned his head. He never looked up. He simply walked by me and said, "And you said it couldn't be done."

I was hooked. Coach and I became really good friends. Everybody needs someone to talk to. During football season I called him between 11:00 PM and midnight to try and loosen him up as he sat in office watching videotape on the last leg of his 18-hour workday. There was no harder worker in America. I knew that he needed a break. Most of the time, we just talked about life. That's just the nature of our relationship. He's as good of a friend as you can have. When I live in Colbert Hills during the summer, Snyder comes over every Thursday night, and we pour a glass of wine and just talk. Every time we eat at Colbert's restaurant, he orders the same sandwich and he visits with the children or anyone who stops by our table. He is an amazing man.

Three things have made the biggest difference in the 166-year history of Manhattan: Kansas State University, the Tuttle Creek Dam, and Bill Snyder. Jon Wefald and Steve Miller hired Snyder in 1988, and the rest is history. Colbert Hills Golf Course wouldn't exist if Snyder hadn't built that football program. Hell, Kansas State probably wouldn't even have football.

—Jim Colbert
Kansas State Football, 1959–64
35-Time Winner on PGA Tour and Senior PGA Tour

Whether it is being a husband to Monica, a father to Livea (12) and Lexie (9), a professional football player, or a teacher and coach of young men, I am blessed for the values that coach Bill Snyder instilled into me many years ago, which continue to touch virtually every aspect of my life each day. For the first 18 years of my life, my parents, Jim and Marcia, were a part of my life virtually every day as I grew up in Smith Center, Kansas. Their love, guidance, emphasis on hard work, and on being a good person set the foundation for my life, and I am forever grateful. However, it becomes equally difficult to fully define Coach Snyder's impact upon my life simply because his teachings also became a part of my existence.

Coach Snyder instilled a vision and mind-set into his players, which combined with hard work and commitment, gave us the opportunity to succeed on the football field at Kansas State University while the many life lessons Coach Snyder taught us along the way positioned us for success long after we left Manhattan.

One day I am going to tell my grandchildren the story of how I was fortunate enough to play for one of the greatest, if not the greatest, college football coaches to ever live. I will tell them about how I enjoyed a certain degree of success at Smith Center High School, about how I had always dreamed of playing major college football, and about how Coach Snyder was the only Division I-A head football coach who gave me that opportunity. I will tell them about how Coach Snyder transformed Kansas State from the worst program in the history of college football into one of the best programs in the country and how he told me, "You need to come here" and how grateful I was to be at the right place at the right time. We became a national powerhouse. My junior year, we were within a whisker of playing for the national championship. But above all else, I will tell my grandchildren about how Coach Snyder taught us to build and maintain the work ethic and drive necessary to separate ourselves and become successful.

There was no magic wand for Kansas State football. Coach Snyder came to Kansas State with a vision and he instilled a mind-set into the football program, the university, the state of Kansas, and K-Staters across the world. Coach Snyder set expectations for us and taught us that we could accomplish our goals, but he emphasized that there were no shortcuts, which is what made him so great. Outside of his innovations on the offensive side of the ball within the X's and O's and his penchant for identifying and grooming young talented coaches was an insatiable desire to develop and maximize the talents of his players. He demanded the very best out of everyone every single day. There is a small defining line between success and failure, and he knew that when everybody unselfishly committed themselves to those values and consistent improvement, we could achieve something special. Those little things over time just became something bigger, which is important for us to remember in all areas of our lives.

Although the outside expectations for Kansas State grew over the years, Coach Snyder's expectations for us remained the same and he never deviated from his approach. He was always consistent. So many coaches in Coach Snyder's position might've used Kansas State as a springboard for another job. He didn't leave. He said that we were a family. He loved the Kansas State people. It is important that we never forget his greatness and loyalty.

From the very beginning, Coach Snyder gave young men the opportunity. He asked us to work hard. He said, "Here is how you're going to develop and be successful."

Coach Snyder knew the way. He showed us the road map and shared a value system that would help guide us to success beyond football. Now I share those same values with my own children.

—Mark Simoneau
Kansas State Linebacker, 1995–99
2012 College Football Hall of Fame Inductee

I have enjoyed many blessings in my life, one of which was being able to play college football. As a naïve high school senior, I was recruited to play football at Kansas State. I had no idea of the impact coach Bill Snyder would have on the football program and, more importantly, how he would eventually influence my own life.

By now everyone knows the name Bill Snyder and his importance within the history of college football. Shortly after his hiring in November 1988, he initiated the process of building the foundation for Kansas State. Under his watch the program went from being called "Futility U" by *Sports Illustrated* to becoming one of the best college football programs in the country.

I was fortunate to be at Kansas State between 1990 and 1994, as Coach Snyder laid the groundwork for an incredible run in which he led Kansas State to 19 bowl games and earned numerous Coach of the Year honors. I was a starting linebacker on the first bowl team and served as a team captain on the second bowl team, and the program eventually went to 11 straight bowl games under Coach Snyder.

Playing for Coach Snyder was and, always will be, an honor. Not only is Coach one of the greatest head coaches in college football history, but he is also one of the best teachers. In those important formative years, Coach not only developed us to win football games, but he also developed us to be successful in an area even more important—life.

No one was driven to win more than Coach Snyder, but he believed that his calling was much greater than wins and losses. Coach focused on developing leadership—a trait that would enable us to be quality leaders for our families, in our communities, and guide us as we worked to make a positive impact upon society.

Football is the greatest team sport in the world and football teaches us so many valuable lessons. Coach Snyder took it one step further and applied our lessons to all areas of life. Little did I know, the virtues that Coach Snyder instilled into us—hard work, a commitment to daily improvements, an attention to detail, and a drive and determination to be the very best—would carry over to this very day in whatever we do.

Coach taught us to dream, to believe, and not to limit ourselves. On October 20, 1993, we were a nationally-ranked team and beat Oklahoma for the first time in more than two decades. I remember the postgame celebration and how Coach stopped by our lockers to congratulate the defense on our performance. We went on to become the first Kansas State team in history team to finish a season in the national rankings.

Coach believed in us and helped us to play beyond our capabilities. He truly pushed us to our limits in an effort to develop toughness along with an expect-to-win mentality. Although some of our opponents perhaps possessed superior talent, our team was always better prepared and carried a belief that we were the tougher and more-determined team on the field.

Although Coach Snyder engineered the greatest turnaround in college football history, he achieved an even greater accomplishment: he gave thousands of young men such as myself the necessary foundation to reach our dreams. Coach Snyder is and will always be my Coach. I still call him "Coach," and that will never change.

—Kirby Hocutt
Kansas State Linebacker, 1990–94
Texas Tech Athletic Director

I met Bill Snyder when he was hired as offensive coordinator at the University of Iowa in 1978. In 1988 he became the 32nd head football coach at Kansas State University. He retired in 2005, returned to the sideline in 2009, and recorded 215 victories, two Big 12 Championships, and took Kansas State to 19 bowl games over two tenures prior to his retirement in 2018.

Those who perhaps gauge Coach Snyder's success in terms of wins or titles fall short of understanding the true magnitude of his impact upon Kansas State University. Not only did Coach Snyder positively affect the team's on-field results, but he transformed the attitude, confidence, respect, resolve, and expectations in all areas of the Kansas State community, which in turn positively influenced the pride and perception of the entire university.

Coach Snyder's impact is also apparent in the vast array of facility improvements on campus. His enduring influence is embodied in the spirit and determination to excel academically, athletically, and individually, which is now the expectation of the Kansas State family. Coach Snyder created this culture by always doing the right thing and through his devotion to an unwavering belief in the value of personal growth through discipline and a commitment to daily improvement. The true measure of Coach Snyder's legacy isn't found in his coaching records, awards, accolades, or new facilities. It exists in each of our hearts, minds, attitudes, and commitment to personal achievement. It flourishes in the Kansas State family through the enduring impact he has had on the profile and prestige of the university.

At his introductory news conference as Kansas State head football coach, Bill Snyder said, "It's a tremendous challenge here, and I think the opportunity for the greatest turnaround in college football exists here today…and it's not…and it's not one to be taken lightly."

Thank you is perhaps the most powerful phrase in the English language. We say thank you to Coach Snyder for all that he has meant to us. His thank you to us lies in how his profound influence will serve to guide each of us in the years ahead.

In order to understand Coach Snyder's success as head coach, it becomes important to appreciate the people, experiences, opportunities, and decisions that influenced his life. In our 40-plus years of friendship, I believe the word that best epitomizes Bill is *humility*. After Kansas State beat North Texas State for the first victory of Bill's career, I called and excitedly congratulated him on his success. Bill replied, "It was going to happen sometime" and was unemotional and pragmatic. To Bill, the success has never been about the moment or him individually.

Thank you, Coach Snyder. You turned opportunity into reality and forever changed our lives.

—*Thomas D. Ross*
Longtime Friend

Coach Snyder attended our Wednesday night formal dinner as a guest speaker at Pi Kappa Alpha fraternity in the early 1990s. We listened attentively and were so happy and proud that he spent time with us and talked to us. We saw Coach Snyder on this giant pedestal, so it was awesome to be in the same room with him. I always admired Coach Snyder because of his ability to turn a football program, which was destined to lose and on the verge of being kicked out of the conference, into a winner by instilling strong values and work ethic into young men. At a time when Nebraska, Oklahoma, and Colorado had the blue-chip recruits, Coach Snyder taught his players that if you worked harder, studied harder, trusted the coaches, were in the right position, and never gave up, that you could come out victorious at the end of the day. He taught two generations of football players that it didn't matter where you came from. He believed you were great, he believed in you, he wanted you at Kansas State, and you would practice every day, earn your degree, and win at life. He is a leader of men and he changed the mind-set of an entire university and an entire group of people in the state of Kansas that wore purple instead of blue and red. He completely replaced the loser mentality with the 16 Wildcat Goals for Success and encouraged his players to expect to win.

As I got to know Coach Snyder, I felt like he knew everything about me and that I was a close personal friend. I still remember meeting Coach for the first time. Sean Snyder had spoken with his dad, and they asked me to speak to the football team, so I flew in from California on the Friday before the KU game in 2011. Coach gathered around us at midfield inside Bill Snyder Family Stadium. Although I co-starred in a top-rated TV show and had won an Emmy, there was no reason for Coach Snyder to know me. He certainly wasn't in his office at night watching TV, so Sean told his dad a little bit about me before I gave this talk. Coach went on to deliver one of the most memorable introductions in my entire life. He said, "Gentlemen, this is a great Wildcat who started here and made his way to Hollywood, California, and found his success. He is an Emmy award-winner on the TV show *Modern Family*. Please give a big Wildcat welcome to…Eric Summerset."

There was a pause. Sean stood by his dad and shook his head in laughter. In that moment I thought to myself, *Okay, I just have to accept that my name is now Eric Summerset* and I went on and spoke to the team about the specialness of Kansas State. A few days later, Coach sent me a thank you note and he apologized for mispronouncing my name. The next time I saw coach was when I spoke at the Kansas State pep rally the night before the 2012 Cotton Bowl. Coach shook my hand and said, "I just wanted to apologize again in person for calling you Eric Summerset."

I said, "Coach, listen, after that happened, I went to the *Modern Family* producers and said, 'We need to change my name in the credits to 'Eric Summerset.' Then I told my agent, 'Coach Snyder has changed my name to 'Eric Summerset.''" There's a great photo of Coach and I laughing during our little exchange at the pep rally.

What Coach failed to realize was that he had unknowingly began a national trend. After he called me "Eric Summerset," people called me "Eric Greenstreet," "Eric Stonebridge," "Eric Bridgestreet," "Eric Silverstreet," "Eric Stonesand," "Eric Streetset," "Eric Summerstreet," and on and on. I shared my Coach Snyder story during an appearance on *Ellen*. I wanted America to know that not only was Coach Snyder this wonderful man and the first coach to implement the Wildcat offense, but also that Coach Snyder was also the first person to call me by a different name.

After the 2018 season, I wrote Coach a letter. It is an absolute fact that Coach Snyder is one of the greatest coaches in the history of college football. He taught generations of young men about intrinsic values, commitment, unity, gave a blueprint for leading a successful life. I wrote the letter because I just wanted him to know how much he meant to me, the Kansas State people, the entire state of Kansas, and to the world of college football. At the bottom of my letter, I wrote, "With warm regards, Eric Summerset."

My parents Vince and Jamey live in Kansas City, Kansas. My dad owned L & V Outlet in Leavenworth for 35 years and retired around 2000. Dad is now 78 years old and he was diagnosed with chronic leukemia in July 2017. Some days are good, and some days are not so good. When I shared my dad's diagnosis with Coach Snyder, he said, "I'd like your dad's phone number. I'd love to talk to him." My dad said that he spoke with Coach Snyder for a while and that it really brightened up his day.

On October 19, 2019, I flew in from California and visited my parents in Kansas City before I drove to Manhattan for the Kansas State–TCU football game. Just before halftime I visited Coach Snyder in his stadium suite. Coach said, "How's your dad doing?" I said, "He's kind of having a rough day. He wasn't feeling too well when I went over and saw him."

After the game I called my parents, and my mom said, "Coach Snyder called your dad, and they spoke for about 15 minutes." The moment I had left Coach's suite, Coach called my dad. That will forever be the example of how to make an impact on someone's life.

—*Eric Stonestreet*
1996 Kansas State Graduate
2010, 2012 Emmy Award Winner

I have always respected Coach Snyder and I followed him throughout his career at Kansas State. A friend of mine went to William Jewell College and first told me about Coach Snyder. I was excited that Coach Snyder might turn around the program, though so many people didn't believe that he could really do it. Our children, Mauria and Eric, attended Kansas State in the 1990s, and it was incredible how Coach Snyder turned Kansas State into winners. Many years passed, and soon after I was diagnosed with leukemia in 2017, I received a surprise phone call from Coach Snyder, and he offered some words of encouragement. I couldn't believe that he took time out of his busy schedule to call me. He called me at exactly the right time. I'm still battling leukemia. The medication—even the experimental medication—has proven ineffective. Doctors can't believe that I'm still getting around, but I keep fighting every day. And Coach Snyder perks me right up. He has a wonderful way of doing that. When he calls, we talk about everything. It's so uplifting. I'm nobody, and he makes me somebody. I'd like to call him my friend. Bill Snyder is the kindest man I've ever spoken to. I feel blessed to have him call me.

—Vince Stonestreet
Eric Stonestreet's Father

The pages that lie ahead will surely be one of the sweetest journeys of your life if you are ready and willing to receive them. I met Coach Bill Snyder in 2019 after covering him for many years as a national sports-talk radio host. For most of my 17-year career, I had heard about this giant of a man. His character loomed large in the college football world—and still does to this day. The moment I met Bill, I knew we were going to be lifelong friends. Sometimes, you just know. Bill is that good, that golden. Whether you are a CEO, a stay-at-home mom, a die-hard football fan, or a coach, get your pen and paper ready to take notes because anyone who comes into contact with Bill is better for it. His stories are invaluable, and the lessons are unforgettable. I count his friendship as one of the greatest gifts of my life. Through these pages, you will get to know the same man I call one of my dearest friends and you, too, will be better for it!

—Rachel Baribeau
Former College Sports Nation *on SiriusXM Host*

When I hear the name Bill Snyder, a few words or phrases immediately enter my mind: transformational leader, meticulous, loyal, tireless work ethic, development, uber-planner, organized, among many others. I have had the luxury of being able to call Coach Snyder a coworker, a teammate, and even a friend, and his impact on Kansas State University, Manhattan, the state of Kansas, and the world of college football is unmatched.

Being inside the program, I was able to see firsthand the impact he had on every person involved, from players to staff and even his coaches. When Bill Snyder walked into a room, everyone sat a little more straight in their chairs and everyone listened. He made everyone around him better in every sense of the word, and it was truly remarkable.

But as much as I enjoyed the football aspect of our relationship, I truly enjoyed getting to know his family. Sharon is a joy to be around, and naturally my relationship with Sean was one that grew into something special. Family means so much to Coach Snyder, and it showed.

He will always be considered one of the greatest football coaches of all time at any level, but more importantly, he will always be remembered as a loyal, caring individual who made everyone around him better. Simply put, there will never be too many more Bill Snyders in this profession. Or better yet, there may never be too many more Bill Snyders in this world.

—Wyatt Thompson
Voice of the Wildcats, 2002–present

Kansas State is my school. I played there. I bleed purple. I love football and enjoy it when others can experience the greatness of the gridiron. Bill Snyder brought that joy to us. He not only made Kansas State football relevant; he made it a football school—a dream come true for me and my fellow Wildcats fans. From the very first practice I saw in 1989, I believed that Coach Snyder would succeed in building the program. I said, "We are going to win," even though we had not won a game in the previous two seasons. Coach had high expectations for every aspect of the football program. He instilled discipline and toughness and utilized the best strategies and finesse to find ways to win. His Wildcat 16 Goals for Success not only helped players and coaches succeed, but they also set the example for me to be a better person.

Bill Snyder greatly contributed to my successful broadcasting career. I was very young and had no experience or training when I joined the booth in 1986, and we had a small listening audience. As Kansas State experienced success and our listenership grew, so did my creditability as a knowledgeable source among Kansas State fans and sports media, including in Kansas City, which has the biggest market in our region. Without Coach Snyder's ability to put a superior product on the field, no one would've known my capabilities as a broadcaster.

My two sons, Stanton and Landry, grew up engrossed in Kansas State football, and both lived out their dreams of playing for Coach Snyder. Coach Snyder accepted them into his program, taught them how to become better men, and maximized their football talents to help my school win games, which allowed me to experience some of the greatest moments that life has to offer.

—*Stan Weber*
Kansas State Quarterback, 1980–84
Kansas State Radio Network, 1986–present

BILL SNYDER

MY FOOTBALL LIFE
AND THE REST OF THE STORY

Bill Snyder
and D. Scott Fritchen

TRIUMPH
BOOKS

In Fond and Loving Memory of:

Matthew Snyder	*Blair Detelich*	*Ben Griffith*
Troy Miller	*Tad Melichar*	*Bryan Hickman*
Bob Cope	*Dylan Meier*	*Evan Simpson*
Nancy Bennett	*Elijah Alexander*	*Richard Boyd*
Anthony Bates	*David Garrett*	*Mike Lykins*
Scott Marshall	*Bob Elliott*	*Steve Moten*

Each who were valued and loved members of our football family.

Library of Congress Cataloging-in-Publication Data available upon request

This book is available in quantity at special discounts for your group or organization. For further information, contact:

Triumph Books LLC
814 North Franklin Street
Chicago, Illinois 60610
(312) 337-0747
www.triumphbooks.com

Printed in U.S.A.
ISBN: 978-1-63727-093-6

Design by Sue Knopf
Production by Patricia Frey
Photos courtesy of K-State Athletics unless otherwise indicated

CONTENTS

CHAPTER 1

GROWING UP IN
ST. JOSEPH, MISSOURI

"Not many coaches in college football history have the credentials that coach Bill Snyder had during a career that spanned nearly 30 years. The same year that Coach Snyder became Kansas State head football coach, Bob Stull brought his coaching staff from UTEP to Missouri. I was Stull's offensive line coach. Twenty-three years later, I was hired as head coach for the Kansas City Chiefs, and Coach Snyder was still rolling up wins at KSU. AMAZING!!! All done with class and grace. He is truly a great man."

—Andy Reid, Kansas City Chiefs head coach

I am 82 years of age, and my mother remains the most prominent mentor in my life. My mother, Marionetta Owens Snyder, was an amazingly caring woman. From the day of my birth October 7, 1939, in St. Joseph, Missouri, the most significant thing in my mother's life centered around instilling into me a value system that would last the entirety of my life. She was 4'9" and never weighed 100 pounds in her life, but she was the strongest person I've ever known.

Shortly after I was born, my parents and I moved to Chicago, then on to Kansas City, Missouri, before settling in Salina, Kansas, where I began elementary school. One of my earliest childhood memories involved one late-night excursion in Kansas City. I was supposed to be asleep, but I climbed out of my bedroom window, scurried down the street, and climbed into my friend's bedroom window. We played quietly inside his room. It wasn't long before my parents found me and took me home.

Our family moved to Salina when my father, Thomas, a salesperson for the CertainTeed Roofing Company, was transferred to a new location. Today, I still drive by the duplex where we lived on Crawford Avenue, which at the time closely intersected the I-70 interstate. Since then, the growth of Salina has pushed the interstate nearly a mile farther west.

Our home in Salina was located catty-corner to the home of another family with a boy who was several years older than I. Despite my best efforts to play with the older children on our block, they wanted nothing to do with a first grader, but I persisted nevertheless. Then one day, that older boy wound up and punched me. When I ran into our house and told my father, he said, "I want you to go back outside and punch that kid back." When I hesitated, my father grew stern. "Either you go out there and punch that kid," he said, "or I'm going to give you a whipping." So I went outside. The older boy beat me up.

My mother and father separated when I was six years old. My father moved to Omaha, Nebraska, where he died at age 47. Upon my parent's separation, my mother and I returned to St. Joseph and moved in briefly with my paternal grandparents, who owned a large home at the foot of King Hill, which rose a thousand or so feet above their property. From the top of the hill, I could see most of southern St. Joseph. One block from my grandparents' house was the St. Joseph Fire Department station house where my uncle worked as a firefighter. He liked to take me to the second level of the building and let me slide down the old-fashioned brass pole. I enjoyed many hours climbing those stairs and sliding down that pole.

When my parents eventually divorced, my mother and I left my paternal grandparents and moved in with her parents, George and Marie Owens. I was in the first grade. My grandfather worked for the Burlington Northern Railroad and owned and operated Owens Motor Company on St. Joseph Avenue. My grandfather, who was 101 years old when he died on September 20, 1996, served as deacon and Elder Emeritus at King Hill Christian Church. He was so very genuine and never short-changed or deceived anyone in his life. He didn't allow vulgar language on his car lot or inside his office. My grandfather gave me my first job, and I earned 10 cents per car that I washed on his lot. My grandparents, who celebrated their 70th wedding anniversary prior to my grandmother's death in 1986, were of great importance in my life. They taught me about values, living a faith-based life, and always gave my mother and me their loving support.

My mother was hired as a sales clerk in lady's apparel on the third floor of Townsend & Wall, a prominent five-story department store in the downtown district. We moved into a one-room apartment on the second floor of a large home at 508 North Fifth Street, which was owned by a wonderful lady named Mrs. Kellog. Our apartment was one block from the city auditorium and three blocks from the department store, which allowed my mother a short walk to work. My mother received no money from the divorce settlement, and her paycheck served as our only income. She didn't drive, never owned a driver's license in her life, and could not afford transportation. Eventually, she became an inventory buyer for the department store. She traveled each year to New York City to select the latest fashions to ship back and sell at the St. Joseph store. She always went to see the Rockettes or a show when she visited New York City.

Our second-floor, one-room apartment had a bathroom and a small kitchen. I slept on a Murphy bed, which I pulled out from the wall in the living room. My mother slept on a cot that I pulled in from the outside landing and unfolded for her every night. Eventually, my mother was able to purchase a 10" black-and-white television set, which sat adjacent to my bed. We enjoyed watching *The Late Show* while lying in our beds at night. When I put my bed up each morning, my bedroom disappeared.

I attended Hall Elementary School, which was walking distance from my grandparents' home and a bus ride from our apartment across town. My mother gave me 30 cents per day for a bus fare and an additional 25 cents to purchase school lunch. I learned that if I awakened early and walked to school then I could pocket the money. Then instead of eating lunch, I could walk one block from school to the grocery store and buy a package of baseball cards, the ones with the bubble gum. Over the years I collected hundreds of baseball cards, which my mother gave away. The collection would be valued at more than $1 million today.

My mother worked 12 hours per day, six days per week at Townsend & Wall. She enrolled me at the YMCA, which was six blocks from our apartment, so that she did not have to worry about me after school. My mother spoke with the YMCA staff, so they knew my expected time of arrival. She told them to call her if I was late or absent, but I was never late or absent. I really enjoyed the YMCA. There were pool tables, Ping-Pong tables, numerous board games, a basketball court, and a running track on the second floor. However, I most enjoyed the YMCA swimming pool, which began my love of competitive swimming. Eventually, I joined the YMCA swim team, which allowed us to swim competitively at events across the state.

In third grade my mother moved me to nearby Washington Grade School, which was just six blocks away from our apartment. My principal was Ruth Houston, whose sister worked with my mother, so she was particularly caring and mindful of our situation. My third-grade teacher was Helen Cronkite, who was also very compassionate and caring. Her brother was Walter Cronkite, who spent 19 years as CBS Evening News anchor and became known as "the most trusted man in America."

A six-foot high stone wall lined the edge of the front lawn of the home next to us. I spent hours throwing a ball against the wall and fielding it. I played tackle football with the neighborhood boys on the red brick street. We got banged up quite a bit. Nearly all of my activities involved sports or some kind of competition.

The city auditorium near our apartment held crowds of 12,000 people and hosted national basketball tournaments and city high school games. I also saw the Harlem Globetrotters play inside the auditorium. The auditorium served as a premier venue for professional wrestling, featuring the big name wrestlers, as seen on TV, and the wrestlers signed autographs for kids after each match. Since I had no money to purchase a ticket, I usually snuck into the auditorium through a rear entrance. Upon doing so one night, I witnessed a scene by happenstance that crushed my longstanding belief that professional wrestling was real. While walking by the locker room, I stole a glance at four wrestlers, who were laughing with one another over beer and cigarettes moments before they were supposed to step into the ring and fight each other. I never saw professional wrestling the same way ever again.

As I grew older and attended Lafayette High School, my mother once again gave me bus money for the ride a few miles across town, and once again I saved the money and walked to school. I believe that I became frugal over my lifetime because of those circumstances. Twenty-five cents got me a sandwich at the downtown Maid-Rite. One dollar got me two Maid-Rite sandwiches and an afternoon movie at the nearby historic Missouri or Electric Theaters.

I played high school football, basketball, and baseball, and also competed in track and field. In addition, I coached swimming, taught swimming lessons, and swam competitively at our local swim meets. St. Joseph had a very nice baseball stadium where we played some of our high school games. The stadium also hosted Western Association minor league games. I saw Mickey Mantle, Roger Maris, and others play baseball on that field before they were promoted to the major league and enjoyed Hall of Fame careers.

When I began high school, the young people in my neighborhood were juniors and seniors, and some of them liked to drink beer. My mother had a sixth sense for when I was leaving the apartment to hang out with these older friends. She stood at the front door and said, "Absolutely not." She may have been 4'9" and never weighed 100 pounds in her life, but she was so mentally and emotionally strong. I feared my mother in that regard, but deep down I knew she was teaching me to make positive choices, and she always looked out for my best interests. That made a major difference in my life.

Although I loved to play sports, I didn't care as much about academics and I sometimes cut class to visit L.R. Violett's barber shop or to walk home. I had constructed a basketball hoop from a wire hanger with thick string as a net and taped it to the top of the door to my Murphy bed, and whenever I skipped class, I went home and shot baskets with rolled-up socks. Basil Hoehn knew where to find me. Mr. Hoehn, our vice principal in charge of discipline, was very demanding, but he truly cared about students. If Mr. Hoehn discovered that I was absent from class, he usually drove to my apartment and brought me back to school.

Even those times when he didn't come to the apartment, I almost always returned to school for wood shop class. I loved working on the wood lathe. I put different-colored wood together and carved what I believed to be beautiful vases, lamps, and bowls. I gave many of them to family members as gifts. A few of them currently sit on my desk at home. Wood shop class was on the first floor of our high school. Some of my female friends—Paula Eaton, Gayle Riley, Martha Morgan, Eleanor Courtney, and my first wife Judy Friederick— had lockers nearby. We always met at the lockers and talked between classes. They were all very dear friends.

St. Joseph had a "Teen Town" event for high school students on Saturday nights at the chamber of commerce building three blocks from our apartment. It was our introduction to socializing and dancing. The boys stood on one side of the room, and the girls stood on the other side, and every once in a while, someone worked up the courage to ask someone to dance. Since many of my friends were girls, they tried to teach me to dance, but it proved to be an unsuccessful endeavor.

I practiced a sport virtually every day after school. Richard Shrout was my varsity basketball coach. He knew I was from a single-parent home and became more than a coach, which impacted my life and helped shape my perception of coaching as well. I had two different head coaches during my varsity football career—Bob Matheson and then Jerry Hampton. Both coaches were very significant because they cared about young people as well as the sport itself. I played halfback on offense and defensive back on defense. Although we ran a single-wing offense, Coach Mathison flirted with putting the quarterback under center. Then Coach Hampton became our head coach after arriving from William Jewell College, which utilized the single-wing offense, and he kept our offensive scheme intact. Our offensive design allowed me to throw the football. Thus the halfback pass was born, and my teammates called me "Lefty" because I was a left-handed passer. I somehow earned All-City and All-Pony Express Conference honors as a halfback.

It wasn't the last time that I would be a part of an offense that utilized personnel in unique ways. In my coaching career, we really initiated the trend of putting the quarterback in the shotgun alignment and we essentially built a single-wing offense. Whereas the tailback received the ball in the single-wing, we moved the quarterback into that spot to receive the ball. Whereas the quarterback typically handed off the ball to a tailback, our quarterback also posed a constant threat in the running game, which served to our advantage because we now had an additional offensive player in the blocking scheme. We had a blocker for every defender, plus our running quarterback, which gave us a numbers advantage inside the box and consequently allowed us the opportunity to execute successful plays.

Although Chuck Long was one of the best passing quarterbacks in Division I-A history at the University of Iowa, we also utilized Chuck in the quarterback running game at times. However, our quarterback running game steadily became more predominate during our time at Kansas State University. The offensive scheme eventually evolved into what we see today at both the college and NFL level, as teams utilize their quarterback out of the shotgun formation, and the quarterback has the option to ride the running back and eventually give the ball to him or keep the ball and run. We had that offensive scheme in our playbook from the very beginning. We also ran our quarterback on every play which our running back would run Years later, 36-year-old Bowling Green head coach Urban Meyer visited me in Manhattan in hopes of adding the quarterback running game to his playbook. When Urban went to the University of Florida, the offense served him well with Tim Tebow at quarterback.

Our high school football team didn't conduct summer workouts like we see now at the high school level, so I worked as a lifeguard and taught swimming lessons at Krug Park Pool, and the St. Joseph Country Club hired me to coach its swimming team. I quickly discovered that I needed transportation, so I made my first major purchase. I bought a 1946 Chevrolet from my grandfather for $50.

I actually received my first automobile for my 16th birthday. My father, who at the time lived in Omaha, gave me a bright yellow Mercury convertible, but it was a short-lived luxury. Over the course of two short weeks, I became more sociable and came home later and later at night. My mother called my father and said, "Come get this automobile. I'm not asking you; I'm telling you. Come get this automobile, or it is going into the Missouri River." The river was just five blocks from our apartment.

Although I always desired to play football at a major college, I received no scholarship offers following my graduation from Lafayette High School in 1957. Unbeknownst to me, my mother had saved up all of her money over the years for my education, which enabled me to walk on at the University of Missouri. I was the eighth-string quarterback on the freshman football team under head coach Al Onofrio. Obviously, I wasn't in line to become a productive member of the team. Meanwhile, I also performed miserably in the classroom during my first semester. My 12 credit-hour course load included introduction to education, required courses for men, composition, air science, American government, and general zoology. I received one B, two C's, and three F's, and I had 56 class absences.

I returned home feeling extreme guilt due to the fact that I had wasted my mother's hard-earned money. That spring semester I enrolled at St. Joseph Junior College, which did not have a football team, and I played guard on its basketball team. In order to earn tuition money, I taught swimming lessons and worked at Noma Lites, a historic St. Joseph-based company that manufactured Christmas tree lights. It was a simple job. I boxed strands of Christmas lights and pushed them down a circular slide to the store room five stories below. In a mischievous moment, I even slid down that slide myself. Just as I began to feel content working my jobs and attending the local junior college, my plan suddenly changed toward the end of that spring semester.

That's when I met a man named Dr. Norris Patterson, the athletic director and head football coach at William Jewell College in Liberty, Missouri. Perhaps as a favor to Coach Hampton, my high school football coach, Dr. Patterson asked me to join the William Jewell football team. Although I did not qualify for an academic scholarship at this non-athletic scholarship school, I qualified for a National Defense Student Loan in the amount of $400 and I worked two jobs cleaning the dormitory and doing janitorial work at the athletic facility until 10:00 PM each night. Eventually, I was awarded a $300 academic scholarship after I received three A's, three B's, and one D my first semester.

Dr. Patterson had built a highly-successful football program at William Jewell behind his single-wing offense, and I earned starting positions at halfback and defensive back. Suddenly, the left-handed halfback pass became a fixture in our offense. William Jewell finished ranked in the top 10 and top 20 in NAIA over the next two seasons. Dr. Patterson greatly impacted my life by virtue of his demands for discipline, his insistence upon doing things the right way, and his caring and compassionate nature.

My sophomore year, I lived in the dormitory and joined the Phi Gamma Delta fraternity. My junior year, I lived off campus with a friend, George Olendoff, who had been a competitive swimmer with me in St. Joseph. I lived inside the Phi Gamma Delta house during my senior year. Although I played on both the baseball and basketball teams at William Jewell, my passions remained football and swimming. Upon learning that the William Jewell athletic department did not have a swimming team, I elicited the help of my Red Cross advanced life-saving instructor, and we founded the very first William Jewell swim team. She served as the head coach, and I was the assistant coach and a team member.

My major area of study was physiology of exercise, which I really enjoyed, but I discovered that a liberal arts degree required two classes of a foreign language. I took Spanish. Although I learned to read and write in Spanish, I had difficulty speaking the language. Prior to my senior year, I learned that I needed to declare a minor area of study in order to satisfy all of my academic requirements to graduate. I decided to take another Spanish course and declared Spanish as my minor.

I graduated from William Jewell College on May 28, 1962. I was proud of my growth and maturity as a student, which allowed me to redeem my previous failure at the University of Missouri and graduate in a total of four years. My mother was so proud. She gave me a graduation card that featured an inscription: "Loving congratulations, Son, and all good things to you. May you fulfill your high ideals in everything you do. May hope be always in your heart, your future ever bright, and may you reach successfully each goal you have in sight. May every milestone of your life reflect a brilliant star, God bless you, boy, and thank you for the loving son you are. Love, Mom."

I had a great appreciation for athletes in all sports and realized nothing would bring me more joy in life than to remain in athletics. However, I knew my talent level wouldn't allow me to become a professional athlete. That was okay. I had realized my true calling years before in St. Joseph as a swimming coach. It was settled. I had no questions regarding my career field.

I was going to be a coach.

The small town of Gallatin, Missouri, was a one-hour drive from St. Joseph, and fewer than 100 students attended Gallatin K-12. A helping hand from Dr. Patterson made this quaint town and its high school my first official home as a teacher and assistant coach for football, basketball, and track and field. They gave me a salary of $3,600, and I even drove the school bus. Richard Roda, the head football coach, was a good person and he helped me a great deal. A very kind lady, Mrs. Sarah Witt, leased me a room in her home located across the street from the school. She and her husband had lived on a farm outside of town. Following his death, she returned to town and purchased this home. She was a marvelous woman and she loved to cook. I came home each night to find her 6' long and 4' wide dining room table filled with delicious food for the two of us. She did not eat a great deal, and I had never been a big eater, but my mother always told me it was polite to eat everything on my plate, so I sat down at the table each night and finished all that she had fixed for me.

Just before I moved to Gallatin, the high school assistant principal phoned to inform me of my teaching schedule. "You'll teach four classes," he said. "You'll teach three classes of first-year Spanish and one class of second-year Spanish." I instantly thought to myself, *What in the world did I get myself into? I can't teach Spanish.* That summer, I decided to move on.

Through the efforts of Dr. Patterson, Eastern New Mexico University athletic director Joe Dixon hired me as a graduate assistant for the physical education department. Eastern New Mexico University was located in Portales, New Mexico, which was about 100 miles from Lubbock, Texas, the largest community around. My roommate, Ken Copeland, was a graduate assistant swimming coach from Odessa, Texas. He was 5'6" and 380 pounds (yes, that number is correct) and a seriously talented competitive diver. I really liked Ken. Over the course of two semesters, I earned a master's degree in exercise physiology and I aspired to teach in that field at my next destination.

I moved sight unseen to Indio, California, to teach physical education at Indio High School, which was in the heart of the Coachella Valley. Upon my arrival, I found an apartment, settled in, and attended an all-staff administrative meeting at the high school. I learned that the community was heavily populated with Hispanic families who had crossed the border from Mexico to work in the fields, and many of our students primarily spoke Spanish. The school principal shared the guidelines, rules, and regulations with our teaching staff and then he pulled me aside as everyone filed out the door. "We've had a slight change," he said. "One of our teachers is on maternity leave. So I would you like you to teach one of her classes."

"Sure, I'll do whatever you want me to do," I said. "What is the class?"

"Good," he replied, "It's a Spanish class."

On the first day of school, I tried to introduce myself to each of the students as they entered the classroom. I quickly realized that I was going to have difficulty communicating with many of my students. I thought to myself, *Here we go again.*

In a classroom of between 35 and 40 students, there were just five English-speaking students in my class. The Spanish-speaking students knew the language far better than I did, which only added to my initial discomfort inside the classroom. I stayed up until 2:00 AM trying to devise a strategy to best handle our language barrier. Early the next morning, I carried my student roster and mapped out the classroom in groups of five. On the chalk board, I wrote instructions in Spanish. My group-of-five strategy entailed seating four Spanish-speaking students with one English-speaking student. The English-speaking student would teach English to the Spanish-speaking students, and the Spanish-speaking students would teach Spanish to the English-speaking student. I would monitor the groups. I was sick to my stomach every night. I simply wore myself out over the course of the school year. That summer, I decided to move on. I never wanted to teach Spanish again.

Judy Fredrick and I married in 1965 at the First Methodist Church in Indio, and following a brief honeymoon in Laguna Beach, we moved into the Sun Gold Apartments. Judy was one of the female friends that I always met at the lockers in high school. We dated on and off while I attended William Jewell College. After Judy attended William Jewell, she joined me in Indio. Our family grew with the births of Sean, Shannon, and Meredith over the next 10 years.

Although I served as Indio High School assistant basketball coach and assistant football coach, the school initially hired me because of my swimming background. I was head swimming coach. In addition, I coached the local swim team of hundreds of young competitive swimmers and divers. Six-year-old Johnny Peters was one of those children. John Peters, his father, owned the sprawling and extravagant El Morocco Hotel, which was perhaps the finest hotel in the desert. The elder Peters and I struck up a friendship. He was a University of Southern California alumnus and a major university and athletic department donor. Peters also knew John McKay, the legendary USC head football coach. John asked Coach McKay to hire me as a student assistant, Coach McKay obliged, and I became a student assistant on the USC coaching staff, thus ending my initial tenure at Indio High School. I then asked the Indio High athletic department to hire Ken as head swimming coach.

Basically, I helped coach the USC freshman football team with Craig Fertig, a former All-American USC quarterback-turned assistant coach, and I did my best to assist the varsity football team as a scout-squad coach. Although Coach McKay didn't pay much attention to me, I spent a considerable amount of time studying him. Coach McKay was a somewhat stoic man, a quality that people later identified in me, and he possessed an excellent understanding of everything that took place in his program. He was extremely observant. Coach McKay heavily invested himself in all aspects of football on and off the practice field and he was a good teacher of players and staff. As a part of my appointment as a student assistant, I completed 12 hours toward a doctorate in physical education, which I no longer pursued when I left USC after my only season on the coaching staff. One football story that I will never forget occurred prior to the Trojans' season opener at the Los Angeles Coliseum: I couldn't locate our team. I had been under the impression that the team met at our practice locker room, which was four blocks from the Coliseum. After many anxious minutes waiting for the team, I realized I had been mistaken and I ran four blocks through traffic to reach the stadium gate. There I faced another dilemma: I didn't have a team credential in order to enter the stadium. I convinced a stadium employee to go to the USC locker room and find coach Craig Fertig and I was finally able to join the team.

Although I enjoyed my time with the USC football program during the 1966 season, I returned to Indio High School only because they offered me the head coaching position following the retirement of Don Dutcher. I was officially hired as a head football coach for the first time in my career on February 27, 1967. I was an energetic 27 year old who already had built past relationships with many of the returning players. I had a staff of three assistant coaches, and we inherited an Indio High varsity team that recorded a 1–8 record and finished last place in the Desert Valley League the previous season. I told my assistant coaches, "If at any time during the season you drive past my house and the lights aren't on, you can have my job."

Our 30-player roster included 14 returning letter winners and a handful of returning starters. Upon watching film and doing my own research, I addressed our team and firmly told our players that discipline, along with a demanding but fair approach, was necessary for the eventual betterment of the program and that we had no time to waste. Shortly after, our best quarterback quit the team. I pushed our coaches and players very aggressively. I installed the I-formation from the USC playbook, which allowed us to utilize the speed of our tailbacks, and I installed the USC defense. Although we were a small team both physically and in numbers, we had good overall team speed. We just needed to identify and best utilize our strengths. I worked our coaches to the point of exhaustion. Coaches threatened to resign if I didn't ease up.

During the season I rarely slept. I returned home following our Friday night games at midnight and I rested for a few hours before I began preparing for the next opponent. I had a coaches meeting Saturday at noon to outline the week ahead and compare notes. We watched film as a coaching staff near midnight. Then I returned to my paperwork. I worked on football schemes, offense, defense, and special teams until it was time to dress for church and then I resumed work when we returned home. During the first few weeks of the season, I turned out the lights at around 11:30 PM. As we got into the season, I began working well into the early-morning hours. Truth is: there's probably always something left undone. By that, I mean there's some particular piece of information or something about a technique or a player or an opponent that occurs, and you say, "Why didn't I know that?" Covering the most significant information became the goal each day.

The dedication of our players and coaches was rewarded as we finished our first season with a 5–3–1 record. I told our players that they were one of the finest groups of young men that I'd ever been associated with. We had achieved some of our goals, which included building team unity, pride, work ethic, and improvement each and every day.

Ken Copeland, my very good friend, remained as Indio High School swimming head coach. When we had free time, Ken sometimes rented a plane, flew us to Las Vegas to see shows all night, and then flew us back home. Intrigued by the thought of owning a pilot's license, I decided to take flying lessons. In all, I took seven one-hour lessons. I cut my eighth lesson short—and for good reason. As I sat in the cockpit next to my instructor and watched the horizon, he suddenly pulled back on the controls, and we began a steep vertical climb. Then, suddenly, the airplane stalled out, and we were in a virtual freefall, and the nose of our airplane still pointed straight up. My instructor eventually pushed the stick forward, our nose came down, and we regained power and assumed a safe altitude. My instructor looked at me and said, "That is called a stall and that is how you get out of the stall. Now I want you to do that."

"No," I replied. "I want you to put this airplane on the ground." That was my very last flying lesson.

Ken had lost a ton of weight. He credited his weight loss to self-hypnotism. I figured if hypnotism helped Ken lose weight, perhaps hypnotism would enable me to garner sleep without having to sleep, thus allowing me to increase my time on the job. The hypnotist just looked at me. He said that would not work, and I did not attempt it.

After the 1968 season, I was hired by Foothill High School in North Tustin, California, to serve as an assistant football coach with the understanding that I was the head-coach-in-waiting to succeed Ed Bain, our head coach. Foothill High School had a highly-regarded athletics department. It had nice facilities and a very supportive community. With a student enrollment of approximately 2,500, our football program competed in the highest division in the state of California, and we had some really good athletes. After serving as an assistant coach for two seasons, I became head coach in 1971. Over the next three seasons, we amassed a 16–8–3 record.

I enjoyed my time at Foothill High School and I loved our home in Mission Viejo, which was about a 20-minute drive to work. We lived in a small, 1,300-square foot home with a swimming pool nestled in a cul-de-sac high upon a hill that offered a tremendous view and overlooked the major interstate highway and the hills in the valley. We bought our home for $19,000 and sold it for $40,000. One month later it sold for $90,000 and today it is worth hundreds of thousands of dollars. I taught our kids how to swim and tried to get all of them involved in competitive swimming during our time in California.

As becomes the quest for some coaches, I developed a pattern of trying to climb the ladder as quickly as possible in the coaching profession. Although I liked my job, half of my thoughts were on the task at hand, but the other half of my thoughts focused on where I wanted to go next. During my five years at Foothill High School, I attended football coaching clinics nearly all 52 weekends out of the year. Virtually every California university and community college held coaching clinics, which featured speeches and instruction from prominent college and high school coaches and drew audiences of between 200 and 1,000 coaches from around the area. I learned so much and met so many impressive people. I listened to UCLA head coach Tommy Prothro, Coach McKay, and all of their talented assistant coaches. I listened to Marv Goux, who was in the midst of a legendary 26-year career as an assistant coach at USC and who was probably one of the toughest individuals I've ever known. Coach Goux was 5'10" and 185 pounds, he knew every cuss word in the vocabulary, and he was extremely tough as a coach. But he was highly-regarded for his loyalty and work ethic, and his players loved him.

Most of the X's and O's that I learned were a product of these clinics. I took careful notes while listening to each speaker and cataloged all of my notes. I spent endless hours putting all of the pieces together. For as much as the X's and O's piqued my attention, more than anything I wanted to develop a core value system in which principles, organization, people, and attitudes served as the foundation by which a program could achieve success. I truly believed that was the key to developing quality people and quality players. I felt that if five teams ran the same scheme, and one team was successful, and the four other teams weren't successful, then the key to success was more than just a scheme. The key to success also entailed a core value system. The game of football, regardless of level, is an ongoing cycle, and virtually everything executed on the football field was already utilized by a team at some point in time. One scheme might appear to be ahead of its time, but the other teams eventually catch up. Once everyone catches up with that particular scheme, another team throws something else on the table, and so on. Consequently, nothing is totally new. It's all about catching up with the process.

After five wonderful years at Foothill High School, I was hired prior the 1974 season to serve as football offensive coordinator and head swimming and diving coach at Austin College in Sherman, Texas. Vance Morris, a college football teammate, was already on the football staff at the NAIA Division II program and he informed me about the coaching opportunities in both the football and swimming programs. Vance recommended me to football head coach Larry Kramer, who hired me without an in-person interview.

Our family packed up and drove from Mission Viejo to Sherman, where we purchased a home on a spacious plot across the street from a lake. I carved out a baseball diamond with the lawn mower in the backyard where Sean and I spent free time together playing baseball. In the office, I began accumulating thoughts and philosophies, developing concepts, and constructing my playbook. I mapped out and designed plays for hours. I scribbled X's and O's on restaurant napkins or notepads that I carried with me. Some of the plays that I devised over the course of my time at Austin College remained in my playbook throughout my career—the passing game, the running game, and the option game. I just tried to develop a playbook that contained sections of plays that best utilized whatever our strengths happened to be in a given year. Eventually, we had a package against every type of defense possible, and that would fix the talent level of the players we had at the time.

I enjoyed my time and enjoyed the people at Austin College, but we didn't stay there very long. Prior to the 1976 season, I received a call from Hayden Fry, who was entering his third year as North Texas State head coach. He asked me if I was interested in the quarterback/wide receiver coaching position, which I responded to affirmatively. I then mailed him my offensive playbook.

"Coach Snyder is an old-school type of guy, which we all know. So he plays by the old-school rules. Regardless of wherever you come in life, whether you're already on third base or whether you had to start off slow, Coach Snyder makes everyone start out at home. We all have to learn discipline, what it means to respond to adversity, and what it means to earn something. That really teaches you a lot in life rather than always having everything given to you."

—Tyler Lockett, Kansas State wide receiver, 2011–14

CHAPTER 2

SPECIAL YEARS
WITH HAYDEN FRY

"He is the greatest. He did a wonderful job for me for 17 years as an assistant coach. He is extremely intelligent and organized. He is fundamentally the best coach I have ever seen. He had a great career, and I am extremely proud of him."

—Hayden Fry, former Iowa head coach

Hayden Fry left after 11 seasons as head football coach at Southern Methodist University in 1972 and was hired to the same position at North Texas State that offseason. Hayden had spent most of his life in the Lone Star State. He was born in Eastland, Texas, in 1929, played four years as a Baylor quarterback during the late 1940s and, following three years in the U.S. Marines, where Hayden befriended George H.W. Bush, he coached at Odessa High School, where he befriended Texas A&M head coach Bear Bryant. Hayden served as Baylor's defensive backs coach in 1958, spent one year as offensive backfield coach under Frank Broyles at Arkansas, and was hired as SMU head coach in 1962. Over his tenure he took SMU to its first Southwest Conference title in 18 years and made three bowl appearances. After a 7–4 record in 1972, he got a fresh start when he moved 40 miles north from Dallas to Denton to take over at North Texas State.

Hayden inherited a North Texas State program that went 1–10 the previous year and 7–26 over the previous three campaigns. During his third year, Hayden led the Mean Green to a seven-win season. I had read positive things about Hayden and was eager to take that next step in the coaching ranks when I received his call asking me to come interview. I sent him an inquiry letter along with my offensive playbook, which had grown large with hundreds of plays accumulated over several years. Hayden seemed impressed and invited me to interview for the offensive coordinator position. My wife and I made the hour-long trip from Sherman to Denton. At the end of the interview, Hayden offered me the job.

Upon leaving the football building, my wife and I noticed a steady stream of cars pulling into the nearby basketball arena parking lot. We thought perhaps the Mean Green had a basketball game and felt it was a great opportunity to view their fan support. It was only after walking into the concourse and purchasing our tickets that we discovered it was a country music concert for some guy named Willie Nelson. We reclaimed our money and left—a move I now absolutely regret. Unbeknownst to me at the time, Nelson had just released an album that would go platinum by the end of the year. He became one of my all-time favorite music artists.

Shortly after my wife and I arrived home, we processed the logistics involved in a move, and I accepted Hayden's offer. I moved into a dormitory on the North Texas State campus, and the family remained in Sherman so that Sean could finish the school year and we could sell our home.

Hayden was a very outgoing individual. He was friendly, compassionate, and cared about his players and coaches. Although Hayden and I didn't agree on everything, he was always a friend throughout my time at Kansas State until his death at 90 years of age in 2019. As time went on at North Texas State, I thought it could evolve into a destination job, which could allow us to plant roots, put an end to the years of always looking for the next job, and perhaps lessen the strain that the football life had put on our family. Had Hayden stayed at North Texas State, I believe I would've remained there as long as I had a job with him. I had finally learned to be where I was. That meant that I would do the dead-level best that I could and wouldn't focus on anything other than what I coached at that particular point in time. I would take great pride in whatever my responsibilities and assignments were, whether it was coaching quarterbacks or coaching offense. Later, when we went to the University of Iowa, my intent was to stay at Iowa. For nearly 10 years, I didn't look for or respond to offers to interview for other positions.

Numerous people had contacted me over the years. Somewhere it was said that I contacted UCLA when it had a job opening, but UCLA in fact contacted me. I didn't pursue that job or any others.

North Texas State had just one winning season in the previous six years, but I paid little attention to its history. I poured myself into my coaching responsibilities, a virtue I had maintained from the beginning of my career. The expectations that I placed upon myself were virtually limitless. During the night my studious nature entailed sitting in darkness with a pencil and my notepad and watching offenses on reels of 16-millimeter film, awaiting the opportunity for some of these plays to see the light of day. On the football field, my determination entailed hours upon hours of teaching, and I observed repetition upon repetition, trying to ensure that our offensive players utilized proper technique, eliminated unnecessary movements, and remained in sync from the huddle to the pre-snap reads to protection to hitting holes to executing crisp routes and finally completing the play. Although we spent time talking about our expectations for our players, my ideology promoted players developing their own expectations. My unwavering expectation to build and maintain successful programs involved far more than just winning on the scoreboard. My aspirations that I held for myself far outweighed those aspirations directed toward me by other people.

On gameday Hayden carried a penchant for unearthing some play calls that would sometimes baffle me, but he possessed an uncanny knack for knowing the exact moment to utilize those special plays. He loved gadget plays. That was fun for him. I was a far more conservative individual than Hayden. Although his tendency to roll the dice prompted me to cringe at times, it often paid dividends, and I admired that confidence and insight.

Hayden also was a players' coach, and we had good players who really believed in his culture. Hayden wasn't a hard-nosed coach with the players. He walked around practice, patting players on the back and joking with them. His personable nature permeated the locker room. We went 7–4 my first year at North Texas State and then we produced the best season in school history with a 10–1 record that was only blemished by a loss at No. 20 Florida State. Our 9–2 record in 1978 gave North Texas State back-to-back seasons with at least nine wins for the first time in history.

Decision time arrived in 1978 when Hayden announced to the coaching staff that the University of Iowa had offered him the head coach position. He basically asked us, "Do you guys want to go to Iowa or not? If you guys want to go, then I'll take the job." I actually believe that he would've accepted the job regardless, but everybody agreed to join him, though one member of our coaching staff opted to remain in Texas when we departed for Iowa City. I realized that I would be distanced from my family if I joined Hayden at Iowa. That made it a very difficult decision. After all, my family believed that we were probably going to plant roots at North Texas State. Now my plans had changed on a dime. Had I been assured of a coaching position at North Texas State, I would've stayed in Denton. Instead, I went with Hayden. My family remained in Denton. Judy and I divorced in 1979.

Iowa came off a 2–9 season and hadn't experienced a wealth of success for several years prior to our arrival. Forest Evashevski (52–27–4 between 1952–60) took Iowa to its only two bowl games (1956 and 1958 Rose Bowls), but the previous two head coaches, Frank Lauterbur (4–28–1 between 1971–73) and Bob Commings (17–38 between 1974–78), collectively produced 21 wins and 66 losses.

However, Hayden, who inspired success, instilled confidence into the Iowa people. Downtrodden players beaten down by mediocrity flipped their mentality under Hayden and prepared for success, trusting that he could maximize their capabilities and cultivate a winning culture.

Home attendance figures at Kinnick Stadium steadily climbed alongside the program's success. Fans had a major impact on that success and were positive about all aspects of the program. Iowa City was all about the Hawkeyes. That was the premise of the city's existence, and the athletic department boasted several successful programs. Lute Olson led Iowa to a 20–8 record, a Big Ten Conference title, and an appearance in the 1979 NCAA Tournament during our first year in Iowa City. Dan Gable was in the midst of leading the Iowa wrestling program to 15 NCAA Division I titles and 21 Big Ten championships during his legendary career. Iowa athletic director Bump Elliott knew quality football as the former University of Michigan head coach had taken his team to the 1964 Rose Bowl. Iowa was a highly-regarded academic institution with a passionate fanbase and loyal student body.

Iowa possessed quality in-state high school football talent yet was limited in numbers due to population. We did, however, attempt to recruit nationally. Shortly after our arrival, Hayden directed me to recruit in California, where I had resided as a high school coach. I was fortunate to bring in a pair of junior college commitments in quarterback Gordy Bohannon and wide receiver Keith Chappelle. Both from Pasadena City College, they became immediate starters. Our coaching staff had a history in Texas, which proved to be an effective asset. I also found success, in particular, between the Iowa border and Chicago, as I found Chuck Long, who became perhaps the finest quarterback in Iowa history, and wide receiver David Moritz, who developed into a 1983 first-team All-Big Ten selection.

During the offseason, our players grew vastly under the guidance of Bill Dervich, our head strength and conditioning coach. Bill was demanding yet a good person and highly successful. Our players responded well to him and thus became better conditioned and stronger.

Our coaching staff was composed of good men with integrity and strong intrinsic values, who always did the right thing and didn't cheat or violate NCAA rules. Bill Brazier served as defensive coordinator and defensive secondary coach and was as fine of a coach as I've ever been around. He made productive opposing offenses non-productive. Bill was a personable man who carried a matter-of-fact tone and possessed great intuition regarding defensive football. He was the oldest assistant coach and was as highly respected as any coach on the staff. Hayden trusted Bill with the entirety of the defense, which allowed Hayden to focus on the offense.

Kirk Ferentz joined the coaching staff after the departure of our offensive line coach following the first season. Tired of hiring coaches, Hayden directed me to find an offensive line coach, which led me to contact and introduce myself to Joe Moore, who at the time was probably as prolific of an offensive assistant coach as there was in the nation. Joe recommended Ferentz, who had served as a graduate assistant under him at Pittsburgh and who was the current offensive line coach at Mass Academy. I flew Kirk into Iowa City and introduced him to Hayden. That was an excellent hire. Kirk was so knowledgeable about offensive line play. The coaches and players instantly bought into his capabilities. When Hayden retired following the 1998 season,

Iowa hired Kirk as its head coach. Kirk continues to enjoy an accomplished career with the Hawkeyes.

Del Miller had served on the previous Iowa coaching staff as a graduate assistant, and Hayden retained him as an offensive assistant before eventually promoting him to wide receivers coach, which enabled me to focus on our quarterbacks. First and foremost, Del was an awfully good person and cared about our players. He sought to assist in their development on and off the field. Del was very conscientious, knew the game of football, and was precise in his teaching.

Hayden hired Barry Alvarez from the high school ranks after our second year at Iowa. Barry had a good relationship with his players and a strong knowledge of the game. Of course, Barry went on to become a very successful head coach and then a very successful athletic director at Wisconsin. Hayden also hired Dan McCarney off the previous staff as the defensive line coach. Dan was a hard worker, a very outgoing individual with a dynamic personality. He believed in hard-nosed football and was a strong, aggressive coach but still very personable with his players. Dan eventually became head coach at Iowa State.

Bob Stoops, who had been a very aggressive safety for us at Iowa, joined the staff as a graduate assistant. An aggressive, knowledgeable, and caring coach, Bobby invested himself into defense most of his coaching career, but he had a good understanding of the offense—a virtue that served him well as he became the winningest head coach in Oklahoma history. His father was a highly successful high school coach and had taught him well.

Carl Jackson maybe wasn't a name coach, but he was a highly-respected running backs coach. We had been hired at North Texas State at about the same time. He could be as aggressive of a coach as he needed to be but yet was a mild-mannered, caring person. Donnie Patterson, our tight ends coach, served on the coaching staff until Hayden retired and then he took over a head coaching position at Western Illinois. Donnie always invested himself in the players and was a great communicator and learner. All of our coaches were very proficient teachers, great family men, worked well under pressure, and cared about their young men.

Although Iowa finished 5–6 in 1979 and 4–7 in 1980, Hayden remained upbeat after the losses and bred a positive environment. Sometimes it almost seemed like he forced the players to believe that they were going to be successful. We believed in the program and the system. We had good players who carried a strong intrinsic value system and invested themselves into the mantra of daily improvement. Consequently, the winning culture and player development was steadily enhanced, and the program took a significant leap. Iowa posted an 8–4 record in 1981, tied Ohio State as Big Ten Conference co-champions, and appeared in the Rose Bowl for the first time in 23 years.

At about the same time that Iowa began its ascent, we recruited a young man named Chuck, a 1980 all-state quarterback from Wheaton, Illinois, who led his high school team to the state championship. Wheaton North High School averaged just five or six passing attempts per game, as Chuck operated a run-oriented offense, but Chuck was a talented passer and leader. That was evident when I studied film of every game in Chuck's high school career. For all of his talents, Chuck was such a good person, mild-mannered and overly humble, as were his parents. His quality character made this an easy decision.

The same held true for a young man named Larry Station, a standout linebacker at Omaha (Nebraska) Central High School, who we also recruited to the Hawkeyes. A genuine and intense individual, Larry had committed to the University of Nebraska, but he listened intently as I discussed the positives and many opportunities at Iowa. He took notes and diligently compared the two schools and what they provided for him. Larry graduated from Iowa as a two-time All-American. I would've admired Larry even if had he not chosen to attend Iowa. We would still have remained friends for a long time. We were also fortunate to recruit and land another talent from Omaha Central by the name of Sean Ridley, who was even more highly recruited than Larry. Sean was a very talented young man. Chuck Long, Larry Station, Sean Ridley, and Matt Whitaker were among my proudest recruiting efforts at Iowa.

Chuck redshirted his freshman year and became our starting quarterback in 1982. At 6'4", Chuck possessed ideal height and steadily increased his weight to 217 pounds. He flourished behind a tremendous ability to make proper reads, which coupled with excellent accuracy, allowed him to locate and connect with his targets and execute plays with a high degree of success. However, his leadership proved paramount. I greatly appreciated Chuck's character. I wanted a good person who had quality leadership traits with a strong intrinsic value system and was willing to promote that value system within the program itself. His personality bled into his leadership capacity. He quickly earned the respect of all of his teammates and coaches.

Chuck was surrounded by talented players as well, including David, who boasted admirable confidence, quality skills and an extremely high degree of toughness. David, who I recruited out of the Chicago suburbs, emerged as an All-Big Ten selection while leading the team in receptions in 1982 and 1983 and was a 10th-round pick in the 1984 NFL Draft. Jonathan Hayes was a tremendous tight end for us from Pennsylvania and a second-round pick in the 1985 NFL Draft.

Hayden increasingly leaned on the passing game as Chuck continued to progress in the system. Hayden, who had been a quarterback at Baylor (1947–50), was an aggressive play-caller and thrived on long-yardage pass plays—and Chuck and the offense delivered. Chuck and his teammates led Iowa to a bowl season in each of the four years he was a starter. The Hawkeyes captured the Big Ten title in 1985—a league championship aided by his heroic last-minute drive as No. 1 Iowa beat No. 2 Michigan 12–10 when Rob Houghtlin hit a game-winning 29-yard field goal with four seconds left in the game in Iowa City. It was the first time we had beaten a Bo Schembechler-coached team.

Chuck finished his All-American career with 10,461 passing yards, becoming just the second player in college football history to pass for 10,000 yards, and was as fine a passer as I ever coached in terms of productivity. In terms of getting the most out of a player, he'd be right at the top. With regard to his game management, he was probably as good as any. After finishing seventh in the 1984 Heisman Trophy voting, Chuck finished as 1985 Heisman Trophy runner-up to Bo Jackson in the second closest vote of all time.

Prior to the 1985 season, I received a phone call from a friend, Tom Ross, who had played football at Iowa and owned a lumber company in Des

Moines. I had met him at booster club meetings in the Des Moines area. Tom and his wife, Gay, had a friend named Sharon, who was principal at Wright Elementary School in Des Moines. Tom called me and said, "I'd like for you to come to dinner with us. We're inviting Sharon also."

Sharon and I got to know each other, began dating, and were married on May 4, 1985 at Plymouth Congregational Church in Des Moines. I told Sharon that this likely wouldn't be a normal type of marriage due to the long hours as a football coach, but I cared about her. From her first marriage, Sharon had one son, Ross, who was in elementary school.

Shortly after our wedding, we settled into a home that was designed by Sharon's father, Harold, who was an architect in Des Moines. It was a three-level house perfectly nestled next to the Iowa River, which bordered Iowa City. We liked the house so much that years later we had her father design the exact same house for us in Manhattan. We have lived in that house for 30 years.

Iowa continued to succeed after Chuck completed his career and became the 12th overall pick in the 1986 NFL Draft. After finishing 9–3 in 1986, the team went 10–3 in 1987, ending both seasons with Holiday Bowl victories while beating opponents with a vaunted passing attack that often operated out of no-back formations. At this time, my playbook had become quite substantial, but Hayden still drew-up some plays and said, "This looks good. Let's run this."

Our starting quarterback, Chuck Hartlieb, was a 4.0 student and threw the football well. He set a school record with seven touchdown passes against Northwestern. Long may have thrown the football a little bit better than Hartlieb, but both were excellent leaders, worked diligently, and were highly successful on and off the field. Our quarterbacks earned first-team All-Big Ten honors five of my last six seasons at Iowa.

Regarding the playbook, when you like something, you keep it, and when you've been in the profession for a while, you gather a large amount of information. Even though we had virtually everything in the playbook, each year we tailored it to our players' capabilities. However, if somebody emerged during a season that allowed us to enhance our offense with some different structure, it was all right there in the playbook, and we could do it.

I spent a great deal of my time consumed with helping our players grow in their faith as young men, family men, students, and athletes. I always tried to teach an appropriate value system. As a part of that value system, I tried to impart the importance of investing in hard work, being a good teammate, doing things right, helping others, and studying the game in a thorough and intelligent manner. Schematically, I sought to be different on the field and carefully define proper execution in any phase of the game, which could take advantage of an opponent's schematic system. We sought success by virtue of unique, innovative offensive ideas that maximized our player capabilities and effectively countered the opponent's defensive strategy.

It was an unceasing search and analysis of information, but the tireless quest proved necessary within the competitive environment in such a strong conference. I don't remember when I stopped eating lunch, but I didn't eat lunch at North Texas State or at Iowa. I've never eaten breakfast in my adult life. My mother always ensured that I ate breakfast, but that daily practice ended when I left home. As a coach I realized that working while everybody was gone over the lunch hour enabled me to accomplish more without interruption; so I didn't eat lunch. I'll occasionally eat lunch now, but eating food makes me sleepy, and I prefer to be alert. Since I was able to accomplish uninterrupted tasks by foregoing lunch, I opted to dedicate the dinner hour toward further maximizing my productivity, limiting myself to a late-night meal at home before bed. Not one doctor that I've ever had has been in favor of my meal schedule. Caffeine kept me going through the day and evening. I had never been a big coffee drinker, but I became one at North Texas State and drank coffee late into the day. By the time I left the office, I'd have 10 cups on my desk—all either half or three-quarters full.

Under Hayden and his positive approach and our commitment to constant improvement arrived a lengthy string of success, as Iowa posted at least eight victories each year over a seven-year span—the greatest seven-year stretch in school history. That streak ended with our 6–4–3 record in 1988, as we tied Michigan State (10–10), No. 15 Michigan (17–17), and Ohio State (24–24). I don't know of any other team in college football history that has had three ties in one season. That doesn't mean we weren't as good, but it was a feather in the cap to tie the talented Wolverines, Buckeyes, and Spartans.

Prior to one of our games during that 1988 season, Hayden introduced me to Gary Bender and Dick Vermeil inside of his office. At the time, Gary and Dick were ABC football commentators. Of course, Dick previously had been a longtime NFL head coach and later took the St. Louis Rams to a Super Bowl XXXIV title and then coached the Kansas City Chiefs. I really appreciated the opportunity to speak with Gary and Dick in Hayden's office. We talked for about an hour. I later learned that Dick graciously said that I had as good an offensive mind as any coach he had ever met, which I appreciated a great deal. Dick and I later became friends, and I spent some time with him when he was in Kansas City. He was a very pleasant guy, down to Earth, and never took himself too seriously. He was a very bright mind and a very talented coach. Throughout the years, Dick always said some very positive things about me publicly, which I appreciated a great deal. "No football coach did a better job of coaching football players than Bill Snyder," he said. "No football coach. No coach of the year. No national championship team. None of them."

I loved the people at Iowa—the people within the university and the people within the community. Iowa is a special university, and many good friends remain in Iowa City.

About six or seven games into the 1988 season, I received a phone call from a man who introduced himself as Jim Epps. He said that he was the assistant athletic director at Kansas State. And he asked me for a couple moments of my time.

"Coach Snyder's preparation is legendary. Leading by example, he taught me the valuable lesson of winning before I ever took the field. He analyzed my performance, our team's performance, and his own performance, searching for ways to improve and gain an edge. It was never more evident than in film study meetings, when every step a receiver took on a pass route and every quarterback drop back, could be paused, reversed, and replayed multiple times to determine proper techniques and reads. The legendary preparation often led to lengthy meetings that were also legendary."

—Tom Frantz, University of Iowa tight end, 1976–80

CHAPTER 3

COMING TO MANHATTAN

"What's bewildering is how this story somehow got lost. I don't know if it was because it was Kansas State, but when you hear about some other programs improving, you'd think they had the greatest turnaround in college football history, and they're not even close to what Bill Snyder did at Kansas State. Not even close. It was a frigging miracle. We lied and said there were 15,000 people in the stands. I knew there weren't. It was comedic."

—Steve Miller, former Kansas State athletic director

At the time, I was not aware of Kansas State's football history. The University of Iowa was coming off back-to-back wins at Arizona and at Iowa State when Kansas State visited Kinnick Stadium in Iowa City on September 26, 1987. In the midst of our 38–13 victory against the Wildcats, it became apparent that Kansas State possessed a seemingly hard-working team that maybe didn't harbor all of the talent in the world. However, my focus rested upon our own players' performance on the field and not on Kansas State's circumstances.

Interestingly, when Iowa visited Kansas State in Manhattan on September 10, 1988, one of our team's biggest challenges became the stadium's football field. The worn, rock-hard artificial turf surface featured a sizable arc and peaked in the middle. Our players slipped and skated across the midfield Wildcat logo—an unsuspecting purple-and-white hazard bore from layers of smooth paint. The hinderance was minimized by spreading skill position players to the edge of the field while ballcarriers ran downhill, across the slope, and toward the boundary before turning upfield.

Overlooking a stadium crowd caked with as much yellow as purple—I later learned there had been a total attendance of 21,000 at the game with a large portion of the fans from Iowa—I helped direct the Iowa offense from a sliver of space inside a small visitor's coaching area in the press box. Its thin walls strained to silence those conversations from others in the adjacent boxes.

Weeks passed after our 45–10 win at Kansas State, and I was consumed with Iowa's late-October and early-November stretch against Indiana, Northwestern, and Ohio State when one day the phone rang in my office. Jim Epps, the assistant athletic director at Kansas State, introduced himself. He asked me if I'd be interested in interviewing to become their next head coach. I said, "I can't address that now when we're in the middle of our season."

And I left it at that.

Then Jim called back and said that they would wait to visit with me about the job after the season. I told him that it wouldn't be appropriate on their part because if they waited that long and weren't impressed with me or I with them or I wasn't interested in the job, Kansas State would have lost the opportunity to invest its efforts in many other possible coaching candidates. I figured that was the end of it.

Later in the season on a Sunday during an open week, somebody I didn't know knocked on the front door at our home. It was Kansas State athletic director Steve Miller and associate athletic director Chris Peterson. They flew from Manhattan to Iowa City, found my address, and drove to speak with me about the job. They came inside and talked for a couple of hours about the football program and some of the challenges it had faced. I basically listened. Sharon wasn't actively involved in our conversation, but I'm sure she heard a lot of it. They told me that if I could enact a turnaround at Kansas State that it would be the highlight of my career. I eventually said, "I'm not interested, but I appreciate you for asking me to interview."

"Do you have two extra bedrooms in your home?" Steve asked.

"Why are you asking?"

"Because Chris and I aren't leaving," Steve said, "until you tell us that you'll at least visit."

Finally, I said, "Okay, I'll consider coming to look at it after our season."

However, my biggest concern was the Iowa football program. We had spent 10 great years surrounded by many wonderful people and we had a great life in Iowa City. We had helped build a quality football program, won a Big Ten Conference title, and appeared in eight straight bowl games. Loyalty had been a prominent value in my life. I had no intention of leaving.

Because of Kansas State's persistence, I eventually decided to visit Manhattan. Hayden Fry told me what I already knew: that Kansas State was not a good program. "But," Hayden graciously said, "you can be successful anywhere you go."

I flew into Manhattan on a private plane owned by a Kansas State donor named Fred Merrill, who later became a very dear friend. I was swept onto campus, where a host of people greeted me inside the Legend's Room at Bramlage Coliseum. It quickly became apparent that this wasn't going to be a sit-down discussion with a handful of people. This became a two-hour presentation by Kansas State University officials, friends of the program, athletic department administrators and employees, professors, and student-athletes outlining the many positives of the university. The state of the football program was a major concern, and yet the Kansas State people believed something positive could happen. If I took the job, I would be the third head coach in five years. Kansas State University president Jon Wefald introduced himself to me and said, "This can be done."

Kansas State was founded as Kansas State Agricultural College in 1863 and was the first operational land-grant university in the United States. In July 1986, Jon arrived as president of Kansas State University. The university was struggling in several different aspects. Enrollment had dipped by 15 percent over the past decade and was at approximately 15,000 when Jon assumed his role. Jon had a plan. He wanted to boost university fund-raising, increase on-campus construction, and build a new library and an art museum. He also wanted Kansas State to become a prominent research university and be nationally recognized for academic achievements. Although Kansas State had a tradition of success in men's basketball, Jon also believed that Kansas State could have a winning football program. At the time, I did not know that 18 previous candidates for head football coach had already turned down the job.

There are days that I'll always remember. This was one of those days. At my request, I escaped for an hour-long afternoon stroll along the sidewalks of the Kansas State campus and casually stopped groups of one, two, three, or four people simply to inquire about the university. No one knew who I was or why I was there, and I didn't tell them. I asked them about the community, the university, the faculty, the student body, academics, and the athletic program. I was struck by the graciousness and sincerity of all of those people. I probably visited with more than 60 people during that hour, and despite frigid temperatures, they took the time to politely answer every question, which sent a major message to me. I've always believed that people make the difference. Upon my return to Bramlage Coliseum, I told Jon: "I may be interested."

He replied, "Well, if I may ask, what made you change your mind?"

I said, "The people."

My feelings toward the Kansas State people were strong from the very beginning and remained constant. As I shared so many times through the years: we came to Kansas State University because of the people and we stayed because of the people.

Shortly after I returned to Iowa City, Sharon and I discussed the possible move at length. Although we had roots in Iowa, Sharon agreed to move to Manhattan. Like myself, she knew little about Kansas State or Manhattan and she had never in her life been a big football fan but had recently started to enjoy it. "We'll be fine wherever," she said. "So if that's what you want to do, we'll do it."

I phoned Steve and accepted the position, thus inheriting the worst football program in Division I-A history. Kansas State was 299–509–41 in 93 years and was the only college football program to lose 500 games. Kansas State had recorded one win in its last 38 games. Kansas State was also winless in 27 straight games, the longest active drought in college football. Kansas State was a two-hour drive along Interstate-70 from Kansas City— after which you hung a right at Exit 313, then drove another 10 minutes along a two-lane highway, and crossed a bridge into the city of 37,000. We had been a part of one turnaround at North Texas State, as the Mean Green achieved its winningest four-year stretch in school history. Iowa went from 11 straight losing seasons to a Big Ten championship. Kansas State was different. Kansas State had lost 60 more games than any other program in history. That stuck. It would be a challenge. Virtually everyplace I'd coached had been a challenge, but I wasn't fully aware of the multitude of challenges that awaited me at Kansas State.

The football program was flat on its back.

Hayden supported my leap into a new adventure. "I hate for you to leave," he said. "But you'll do well. Let me know if I can help."

The night before my introductory news conference at Kansas State, I slept like normal—not very much. Although I had consumed myself with plotting the initial steps for the Kansas State football program as I accepted the head coaching position, the necessary steps to begin the process seemingly grew while Sharon and I flew into Manhattan for a morning news conference on November 30. Standing at the podium in the Legend's Room, I thanked Steve, Jim, and Jon, along with those people who I had met that cold day when I visited the Kansas State campus. I never wrote speeches. My only desire involved outlining my mission and answering questions because ample intrigue surrounded this vast undertaking. I said:

> I'm so proud to be here. This is certainly a delightful day in my life. It's an exciting day. This is a task. It's a monumental task. It's one with tremendous challenges. It's the greatest challenge in my life, and I am certainly proud and I'm honored. I could not be happier with the people that were responsible for having me here today. The president and athletic director of this university have proven to me beyond a shadow of a doubt that Kansas State University is ready to move forward. I have never been any place in my life where I wasn't concerned about people. I'm really going to care about the coaches I bring in and the players. I want all of them to live a quality life while they are here at Kansas State.
>
> The state of Kansas and Kansas State University, the state of Iowa and the University of Iowa parallel each other in so many ways. It's an amazing parallel. There was also a tremendous challenge there. The circumstances were identical. And I think that the opportunity

for the greatest turnaround in college football history exists here today, and it's not a challenge that can be taken lightly.

I have no timetable. I want to establish a firm solid ground with which to work from with no shortcuts. I will not do that and I will not be pressured to do that. This will be an honest program—top to bottom. A lot of people work extra hard to get the job done, but sometimes maybe they don't do it quite as intelligently as they should have. We're going to do this within the restraints of every major college football program in America.

Those Kansas high schools and junior colleges are good programs, and I pray that they'll wait because I'm coming. As of about 5:00 PM, December 31, I will be at Kansas State University wholeheartedly, lock, stock, and barrel. I'm going to do all I can do for everybody, and if the ship sinks, then I'm going to be the one to sink it.

When you think about it, exactly how many football programs get to be the losingest program in college football history? That's profound. The bar wasn't overly high in attaining a semblance of success relative to the previous 100 years. I never believed that on a scale of one to 10 the quest to reach success would be a 10. Success really wasn't that far out of sight. Skeptics could opine, "It's been this way for 100 years and it's going to continue to be that way." That was a reasonable statement. My only prediction was that we would win. I had no idea how long it would take, but we would get it done. On a scale of 1 to 10, I felt the task of persuading recruits to come to Kansas State would be a 20. Yet I felt confident that Kansas State could win four, five, or six games a year, reach a bowl game once in a while, and perhaps win seven or eight games every four or five years. In my eyes, that would represent the greatest turnaround in the history of college football.

I refused to be rushed and I didn't believe in shortcuts. A program had to be based on firm, solid ground, and I was going to do it right.

Over the next two days, we hopped between western Kansas and Wichita, Topeka, and Kansas City, and I introduced myself to Kansas State supporters—friendly and genuine people who had a vested interest in the football program and who were curious about me and my vision for the program.

When I returned to the University of Iowa, my primary focus centered on preparation for the Peach Bowl while I also regularly spoke with Jim, who graciously aided in tackling various football-related tasks at Kansas State. It proved to be an especially busy few weeks and it was difficult to accomplish everything necessary in any given day. I don't know that football coaches ever become comfortable, but we were in a comfortable environment at Iowa, and my family enjoyed all aspects of the community. After years of striving to take that next step or find that next job, I was a 49-year-old coach who had become emotionally invested in the desire to finish my career in Iowa City. People might've knocked on the door to present a coaching opportunity, but I had never responded. Kansas State was just different.

We decided that the family would remain in Iowa City so that Ross could complete the school year, which made sense, as we didn't yet have a home in Manhattan, and I was going to be extremely busy. The day we returned home from the bowl game, I left for Manhattan.

"If it wasn't for Coach Snyder's offensive plan of attack and mainly the quarterback shotgun, which we introduced in the 1981 season, we probably wouldn't have won the Big Ten championship. Every one of us defensive players stood up when our offense took the field during games because we always heard all week about the plays that Coach Snyder had drawn up for that particular game. No one wanted to miss it. Coach Snyder brought new life to the football field with his new high-flying offense."

—James Pekar, University of Iowa defensive lineman, 1980–81

CHAPTER 4

BUILDING THE FOUNDATION

"Bill Snyder is a great guy. He is one of those people that other people don't quite appreciate because of the fact that he is not an outgoing guy. He is not a guy that promotes himself, but he is a great football coach. He is a guy I admire very much both as a person and as a football coach. Bill and I spent a lot of time together on different Nike trips, and we talked a lot. I hope we have young people who are coming into it with the same type of commitment to what college football is all about and not necessarily how much money they are going to make. Bill was never that way."

—Joe Paterno, former Penn State head coach

There was no order of business. There were just so many issues. Not a moment passed that I wasn't addressing some aspect of those issues. If we solved one problem, it didn't mean we had a good day. The problems were countless, they were ongoing, and they might've seemed insurmountable to most people. When another significant issue arose, it was difficult to drop everything and deal with it. We had to focus on everything at the same time. The problems didn't slow down. They persisted from the time I awoke until I laid down late in the evening. I was in my office seven days a week, 16 to 18 hours each day. It was a minimum of 16 hours, I can assure you of that.

This was the state of the Kansas State football program. And the challenges were far beyond what I had anticipated when I accepted the head coaching position. Steve Miller introduced me to some, but not all of the areas in and around the football facility during my initial visit at Kansas

State. I conducted my own top-to-bottom tour of the entire facility when I returned. I had not been to the facilities at every college football program in the country. But I do not believe there were facilities anywhere that were any worse. We had gravel parking lots. The team meeting room consisted of a concrete slab and flimsy plastic folding chairs that could barely hold a 100-pound man. It was far from the attractive, warm, and functional appearance I desired for our players, coaches, families, and guests in what we eventually named the Big 8 Room. The assistant coaches' offices were too small, and there were two or three coaches in each office. The weight room measured roughly 15' wide and 45' long—less than the size of a small high school weight room. The to-do list was immense and came down to this: we needed to reconstruct the football facility, level the football field and replace the AstroTurf, reconstruct the press box, and improve the cosmetics of the stadium. This was going to cost around $8 million. We needed to accomplish these tasks on the smallest athletic budget in the Big 8 Conference and perhaps the country. In all actuality, the Kansas State athletic department faced about a $5 million deficit. All of this was in addition to having only 91 scholarship players in the program. No matter what football program enhancement I asked of Steve, he answered, "Yes."

Shortly after I arrived, I served as a building contractor of sorts, at times prodding the construction company to remain on schedule, and I addressed the program's numerous other needs in my office each day while slowly becoming accustomed to the constant banging and sawing inside the facility. Then one day, all construction stopped. I walked around and couldn't find a single construction worker, so I phoned Steve. "Steve," I said, "did you know that the construction has stopped?"

"I hate to tell you this," Steve replied, "but we ran out of money. We can't continue this project."

"Well, I'll get you the money," I said. "I'll write a check. How much do you need? I'll give it to you."

The Kansas State athletic department owed the construction company nearly $100,000. Of course, I didn't have those funds in our bank account. I had decided that I would borrow the money. I was determined to take any necessary steps to ensure the completion of the facility project. Steve understood my concern and elicited the financial support of some very special individuals who quickly became very dear friends to me: Jack and Donna Vanier and Howard Sherwood.

Although the graciousness and generosity of Jack and Donna and Howard was so vital to the football program, their friendship was even more meaningful to me. Jack and Donna lived on a ranch outside of Salina and owned an amazing amount of acreage throughout the Midwest. Despite owning all of the ranch land, Jack was a very unassuming individual with great humility. Jack always wore an old flannel shirt and blue jeans. Jack was Jack. Upon learning of our financial concerns, Jack rolled up his sleeves and went to work. Jack was fundamental to everything. He didn't give us a dollar figure. Jack asked, "What do you need? We'll make this happen."

And Jack never asked for a single thing in return. The generosity enabled construction to continue on the football facility, which was eventually named the Vanier Football Complex. When we first arrived, there were three holes in a wall inside my office, which had poor carpeting and an old desk. I covered the holes with putty. I did not need a CEO office. I made sure every other building renovation was complete before any construction worker touched my office. When finally completed, the $1.5 million football complex featured a picturesque Big 8 Room, upgraded locker rooms, a 7,500-square foot weight room, classrooms equipped with updated video equipment, a training room, new assistant coaches offices, and a players' lounge.

We had a trophy case, and it had one trophy inside of it—the second-place trophy from the 1982 Independence Bowl. It was the only bowl game Kansas State had participated in during the entire history of the football program. I wanted to dispose of the trophy, but I did not because there were still people in the Kansas State athletic department who had earned the right to be represented by their football team in a bowl game. I did not want for them to think that I did not recognize that they had achieved something special. Eventually, I gave the trophy to Joan Friederich, our longtime administrative assistant for assistant football coaches. Joan was the final person in our program who had been at Kansas State during the 1982 season.

However, the obstacles remained ongoing. A Nebraska-based stone company announced a two-week delay on the shipment of the tons of limestone rock needed to cover the outside surface of the football complex. I phoned that company's president, and he sped up the limestone arrival time. A chair company announced a delay on the shipment of chairs for the team meeting room until August 15, which was three weeks after we were to start meetings. One company set to assist in construction backed out of its contract. I phoned the steel company to expedite fabrication and confronted the lagging building contractor, who graciously responded rapidly. It was that way with virtually everything.

Throughout my career, I never wanted a Taj Mahal and I requested only those enhancements absolutely necessary to help our program succeed. There were no frills. I always believed that principles, values, people, and attitudes were most necessary for success. An institution should be centered upon education, not athletic facilities. Unfortunately, college football has largely overshadowed that virtue in today's society. I believe that downgrades an institution's academic environment. I've always been opposed to building just to build and have shared that with the Kansas State faculty over the years. But when I arrived at Kansas State prior to the 1989 football season, the program was literally scraping to survive.

Kansas State gave me a five-year contract with a base salary of $85,000. Considering at the time that when I went to Gallatin High School my salary was $3,600, I thought it was very gracious. Dollar figures weren't significant to me. I left my original contract at Kansas State unsigned in a desk drawer over the first two years. I told Steve, "I don't want to sign a contract. If I'm not getting the job done, I don't want you to feel obligated to have to pay me or keep me."

Eventually, Jon Wefald discovered that I had not signed the formal contract and asked me to do so. So I finally signed the contract. During all of my time at Kansas State, I never asked for a raise. Not once. I received a few raises, but I didn't want it to be about the money except when it came to paying the assistant coaches.

By now, I had trained myself to work through the lunch hour and to work through the dinner hour because I needed that time and I needed every bit of it. Of course, eating makes me sleepy, so meal displacement was highly beneficial. Had I eaten those meals, I would've slowed down tremendously and I couldn't afford to slow down at all. I don't dislike sleeping. I could grow fond of it, but it's never been a necessity for me. In this profession, you learn to go without certain things, and sleep is one of them. Throughout the day, I invested myself in one issue, then progressed onto the next issue, and the next one. Too often, sudden problems arose in one area, diverting my focus from another area. It became a taxing process.

Fortunately, I had Joan. Hired as an administrative assistant for assistant football coaches in 1973, Joan became administrative assistant to the head football coach in 1980 and served in that capacity under previous head coaches Jim Dickey and Stan Parrish. Joan was an amazing asset to the football program for 42 years all the way up to her retirement following the 2016 season. Joan was a protector, knew the entirety of our football program, and wasn't afraid of extra hours. She was so very special to our staff and our players daily. I always asked our players to come by Joan's office to say hello each day. She loved that and kept a full candy jar for the players when they stopped in. Shortly after I arrived at Kansas State and while I was visiting supporters across the state of Kansas, I called Joan and asked her to contact every returning football player and tell them that we were going to have a meeting when I returned.

Among the issues facing the football program at a time when a Division I-A football program could have 95 scholarship players, Kansas State only had 47 players on scholarship. While major college football teams had 100-plus players on their roster, we had about half of that total. Many of our players faced academic issues, and some were academically ineligible. Some players had transferred or were seeking a transfer, some players had quit the team, and some players had quit football altogether. All of these Kansas State players had one thing in common: they had never won a college football game while at Kansas State.

All of the players were quiet when I introduced myself in that first meeting. I told them, "This conversation today is going to be about you. This football program is about you. I'm not here to cast blame on anyone and certainly not your previous coaches."

Some of the players had been a part of the teams that had finished 1–10, 2–9, 0–10–1 and 0–11 over the previous four seasons. I anticipated that the players would discuss the team's on-field performance or that they needed more players or what went on with the previous coaches. Instead, the players revealed to me how failure on the football field had negatively impacted their college experience and their lives. One young man raised his hand. He said, "Coach, we have an area called Aggieville where everybody goes after football games, and none of us go there because we're too embarrassed."

Another young man said, "Coach, we don't go to class on Monday because we're too embarrassed."

Then another young man said, "And Coach, we don't go to class on Tuesday either because we're too embarrassed."

Finally, a young man said, "Coach, a bunch of us don't even go to class on Wednesdays either."

That first meeting with the returning players left an impression upon me. It reiterated to me just how much losing had beaten down these young men, impacting their personal and academic lives.

That included a young wide receiver named Michael Smith. Michael had been a walk-on who had packed up his dorm room and returned to his parents' home in New Orleans immediately after the 1988 season. I called Michael on Christmas Day, told him that I'd love for him to come back to Kansas State, and promised him a scholarship. Michael returned to the program and finished his career as one of the finest wide receivers in program history.

I also met with the outgoing senior class—22 young men who dearly loved the opportunity to compete in football at the college level and yet had experienced absolutely no success. Worried about how these young men might proceed with the rest of their lives after having been so impacted during their football careers, I informed those departing players that the Kansas State football program would always be there for them. I told them that I would do anything to help them achieve future personal success and that the football program would aid them—whether it be locating employment or writing recommendations, and we would support their academic progress. "Do not allow the outcome of your football career to impact the quality of people you are," I said. "There are so many more important things in life like your family, your personal life, your academic achievement, and your future career."

Weeks progressed and many current players attempted to leave the program. We were able to convince several to remain, and yet some ultimately decided not to stay. It was an ongoing cycle. We attempted to reach the players. Every one of them was valuable to us.

Then one day, things almost turned tragic. A Kansas State player attempted suicide.

I left the building and was headed to my car when a young man approached me in the parking lot. "Coach, he said, "I need to tell you something. One of our players is distraught, and he's attempting suicide as we speak."

"How do you know that?" I replied.

"Because he told me what he was going to do."

"Where is he?"

"He said that he's going to Tuttle Creek Lake."

I climbed into my car and was off.

I didn't know the type of vehicle this young man drove or exactly where he would be, but I wound around the small road surrounding the lake and searched every nook and cranny until I finally came upon an automobile tucked beneath some overhanging trees. The vehicle was running, and I spotted a hose fastened from the exhaust pipe into the driver's window. The young man sat in the driver's seat. At first, he wouldn't acknowledge me as I knocked on the window. I continued to knock. "Please roll your window down!" I said.

Finally, he rolled down the window. Then I asked him to turn off the vehicle. And then we began to talk. As the exhaust fumes dissipated, I convinced him to follow me to my office. Finally, he said, "Okay, Coach, I'll come with you."

I followed him into town, and we sat in my office and gradually addressed some of the issues he was experiencing. I told him, "I will do everything I can to make things better for you if you make the same effort."

Although the young man, a senior on the football team, told me that he would make an effort, I remained concerned that he had just attempted to take his own life, so I contacted his roommate. "If anything happens," I said, "here's how to get ahold of me."

The young man worked through the issues troubling him and finished his football career at Kansas State. He moved away, got married, and raised a family. We remained in contact for a long time, and it pleased me to see him do well.

My concern for the lives of our young people in the program remained ongoing. I addressed some of the academic difficulties with professors on campus. I told the deans, assistant deans, department heads, and professors that they had my full support, adding that I would never request special favors for our players but hoped that they would be treated the same as all other students. It was important to me that I initiated contact with the faculty as our football program worked to create a process by which our players could succeed in all areas of their lives.

The process of assembling a coaching staff remained an ongoing venture as well. I didn't interview a large number of candidates for the staff. Some of them were coaches eager to take a step up from lower-division programs, some were unemployed coaches, and some carried a University of Iowa background. Like everything else surrounding the program, building a coaching staff required time. The coaching meetings began small and gradually grew as new assistant coaches arrived. The coaches all shared a similar sentiment. They said, "Wow, we didn't know the program was this bad off." The development of the coaching staff was as complex as the development of the players in the program. Several coaches arrived at Kansas State, discovered the major issues facing the program, realized it wasn't going to be an overnight fix, and searched for another job.

When Hayden Fry and I arrived at the University of Iowa, Hayden retained Del Miller, a graduate assistant from the previous Iowa coaching staff, and Del eventually became our wide receivers coach. Del helped me coach quarterbacks and wide receivers for nearly 10 years at Iowa. He possessed a tremendous understanding of the offense and was outstanding at quarterback and wide receiver development. I asked Del to join me at Kansas State and brought him on as offensive coordinator.

Bobby Stoops played safety for us at Iowa and had begun his coaching career as an assistant coach at Kent State, and I brought him in to coach the defensive secondary. Tom Grogan, who had been a quarterback for us at Iowa, graduated and joined an architectural firm in Kansas City. Tom was a very bright young man and expressed a desire to join the staff. I hired him as our quarterbacks coach.

Bobby Cope had coached at many places and had left his job as head coach at Pacific University. We had mutual acquaintances, and Cope came highly regarded with previous coaching experience as a defensive assistant at Ole Miss and Purdue and he had also served as defensive coordinator at Arkansas. Cope was a tremendous individual and just enjoyed coaching. I flew him in for an interview and hired him as our defensive coordinator.

I extended an interview opportunity to every member of the previous Kansas State coaching staff, but just a few of them applied for a position on our staff. I retained former Kansas State offensive tackle Dana Dimel, who had served as a graduate assistant on the previous staff, and he assumed an identical role for us that first year. Dana eventually became our offensive line coach.

Although I had my ideas regarding our overall operation, I gathered thoughts from the coaching staff, and we implemented several of those ideas. I understood that coaches wanted to incorporate their own philosophies, and that just came with the territory, as coaches had their own way of operating, and I had great respect for them and their thoughts. The coaches, to their credit, sought to put their own touches on the blueprint. My concern, though, stemmed from one defining characteristic: this program was unlike any program that any of us had ever experienced in our careers. Bobby Stoops was a young safety when Hayden and I arrived at Iowa, so Bobby encountered some of those difficult times when we rebuilt the Iowa program, but Kansas State was without comparison. The multitude of challenges trumped anybody's experience, including mine.

One of our first coaching staff meetings detailed assigning recruiting territories and formulating a plan to land high school and community college prospects. The coaching staff wore out the phones and traveled constantly, visiting their own familiar areas. Most of our coaches maintained a common belief: we must recruit the best possible prospects. Given the state of the program, I was reluctant to chase five-star players, but finally said, "fine." To our coaches' credit, they succeeded in getting a few of these youngsters to visit the campus, yet I carried this fear—and it was reaffirmed rather quickly— that things would quickly go south when these top prospects stepped foot onto our campus. All of these highly-regarded recruits immediately wanted to go home. That coaches had focused their energy on the five-star players, who absolutely weren't going to attend Kansas State, and it set us behind in recruiting other prospects. We were no longer going to waste our time recruiting five-star players. We altered our philosophy and found young men who met our expectations and yet we believed we had a chance at them joining our program.

I was honest with the young people who visited Kansas State. I didn't want them to step foot inside our facility and say, "Oh wow, this is not what I expected. I'm not coming here." I told them ahead of time, "Listen, here's what you're going to see," and I likely painted a darker picture than what actually existed. In the next breath, I outlined the plans for facility enhancements along with the athletic department's commitment to the program and touted the fact that they could potentially compete for a spot on the field given our small roster size. "We are identified as the worst program in college football history, but we have the opportunity to stage the greatest turnaround in college football history, and you have an opportunity to be a part of that," we told them. "It will carry great meaning as you go through life because you will be identified as a person who can make very positive things take place in a very dark environment."

We continued to communicate this idea to our recruits. Sometimes, it wasn't so easy. One evening, I traveled to Wyoming for an in-home visit with a recruit and his family and spotted reporters and photographers standing outside the house. I thought to myself, *This is crazy. Maybe everyone is here because he's going to commit to us tonight.*

Shortly after, those reporters and photographers surrounded Colorado head coach Bill McCartney as he exited the front door. That pretty much took the spark out of my visit. After McCartney left, I went into the house and spoke with the young man and his family about Kansas State. The youngster went to Colorado.

Although we had some young people from Missouri, Ohio, Texas, Nebraska, New Jersey, and Pennsylvania commit to play for us, much of our recruiting success was in our own backyard within the state of Kansas in communities such as Salina, Lebanon, Leonardville, Topeka, Hoisington, Manhattan, and many others. Maybe some of the youngsters were undersized and perhaps they weren't as athletically gifted as five-star prospects, but there was the potential for exceptional development during their college careers. Similarly, it became paramount to locate young people with a strong value system, who were extremely hard workers, who did things the right way, who we felt wouldn't give up, who would be conscientious students in the classroom, and who possessed the capabilities for great improvement and development in their athletic skillset. Together, these individuals might promote positive change within the program. Young people in the state of Kansas and the Midwest didn't have the opportunity to fully invest themselves into high school football 365 days a year like players in Texas, Florida, California, and Pennsylvania. The young people in the state of Kansas— many of whom played football, basketball, baseball, and track and field— possessed a greater capacity to improve their football skills at the college level. That became our recruiting focus. And it became effective for us.

The first in-state player to commit to play for us was a tight end named Brad Seib out of Hoisington, Kansas. Brad was one of young guys you loved dearly. Brad wasn't a highly-recruited individual, but I liked him as he was a young man of character just looking for an opportunity. You take a young person like Brad and a highly-touted recruit, and because of Brad's intrinsic values, he might go to a much higher level and reach his potential or beyond, whereas maybe a higher-profile athlete might never get there. Brad played to his potential, to his full capabilities, and wanted this program to be successful. The same can be said about so many of those players.

For the better part of two decades, we found numerous under-recruited players who carried that capacity for development, who were committed toward making daily improvement, and who possessed those intrinsic values that allowed them to grasp the process of becoming a little bit better each day of their lives. Several of those youngsters evolved into some of the most prominent players in the country and in our program's history.

"When Coach Snyder met with us outgoing seniors upon his arrival, he called us a beaten down group of young men. We told him how pained we were by losing and how we were too embarrassed to wear our lettermen's jackets on campus and how we hoped that he could get things turned around. He didn't have to talk with us, but he did. I know the conversation affected me and I think it affected him as well. Coach Snyder turned it around. I'm proud to say not only did I play at Kansas State, but my sons did as well."

—Mark Porter, Kansas State kicker, 1985–88

CHAPTER 5

THE FIRST STEP

"I took my first full-time coaching job at Iowa in 1981, and Bill was our offensive coordinator. It was a magical time in Iowa football history, and I was fortunate to work closely with such an outstanding coach the next eight years. I had my doubts when Bill accepted the Kansas State job, but with his thorough knowledge of the game and of people coupled with an extremely strong will, he has accomplished what most sound football people said would be impossible. Bill is meticulous in all that he does and has a determination to reach his goals that is rare; as a result, he leaves a lasting legacy. I am very appreciative of the eight years we worked together and very happy for the unparalleled success he created and experienced at Kansas State—he has earned every bit of it."

—Kirk Ferentz, Iowa head coach

We were not a mentally or physically well-conditioned football team. Some of it was probably due in part to the transition time between coaching staffs. Without guidance, young people weren't invested in the conditioning process. Some of it was simply because young people were seeking a different avenue, a place to be other than Kansas State.

Upon our arrival, our goals were simple. We wanted our players to push themselves mentally and physically like never before while instilling the self-discipline necessary to have an opportunity to succeed each day in all facets of their lives. We attempted to instill strong work habits. Our players ran and ran and ran some more. It became evident that some individuals weren't interested in putting in the enhanced work, and many of those players left the program. However, we also possessed many special players because they didn't give in, they fought the battle, they believed in the process, and they ultimately created *The Foundation* for success because they were involved in gradual day-to-day improvement throughout the course of the year. Consequently, they established the basis for the program to become better. Eventually, most of these players bought into our coaches and the process.

These 68 players became known as *The Foundation*.

I addressed our value system with each player and the expectation that they would commit to be quality people, to invest in hard work, to do right, and to improve their academic focus. I had individual conversations with each player to learn about him, his parents, his family, and his home life. I wanted the families invested, and we contacted them immediately—first by mail and then by phone call. I assigned each coach to call his players' parents every two weeks to share their son's progress. I wanted to learn about each player's interests and field of study. I quickly discovered that many players had no career aspirations upon completion of their degree. We put into place a program that focused on our players' future outside of football. We had professionals from various companies visit with our players about virtues like quality of character, as they outlined different career fields, so players might better define a direction for their education.

It was important to me for our players to become strong representatives of the football program, our university, and the Manhattan community, as well as their own families. Behavior issues had been a problem in the classroom and in Aggieville, a social area in Manhattan, so we put into place some program guidelines to promote self-discipline and small measures of individual sacrifice. Whatever our players wanted to achieve in life was going to require sacrifice and the discipline necessary to succeed. We introduced to our players *Cat Time*, which meant everything and everyone must be in place three minutes ahead of schedule for any scheduled event we held. Players who failed to attend a class met at the stadium at 6:00 AM to perform some taxing running to reinforce the importance of class attendance. We asked our players to sit toward the front of the classroom, sit up in their chairs, and keep their eyes on the lecturer or speaker. We had individuals visit the classrooms to ensure that our young people were doing exactly that.

We placed signs on the doors to our football complex that read "Please Wipe Feet Before Entering" and explained that it was important for us to respect our property and our custodian's efforts to maintain a clean environment. Personal sacrifice also involved not wearing hats or earrings inside of the football complex. Such a guideline probably isn't so prevalent in today's society, but nevertheless, I don't know if I'd do it any differently today. I explained to our players, "I have nothing against hats or earrings, but when you're inside the building, this is about our family, the game of football, and developing ourselves. Going without hats and earrings are a part of the sacrifice and self-discipline that one has to make in order to accomplish something special." I was raised knowing that men politely took off their hats inside.

Players also couldn't have their hair flow out from underneath their helmet. Again, hats, hair, and earrings don't make one a bad person. It was simply a matter of making sacrifices and creating a unified group. To reinforce discipline, we instituted a punishment called "The Price of Irresponsibility." If a player lost his playbook; had an unexcused absence from study table, a doctor's appointment, treatments, practice, or a meeting; skipped a class; or wore a hat or earrings into the football complex, he suffered "The Price of Irresponsibility." He reported to the football field at 6:00 AM and performed what we called 8-8-8s. The 8-8-8s involved running the stadium stairs eight times, performing up and downs for 800 yards, and running around the field eight times under the guidance of a member of our staff.

So many people would say, "You're taking things way too far," but we had places to go, and we needed to get there quickly. And we needed to develop the discipline and commitment needed for daily improvement over the long haul. We explained that when we lose pride in our performance, we lose pride in our capacity to do things right. When that pride goes, discipline is right behind. We geared everything we did toward reinforcing the discipline, commitment, and hard work necessary to benefit the program and our young people over the course of their lifetime. We ordered matching blazers, and coaches and players would also wear those and ties to away games. We would be well-mannered and we would be gentlemen.

Sitting at my desk, I asked myself the fundamental question: *what do these young people need, what do we need, and what does the program need in order to become successful?* I thought of far more values than could fit on a piece of paper. The values weren't rocket science. They centered on the values that most parents try to teach their children and that we needed in order for our program to be successful. You can go into any locker room across the country and see a bunch of words painted on the walls, words like "commitment" and "discipline" and "hard work." It was important that those virtues that we emphasized didn't eventually just become words. We wanted to utilize these goals on a daily basis. We wanted our players to grasp each concept and value and we wanted our players to experience them each and every day. These characteristics became known as the 12 Wildcat Goals for Success (and later it grew to become the 14 Wildcat Goals for Success, and then it grew to become the 16 Wildcat Goals for Success).

We reinforced a specific goal with an activity each day. For instance, one of the Wildcat Goals became known as "Expect to Win," which we emphasized by putting players in an arena to compete not just on the football field, but also during the out-of-season program and inside the meeting room. This might entail a one-on-one drill on the field in front of all of the players, it might be a question-and-answer session in the meeting room, but I wanted to put our young people into a position where they had the opportunity to be successful and where they realized that they had that opportunity to succeed.

One of our goals became known as "Unity—come together as never before." We implemented a unity sharing program in which we divided our players into groups, and each group interacted with another group. Each player from one group matched up with each player from another group. In this exercise, I gave the players a topic. Some of the topics were light, but for the most part, I gave them pretty heavy and very personal topics—things you probably wouldn't normally share with anybody other than your family and closest friends. So, over the course of a two-minute period, our players were put into a position where they shared thoughts that were very precious to them with several fellow teammates. What transpired was that sense of unity, that friendship, and that trust for each other, along with that willingness to share privileged information because you trusted that your partner would handle it appropriately. Over the course of the season, every player had had a one-on-one conversation with every other player on the team.

This unity exercise was for each youngster—regardless if they were from a big city or small town, the suburbs or inner city. Some players became invested right away, and others were very cautious and not as open. We understood this would be a learning process. Each day the players became more and more invested, and we readdressed it while discussing the daily improvement within our football program. We strived to become a little bit better each day, and this was one of the elements in that process. Each day, players became a little bit more trusting of their teammates and we expounded upon the process of implementing unity into their own personal lives. It all worked hand in hand.

Soon after arriving in Manhattan, I decided that the football program needed a new logo. It was my thinking that players understood that things had to change. The players didn't really know what needed to change, but they just knew that they needed change. Kansas State fans were the same way. Everybody knew something had to change. I believed a new logo for the program was an important part of it. It was significant to me that a player couldn't see the previous Kansas State logo and say, "This is the same old stuff" and then relate that feeling to their previous difficulties on the football field.

I spoke with Jon Wefald and Steve Miller about this plan. I told them: "I don't want to disrupt the current university logo, Willie the Wildcat, which I truly love, but I'd like to create a logo just for the football program. One that doesn't disrupt anything with the university. Our football program needs to demonstrate a new identity."

They both approved the change, so I called the Kansas State art department and became introduced to Tom Bookwalter. I'm not afraid to be a copycat, so I showed Tom the University of Iowa logo and told him that I wanted our logo to be based on that logo with no words or letters. I wanted people across the nation to see this logo and know that it represented Kansas State football. We were the Wildcats, and I wanted that to come across with a stronger logo. The new logo became known as the Powercat.

Tom did a great job and brought me three or four drawings at a time, and I'd say, "No," "Maybe," and "Let's tweak this a little bit." I still have those drawings, in a box somewhere. There were a significant number of drawings and they crept closer and closer toward that desired image.

Finally, we created a logo that hit the target.

I had told our players that we were creating a logo to identify the Kansas State football program. I introduced the completed Powercat logo to them during a meeting and said, "This will be your decision. This is your team. I want this to be your decision." Our players were overwhelmingly in favor of this new logo, and the rest is history. Eventually, the university decided it wanted to adopt the logo campus wide, but I strongly opposed the move because I didn't want to be seen as the person responsible for replacing Willie the Wildcat. I liked Willie the Wildcat, but he just didn't fit what we needed for our program at that time.

I hired a company to manufacture Powercat license plates for our players. I told the company that it could produce these license plates to sell to the public, but these Powercat plates could not be publicly distributed until after we gave them to our football team. During a meeting we handed these license plates to our players and said, "You get to be the ring bearer, and if you'd like, please put this license plate on the front of your car and broadcast the Powercat." We gave Kansas State University the rights to the revenue generated by the license plates, which have been responsible for millions of dollars in sales over the last 30-plus years.

Once we had decided upon the Powercat, I approached our contracted athletic apparel company because it was time to change our uniforms. I wanted our primary color to be a darker shade of purple because it demonstrated strength over the lighter purple, which had been previously utilized by the football program. I wanted our uniforms to express class, strength, and aggressiveness. I structured the Kansas State football uniforms off of the Dallas Cowboys uniforms. The Cowboys were highly successful at the time, and I wanted our uniforms to promote that identity of success. Whereas Kansas State football previously utilized the color white on its pants, I wanted our players to wear silver pants to reinforce that desire for change. I wanted the Powercat displayed on each side of a silver helmet with dark purple uniform tops and silver pants for home games and white uniform tops with silver pants for away games.

I wanted our changes within the football program to permeate the Kansas State fanbase. When I arrived in Manhattan, I was not aware that the Kansas State average home attendance had been about 13,000. I also did not know that the Kansas Board of Regents had contemplated the future of the Kansas State football program. An NCAA rule stated that Division I-A football programs must maintain an average home attendance of 19,000. Kansas State had fallen below that threshold. From what I understood, the Kansas Board of Regents discussed two options—either drop Kansas State to a Division I-AA classification or dissolve the football program. Some people suggested the University of Arkansas could replace Kansas State in the conference. Of course, such a move would've been dire to the Manhattan economy and subsequently would have a dramatic impact upon the overall population and growth of the community.

The Kansas State football program needed its fans, but I realized that these fans had not seen a Kansas State football victory in a long while. Many of them were beaten down much like our players, and they had been overcome by this sense of darkness regarding the program. We had to change that. I traveled across the state and said, "We need you to be a part of this program and we need you in the stands, and your support will help define the success of the program."

I wanted our players to feel supported. Our players lived in a reasonably small community, so they were around the people, and it just made sense that they needed the support of the community, the university, and the people in the state of Kansas. I met with Manhattan city representatives, I met with the student body governing board, and I invited students to the stadium and told them, "It is necessary to have you actively involved with our program because we cannot succeed without your help."

We obviously understood it would be difficult to win games in the Big 8 Conference with Colorado, Nebraska, and Oklahoma always among the top teams in the country. That's a tough enough schedule. When we arrived in Manhattan, Kansas State was scheduled to play a televised game against Oklahoma in Tokyo, Japan, on December 4, 1990. But Oklahoma was on

NCAA probation and was prohibited from playing on TV for one year. Prior to the Tokyo arrangement, our game against Oklahoma had been scheduled for Manhattan in 1990. Instead, we agreed to move the game to Oklahoma. In fact, we opted to play Oklahoma in Norman our first four years in 1989, 1990, 1991, and 1992 because Oklahoma gave us $350,000 per visit, and our football program was dearly in need of money. At the time, playing Oklahoma in Norman was more profitable for us than playing Oklahoma in Manhattan.

Kansas State also had scheduled itself for many non-conference road games against many highly-prominent college football programs over the course of the next few seasons, including Tennessee, Clemson, and Georgia. One of the early tasks involved dissolving as many of those existing non-conference road-game contracts as possible. It proved to be an arduous process for Steve—Kansas State had originally scheduled those road games for a much-needed payout to help support the athletic department—but it was in the best interest of the football program to find home games against less-formidable opponents to build our players' confidence, get fans in the stands, and give our players and opportunity to succeed. A few non-conference road opponents—Arizona State (1989), Washington (1991), Utah State (1992), and Minnesota (1993)—did not allow us to void our contract.

During the spring, we spent a great amount of time having post-practice dialogue with players after actual practice, addressing the pluses and minuses of the practice itself, outlining the needed improvements and how we might make those improvements, and identifying positive aspects and ways we could continue to build upon those areas. We addressed academics every day, we addressed our value system and the necessity to do the right things, and we addressed those Wildcat Goals. We addressed one, two, or three of those goals every day at the end of practice.

Truly, we had to learn how to practice and we barely had enough players for all-out scrimmages. The youngsters now will look back and tell you there was great value in that process, but at the time, they were often disgruntled because of the length of time and how hard that we practiced. Virtually every moment of every day was structured. We had a set practice schedule that encompassed 2 hours and 47 minutes. They were long, hard practices organized so every player was practicing the entire time, and nobody was standing around. Our players were engaged in some activity virtually every minute. First of all, I wanted us as coaches to teach our players as well as we possibly could, which meant organizing a routine that emphasized instruction about techniques and fundamentals of the game itself. Conditioning was imperative, and it wasn't as much about physical conditioning as it was about mental conditioning. When you're running 20 100-yard sprints one after another, it takes a certain mental capacity to accomplish that task.

Our practice sessions were composed of seven minutes, then three minutes, then 13 minutes, and so forth. Practices were designed that way because it required thinking, awareness, and efficiency, and it was important to be different. All around, I wanted our players to see change. When you added the post-practice meeting time to our schedule, the totality of our practices went beyond three-plus hours. This was before rule changes limited practice time.

I'd never purposely violated NCAA rules, but we unknowingly violated an NCAA rule regarding the length of time that we occupied the practice field many years later when rules were established limiting practice time considerably. We were on schedule with the allotted practice time, but I hadn't also figured in the time that I spent visiting with our players afterward on the field about topics other than football. I didn't believe that post-practice discussion period counted as actual practice time. Thus we committed a lower-level NCAA violation and were forced to forfeit a few practice opportunities. I soon restructured a few things so we could achieve all that we needed to achieve to adhere to those NCAA guidelines.

While our tiny weight room hindered the quality of our weight training, we incurred other obstacles. Since we were in the process of a $1.6 million renovation for our building and for new artificial turf, we practiced at old Memorial Stadium on campus or on a grass pasture field several blocks from the football complex. We were committed to accomplishing our daily goals despite some undesirable circumstances.

Over the course of winter conditioning and spring practice, some players decided that they couldn't comply with our standards and left the program. Sixteen players left the first day of winter conditioning. We only had a handful of defensive linemen. Each time a player left, I repeated to our players that it took a special person to become highly successful in life, and sacrifices were a big part of that endeavor. Our players eventually improved their discipline, fundamentals on the football field, and eventually the mental aspect necessary to take steps toward success followed.

During the summer, I received a phone call from a writer named Douglas S. Looney, who wanted to visit Manhattan and write a story about our football program for *Sports Illustrated*. I said, "Respectfully, no. I'm not ready to do that. We haven't done a thing yet." He called two or three more times. Finally, I said, "I appreciate your persistence," knowing it would be a negative article about Kansas State football. I allowed him to visit for an interview—provided that he promised to write a positive article when we did become successful. Doug kept his word and did so.. Of course, he never mentioned the title of the story, "Futility U," which painted a picture of all of the program's struggles. He wrote: "When it comes to college football, nobody does it worse than Kansas State." In the story, he also asked, "Why bother?" He questioned why Kansas State even played football. I told him, "You have to promise me when and if the football program changes and we become successful that you'll come back and write a positive story about Kansas State." He said that he would do so.

Our purpose was simple: we wanted to at least initiate and hopefully culminate the greatest turnaround in college football history.

My friends were always positive with me. The media wasn't so much. Many sportswriters insisted that there was no chance to turn around the program. A few were upset with me when I closed our practices to reporters. One sportswriter in Topeka published an article every week criticizing my decision to close practices. Other media outlets also wrote a few negative stories about the program. What I appreciated so much was that Kansas State fans—and even a few newspaper advertisers—took issue with the negative reporting and made their concerns known to the media. Some companies pulled newspaper advertisements. Nevertheless, I compromised and allowed reporters to observe the initial phase of our practices, which entailed individual player drills. The reporters attended a few of the practice opportunities and then stopped coming. I said, "You wanted open practices, and now that they're open, you're not coming? Make sense of this."

Honestly, I didn't read a lot of stories and I discouraged our players from reading them. If the newspapers said that you're good, you might start believing what you read. I didn't want the media to have any impact on our football program. Really, I had nothing against the media whatsoever. I was just protective of our football program.

We were with our players virtually 24 hours a day during fall camp. Our days were packed from early morning to late at night. Coaches rotated and stayed with our players in the dormitory. We had two-a-day practices with a meeting in the morning and afternoon, along with strength work and a final meeting at night. Each nighttime meeting featured a guest speaker—perhaps a professor, a university administrator, a community leader, or a campus police chief. I wanted our players to be well-rounded and informed.

It became apparent over the course of preparation that our players had bought into that virtue of daily improvement. As we entered the football season, I told our players that I wouldn't address their season based upon the results on the scoreboard but rather based upon their acceptance and execution of getting better each and every day.

Several individuals emerged in providing various forms of leadership during our initial season. Brooks Barta was really a quality leader for us and had 436 total tackles in his career. He was an intelligent linebacker who didn't make mistakes and provided tremendous leadership because of his passion for the game and his desire for us to succeed on every play. Defensive end Reggie Blackwell was a player we knew would advance himself. He played hard and was aggressive and astute in his knowledge of the game. Tight end Russ Campbell brought size and skills at the tight end position and was significant to our passing game. Offensive guard Chad Faulkner was destined to be successful and was a good leader within the program. He was a quality player who performed well and was selfless in his desire for the team to succeed. Running back Eric Gallon was a talented player and hard worker who recovered from injury and became our all-time leading rusher at that time. Frank Hernandez and Michael Smith were two talented wide receivers who provided leadership and were special people. These players, and so many more, were engrained in the team aspect of the program to a high degree and were teammates first, which was an integral part of our value system.

I strived to make that first game week as Kansas State head coach nothing out of the ordinary for me. I didn't try to project what this first-game experience would be like but instead focused on the organization and my mission, as we headed to open the season at Arizona State University. I focused on the ballgame itself, the players, and all of the logistics—the hotel, the food menu, the meeting space, the eating space, the table arrangements, the busses, the travel time to the stadium, the preparation time inside the locker room, the individual position group meetings, the final group meeting, and the team warmups. I wanted to make sure that we were well organized, that all issues were addressed, and that we were well-tuned on all aspects of the travel itinerary.

I thought we could achieve success against Arizona State. I knew that I had to maintain that approach in order to be genuine to our players so they could adopt a similar feeling. There are certain things said inside a locker room prior to virtually every ballgame and there are other things that are exclusive to that particular opponent. I readdressed those things that needed to take place for us to be successful and tried to be as specific as I could toward our players. As for motivation? Throughout the players' time in football, they might've had coaches yelling and screaming to try to keep them motivated. That wasn't my style. This wasn't about how motivated I was to succeed—it was about how motivated our players were to succeed. I wanted our players to learn how to self-motivate. I did try to build our players up to realize we had to do the very best that we could and be as good as we were capable of being, and good things would happen. You're never without the opportunity to be successful. I never said, "Win." I talked in different terms. It was about constant improvement and performing to the best of your capabilities. We faced one challenge in particular prior to our season opener. Only about half of our players had ever played in a major college game. This would also be the first college football game for 22 freshmen players.

When we went onto the field, I sensed a proper level of enthusiasm among our players. Our fans expressed genuine excitement about the team, our coaches, and our new uniforms. Although the official attendance was

68,606 at Sun Devil Stadium, I didn't pay attention to the crowd. I couldn't hear a thing through my headset other than the communication with the coaches. I was focused on the next step. On the very first play of the game, one of our defensive backs, William Price, intercepted a pass, and our offense marched down the field, missed a field goal, and then went into the tank and lost 31–0.

When we returned to the locker room after the game, I told our players and coaches that we went into the ballgame with the attitude that we could be successful and I was pleased with that attitude. On the very first drive, we put ourselves into position to take the lead against a highly-regarded football team. Even though we missed the field goal, we played well for most of the first quarter. However, when Arizona State eventually scored, we immediately fell back into that feeling of inferiority, we lost our mental edge, and we fell back into that here-we-go-again scenario that our players knew all too well. "What I hope you take from this is that we proved that we can be successful to a certain degree," I said. "And that success is based upon our attitude that we possess in any area of life."

Although our players still had not won a game in a long while, they believed that they should be able to beat Northern Iowa, a Division I-AA opponent, in Manhattan. We showed some improvement from the season opener, felt good about ourselves, then became overconfident, and gave up the decisive score in a 10–8 defeat. One week later, we took more positive steps but suffered a 37–20 loss to Northern Illinois.

That brought us to the week of the ballgame against North Texas State. It had been more than 10 years since I had been an assistant coach at North Texas State. They were really an exceptional Division I-AA football team and were very competitive. I emphasized to our players time and time again that we couldn't take a lighthearted approach toward this opponent. And really, why would we take a lighthearted approach toward anybody?

Even though I could see progress, I was frustrated. Hardly a day went by that a player didn't encounter some sort of academic difficulty, that the athletic department lacked enough money to complete a scheduled task, or that a coach wondered if he was ruining his career at Kansas State. Some coaches looked to be someplace else for fear this was a dead-end stop. Still, we continued to strive for gradual improvement each day on the practice field, but some players suffered from those here-we-go-again moments.

Our players fought to put that here-we-go-again mentality to rest at a critical juncture late in the fourth quarter against North Texas State. We suffered a couple of fumbles and faced some adversity. We led 14–10, and North Texas State faced fourth and 19 from their 47-yard line with less than two minutes remaining in the ballgame when their quarterback threw a Hail Mary pass for a touchdown. Suddenly, we trailed 17–14. I was afraid our players believed that we were destined to lose, and that somehow, someway, it was going to happen. It was crucial to let them understand that we had come this far and that we could win this ballgame.

We had one final drive and needed to travel 85 yards with 91 seconds remaining in the ballgame. The drive was representative of the tough-mindedness demonstrated by our quarterback, Carl Straw. Carl hurt his hand in the ballgame, and it had affected his performance, but had I attempted to take him out of the game, I don't think he would've come off the field because he was just that competitive of an individual. Before that final drive, I gathered our players and asked them what plays they liked the most and I utilized most of those plays. Carl completed pass after pass to Michael. I felt awfully good about Michael. He was a talented individual, who had a good knack for the game, knew how to execute, had good movement in his route running, and could catch the ball and run well.

Michael caught a pass and went out of bounds at the 12-yard line with four seconds remaining in the game. I called a timeout and asked the players, "What do you feel best about?" We had noted in our film study that North Texas had a cornerback who had a tendency to play several yards off the ball in the defensive backfield, which would increase our chances of successfully executing a pass underneath him. Frank, a talented wide receiver, believed that he could get open in the end zone and he did. Frank lined up split to the left, ran an excellent route and cut to the left, but it was actually well covered. Carl threw the pass, and Frank showed great concentration as he caught the ball just inside the front left pylon in north end zone and had the presence of mind to keep his feet inbounds just long enough to score. Had Carl thrown the ball six inches in either direction, it would've been an incomplete pass. It was great execution.

I remember the fans. Our Kansas State fans didn't know what to do. Kansas State had not won a football game since it beat Kansas 29–12 on October 18, 1986. Kansas State had lost 16 consecutive games and had gone winless in 30 straight ballgames, and we had just beaten North Texas State 20–17. Our fans had gone 1,071 days without witnessing a victory. Little did I know this was the 300th victory in program history. For a moment, the crowd of 26,000 inside the stadium fell completely silent. Our fans, many who had never before experienced a win, didn't know whether to run onto the field. All of our players were like, "What do we do?"

I jumped into the arms of Jim Leavitt, our linebackers coach—there's a picture of that somewhere—but by the time we entered the locker room, I was back to myself again. At the moment, nothing was more important than the fact that our players and fans were excited. There wasn't a member of our student body who had experienced a win, and there wasn't a player who had experienced a win. We had a large bell just outside of our football complex on the north side, and Kansas State had a tradition to ring the bell following a victory, but nobody had ever heard it before, so a couple of our players ran over and rang the bell.

I don't know how long it took to finally get into the locker room. First and foremost, I applauded our players for their accomplishment and particularly in the way that it happened—that they had taken the lead, fallen behind, and had the opportunity to say, "Here we go again" and yet they didn't possess that mentality. Instead they stepped onto the field and executed that last drive. That was a major step in their improvement as it related to their approach, mental attitude, and their persistence. Then I addressed our necessity to build upon this ballgame and correct our mistakes. It was important to me to keep our players mentally balanced, so they didn't think, *We won; it's over* but rather to be positive about the victory and understand there's still so much to accomplish. As I said after the game, one win is not going to make the total difference. It just eases the pain. That victory meant a lot with regards to Kansas State people feeling that we're a little bit closer to believing it can happen. After that ballgame, I believed that Kansas State people were beginning to think, "Yes, we can."

I witnessed a consistent change in our players and I believe it was a combination of things. There were ongoing changes. We got beat bad by some teams, but each week we were playing better. I was confident that our players understood and respected the concept of daily improvement. The way all of this worked out was important. If you went in and tried to bite it all off in one chunk, more often than not, those plans don't work out, and consequently you give in. Young people and old people as well—all of us—give up on goals. The National Education Association in a study many years ago indicated that 100 percent of people set goals, and approximately 50 percent of the people actually have a process geared toward achieving those goals, and only 5 percent achieved the goals that they set for themselves. I never talked about wins. I talked about how improved we could be, what we needed to do in order to be the best we could be, and what it would require to become just a little bit better each day. Although we finished that first year with a 1–10 record, our players did as they were asked and improved virtually every single day of the season. In fact, they carried a curious air of confidence atypical of a one-win football team. After the season, everyone told me, "You need to leave, or your career is dead."

I replied, "To the contrary, I've never felt more confident than I do right now that we can have a successful program."

"On the morning of September 30, 1989, I told Coach Snyder that I wouldn't be able to play because my car was stolen during the night, and my dad was going to kill me. Coach told me everything would be okay. I went out and had eight catches for 114 yards, including four receptions on the final drive, and my best friend Frank Hernandez caught the winning touchdown with no time left on the clock in a 20–17 win over North Texas State, ending the longest losing streak in college football. Afterward, police found my car in Emporia. Coach was right. Everything turned out okay."

—Michael Smith, Kansas State wide receiver, 1988–91

CHAPTER 6

EARLY CLIMB

"Bill is a good friend of mine and someone whom I greatly admire. Bill engineered one of the greatest turnarounds in college football, turning Kansas State's program into one of the top in the country. I have many good memories of our relationship."

—Tom Osborne, former Nebraska head coach

We won one game, but we quickly hit reality after the enthusiasm, joy, and excitement wore off from that lone win during the 1989 season. We ended our first season with seven straight defeats and suffered 10 total losses, which tempered our players' attitudes. It was still so easy for them to drift back into those moments of negativity and failure. As a coach, there existed a fine line and a temptation to be overly positive. It would have been easy to pat a player on the back regardless of his performance and say, "Hey, you're doing fine" after he missed a tackle or cut a class. It was important to be honest. If a player did something good, we told him it was good; if he did something great, we told him it was great; if it was not so good, we told him it was not so good; and if it was horrible, we told him it was horrible. It promoted an environment of trust among the players. It was necessary to define an issue, no matter how small, and attempt to correct it.

Many of our issues from the first season carried over into our second season. Although we stressed to our players the importance of living a positive life as it related to individual development, several players suffered difficulty both in their academics and in their behavior on and off the field. Meanwhile, the financial status of our athletic department remained an issue as well despite the fact our average home football attendance increased to

26,726 per game. Although our issues were not as numerous as they had been during the first year, we still had to strive for daily improvement amid the ongoing complexities, difficulties, issues, and problems that existed in and around our program.

Our players became stronger and better conditioned during the out-of-season program, and yet some still lamented: "Don't we work too hard?" Some players adopted a proper work ethic quicker than others and truly made the daily investment necessary to elevate their overall development on and off the field. At the same time, our players expected to see positive results, which was only human nature. Our players, coaches, and fans experienced some growth during the 1990 season. We won our first two games against Western Illinois (27–6) and New Mexico State (52–7), which represented more victories than the program achieved over the entirety of the 1987, 1988, and 1989 seasons. A step in the right direction. A team, no matter how successful, always ran the risk of showing no additional wins despite its improvement. Over the course of those first two ballgames, we became a better team.

Although I was concerned how our players would respond following our loss to No. 8 Nebraska (45–8), their hard work was rewarded in a victory against Oklahoma State (23–17), which marked our program's first Big 8 Conference win since 1986. Our victory against Iowa State (28–14) marked our first homecoming win since 1981. It was always difficult to end a season with a defeat, and the fact that a season of continual improvement finished with a lopsided loss at eventual national champion Colorado (64–3) was major. Bill McCartney did things the right way and did a wonderful job with the University of Colorado. I had a great amount of respect for Bill and thought he was a fantastic person as well as football coach.

Part of the difficulty resided in the fact that our players perhaps questioned their improvement over the course of the season when staring at the scoreboard in Boulder, Colorado, and they had to wait another nine months before having an opportunity to win another game. As I stood in the locker room, I felt our players' disappointment and told them that I had not done due diligence to prepare them for the game. Although Colorado was a tremendous team, I also knew that we didn't play to our full potential. When I asked for every player who had given their best effort to stand, no one stood, which was important because I did not want our players to find fault with each other. We were a family. We had to come together, work through our issues over the offseason, and come out the other end a stronger and improved team.

Yet our 5–6 season record represented growth. We won more games in 1990 than the program won during the previous five seasons. We won the most games by a Kansas State team since 1982. We lost two road games—at Northern Illinois (42–35) and at Kansas (27–24)—by a total of 10 points, meaning we were excruciatingly close to a winning record and a possible bowl game. I reminded our players how far we came to reach a five-win season—something our players previously could have only dreamed about. Our 1989 team was ranked 100th in the nation, and our 1990 team ranked 59th—a 41 spot improvement. Although I knew we improved during our 1–10 season, no one outside of our program probably saw the tangible results. One year later, our fanbase and the football world recognized our improvement. When I was fortunate enough to be named 1990 Big 8 Coach of the Year, I emphasized that it was a team award and I accepted the honor on our behalf of our team.

Sean, my son, came to Kansas State as a walk-on (even though he deserved a scholarship) prior to the 1990 season. Sean grew up playing soccer, became a first-team all-area punter and kicker at Greenville (Texas) High School, and Hayden Fry thought enough of Sean to offer him a scholarship at the University of Iowa prior to the 1988 season. I told Hayden to award a scholarship to Sean only if he felt that he was deserving of a scholarship and not because of our relationship. Hayden believed Sean could be an asset to the Iowa program. After Sean redshirted his freshman season, he became a starter in the 1989 season for the Hawkeyes. I believed that Sean could have a successful career at Iowa, but I told him that I would love to have him at Kansas State if he opted to transfer.

Sean is one of the loves of my life, and my feelings toward him have nothing to do with football. He is an absolutely amazing person, as are all of our children. The oldest of five children, Sean stepped up and provided leadership for Shannon and Meredith when his mother and I separated during my last year at North Texas State. He always possessed strong intrinsic values. All of our children are special, and I spoke with them daily when I was at the University of Iowa—we still speak daily today—but it was special for Sean to eventually join our program at Kansas State.

However, I did not initially put Sean on scholarship when he arrived at Kansas State and I did not hide that fact from the players on our team. Although I knew all about Sean's ability as a punter and he was certainly worthy of a scholarship, I believed that our players would deem him worthy of a scholarship when he proved his skills on the field and not just because he was my son. After Sean sat out the 1990 season due to NCAA transfer rules, he proved his skills to the team, emerged as our starting punter, and faced no animosity from his teammates. I admired Sean's dedication in all areas of his life. He studied hard and practiced hard. He was and continues to be a loving husband to his wife, Wanda, and his family.

As a junior, Sean ranked 27th nationally in averaging 40.5 yards per punt and was named 1991 Big 8 Newcomer of the Year by a vote of the league's coaches. As a senior, Sean was named a 1992 consensus All-American, the first such distinction by a Kansas State player since Gary Spani in 1977. Sean established school records for punting average in a game (52.8 yards), in a season (44.7), and in a career (43.0). Although Sean finished his career as the most prolific punter in Kansas State history, became a member of our inaugural Ring of Honor Class in 2002, and was a 2016 inductee into the Kansas State Athletics Hall of Fame, he would have held every NCAA punting record had he not punted 12 times into a stiff wind at Oklahoma State during the final game of the 1991 season. Sean entered the game on pace to beat Reggie Roby's NCAA single-season record of 49.8 yards per punt before that wind greatly impacted his season-ending statistics.

After Sean spent two years in the NFL—he signed as an undrafted free agent with the Phoenix Cardinals in 1993 and signed with the San Diego Chargers in 1994—I hired Sean as a part-time assistant coach. Once again, Sean proved his skills within the program, and his responsibilities steadily grew over the course of his 26-year tenure at Kansas State. After Sean served as senior associate athletic director for football operations, I promoted him to assistant head coach and special teams coordinator prior to the 2011 season.

He was recognized as national Special Teams Coordinator of the Year in 2015 and 2017.

Success can create issues. That was our plight entering the 1991 season. Many of our assistant coaches entertained job offers from more prominent programs while less successful programs sought potential head coaches to improve their teams. We were the lowest-paid coaching staff in the Big 8 Conference, myself included, and some promises for salary raises fell through simply because no funds were available in the athletic department budget.

Prior to the 1991 season, we hired Mark Mangino as a graduate assistant on the recommendation of John Latina, our offensive line coach. Mark grew up in New Castle, Pennsylvania, less than 50 miles from where Bobby and Mike Stoops grew up in Youngstown, Ohio. Mark worked for the Pennsylvania Turnpike Commission for more than a decade, had been a high school offensive coordinator, and then served as a high school head coach for one season before he packed up his family and moved to Manhattan. John told me that Mark was a highly organized and intense individual and believed that Mark could be an asset to our program. Over Mark's time with us, he served as recruiting coordinator and running game coordinator while I promoted him to assistant head coach in 1998.

Kansas State entered the 1991 fiscal year with an operating debt of $3.5 million. Eventually, I was able to increase our assistant coaches' salaries by more than 25 percent. Our coaches had to take care of their families. Salaries were a point of contention within our program long before college football assistant coaches began making $1 million per year.

After serving as the defensive coordinator during our first two seasons, Bob Cope left to become an assistant coach at Southern California. At about that same time, Coach McCartney offered Jim Leavitt, our linebackers coach, the same position on his coaching staff at Colorado. Jim came close to leaving us. In an effort to retain Jim on our staff, I elevated him to co-defensive coordinator with Bobby Stoops, our defensive secondary coach. Bobby was fine with the joint defensive coordinator roles. Bob and Jim both had great defensive minds. Together they got the most out of their players and had good chemistry. Over the next several years, they built and led staunch defensive units that mightily contributed to our success and ranked in the top 25 annually. Our defenses embraced the personality of their coaches. Bob and Jim were very aggressive coaches, and, consequently, we had very aggressive defenses.

We continued to expound upon the plan for our program, and it encompassed virtually everything. We invested in our players, their education, their families, the Kansas State academic community, the Manhattan community, and our fanbase. We steadily gained supporters from all areas, and families across the nation began allowing us into their homes to explain our process of achieving success, how their sons could play an important part in that pursuit, and most importantly how we would help guide their sons toward highly successful lives. Although we were still nowhere near a fully-scholarshipped program, we crept closer. We were able to receive an additional $100,000 to our recruiting budget. Our $2.1 million facility construction project neared completion. Before the season, we also installed new artificial turf by virtue of a $1 million donation from Dave and Carol Wagner of Dodge City and we eventually named the football field in their honor.

In order to thoroughly address each area of our program, we met as a coaching staff at 8:00 AM and again at 1:00 PM each day. Dependent upon the amount of information we needed to cover, each meeting could consume one hour or it could consume a few hours. The morning meeting addressed academic issues, behavioral issues, and our players' positive achievements within a given realm of their life. We also received a daily report from our academic staff, our support staff, our director of strength and conditioning, our equipment manager, and our trainers. It was important for everyone to be on the same page with anything that transpired within the program. Then our coaching staff turned its attention to every area of our special teams units. Before we had a special teams coordinator, our assistant coaches split the responsibilities and were charged with specific segments of our special teams.

I met with our entire offensive coaching staff following the morning meeting. I met with our entire defensive coaching staff following the afternoon meeting, which also consisted of reports from our trainers that outlined the practice limitations for any player recovering from an injury. In between our staff meetings, each assistant coach provided me with a written outline detailing the agenda for their afternoon position meeting. Our coaches worked extremely long hours, and I appreciated their preparedness. Given their depth of responsibilities, it could be easy to overlook a certain detail, so a written outline safeguarded any possible omission.

A unique twist maximized the structural organization and efficiency of our daily players meeting between 2:48 and 3:48 PM. Due to space limitations within the football complex, we designed an overall team meeting room, which partitioned into two rooms and then partitioned into eight smaller rooms. Grouped by position and arranged in order of depth chart, our players sat in chairs that swiveled 360 degrees. For offensive and defensive meetings, we simply unfolded an accordion wall to separate the two groups. For position meetings, we unfolded additional accordion walls to create smaller rooms for our coaches and their players. Our players attended a team meeting, an offensive or defensive meeting, and a position meeting without leaving their seat. Probably no team in college football made better use of its resources and time relative to the development of its student-athletes.

I believe that I met Kevin Saunders for the first time prior to the 1991 season. Kevin was a Kansas State alumnus from Smith Center, Kansas. Kevin was a miracle and he had a very special story. Kevin had been involved in a grain elevator explosion in 1981, and emergency responders found him several hundred feet away from the blast. Kevin had broken virtually every bone in his body and was given a 1 percent chance of survival. Kevin persevered and, though he would never walk again, he became a national inspiration and won numerous gold medals in the Paralympic Games and more than once was named Outstanding Male Athlete at the National and International Games. In 1989, Senate Majority Leader Bob Dole recommended Kevin as the first person with a disability to serve on the President's Council on Sports, Fitness, and Nutrition, and Kevin served under George H.W. Bush and Bill Clinton.

We were so inspired by Kevin's story. I was able to meet with Kevin and I invited him to our locker room prior to a game so he could share with our players his amazing experiences and never-give-up approach to life that enabled him to succeed at the highest level. Soon after, I asked Kevin to serve as a motivational coach for our team, and he helped our players with goal-setting and athletic and personal development through the 2005 season. Kevin is truly an amazing individual.

Over the course of the season, it became apparent that we gradually improved in all aspects of the program. Our players were stronger and better conditioned. Our coaches continued to gain more familiarity with our opponents and learned more about our own players. We were learning to practice well and practice with a passion. We became mentally stronger, tougher, and more dedicated to our educational and personal lives. As for motivation? We were picked to finish dead last in the Big 8. It quickly became evident that we possessed the will and desire to overcome adversity. We allowed a touchdown late in the game during our season opener and trailed Division I-AA Indiana State 25–24, but we did not give in. When they attempted a two-point conversion, William Price, one of our cornerbacks, intercepted the pass and dashed all the way to the opposite end zone to give us two points, and we won 26–25.

Subsequent victories over Division I-AA Idaho State (41–7) and Northern Illinois (34–17) emphasized the success-breeds-success adage, and our program opened a season with three straight victories for the first time since 1982. Our players' enthusiasm quickly faded the following the week when we visited No. 4 Washington, which was one of those non-conference opponents that would not allow us out of our pre-existing contract. Washington came off a 36–21 win at Nebraska, ending the Huskers' 20-game home winning streak, and was probably the most talented team in the country. We were dominated every way possible in a 56–3 loss. They scored a touchdown on their first possession, had nearly 500 yards in total offense, averaged 7.6 yards per play, and scored on a punt return. We were sacked eight times, had negative-17 rushing yards, suffered two turnovers inside their red zone, and scored our only points on a field goal that ended the first half. We were ready to go home.

I knew it was important to remain consistent in all areas of our program. Since we had arrived at Kansas State, we made a special effort not to build up the Sunflower Showdown to a point that could cause our players to suffer a letdown over the course of the game or during the ensuing week. I insisted that the University of Kansas was one of 11 games on the schedule and told the media that every conference game commanded equal significance. However, I was hardly naïve. Obviously, the KU game was of paramount importance to our fans and our in-state players. In addition, it served as our Big 8 season opener and homecoming game that year. Our players were not in short supply of motivation during the week leading up to the game. Since our arrival, we had not beaten the University of Kansas, and nobody in the media gave us a chance in the game. Kansas State and Kansas were both 3–1 for the first time since 1974, and it was just the third time since 1933 that both teams carried a winning record into the Sunflower Showdown. Kansas averaged nearly 500 yards per game, and the media believed that KU would run away with the game. We told our out-of-state players, "If you want to play this game for somebody, play this game for your in-state teammates."

Similar to the 1991 season opener, we again faced adversity toward the end of the game. Trailing 12–3 in the fourth quarter, our defense held Kansas on fourth and 1 at our 6-yard line, and our offense drove 94 yards on 14 plays for a touchdown with three minutes, 58 seconds remaining in the game. Then when our defense absolutely had to force a three-and-out, it responded, and a punt gave us possession at our 34-yard line with 2:55 left. We had a crowd of 40,856 at our stadium, and our players and fans seemingly fed off of each other's energy.

Paul Watson, our senior quarterback and a native of Kansas City, Missouri, wore a black shield over his helmet to protect his eye as it healed from a BB gun accident a couple of weeks prior. We committed six turnovers, and he suffered an interception, a fumbled snap, and a bad pitch, which meant that he stood next to me on the sideline late in the third quarter. Kansas took over possession five times on our end of the field, and our defense responded every time. Paul was good with the offensive system, went through his progressions, and did not panic regardless of the situation, which contributed to my decision in eventually allowing him to return to the field. Just when it appeared we were stuck, Paul completed a third-down pass to Russ Campbell, our tight end, for a 22-yard gain to the Kansas 35. Plenty of time remained on the game clock. Although a field goal would give us a one-point lead, we did not want to create an opportunity for Kansas to respond and kick a game-winning field goal.

A few seconds later, our players executed one of the more memorable last-minute plays in program history, which enabled us to complete one of the greatest comebacks in program history. Paul completed a pass to Andre Coleman, our speedy wide receiver, inside the 5-yard line, and Andre outran everybody to the end zone for the go-ahead touchdown with 1:58 remaining. Although we led 16–12, we knew it was still anyone's game to win. Kansas drove to our 9-yard line, but we forced the Jayhawks into an incomplete pass in the end zone as time expired. I was so proud of our defense because twice in the game we let Kansas inside our 10-yard line, and both times they had to settle for field goals. Our ability to respond very positively to adversity on both sides of the ball pleased me greatly, and it served as another small step in our process.

Every game was significant, which made our victory and the fashion by which it took place significant, and it pleased me to see the victory's outgrowth and the excitement among our players and fans. Our fans stormed the field and tore down the goalposts, which at the time did not necessarily thrill me because some major games were still ahead of us. Plus, everybody in the country would see the gesture and think, *Wait, they tore down the goalposts for beating Kansas?* I feared that it might suggest we had limited expectations for our program. Our program was 4–1 for the first time since 1969, and we took possession of the Governor's Cup Trophy for the first time since 1986, following some brief congratulatory comments by Governor Joan Finney inside our locker room. I made some stern comments to the media during my postgame news conference regarding the lack of respect they continued to show toward our players despite their collective and individual efforts to consistently improve. Our players did not deserve criticism week after week. Nobody gave us a chance.

A countless number of steps remained in order for us to reach our goals. Beating Kansas was certainly one of those steps. However, we couldn't get to where we wanted to go unless we could win at No. 9 Nebraska. We entered the game as a 35-point underdog against Nebraska, which had beaten us by double digits every year since 1979. Our program hadn't won a road game since 1985. Yet we led 31–24 with less than seven minutes remaining in the game before Nebraska scored a pair of touchdowns on drives that covered 80 and 60 yards. We needed to respond with one final touchdown to win the game. During perhaps the finest performance of his career, Paul completed 26-of-46 passes for 340 yards and two touchdowns and no interceptions. Michael Smith, who at the time held all of the receiving records at Kansas State, had 10 catches for 172 yards in the game while adding to some career marks that recognized him as one of the finest receivers in Big 8 history. We drove the field and reached the Nebraska 7-yard line in the final minute. On fourth down, a defensive back ripped the ball away from Russ Campbell before he could complete the catch at the goal line with 36 seconds left. We suffered a 38–31 loss while scoring more points and recording more total yards than any Kansas State team in history against the University of Nebraska. The crowd of 76,209 at Memorial Stadium gave our players a standing ovation as they ran off the field, but we did not accept any moral victories. Outsiders perhaps believed that our expectation level was so low that playing close was acceptable. It wasn't. Had we scored the touchdown, we would have gone for two points to win the game.

Nebraska, Colorado, and Oklahoma were always three of the top teams in the nation. We entered as a 22-point underdog at home against No. 16 Colorado before losing 10–0. One season after we surrendered 64 points to Colorado, our defense put together its best collective performance since we arrived in Manhattan. We held one of the nation's most productive offenses to below 350 total yards and held Heisman Trophy candidate Darian Hagan to just 122 passing yards and 46 rushing yards without a touchdown. Colorado's only touchdown was a product of the ideal field position we afforded them when we turned over the ball inside our red zone.

Representatives from the Copper Bowl and Freedom Bowl attended the game, and we faced an interesting situation with a 4–3 record heading to meet No. 21 Oklahoma in Norman, Oklahoma. An NCAA rule went into effect for the 1991–92 bowl season that required teams to win six games against Division I-A opponents in order to become bowl eligible. Shortly after we arrived, we replaced a 1991 non-conference road game at Wisconsin with a home game against Division I-AA Idaho State, which was better suited for us to establish a foundation for our team. That gave us two Division I-AA opponents on our schedule, and we had no time to find a Division I-A opponent prior to the season. We had requested a waiver from the NCAA Postseason Football Subcommittee to allow our Division I-AA games to count toward bowl eligibility, but they declined our request. That meant that we had to win our four remaining games in order to reach the six Division I-A victories required to participate in a bowl.

Our ensuing 28–7 loss at Oklahoma effectively knocked us out of the bowl picture. On a 24-degree day that featured blowing snow, we traveled inside the Oklahoma 25-yard line five times and failed to score a point. Yet even after this difficult stretch during the middle of the season against Washington, Kansas, Nebraska, Colorado, and Oklahoma, our players remained enthusiastic despite not gaining bowl eligibility. We finished out the season with victories at Iowa State (37–7), against Missouri (32–0), and at Oklahoma State (36–26). The victory against Iowa State snapped our program's 30-game road losing streak and marked our most lopsided Big 8 road victory since 1955. Against Missouri, we shut out our first opponent in 16 years. We finished our season with a victory for the first time since 1984. We won three straight Big 8 games for the first time since 1969. Our 4–3 record in conference play marked the program's first winning record within the conference in 21 years. It was encouraging to me because it identified that we might've gotten away from that here-we-go-again mentality and realized that we might have a bad game or a really bad game, but that didn't mean it would negatively impact us in the other games. Every coach in the country told their players not to allow a defeat to affect their performance the following week. We always argued that we must also instruct our players not to allow a victory to negatively affect the outcome of the following game.

Our 7–4 record in 1991 marked our program's fifth winning season since World War II and our most victories in a season since 1954. Our program brought $3,921,798 to the athletic department—$410,000 more than originally budgeted. However, my thoughts were elsewhere. My mother and 97-year-old grandfather both were hospitalized in St. Joseph,

Missouri. When I coached at the University of Iowa, my mother had been diagnosed with breast cancer, and I admitted her for cancer treatments at the University of Iowa hospital, which was located across the street from Kinnick Stadium. After surgery, my mother regained her health and returned home to St. Joseph. My mother's cancer had now returned. At the same time, my grandfather George fell ill at his home. It was a difficult last few weeks of the season for me.

Although we were a seven-win team with no bowl game, the college football world still recognized the positive steps by our program. When ESPN honored me as its 1991 NCAA Division I National Football Coach of the Year and the Big 8 honored me as its Coach of the Year for a second straight season, I made an extreme effort to ensure that our coaches, support staff, players, and fans understood their own significance in the achievement. It wasn't a Bill Snyder award but rather a family award. It was everyone. More than 100 players, 40 staff members, and thousands of fans played a role. Awards were not the ultimate outcome by any stretch of the imagination, but they were an attachment to our good fortune, and it was important that everybody felt that they played a part in it. Our families and my own family were a part of it because they too made great sacrifices.

Shortly after the season, I accompanied former Kansas State athletic director and top fundraiser Ernie Barrett to Las Vegas to meet with Jim Colbert, a Kansas State alum and one of the top professional golfers in the PGA. Although I had never met Jim, Ernie hoped that he might make a financial contribution to the Kansas State athletic department and football program. During dinner, Ernie told Jim that Kansas State won seven games during the season. Jim told me that if another school came knocking to seriously listen because there was no way that anybody could win consistently at Kansas State. I remembered that.

The most painful period of time in my life began February 15, 1992. That's when I received the phone call that Meredith, who was a senior in high school and living with her mother in Greenville, Texas, had been severely injured in an automobile accident just before midnight. Meredith never had alcohol in her life but got into a vehicle with a young lady who had been drinking and had personal problems and wanted to talk with my daughter.

The driver lost control of the vehicle, and Meredith was thrown through the windshield and from the vehicle about 50 feet into a tree. She suffered a crushed spinal cord, shattered vertebrae, and a broken neck. She was hospitalized and breathed through a ventilator at Presbyterian Hospital while awaiting surgery. We drove through the night from Manhattan to Dallas and sat in the hospital waiting room. A doctor entered the room and said, "Coach, your daughter will never walk again the rest of her life."

I politely responded, "Yes, she will. Doctor, you don't know my daughter."

I believed in my daughter's will and determination. She would not be defeated.

We were absolutely devastated. Meredith was moved to the intensive care unit in a coma. We stood at the foot of her bed day after day, and she did not respond to any of our voices. Several days later, I saw the big toe on her right foot move, as I stood at the foot of her bed. The nurse insisted that it was an involuntary twitch. I politely said, "No, something is going to happen here." Several days later, Meredith began to move, then she eventually awoke, and then she eventually spoke. We moved her into the Dallas Rehabilitation Institute, where she improved over the course of six weeks. Then we moved her to a rehabilitation center in Southern California, which was regarded as one of the best rehabilitation facilities in the country.

My mother and grandfather remained in poor health. So I tried to prepare for the season, recruit, and travel between Manhattan, St. Joseph, and California. I traveled virtually every day. Meredith steadily progressed over the course of several surgeries. Eventually, she took her first step with the help of a cane and a physical therapist, but it was very difficult for her. Eventually, they got her up on snow skis at a rehabilitation retreat.

Meredith was and is an amazingly wonderful young lady. She is very special. Three months after her accident, she miraculously graduated with her class at Greenville High School. She walked across the stage with a walker. A few weeks later, she was able to walk 30 feet without a walker. We refused to put any limitations on her. Her courage and dedication epitomized our program's foundation of finding a way to become a little bit better every day. She is an unbelievable fighter. I always said that if I had a football team full of Merediths, we would never lose. Six years later,

I escorted Meredith across the stage when she accepted her college diploma at Kansas State University.

It remains one of the greatest days of my life.

One of our challenges when we first arrived at Kansas State was convincing players to stay in the program. Many players left. Over the years, several others followed. One day prior to the 1992 season, I chased down Eric Gallon in our football facility parking lot and got him to stay. Eric was a tough young man, and his 1,102 rushing yards in 1991 were the second most in program history. But Eric tore an anterior cruciate ligament in the spring prior to his senior season, which meant a nine-month recovery and the possible end of his career. Several days after Eric had reconstructive surgery on the knee, I saw him put all of his belongings in his truck in the parking lot. I approached him before he could leave. We talked for quite a while inside his truck. He had too many things at stake, and too many people cared about him. I believed that he could return at some point during his senior season. He stayed, and the rest was history.

Over the summer, Douglas S. Looney wrote a positive story about our program, as he had earlier promised if we had shown improvement, and the headline in *Sports Illustrated* read: "The Power of Positive Thinking." Coming off our program's best season in 37 years, we faced a challenging spring and summer. The media latched onto any rumor regarding prominent teams across the country contacting me about a job. I received a handful of phone calls from Division I-A programs. My contract ran two more years, and people believed that I might leave to take over at the University of Iowa whenever Hayden Fry retired. I reiterated to the media that I was not thinking about leaving Kansas State. I also reiterated that my goal was to bring about the greatest turnaround in the history of college football.

Heading toward the season, we had to keep everybody's ego in check and re-emphasize to our young people the process by which we reached our mild success. So often in life, when we diligently work toward achieving success, we tend to lose track of those things that allowed us to attain that success. We can begin to take things for granted. Meanwhile, during the offseason, we knew that we could not risk suffering the same fate as it related to bowl eligibility in future seasons. We changed our non-conference schedules to ensure that we played only one Division I-AA opponent each season.

It was extremely hard for me to coach during the 1992 season. It wasn't the top priority in my life. Meredith, my mother. and my grandfather were my major priorities. I juggled a lot of balls. We were picked fifth in the Big 8. We finished with a 5–6 record. Midway through the season, our offense ranked 107th out of 107 teams in the country. In a 54–7 loss at No. 9 Colorado, our offense finished with 16 yards of total offense, the worst by a Big 8 team in history. We finished within striking distance at Utah State (28–16), at Oklahoma (16–14), and at Missouri (27–14). The loss at Utah State, which again was one of those non-conference road games that had already been scheduled, was probably our worst loss during the first four years. I did not believe over the course of the season that we played with the attitude and edge that we played with during the previous season. We finished with a 5–0 home record for our program's first undefeated season at home since 1934. Our fans tore down the goalposts after a 22–13 win against Iowa State during an ESPN Thursday night game. But we lost on the road to a Missouri team that had previously won only one game all season.

Our final game of the season against No. 11 Nebraska at the Coca-Cola Bowl in Tokyo, Japan, proved to be memorable experience. The story behind the game was interesting in itself. When we first arrived at Kansas State, we were scheduled to play against Oklahoma in Tokyo, but then Oklahoma went on probation, and the game was cancelled. We agreed to play Nebraska and moved the originally-scheduled game on October 17 in Manhattan to December 5 in Tokyo. Both schools received $400,000. Half-jokingly, I said we wanted to play Nebraska as far away as possible so the newspapers in the United States would not know the score.

Nebraska and Kansas State shared the same airplane to Tokyo. The 360-passenger flight refueled in Vancouver, British Columbia, then was in the air for 10 more hours to Japan. One side of the airplane would be exposed to sunlight during the entirety of the trip, and the other side would be dark. Well, the story came out that I asked for our players to occupy the side of the plane that wouldn't be sunny, so our players could get proper sleep. It wasn't to put Nebraska at a disadvantage, but indeed if we could have the shady side and not be exposed to sunlight the entire trip and still enjoy the view, we would take it.

I was always big on the meals that were served to our players. Among other things, I never allowed our players to eat butter. When we were over there, the meal staff served our players pats of butter. I asked them to please replace the butter and serve our players margarine instead. The media latched onto that story as well during our trip. All week I was concerned about the 15-hour time difference and the fact that our players also had to study for final exams.

Even though we lost against No. 11 Nebraska (38–24), we had a chance to win the ballgame, and I was pleased with our players' effort at the end of a long season. The people at the hotel were wonderful, the Japanese people were wonderful, and our experiences in the country were wonderful. However, I was displeased with the game's producers because they refused to dignify us as the home team despite the contract agreement and they failed to show our players and coaches the same respect that they extended to Nebraska. Right up until kickoff, the game's producers broke promises and even refused to give Kansas State the home sideline even after Tom Osborne willingly offered to switch sides. It quickly became apparent their sole intent was to showcase Nebraska. Afterward, the game's producers would not allow our team to be a part of the postgame ceremony. They only invited myself and Andre, who had been named Kansas State's MVP of the game, to remain on the field. I told them, "If you don't want my football team, then you don't want me." We changed our clothes and were on our way to the airport before the postgame news conference even began.

Still, I maintained my belief that the experience of playing a neutral-site game against a formidable foe during the final game of a season would benefit our program moving forward. Our 18 wins over the first four years were the most by Kansas State in a four-year span since 1931. I was perhaps most interested in seeing how our players responded over the course of the next several months as we attempted to take all of the necessary steps to ensure we did not repeat the difficulties we experienced in the 1992 season. There was still so much left for our program to accomplish.

"Coach Snyder believed in family and that if we worked as one unit we would succeed. He taught me and his first team, The Foundation, how to win. Coach Snyder instilled that never-give-up attitude, so when North Texas State scored a late touchdown, we didn't retreat to the sideline and accept the loss. We came back and broke the longest losing streak in college football. Although we won only one game in 1989, that small taste of victory started the greatest turnaround in college football history."

—Marcus Miller, Kansas State defensive back, 1986–89

CHAPTER 7

FIRST EVER BOWL VICTORY

"Bill Snyder isn't the coach of the year and he isn't coach of the decade. He's the coach of the century."

—Barry Switzer, former Oklahoma and Dallas Cowboys head coach

Our football facilities took a step forward prior to the 1993 season. Our athletic department had been able to secure $5.5 million in private donations for our 94,000 square-foot indoor facility ($2.2 million) and new press box ($3.3 million), and those projects were completed before the season opener. In all, our facility enhancements since our arrival had totaled about $8.1 million, and all but $2 million came from private donations. What was amazing was that 25 years prior to the new construction they had built the entire football stadium for just $1.6 million.

The visible enhancements were very significant for our players and the program. Considering the previous facilities, this was prominent. Many universities might have had better facilities, but for people who had been around our program since the beginning, the results of the hard work were rewarded. Our indoor facility—133 yards long and 76 yards wide—was the largest in the Big 8. The press box featured a total of 22 suites, and the $450,000 generated from those suites helped pay for the project. The suites helped reward people who had been so gracious to our program. I wasn't interested in a Taj Mahal. All I wanted were comfortable facilities that were functional and beneficial for our players and our program. The commitment by many people helped us to achieve that goal.

Kansas State graciously awarded me a 10-year contract, as Kansas State had sought continuity within its football program for many years. I received $115,000 the first year of the contract and was grateful for the trust of our administration as we continued to move forward.

Our players showed dedication and initiative in conducting player-led practices in 105-degree temperatures during the summer, and I was so proud of how our players answered the call when a catastrophic flood hit the Manhattan area in July, leaving about 70,000 people homeless across the region. The people in the Manhattan community are resilient, and many stepped up to help with flood relief. Every one of our players helped with sandbagging efforts seven hours a day for three days straight. I was proud, but not surprised, of their selflessness during a time of need for so many people.

During the summer, our head strength and conditioning coach Jerry Palmieri went to Boston College, and we promoted Rod Cole to the position. Rod had been Palmieri's assistant since March after serving as an assistant coach at Dodge Community College. Rod spent 14 years on our staff and earned the Big 12 Conference Strength and Conditioning Professional of the Year Award in 1997 and 1999.

Our football team experienced some turnover as well. Our 1992 starting quarterback, Jason Smargiasso, opted not to return to the program. However, we believed that we had a capable quarterback in Chad May, a junior who had transferred from California-State Fullerton and sat out the 1992 season due to NCAA transfer rules. Chad really had a nice arm and was a fit schematically. What I really appreciated about Chad was his competitiveness. I thought he was going to be a good player for us. Every quarterback is different in his own right, but Chad just wore it on his sleeve more than others. He had such confidence. He knew he could throw the ball and he had confidence in his teammates as well. We weren't the type of program where any one player was going to define our success or failure for our team or program. Michael Bishop probably came closest to that, but Michael had a lot of help, and so did Chad.

We began two-a-day practices on August 12, and basically it was all football between 7:00 AM and 11:00 PM until the beginning of the fall semester. We had lost our top passer, rusher, and receiver; the starting front seven on defense; and Sean at punter. People had questions. Nebraska was a heavy favorite in the Big 8 Conference, and Kansas State was picked to finish seventh in the conference standings only ahead of Iowa State.

Motivation comes in many forms, and the best kind of motivation for our players is self-motivation. They carried an appropriate amount of motivation into the season, and we were fortunate enough to start off with wins against New Mexico State (34–10) and Western Kentucky (38–13). Those ballgames preceded a matchup against the University of Minnesota at the Metrodome.

Although I knew it had been a while since Kansas State had won a non-conference road game, I did not know that the program's last non-conference road victory was in 1979. We practiced a good portion of the week in the indoor facility and brought loud speakers inside to simulate crowd noise for our players. We left the day of the game at 10:00 AM for a 7:00 PM kickoff in part because we couldn't conduct our normal Friday night walk-through of the stadium because the Minnesota Twins hosted the Toronto Blue Jays, and also it saved the athletic department a substantial amount of money on hotel expenses.

Minnesota quarterback Scott Eckers led the country in total offense, passing for 823 yards in the previous two ballgames, which would provide a test for our defense. We played nickel coverage throughout the game and were able to intercept a couple of passes and limit the quarterback's effectiveness. Although we took a 17–0 lead, we let our foot off the pedal. We led 24–13 in the fourth quarter, but Minnesota came back to take a 25–24 lead. Eventually, we led 30–25 late in the game and were able to hold on for a victory. Minnesota faced fourth and goal at our 2-yard line with 52 seconds remaining, and our defense held, allowing our offense to run out the clock. The win at Minnesota was the defining road game to that point in our journey. It was very meaningful and highly motivational.

Our players and fanbase were energized as we took another step with a 10–9 victory against the University of Kansas. It was a chilly and windy day. We led 10–0 before we tempered our performance level again. But once again our players responded late in the ballgame for the victory, and our fans took the goalposts down again. We had the good fortune of having bowl representatives from the Orange Bowl and Copper Bowl in attendance to watch Kansas State start off a season with a 5–0 record for the first time since 1931. We also moved into the national rankings. We were ranked No. 24 in the CNN/*USA Today* poll, which was our program's first national ranking since 1970. I thought we deserved the recognition but remained cautious about overconfidence.

Kansas State hadn't beaten the University of Nebraska in 25 years. We were 28 ½-point underdogs when we visited the sixth-ranked Cornhuskers. Our players read the newspapers. They knew everybody outside of the locker room had counted them out. But they were competitive, and nothing scared them away. The night before a ballgame, I might write down, "I think we'll do well," but this felt different. We bussed to Lincoln the night before the ballgame, walked around the stadium, ate in the hotel, and conducted our Friday night meeting followed by our special teams meeting. All along, I just had this strong feeling about the ballgame. We always had a mandatory movie the night before a game. Each week, I selected two or three movies, and our players voted for their favorite. These movies pushed the themes of competitive spirit and motivation. Based upon our week of practice, the attitude of our players in meetings and on the practice field, and our players' consistency and spirit, that Friday night I did something that I had never done before. I wrote in a note to myself: "I believe we are going to win this ballgame."

Well, we certainly had the opportunity. However, we lost a fumble in our own territory, and Nebraska scored, and then we were penalized, and Nebraska got great field position following our punt and scored. We essentially gave them two scores. Twice we had the ball inside the 5-yard line and couldn't score. We were our own worst enemy. We trailed by 17 points at halftime.

What I did not fully realize at the time was that we were witnessing the most prolific passing performance by a quarterback in the history of the Big 8 Conference. Chad had a good strong arm, was extremely competitive, loved to throw the ball, and was an accurate passer. Nebraska featured one of the top rushing defenses in not only the run-oriented Big 8, but also the entire nation. We had everything possible in our Kansas State offensive playbook, everything fit together, and we were well-prepared. One of the things we asked ourselves when we arrived at Kansas State was: "What is it that opposing defenses in the conference don't see each week?"

If Big 8 teams saw the passing game each week and you were a pass-oriented team, then you were old hat when you faced them. If your offense promoted a particular aspect that opposing defenses hadn't seen, then those defenses had to adjust in that ballgame. It isolated the amount of time that they could prepare for that particular scheme to one given week, and they couldn't accumulate the hours of repetitions necessary in practice to counter our offensive attack. We always tried to do something different yet stay within our large playbook. As we studied film, we always picked things that might work against the opponent's defense. In our preparation for Nebraska, we believed some vulnerability existed in its pass defense.

Chad passed for 489 yards against Nebraska, which was a Big 8 record, and our 565 total offensive yards were the most ever allowed in the Tom Osborne era at Nebraska. Anything that anybody accomplished for the first time against an Osborne team was pretty special. Tom is an amazing person and was a great football coach. He was of that old adage: "don't let the same thing beat you twice." If anybody found a weakness in Nebraska's armor, he fixed it in a heartbeat.

We trailed Nebraska 31–28 with seven minutes remaining in the ballgame. I was proud of how we had fought back, but Nebraska scored the final 14 points, and we suffered a 45–28 loss. It was a disheartening loss. I just had such a strong feeling about where our team was at that particular time that it made it all the more disappointing.

Although we believed we were closing the gap on the conference's top three teams—Nebraska, Colorado, and Oklahoma—I made one decision during the 1993 season that some former players still talk about almost 30 years later. The decision occurred in the final seconds against No. 16 Colorado. We couldn't do anything offensively and trailed 9–0 at halftime and then scored a touchdown in the third quarter and missed the extra-point attempt. With 21 seconds left, Colorado led 16–13, and we drove from our 20-yard line to the Colorado 18-yard line. People still talk about whether or not we should have gone for the touchdown on fourth down. Trailing by three points, many thoughts raced through my head. I didn't want our players to believe it was appropriate to settle for less than best, but I also pondered our final status in the conference standings and believed that if we won our remaining ballgames, a tie against Colorado could benefit us in the bowl selection.

I elected to go for the field goal. Tate Wright made a 35-yard field goal, and we ended the game against No. 16 Colorado in a 16–16 tie. It wasn't anybody's decision other than mine. Almost 30 years later, I wouldn't have done it any differently. However, the tie stirred emotions among our players, including our consensus All-American safety Jaime Mendez, who was a senior and a team captain. Jaime came to us from Cardinal Mooney High School in Youngstown, Ohio, which was also home to Bobby and Mike Stoops. After Jaime redshirted the 1989 season, he developed into a passionate player and leader for us. He finished his senior season as a semifinalist for the Jim Thorpe Award and he remains our program's all-time leader with 15 interceptions over his career and recorded a Big 8-record four interceptions in a single game. Jaime was vocal and criticized my decision to kick a field goal after the Colorado game. I always appreciated Jaime and his attitude, and he felt strongly about his opinion. That following Monday, he apologized to me and the team for his outburst, but I always admired his competitive spirit.

The tie really bothered me for several days and weeks because of the impact that it may have had on our players, but I've never shared those feelings with anyone. The tie still turned the heads of voters, and we moved to No. 25 in the Associated Press poll, and the important thing was that we were there. My concern had always been whether our previous 100-year history would cast a vote against us even if we were worthy of being in the polls, so it was a relief that the voters selected our team for its present capabilities. However, we did not have a good week as a football program. During my Tuesday news conference, the media wouldn't let go of the outcome in the Colorado game and also pushed for me to release the terms of my contract, which was a request I wasn't interested in fulfilling for a variety of reasons. The media printed up harsh stories about me and my contract, causing many newspaper advertisers to retract their business. The Kansas State fanbase responded by purchasing a full-page newspaper ad featuring the names of 500 people supporting me, our football program, and the athletic department.

There were just so many issues during the week that it could've easily been distracting. We maintained our focus and prepared for our homecoming game against No. 13 Oklahoma. Our players responded to the eventful week in an appropriate way. It appeared that everything, including the tie, had brought our players to a higher level of intensity, and they prepared themselves well for the Sooners.

Kansas State hadn't beaten Oklahoma since 1970 and hadn't defeated a nationally-ranked team since 1971, and yet we led the Sooners 21–0 heading into the fourth quarter. Our players remained focused, and we won 21–7. Afterward Mitch Holthus, the Voice of the Wildcats, made the comment on the radio about us parting the Red Sea. I always appreciated Mitch. I was always proud of him and I hated it when he left to become the voice of the Kansas City Chiefs. But I did tell Mitch after the Oklahoma ballgame that there was absolutely no comparison between Kansas State football winning a ballgame and the parting of the Red Sea.

My postgame focus was never to hold on to a game for longer than 24 hours. I processed the game for several hours and then began preparing for the next ballgame. However, after the win over Oklahoma, I examined the different possible scenarios to reach certain bowl games. We were the second-place team in the Big 8 and wanted to get to the highest possible bowl.

Our team moved to No. 18 in the national rankings as we prepared for our next game at Iowa State. I came down with pneumonia a few days before we visited Iowa State, but I kept coaching. We led Iowa State 17–6 in the third quarter when a streaker ran onto the football field. For some reason, that incident seemed to change the entire game. How distracting was it? I don't know. But we gave up three fourth-quarter touchdowns in a 27–23 loss, and I felt we were so much better than that Iowa State team. That was as disappointing of a loss as any. It was a very disheartening loss and very painful.

We bounced back with a 31–21 win against Missouri on Senior Day to secure the program's first bowl berth since 1982. It was such a meaningful day for our seniors and their families, as all Senior Days are. Several of those seniors had been in our program since the beginning, and they had been a part of that incremental growth while developing into fine young men with an intrinsic value system that would serve them well in life.

One of the defining moments in our season arrived on our final drive in the regular-season finale at Oklahoma State. Although we scored the game's first 14 points, Oklahoma State scored the next 17 points, so we trailed 17–14 with 58 seconds remaining in the game. The Oklahoma State game was one of many where Chad really stood out. When we absolutely had to have it, Chad marched the offense 80 yards for the win. Brad Seib, our senior tight end, caught a short pass in the back of the end zone with 17 seconds left on the clock to secure our 21–17 win.

I was recognized as Big 8 Coach of the Year and sincerely told our players that it was a team award. I asked our players their preferred bowl destination if we received more than one bowl opportunity. The players voted for the Aloha Bowl in Honolulu. I could understand their feeling. However, our administration preferred that we accept a Copper Bowl invitation instead, to which I agreed because I wanted to play in a bowl game that would be reachable for as many of our fans as possible.

In the early evening of November 28, the Copper Bowl chairman phoned myself and Kansas State athletic director Max Urick to formally extend a bowl invitation. We would play Wyoming, the Western Athletic Conference co-champion, on December 29 at Arizona Stadium in Tucson, Arizona. There was a segment of our players that believed we had been deserving of a different bowl, but I was pleased that we had just taken that next step and were in a position to go to a bowl game. Our initial projection in 1989 was that we would be capable of playing in a bowl game every few years. That projection had become a reality. We still had so far to go, but we were on the right track, and it was significant that most of our players realized that we weren't finished. There were those players who had been with us since the beginning and made that understood to all of our other players. There was a sentiment among our players that this can happen and that they could accomplish their goals, and it became important that that realization spread to the younger players as they joined the program.

What I will always remember is the Kansas State pep rally prior to the Copper Bowl. Our team stayed in a hotel in Tucson, and the property had a large ballroom. I had told Mitch that part of the bowl tradition at the University of Iowa included large pep rallies for their fans. I told him that I wanted to have a pep rally for our fans. I am told there were handmade signs all across the city of Tucson announcing a Kansas State pep rally. At the time, we had no idea how many of our fans would be able to attend. The night of the pep rally arrived, and our team was returning from a bowl event. The streets were so packed with Kansas State people that we had to park the team bus down the street and walk to our pep rally in the hotel.

We later learned there were more than 5,000 people in attendance at the pep rally, and not all of them could get into the ballroom, forcing some to watch on a video screen outside the hotel. We could barely squeeze through all of the people. It was amazing. When we got in front of all of our Kansas State fans, several of our players had tears running down their faces. Our fans were so loud. A few of our players had played in a couple of home football games when only 5,000 people would attend, and now our players were surrounded by that many people at a pep rally. Max Urick stood at the pep rally and said, "As the sun begins to set on Tucson tonight, you're going to see a purple haze on the horizon because they're coming, and they're coming by the thousands."

We made sure the players had read in the newspapers how Wyoming was going to run over Kansas State. Wyoming had a top 25 offense, a 3,000-yard passer, and a young man named Ryan Yarborough, who at the time was the leading receiver in NCAA history. Some people touted this game as a "100-point shootout." However, our players were very energized when they saw 22,000 Kansas State fans in the stadium. We played virtually a complete game offensively, defensively, and on special teams. Andre Coleman gave us momentum with a 68-yard punt return touchdown for a 24–10 lead at halftime, and then Chad found Andre with a pass that he turned into a 61-yard touchdown early in the third quarter. Andre was named the Copper Bowl MVP after recording a career-high 283 all-purpose yards in the final game of his Kansas State career. Kenny McEntyre scored the game's final points on a 37-yard interception return for a 52-17 bowl victory—the first bowl win in the history of the Kansas State football program.

Some of our seniors wept with joy in the locker room. Our 9–2–1 record was the best since 1910 at Kansas State. We finished at No. 20 in the Associated Press poll, our highest finish in program history. We had our first undefeated non-conference season since 1954, improved to 21–2–1 at home in the 1990s, snapped an 18-game non-conference road losing streak, beat Oklahoma, and tied Colorado. Six of our players earned All-America recognition, including Mendez, who recorded a school-record four interceptions during one game.

I always delivered a postgame talk and on occasion spoke off of notes to make sure that I covered all the topics that I wanted to cover, but I hadn't prepared any notes to speak to that sizable of a victory margin. In the end, I asked our players to pay their respects to our fanbase at every opportunity. I asked them to realize what we could achieve when we went about our business in an appropriate way and if we prepared ourselves the best way possible. I thanked our seniors for their hard work, dedication, and perseverance and I told our returning players to remember the hard work required to get to this point and the investment made by our seniors. I challenged them to continue to push our program to that next step.

We returned to the hotel, and Sharon and I spent the rest of the evening with family. While the team flew back to Manhattan the following day, Sharon and I went to watch Barry Alvarez and Wisconsin play in the Rose Bowl. While we were in town, I visited a couple of recruits in Orange County. Having coached high school football in the area, I knew my way around the high schools and I visited the community colleges as well. Our Copper Bowl victory had helped verify to recruits and coaches that we were a step-by-step program, that we were making the type of progress that we intended, that our program was gaining recognition, and consequently Kansas State was becoming a prominent program in college football.

Days after we returned to Manhattan, I left the football complex at around midnight and spotted one car in the parking lot. A man stepped out and walked toward me in darkness. The man greeted me, introduced himself, and said, "Coach, I don't want to take up any of your time, but I had to come tell you that what you've done has been the most meaningful thing in my entire life."

The man told me that he had driven from Goodland, Kansas, and that he had sat in his car waiting for me for quite some time. We talked about him and his family. I said, "Those are some of the most significant things in your life, not a football game." But the man really meant what he said. He was passionate about it, and it was meaningful to him and me.

The visit with the man from Goodland allowed me to truly understand what had gone through the hearts and minds of so many Kansas State people over the years, and it reiterated to me the significance of our climb after all of those hard times in the football program. I had never looked at our achievements in that frame of mind or with that kind of understanding until my brief conversation with this man. I asked him, "Where are you going to stay tonight?"

He replied, "I'm going to drive back home."

Then the man climbed into his car and began the four to five-hour drive to his home in western Kansas. It is something I will never forget.

"Coach Snyder's legacy will undoubtedly last for many generations to come. From the moment that Coach arrived in Manhattan, I believe he felt a personal responsibility to the university, community, state of Kansas for the football program to succeed. He demanded, and mostly received, the very best from everyone who has been associated with the program because he cared enough to make a difference in their lives. Simply put, he makes people better than they were before they met him in all areas of their lives."

—Brad Seib, Kansas State tight end, 1990–93

CHAPTER 8

16 Wildcat Goals
for Success

"Bill Snyder is Kansas State football. He's an icon. He will forever be a legend and forever be remembered and respected in the college football community for what he was able to build in Manhattan, Kansas. I think back to Michael Bishop, Darren Sproles, and so many of those great teams. Even the great teams they had that didn't necessarily have great talent, they were just so well-coached and always showed up."

—Kirk Herbstreit, ESPN

A single set of core values can unify a family, a business, or players and coaches under one vision. If each individual adheres to the goals or values, then team success will follow. In a venture in which multiple individuals contribute to an effort in order to achieve individual or collective success, it takes a community effort that involves the values necessary to achieve those successes. It's that old adage: "It's a team game and it takes all of us." In football, there are 11 players on the field at a time, but in reality, there are more than 100 players. We wanted our players to understand that the values of teamwork and unity were so significant, and that learning not only to invest in their own success, but also in the success of others was an important value in life. These core values involved players, coaches, trainers, student managers, equipment managers, secretarial assistants, and virtually anybody and everybody inside the program. They also included our student body, our university faculty, and our fanbase. Everyone contributed their part to reach the desired outcome for the program.

So often, young people might focus on themselves, their teammates, and maybe a few coaches, but the path toward success involves so many other entities. Some individuals, not only in athletics but in all walks of life, can be self-centered, which is sort of human nature. Self-centeredness occurs in business and in family life. Individuals only focus on their own capabilities without regarding anybody else and therefore fail to recognize the value of assistance provided by others whether it's in business, family, athletics, or in other areas of life. We believe that it was significant to understand the value of togetherness.

We started with what we originally called "Wildcats' Goals for Success," a list of 12 core values, which we increased to 16 goals after the 1996 season. These became known as the "16 Wildcat Goals for Success." These values and principles were not rocket science. Every single one of them came from my mother. She taught me so much about intrinsic values. These are probably values that you attempt to teach your own children or that your parents taught you. We wanted to make these values visible to our players, to the people within our program, and expound upon each of these values on a consistent basis. We did not want to just expose our players to words but rather define a process by which those values could become engrained within their own lives. Understanding that the spoken word is so easily forgotten, we listed the 16 Wildcat Goals for Success on a small laminated card that fit into a wallet and required our players to carry the card with them at all times, except when they were on the football field. Our coaches ensured that our players had the 16 Wildcat Goals for Success in their possession, and we tested our players on these goals on a regular basis. It wasn't uncommon to open a team meeting and hand out a piece of paper that read, "16 Wildcat Goals for Success," and that was numbered one through 16. Our players had only a few minutes to list the 16 goals in order. A score of lower than 100 percent carried a consequence and a retest.

The meaning behind the 16 goals was so significant. Every person on the face of this Earth at some age recognizes these words and understands their function, but does that individual abide by a set of principles, whether it is the 16 goals or his/her own core values? After a while, we can forget our values. Adhering to our values isn't always the convenient thing to do. In the

Kansas State football program, we took every action possible to ensure that our players memorized our 16 goals and we addressed those goals daily.

On the back side of the laminated card was "Beginning of a New Day," which promoted making the very best of each day through sacrifice and improvement.

Beginning of a New Day

This is the beginning of a new day.
God has given me this day to use as I will.
I can waste it or use it for good.
What I do today is important,
because I'm exchanging a day of my life for it.
When tomorrow comes, this day will be gone forever,
leaving in its place something I have traded for it.
I want it to be a gain, not loss;
good, not evil; success, not failure.
In order that I shall not regret the price I paid for it
because the future is just a whole string of nows.

I didn't relate our goals to football as much as I did to living life. If we travel someplace and hand John Q. Smith the list of 16 Wildcat Goals for Success, the last thing in the world that he's thinking about is football. He's probably thinking about how these goals can apply to his own life. Within our program during practice or team meetings, players paired up, and I announced one of our 16 goals, perhaps "Unselfishness" or "Improve" or "Self-Discipline," and our players discussed the topic amongst themselves in pairs. This exercise was called "Unity Sharing." After practice, I elaborated on one of the 16 goals, then the next day, I addressed another one of the goals, and then the next day, I addressed another one. When I finished elaborating on each of the 16 goals to our players, I began the process all over again.

We had 130-plus players in our team meeting, and I pointed to a player and said, "Okay, John, please share with us your thoughts on Goal No. 4." That player stood up and discussed the goal. Every player knew they would be an active participant in discussing each goal. Our players didn't know if we would ask them to discuss a goal on the football field after practice or during a team meeting. It taught our players accountability. Each player was accountable for the assignment, and everybody understood the importance of that responsibility.

Over the years, hundreds of entities have requested for me to discuss the 16 Wildcat Goals for Success, whether it be to members in the Kansas Legislature, the Kansas City Federal Bureau of Investigation, groups within the Kansas State campus, or in school assemblies across the state of Kansas. I enjoy discussing the 16 Wildcat Goals for Success to children in schools particularly because not every household promotes such a value system. I also realize when we're young we don't always pay attention to our parents, but we'll pay attention to someone else. Many parents have sent me correspondence to express appreciation for discussing these values with their children.

Here are the 16 Wildcat Goals for Success:

1. Commitment (to the common goals and to being successful)
Players seek individual success, but it is important that they also strive for the team's collective success. It requires certain actions that are out of the ordinary and probably difficult to achieve, which requires sacrifice. It requires that players care and trust each other, and that each player competes for his teammates with passion. Each of the 16 goals requires a commitment. It's significant to be committed to each goal and to understand its significance and for each player to be committed to his faith, his family, his education, and his future. Virtually everything and anything that touches our lives in a positive way commands a commitment.

2. Unselfishness (There is no I in team.)
It's a challenge to be an unselfish individual. Unselfishness doesn't require giving up everything, but it is the willingness to sacrifice to help others, our family, our teammates, and our program and the willingness to make sacrifices toward any significant venture in our life. Unfortunately, this is said to be a generation of instant self-gratification, and we hear people say, "I want it, I want it now, and if I can't have it now, I'm going to move on to

something or someplace else." By and large, that's a selfish approach toward life. If every member of a football team or organization possesses that mindset, it becomes dramatically difficult to attain the desired collective success. For example, a running back wants to carry the ball every single time or a family member expresses selfishness in saying, "I want it and I don't care if you want it or not," which damages the family. Unselfishness is a highly significant value in life. It equates to the football field when a player says, "I'm willing to make the sacrifices necessary for the betterment of my teammates and the program."

3. Unity (Come together as never before.)
A team or organization is stronger when all of its members pull in the same direction. In most families, a parent might say, "We stay together and we sacrifice for each other." When the Kansas State football team exited the locker room, a player carried a board with the word "FAMILY" written upon it. Tons and tons of our students held boards that read "FAMILY." Unity is so significant. Kansas State University adopted our one-word slogan, "FAMILY," and the outgrowth began from these 16 goals. If anybody asked a student on campus, "What do you like most about this university?" the student probably replied, "It feels more like family than other schools." Numerous recruits researched our university and program before visiting, so they were aware of "FAMILY" and they sat in my office at the end of their visit and said, "I was told Kansas State is like family. Now I understand. This is so much like family." So many of our former players send correspondence and write how significant it was to develop an attitude of "FAMILY" for their lives. Unity is seemingly a simple thing, but just how dedicated or committed are we toward developing this concept?

4. Improve (everyday…as a player, person, and student)
The foundation of our program was built upon consistent improvement. We were a 1–10 football team after our first season, and everybody turned up their noses at our record, which was appropriate, but I told our players, "I'm not going to judge you by the scoreboard but rather in your attempt and success in becoming better virtually every single day during the course

of the season and on through every day of your life." Our players committed themselves to improve every day, and we encouraged them to achieve constant daily improvement in all aspects of their lives. During our meetings, I would ask a player, "What is one of the priorities in your life?" He might reply, "My family." I would ask him, "When is the last time you called your mother?" He might say, "Three weeks ago." I would say, "When you call your mother after this meeting, you will have improved that priority in your life." As a team, we identified our priorities and how we could improve in each particular area. Every day, my question to the young people in our program was simply: "Did you improve today? At what? How did you do it? And how can you become better?"

5. Be Tough (mentally and physically)
Toughness is equated with the game of football. Football is a physical sport, players bang into one another, and individuals have to possess a physical toughness about them when they compete. Although most people equate football to physical toughness, and that is a big part of it, mental strength and mental toughness is also required for the sport. Mental toughness is an attribute of people who strive for success. Mental toughness also allows us to grow. In order to become a better person or better family member, we must define an action and then possess the mental toughness to follow through and work toward achieving that objective. Mental toughness enters into virtually every aspect of our life and it is needed in order to have the capacity to succeed. We train ourselves to have that toughness. It is not a virtue that we necessarily think about. So it becomes important for us to bring an awareness to it. When we carry out the task at hand to accomplish a goal, it creates mental focus, and that in turn breeds the mental toughness necessary for success. Mental strength is available to everyone period. We hear people say, "He's just not mentally tough enough." But he could become mentally tough if he committed himself toward taking the necessary steps.

6. Self-Discipline (Do it right, don't accept less.)
When considering self-discipline, it becomes important to note that the virtue of self-discipline requires mental toughness, commitment, unselfishness, and

many other values. The values all relate to each other. When addressing self-discipline, we would explain, "Understand what is right, do what is right, and do it that way every single time." Everyone reading this book realizes that self-discipline is an important value for their life, but so many people stray away from it and accept less. That's why other values are necessary in order to achieve the self-discipline needed to create a positive result. Often, we don't do the right thing because doing the right thing is harder and we don't possess the mental toughness necessary to do the right thing. Self-discipline is necessary in order to do the right thing on the football field, in the classroom, and in life.

7. Great Effort

To a certain extent, most people can relate to the word "great." "Great" is an elevated performance in a particular area—a great son, a great daughter, a great father, a great mother, a great student, a great offensive lineman. The word "great" defines something extraordinary and special. Virtually everything anyone accomplishes, whether it is something in the classroom, on the football field, or as a family member requires a certain degree of effort. However, the best results are often created through greater effort. A human recognition exists when we identify: I have given all of my effort. Whatever is thrust upon us and whatever we aim to accomplish requires great effort to do it extremely well. One player's talent level might not be as prominent as another player's talent level on the football field, but if the first player gives great effort, he may still succeed, even though he might not be as good as the other player. A team might lose ballgames, but that isn't the issue. The issue becomes: was it your best effort? If the players gave their best effort, they can walk with their head held high. This virtue is relative to all facets of our life. If we're C students, we can probably be B students or A students, but we must always give our best effort. We paid special attention to our players' academics, but I never chastised a young person who received a C in a class if there was an acceptable reason why that young person simply couldn't achieve a grade higher than a C. If I believed the young person gave great effort, I applauded him for his effort even if he was unable to attain a better result.

8. Enthusiasm

Enthusiasm is viewed differently. It's easy to carry enthusiasm into an event or a ballgame. However, when players jump up and down and scream and holler before the game, it beckons the question: did these same players demonstrate a high degree of enthusiasm in the days leading up to the game? It's significant to have a high degree of enthusiasm each day so it might build and bring out the best in each player and on the collective team on gameday. When channeled in proper ways, enthusiasm often helps us to perform at a higher level, meaning bringing enthusiasm during the course of a week becomes doubly important as it relates to individual improvement. Displaying enthusiasm on Monday will enhance our performance on Monday, and therefore we have a greater chance to improve our capabilities Monday. The same process applies every single day of our lives. However, if we don't bring enthusiasm on Monday, Tuesday, Wednesday, Thursday, and Friday, then we have gone a full week without enhancing our performance, which means that we likely haven't improved our performance during the week either. Although possessing enthusiasm on the football field is vital each day of the week, enthusiasm is important in all aspects of life. Approaching goals or priorities with enthusiasm allows us to achieve something special on behalf of our family, our education, our career field, or any area deemed important in our life. When we're on a team, our enthusiasm should promote enthusiasm among our teammates. If we demonstrate genuine enthusiasm, it's going to rub off on our teammate to the right, our teammate to the left, the teammate lined up behind us, and the teammate lined up in front of us. Enthusiasm is contagious, so when our enthusiasm spreads, it helps the process of achieving improvement and success.

9. Eliminate Mistakes (Don't beat yourself.)

One of our goals in life is to eliminate mistakes. That's true in our day-to-day lives and also in athletics. Coaches coach because they want to improve the players, the team, and the program. Players can also set the example. Players correct their teammates with intentions aimed toward improvement. That improvement collectively helps the team and therefore the entire program. The same applies in life. Everybody makes mistakes, but that's not always a bad thing. A mistake, when considered properly, identifies the wrong thing, and therefore draws attention toward achieving the right thing while we work to eliminate the wrong. The process of eliminating mistakes requires self-discipline and mental toughness along with many other values. It promotes the belief: If I eliminate mistakes, life can be pretty good. Conversely, failing to eliminate mistakes causes failures in life and on the football field. The simple question we must ask ourselves is: *Why beat myself?* Eliminate the mistakes. Life is hard enough without contributing to the complexities of it. When we eliminate mistakes, we enhance our quality of life on and off the football field. The first step, however, is to honestly identify those mistakes.

10. Never Give Up (never, never, never)

So often, we hear people say, "Don't give up." Over time, we can take the statement lightly and possibly for granted. So we wrote, "Never Give Up (never, never, never)" to place extra emphasis upon the necessity not to take the easy way out. Now, there can be exceptions to the rule perhaps when a relationship turns afoul despite our very best effort. But never giving up is the goal a vast majority of the time, and that virtue is achieved through self-discipline and eliminating mistakes and so many other values in life. When I was diagnosed with cancer and received outpatient radiation and chemotherapy treatments in 2017, I utilized many of our values during the process and focused on my family and our football program. The dual treatments knocked some energy off the table, but focusing on my family and on football was significant to my recovery. I traveled back and forth from KU Medical Center two to five times per week and still watched our team's practices from the press box because I didn't want to spend each day fretting about my illness. Had I done so, I would've been worse off mentally than physically. There was no time when I thought about giving up. We have a chance when we don't give up, and a chance is all we can ask for in life. We have no chance if we give up.

11. Don't Accept Losing (If you do it one time, it will be easy for the rest of your life.)

If we accept defeat once, it becomes easier to accept defeat a second time and a third time. We cannot accept losing on the scoreboard and in life. When we make a mistake, we must change it, work to eliminate it, and understand that if we accept it, we'll be in trouble the next time a tough decision looms because we have already accepted a defeat. It is monumental for a young person to understand the concept of not accepting losing on and off the football field. If he fails to properly execute a blocking technique, he cannot accept failure and he must continue practicing the blocking technique. If he performs poorly on an exam, he cannot accept failure and he must study more effectively and harder for the next exam. If his family has a big argument, don't accept it. Make it better. That practice is so impactful in everything and anything we do. Too often we put a mistake behind us, but we must work to improve the situation and work to prevent a reoccurrence of the situation. Someone might say, "I keep failing." To me, it sends a clear message: he is accepting defeat because he has failed to make a proper effort toward correcting or eliminating a mistake in that area of his life.

12. No Self-Limitations (Expect more of yourself.)

So often, we believe our ability to achieve success comes with limitations. We grew up with great expectations, but many of those were expectations placed upon us by others rather than expectations we placed upon ourselves. Our parents carried behavioral and academic expectations of us, our teachers had expectations of us, and our relatives and people in our lives had expectations of us. Sometimes we can go through life basing our own expectations upon those set forth by others rather than establishing a set of expectations for ourselves. Although our internal expectations are often similar to outside expectations, our internal expectations should be most significant, and we must not limit our ability to achieve those expectations. Sometimes we place limitations upon our abilities because we simply don't carry the great expectation of attaining success in a given area of life.

13. Expect to Win (and truly believe we will)

The expectation for success centers on honesty. We can ask a player if we're going to win the ballgame, and he'll say, "Yes, we're going to win this game." He said that he expects success. But deep inside, does he really believe it to be true? If not, it will likely hinder his performance. The same applies when we expect success in any area of our life. The foundation for the expectation to be successful is dependent on the belief that we will succeed. It is an honest belief that we can attain success. We say to ourselves, *If I do this, this, and this in the appropriate way, I can succeed.* Expecting to win must align with that belief that we truly will succeed. Sometimes, we expect success in a venture that we directly impact and fall short. Perhaps we became too busy, lacked focus, or lacked proper planning. Whatever the case, we either carried over expectations that success would manifest itself without proper effort or we didn't fully believe success was achievable in the first place. Expect to succeed if we do the right things that lead to that success.

14. Consistency (your very, very best every time)

Everyone talks about striving for consistency, yet so many of us are consistently not as good as we can be. Pretty soon, we generally accept that level of consistency as our level of performance. It's so important to realize our optimal level, then reach that level, and do so every single day with great enthusiasm. We must identify our very best and consistently ask ourselves, *Is that my best today?* If indeed we aren't performing at our best, we must make that correction and perform at our optimal level today and every day moving forward.

15. Leadership (Everyone can set the example.)

Setting the example, right or wrong, is leadership. Someone is likely to follow that example. Many young people in a football program don't view themselves as leaders. Perhaps they're not vocal and they believe leadership is vocal. However, leadership is action, and great leadership is performing the appropriate action. I could remain silent on the football field and in life and I could still establish leadership for others through my actions. Someone is going to follow—right, wrong, or indifferent. Positive leadership is setting the appropriate example. We can provide leadership through our effort. Others will attempt to match our effort. We can provide vocal leadership but must accept the responsibility of following our words with appropriate action. Virtually everything and anything we do sets an example for someone, and I view that as leadership. The more positive things we achieve, the greater leader we become. Our players always voted for team captains and player representatives before the season. The process allowed our elected leaders to recognize that their teammates responded positively to their actions. Sometimes the most vocal players didn't receive many votes. Being a good leader is truly being committed, it's doing the right things, it's making self-sacrifices, it's being a coach on the field and a coach in life. A leader representing our program was a leader 24 hours a day, seven days a week, and was an active participant in helping guide his teammates to do the right thing.

16. Responsibility (You are responsible for your performance.)
We are responsible for ourselves and our decisions in life. So often, someone might perform a wrong action, then reply, "Well, this person did this" or "He caused me to do that." That individual is attempting to find reason, not be responsible for his own action. It's so easy to attempt to avoid the responsibility for mistakes. Taking responsibility for our own actions can be difficult for younger people, in particular, to accept. Nobody wants to be guilty of a mistake, so they cast the fault on someone else or on some other entity. In the end, the mistake falls on our own shoulders, and it is our responsibility. The sooner we accept the responsibility for our own actions and thoughts, the sooner we can focus on doing the right thing.

"Without Coach Snyder, I wouldn't be in the position I am today. Without his mentoring and his leadership, his wisdom, and knowledge, I wouldn't be the man or the football player that I am. Coach Snyder and his program gave me an opportunity to play football, and in doing so, I learned so many things about being a great player, but I learned tenfold more about being a man."

—B.J. Finney, Kansas State center, 2011–14

CHAPTER 9

THE NEXT STEP

"We named Bill Snyder as 1995 Citizen of the Year for Manhattan Chamber of Commerce. Why? Because in my lifetime, Coach Snyder has done more than any one person to build the Manhattan economy. Before Coach Snyder, there were 16,000 people in the stadium and no excitement on Saturdays in Manhattan. Under Coach Snyder, a Kansas State football game became a three-day event, and some alumni bought second homes. I don't know if there's a way to quantify what Coach Snyder means to Manhattan, but the results of his tireless efforts to build a winning culture didn't stop on the playing field. Bill Snyder transformed Manhattan."

—Dennis Mullin, chairman/CEO of Steel and Pipe Supply Co.

My mother passed away on April 16, 1994 at a hospital in St. Joseph after her lengthy second battle with breast cancer. She was 77 years old. Her cancer had returned nearly a decade following her original diagnosis—back when she came to stay with us for a while when I was at the University of Iowa. I drove from Manhattan to St. Joseph virtually every week to visit my mother and Grandpa Owens. My mother was the most significant person in my life. Even though we saw it coming, it was so painful. She was suffering, but selfishly I didn't want her to go. It was a very painful and emotional time—and not just for myself but for many others because she was such a wonderful woman and had touched many lives.

After my mother retired from Townsend & Wall Department Store in 1983 after 35 years of service to the company, she wanted to move closer to her parents, but she wouldn't allow me to purchase her a home. She wanted to move out of our original one-room apartment into a slightly larger one-bedroom apartment on the second floor of a friend's home. My mother was a very humble lady.

My mother had purchased a burial plot in St. Joseph Memorial Park, which is also known as Memorial Park Cemetery. I went to the cemetery and found a different plot for her, which was located on the highest spot of a small rolling mound that rose above an otherwise flat grassland. It was where she was laid to rest following funeral services at 10:00 AM on April 20 at King Hill Christian Church. She and my grandparents had been members of that church virtually their entire lives.

I still miss her dearly—and always will.

In 1993, we won the most games at Kansas State in 83 years, we won our first bowl game, and we finished ranked in the top 20 of both major polls for the first time in history. I thanked our players, coaches, and support staff for their daily investment that allowed us to have success during the 1993 season, but we knew that we needed to maintain that get-better-everyday mantra if we wanted to get anywhere close to where we desired to go. Heading into our sixth year, we were still the new kids on the block in the college football world, so to speak. We were not an empire by any stretch of the imagination, but we knew how empires had fallen—and it normally happened from within.

I was concerned entering the 1994 season. Because we had reached a certain level of success, some players began taking things for granted, and that manifested itself in behavioral issues. Some of our young people missed classes, and some players ran into trouble at night in Aggieville. I was fortunate to be named Big 8 Coach of the Year for the third time in four seasons by the Associated Press and I attended awards ceremonies as a finalist for the 1993 Bear Bryant National Coach of the Year Award and 1993 Kodak National Coach of the Year Award. I spent time recruiting and speaking at numerous engagements across the country. With my travels, I had to discipline players and resolve other issues within our program over the phone. Meanwhile, other schools zeroed in on some of our assistant coaches, but we were able to increase salaries in order to retain them. Although our total season attendance grew from 138,000 in 1992 to 217,000 in 1993, the additional ticket revenue only generated a portion of the money needed to cover the cost of the stadium construction projects completed over the course of the previous year.

I felt good about the opportunities for our team if we worked diligently each day to reach our goals. This was our most experienced team with 15 returning starters, including 10 first- and second-team All-Big 8 selections from the previous season. Many of our returning players were good leaders and provided a foundation through their work ethic. For the first time since we arrived at Kansas State, we returned a starting quarterback. In 1993, Chad May led the Big 8 in passing yards and set four conference passing records and he entered his senior season regarded by many as among the top quarterbacks in the country. Kevin Lockett, the top returning wide receiver in the Big 8, earned first-team Freshman All-American honors with 50 catches for 770 yards and four touchdowns in 1993. Coupled with fellow wide receivers Tyson Schwieger and Mitch Running, our passing game was prominent enough for us to be competitive in every game, and it was a major factor in our success. Senior running back J.J. Smith was the only Big 8 returning player who recorded 700 rushing yards and 200 receiving yards in 1993.

We returned seven starters from a defense that finished third in the Big 8 and held Oklahoma and Colorado to a combined 164 rushing yards on 73 carries. Linebacker Percell Gaskins was 1993 Big 8 Newcomer of the Year and he joined seniors Kirby Hocutt and Laird Veatch at linebacker. Our biggest question was in the defensive secondary. We needed to replace all four starters: Associated Press All-Americans Jaime Mendez, Thomas Randolph, Kenny McEntyre, and Kitt Rawlings.

After finishing the previous season as a nationally ranked team, we entered the 1994 season unranked. I believe that sent a message to our players, and they were highly motivated. They responded appropriately during the non-conference season with victories over Louisiana-Lafayette (34–6), Rice (27–18), and Minnesota (35–0), which marked our fourth shutout win in four seasons.

Our players enhanced their motivation during a 21–13 victory at Kansas in ESPN's Thursday night TV game. The win was significant for several reasons. First, it was the program's first win in Lawrence since 1969; second, we were the two major schools in the state; third, our in-state players had bragging rights for a year; and fourth, we were competing for the most talented players in the state. The crowd of more than 48,000 at Memorial Stadium was about half purple, and afterward some of our fans went onto the field and tore down a goal post, for which we later apologized to the University of Kansas. I could understand the excitement of our players and fans due to the fact that Kansas State had not beaten Kansas two consecutive times since the 1950s.

I believe we did a good job of getting the KU game out of our system and preparing for No. 2 Nebraska the next week. Our players were aware that we had reached our highest national ranking in history at No. 16 in the Associated Press poll. It was also brought to our attention that we were No. 1 in *The New York Times* computer rankings. Although Nebraska starting quarterback Tommie Frazier would miss the game due to injury, I cautioned our players that we could not take any team for granted—and certainly not a team of Nebraska's caliber. Our players were confident that they could play well in the game.

During the week, the media ran stories about the fact that we didn't wear the color red inside the football complex. Our reasoning behind that decision was simple. At the time, the two most prominent programs in college football were probably Nebraska and Oklahoma, and their school colors were red. We had brought this to the attention of our players, so they would be mindful of the color red and respond appropriately. If we wanted to reach some of our goals, we had to compete against those teams in red.

One of our seniors, Mike Ekeler, knew plenty about the color red. At 5'10" and 200 pounds, Mike was a little undersized at the linebacker position, but by the same token, he was an outstanding special teams player and a tough-as-nails competitor who prodded his teammates to match his energy on the field. Mike came to us from Blair, Nebraska, and he was one of many Nebraska natives who were extra motivated because Nebraska had never offered them a scholarship. Mike expressed leadership in how he conducted himself, and his teammates responded in a positive way. For that reason, Mike was the first player I ever personally hand-selected to serve as a team captain. Mike just loved to compete. Our fans loved him. Mike was a unique individual and took his passion for the game of football to another level. He shaved his head into a mohawk during Nebraska week, completely shaved his head during Colorado week, and shaved off his eyebrows during Oklahoma week.

It was important for our players to really focus and to not allow themselves to be caught in any outside distractions during the week. The media called this the biggest game in program history. It was the first home game to be televised by a major television network since 1982. Our stadium staff added 3,000 folding chairs behind the north end zone and set up additional bleachers along the edges of the stadium to accommodate a few thousand more fans. I was told it was the first time every hotel room in Manhattan and Junction City had been sold out, and that almost every hotel room in Abilene, Salina, and Topeka had been taken as well. Almost every national college football writer in the country filled our press box, and representatives from the Fiesta Bowl, Sun Bowl, and Aloha Bowl also attended the game.

The 1994 season was the first time that we felt we had the opportunity to go undefeated if we did everything as well as we possibly could on the field. That made our 17–6 loss against Nebraska vastly disappointing for our coaches, players, and fans. We recorded a season low 242 yards of total offense and committed 12 penalties. We were unable to score deep inside Nebraska territory twice in the first half when we missed a field goal and threw our first interception of the season. Even then, we only trailed 7–6 at halftime. Nebraska averaged a nation-leading 430 rushing yards per game, and we held them to a season low 210 rushing yards. I felt that we let this game slip away, but I did not believe there was a loss of confidence among our team. It served as a good teaching game that allowed us to truly identify and try to correct mismanaged or poorly executed situations.

One week later, we were tied 21–21 at No. 2 Colorado with 10 minutes remaining in the game. We always seemed to have difficulty playing in Boulder, Colorado, but I do not believe the high altitude ever affected our players. We trained well for it. Colorado had outscored its opponents by an average score of 41–19, but this was a pretty even ballgame. Three times we failed to score deep in Colorado territory, which we could not afford, and we suffered a 35–21 loss when Colorado's talented quarterback Kordell Stewart ran for a pair of touchdowns to end the game.

Starting with a 37–20 win at No. 25 Oklahoma, the program's first win in Norman, Oklahoma, since 1970, we won our final five games of the regular season. We were ranked at No. 11 in the Associated Press poll during the final three weeks and reached nine victories in back-to-back seasons for the first time in history. Consequently, our program was recognized for a team award when I was named 1994 National Coach of the Year by CNN.

The Big 8 standings finished with Nebraska (7–0), Colorado (6–1), Kansas State (5–2), and Oklahoma (4–3). Although we had passed Oklahoma and recorded five conference wins for the first time in decades, we told our players, "We still let two wins get away." Even though we finished the regular season at No. 11 in the Associated Press poll and our two losses were against Nebraska and Colorado, we did not control our own destiny. That gave bowl committees the opportunity to invite teams other than Kansas State. Consequently, unranked Notre Dame, which had a 6–4–1 record, was selected to play in the Fiesta Bowl. We were invited to play Boston College in the Aloha Bowl on Christmas Day. Our players had already voted to play in the Aloha Bowl if we weren't invited to a more prominent bowl game because they liked the idea of going to Hawaii, but we were disappointed. Nearly everybody in the country believed that we deserved to be in a more prominent bowl game.

I was concerned from the very beginning. Whether it was the 1994 season or later seasons, high rankings could promote the attitude that we've arrived and cause our players to lose sight of the necessity of daily improvement in every aspect of their lives. That could get a team into trouble. We had eight All-Big 8 selections, the most of any Big 8 team, but I was concerned that given our increased fame we could lose our way and not possess the same desire and passion that was required in order for us to reach our current level. At the same time, Boston College had a 6–4–1 record and finished fourth in the Big East Conference, so we feared that our players might go through the motions and view the bowl trip more as a vacation.

We realized that virtually nobody on our team had ever been across the ocean, so we wanted them to appreciate their experience while also maintaining focus on the game when we were on the practice field in Honolulu. I believe that we had productive practices while also spending time touring the island and participating in a few bowl-related activities. We had the opportunity to visit attractions such as the USS Arizona Memorial at Pearl Harbor. I believe our players gained an appreciation for those men and women who served and continue to serve to protect our country. When we weren't practicing or visiting attractions, I watched tape virtually every minute inside my hotel room. Our players also spent some time on the beach, which proved to contribute to our undoing in the football field. The day before the bowl game, Chad suffered what appeared to be a significant injury. Apparently, Chad had wiped out while surfing a large wave, and the force of the wave drove his head into the sand. There was some concern that Chad had broken a bone in his neck. The X-ray turned out negative, but Chad experienced significant soreness and stiffness. He played the final game of his career unable to move his neck. Chad established 10 Big 8 records and finished 11th in the voting for the 1994 Heisman Trophy, but we didn't play to our capacity in the bowl game. We managed just 124 yards of total offense and scored our only points off of a blocked punt return in a 12–7 loss in the Aloha Bowl against a very good Boston College team. We had the opportunity to finish as a top 10 team but lost the game. It was a very disappointing way to end the season.

It was important to be consistent. That has always been my nature. It's a trait that I credit to my mother. Consistency was extremely important, and we needed our young people to understand what it entailed. We can say things, but do we demonstrate it? My vision of consistency didn't address whether or not we made changes. We always changed or adjusted when we found something to be more efficient or successful, whether it be on the field or off the field within our program. However, it was important for everybody within our program to adopt positive habits. We emphasized to our players the importance of being on time at all times and being consistent about improving in the classroom, on the practice field, and in all areas in which they conducted their lives. Through consistency develops trust. I truly believe that our players trusted our process, what we did, and what we said. Did they always want to do it that way? Did they always want to work that hard? No, but there was no doubt we were consistent about our expectations. And we believed that was a very positive thing.

Fortunately, a majority of our players were learning to be consistent, and many had begun to see results of that effort to become better each day. We returned eight All-Big 8 players, including five first-team selections, which were more than any other team in the conference. We returned three of the top eight wide receivers in the league in Kevin, Tyson, and Mitch. Although Kevin was the fastest player in Big 8 history to reach 1,000 receiving yards in a career, Tyson also earned first-team All-Big 8 honors and led the league with seven touchdown receptions. Tyson was a former walk-on who was a competitive young guy and understood the game well. All of his life, he had been told that he was too small and too slow, but he had excellent hands and he could always find a way to get open. Mitch was extremely intelligent and ran routes almost to perfection. He didn't have great speed, but he studied diligently and knew how to get himself open.

We returned eight starters from a defense that ranked fifth in Division I-A in allowing just 14.2 points per game. Many people ranked our returning defensive secondary as the best in the nation after they allowed just seven touchdown passes all of the 1994 season. Joe Gordon was the first sophomore cornerback to earn All-Big 8 distinction since 1984, Chris Canty earned 1994 Big 8 Defensive Newcomer of the Year, Chuck Marlowe earned All-Big 8 honors at safety, and Mario Smith was one of our defense's hardest hitters at the other safety position. We also returned third-team All-American defensive tackle Tim Colston and a pair of great defensive ends in Nyle Wiren and Dirk Ochs.

The obvious question was how we would replace Chad. Although Matt Miller attempted just 12 passes while serving as Chad's backup during the 1994 season, we felt confident in Matt's abilities. Matt transferred to Kansas State from Texas A&M and engrained himself in our offense while sitting out the 1993 season due to NCAA transfer rules. Matt was a little bit different than Chad, but he was competitive like Chad. And like Chad, Matt could throw the ball with accuracy, but he had better mobility, so we could utilize him more in the running game, which he cherished. He was a very outgoing young guy, so it was somewhat easy for him to accept some leadership responsibility at the quarterback position, and our players responded well to him.

We did our best to keep our players' focus on football and emphasized every day the importance of not allowing any possible distractions to seep into our football complex. There was talk from the outside about how we were picked as high as No. 2 in the Big 8 during the preseason. Although our players were already motivated for the season, their motivation perhaps jumped a notch when we were not included in the preseason national rankings. We were going to have to earn it, as it should be.

Every year, we knew we would face some adversity, but that was particularly true during the 1995 season, as twice we were forced to come from behind in the final minutes to win on the road, which made a dramatic difference in our final record.

After a season-opening 34–7 victory against Temple, we learned a valuable lesson while playing at Cincinnati. We felt that our players did not take Cincinnati seriously and we allowed them the first two touchdowns of the game. We threw an interception on each of our first three possessions and had just 63 yards of total offense in the first half. In the second half, things began to change for the better. Our defense shut down seven Cincinnati drives that began in our territory, and Matt threw two touchdowns to Kevin in the final five minutes of the game. I still remember his final touchdown pass quite well. We trailed 21–17 with 38 seconds remaining when we drove the ball 59 yards to set up a final play opportunity at the Cincinnati 22-yard line. Matt rolled to his left and threw the ball across his body to Kevin, who caught the pass at the far sideline and stepped into the end zone as the game clock on the scoreboard hit all zeros. The 23–21 win was our program's biggest comeback victory since 1983. It was an amazing comeback. We learned anybody could beat us if we didn't do the things we needed to do as well as we could and if we took ourselves or our opponents for granted.

We went out and beat Akron (67–0) and Northern Illinois (44–0) and then we opened our Big 8 season with shutout victory against Missouri (30–0). We scored 141 consecutive points and recorded three straight shutout victories for the first time since 1933. It moved our team to No. 8 in the Associated Press poll, which was our highest ranking in history. However, our players knew that we still had things to improve upon. By now, our players' approach was: *Is there anything we can do to satisfy this guy?* My question to our players was, "Why would anyone want to stop trying to become better at his craft?" The sky was the limit, and therefore we could never reach a point where we could not become better. These games were important as well because they enabled us to play our second-, third-, and fourth-team players. Everybody invested themselves and made sacrifices, and we wanted our backups to be able to do well. Over that stretch, they were in the games a significant amount of time. Sometimes our starters made few mistakes, but our reserves perhaps didn't execute as well, so it always gave us something to address that needed to be improved upon for the next week

After our win against Northern Illinois, it was brought to my attention that I had become the winningest head coach in the history of Kansas State football. We were 40–13–1 since our arrival in Manhattan. Mike Ahearn accumulated a 39–12 record between 1905–10. I never really paid attention, but the accomplishment certainly meant something to myself and our staff. To be at a school and a program that you care about and win 40 games, it shouldn't be that significant to a coaching staff. But to be in that position made me feel very strongly about everybody who had been in our program and how far they had come. It wasn't Bill Snyder who had won 40 games; it was an awful lot of players, a lot of coaches, a lot of support staff, and a lot of fans. It was "The Family."

At about this time, the media began criticizing our non-conference schedule. What many people did not understand was our belief that we needed these hand-selected, non-conference games in order to give ourselves the best opportunity to build a foundation and to allow the most players possible to see the field. Other reasons we insisted on playing as many non-conference games as possible at home: it was vastly important to the financial well-being of the Manhattan community. From the very beginning, it was always important for us to save money, and playing home games with fans in the stands generated more money than when we traveled with a financial guarantee and, of course, gave loyal fans the opportunity to see their team play. Eventually, we had no home-and-home agreements with non-conference teams. Instead we played nearly all of our non-conference games at home. From the very beginning, business owners shared with me the financial significance of a home football weekend. As the years progressed, the impact of home football games grew. At one point during our tenure, a home football weekend was responsible for $20 million in revenue for Manhattan. That is why I was so very concerned for the Manhattan economy during the 2020 season. Kansas State played just five home games during the shortened season, and COVID-19 guidelines limited game attendance. That meant fewer fans came to Manhattan, which meant less money for hotels, restaurants, retail stores, and local businesses. The 2020 season greatly impacted the local economy.

We played away from Manhattan one time during the first five weeks of the 1995 season. Our first Big 8 road game served as another eye opener for our players. We trailed Oklahoma State 17–14 midway through the fourth quarter and needed an 80-yard touchdown drive in the final minutes in order to leave with a 23–17 victory.

The next week we traveled again. This time we bussed to Lincoln to face No. 2 Nebraska. Nebraska owned a nation-leading 19-game winning streak. Frazier and running back Ahman Green led an offense that ranked second in the nation in averaging 55 points and 626 total yards per game, and that also led the nation in averaging 466 rushing yards per game. Nebraska had beaten its opponents by an average of 41 points. Matt left the game due to an injury, and we trailed 35–6 at halftime. However, Brian Kavanagh stepped in and threw a pair of touchdowns, and we actually outscored Nebraska in the second half of a 49–25 loss. Our defense also held Nebraska one touchdown below its scoring average, 288 yards below its total yardage average, and 276 yards below its season rushing average.

There was a lot of outside noise during the next week as we prepared to play Kansas in Manhattan. People were calling it the biggest Sunflower Showdown in history, but my belief was that every game against the University of Kansas held some special significance for so many of our players. The difference this time was that both of our teams were ranked nationally. Kansas was ranked sixth and started out with a 7–0 record for the first time since 1968, and we were 14th nationally with a 6–1 record. Even though we had beaten Kansas in back-to-back seasons for the first time in history, I knew we would have our hands full. Just as our players and coaches were emotional about the matchup, I knew their players and coaches were emotional about the game as well. It quickly became evident to me that we wouldn't allow one game to beat us in another game, which we had been guilty of from time to time. We gave up one touchdown in the first quarter and kept Kansas off the scoreboard the remainder of the game in a 41–7 victory. It marked the highest-ranked opponent that our program had defeated in our history and it was also our greatest margin of victory over KU since 1955. We achieved these feats in front of a crowd of 44,284, which was the largest crowd ever to attend a football game in the state of Kansas. It wasn't as though we had a psychological or emotional advantage over the University of Kansas, but we just played very well. It was a good game for the rivalry.

I believe we took another step with our 49–10 victory against No. 25 Oklahoma in Manhattan. Here was Kansas State, which had defeated Oklahoma just 13 times in 80 meetings, and we had now won three straight games in the series for the first time since 1927 while also handing Oklahoma its worst loss in 50 years, which was highly significant. We continued one of our best starts to a season in history with a 49–7 win at Iowa State. In a game that featured sub-zero degree temperatures, Matt threw three touchdowns, and his 22 touchdown passes set a Big 8 season record.

Since the Nebraska game, we had outscored No. 6 Kansas, No. 25 Oklahoma, and Iowa State by a combined 139–27 score and we had held seven of 10 opponents to 10 or fewer points. That made our 27–17 loss to No. 9 Colorado on Senior Day very disappointing, particularly because we led 17–13 with three minutes remaining in the game. Once again, we had controlled our own destiny, and our loss took our fate out of our hands. We had been in a position for the Cotton Bowl but had dropped into a three-way tie with Colorado and Kansas for third place in the Big 8. That placed us in the Holiday Bowl in San Diego against a very quality Colorado State team.

This was a busy time for our program. I was fortunate to be a finalist for National Coach of the Year by the Football Writers Association of America and Football News. In December, I received a call from UCLA athletic director Peter Dalis regarding my interest in replacing retired head coach Terry Donahue. I had great respect for Terry's efforts and how he ran the

My caring mother holds me at a local
park.

My loving grandmother—(Marie) Owens.

My beautiful mother—Marionetta
Snyder.

I miss my mother every day.

My amazing grandparents hold our son Sean.

My son Sean practices his football skills in Mission Viejo, California.

Shannon, Sean, Meredith, and I pose for a portrait when my children were at a young age.

Sean, Shannon, and Meredith go boating in the Iowa River.

Sean poses during his freshman year photo day at the University of Iowa with Sharon, Ross, and Whitney.

I speak at the press conference announcing my hiring as Kansas State head coach in November of 1988.

My first coaching staff in 1989 worked tirelessly to turn around the Kansas State football program.

I walk the football field in 1991. It was a breakthrough year, in which we helped lead Kansas State to just its second winning season since 1970.

After an All-American playing career at Kansas State, Sean, my son, coached alongside me and had myriad responsibilities, including overseeing our special teams.

I have great fondness for Jim Leavitt. A coach on our original staff, he went from being our linebacker coach to defensive coordinator and then became the South Florida head coach.

Kansas State quarterback Matt Garber throws a pass during our 1992 Coca-Cola Bowl football game against Nebraska in Tokyo. Even though we lost to No. 11 Nebraska (38–24), I was pleased with our players' effort at the end of a long season and enjoyed the experience in Japan. (AP Images)

Michael Bishop and I discuss strategy during a timeout. Bishop, the runner-up for the 1998 Heisman Trophy, earned the Davey O'Brien Award as the nation's best college quarterback.

Travis Ochs corrals Eric Crouch on fourth and 8 to preserve our 40–30 victory in 1998 against Nebraska, a team we hadn't defeated since 1968. (AP Images)

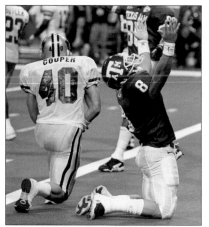

Texas A&M's Sirr Parker, who also scored the game-winning touchdown in the second overtime of our 36–33 loss in the 1998 Big 12 Championship Game, celebrates after tying the game in the fourth quarter. That crushing defeat ended our undefeated season and a chance at a national championship. (AP Images)

After narrowly losing 27–24 to Oklahoma in the 2000 Big 12 Championship Game, I congratulate my good friend and former assistant, Bobby Stoops. (AP Images)

Kansas State defensive end Monty Beisel (44) and safety Thane Bernbeck (34) carry the 2001 Cotton Bowl trophy after we defeated Tennessee 35–21. They were part of a defensive effort that allowed Tennessee to complete just seven passes. (AP Images)

I receive an award at Bill Snyder Family Stadium along with (from left to right) Jon Wefald, daughters Meredith and Shannon, wife Sharon, son Ross, and grandson Matthew (in front).

Sharon and I are honored prior to a game.

Running back Darren Sproles, who set 23 school records during his Kansas State career, runs for some of his 235 rushing yards against previously undefeated Oklahoma during our 35–7 win in the 2003 Big 12 Championship Game. (AP Images)

Following the 36–28 victory against Missouri that capped my first tenure at Kansas State, I did not anticipate Jordy Nelson (left) and Jeromey Clary (right) hoisting me upon their shoulders after the game and carrying me off of the field.

I stand next to Governor Kathleen Sebelius while she signs a proclamation about the Kansas Mentors program in 2006. Mentorship is something on which I place incredible value. (AP Images)

The value of family was always important to our football program, and the university even adopted it as a slogan. (AP Images)

Modern Family actor Eric Stonestreet is a 1996 Kansas State alumnus who loves his Wildcats. He even spoke to our team on the field after a practice early in the 2011 season. (AP Images)

We celebrate capturing a share of the 2012 Big 12 Championship with Oklahoma. By virtue of our tiebreaking win against Oklahoma during the regular season, we secured our conference's automatic Bowl Championship Series berth.

Tyler Lockett, who is part of a great Kansas State family, celebrates his second touchdown during the first half of the 2013 Buffalo Wild Wings Bowl. (AP Images)

After our players possessed ample motivation and a strong desire to beat a traditional powerhouse like Michigan, I celebrate our 31–14 win against the Wolverines in the 2013 Buffalo Wild Wings Bowl. (AP Images)

I instruct Collin Klein, one of the greatest quarterbacks to ever play in the Big 12, during the Fiesta Bowl in 2013. (AP Images)

After our 34–19 win against Kansas in 2016, the players hoist me on their shoulders to celebrate my 200th win at Kansas State.

After our 200th career victory, my family holds a poster created by the Kansas State student body.

Grandchildren Katherine and Sydney (in front) and daughters Whitney and Shannon watch a spring football game from the end zone.

Sharon's family, our children, and grandchildren attend Whitney's graduation from Kansas State University.

On the wedding day for Sharon and I, we pose with best men Tom Ross (far right), Carl Jackson (upper right), Bill Brashier (upper left), Gay Ross (matron of honor), and our four children—Shannon, Meredith, Ross, and Sean (left to right).

Daughter Shannon and husband James celebrate their marriage at First Presbyterian Church in Manhattan.

This is a portion of my Pinocchio collection. The story and film have great symbolism and offer many lessons.

I was raised in a small section of this apartment on 508 Rubidoux Street in St. Joseph, Missouri.

Grandson Matthew, daughter-in-law Wanda, and granddaughter Katherine wear their formal attire.

Daughter Shannon poses at her wedding with daughter Meredith's three boys—Gavin, Tylin, and Kadin—who served as groomsmen.

Sean receives the Ring of Honor from President Jon Wefald prior to a football game.

I watch a football game with granddaughter Lou, who is Whitney's first-born child.

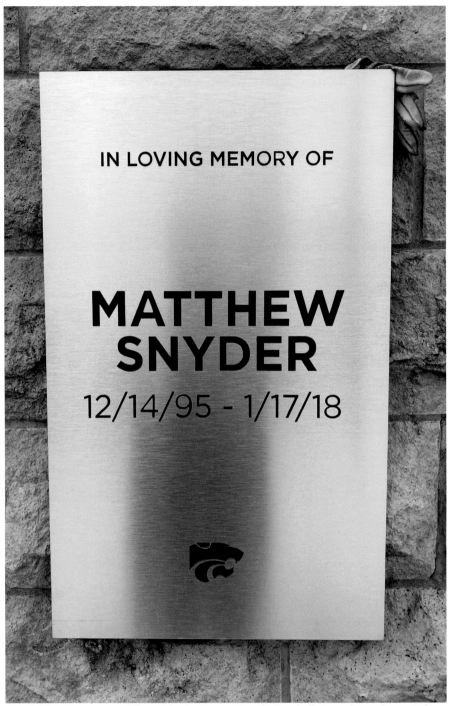

IN LOVING MEMORY OF

MATTHEW SNYDER
12/14/95 - 1/17/18

One of five plaques posted outside the Vanier Family Football Complex in honor of ex-K-Staters affiliated with the football program who lost their lives at an early age, this one honors Matthew, our grandson.

We pose for a family picture in New York at my induction into the College Football Hall of Fame.

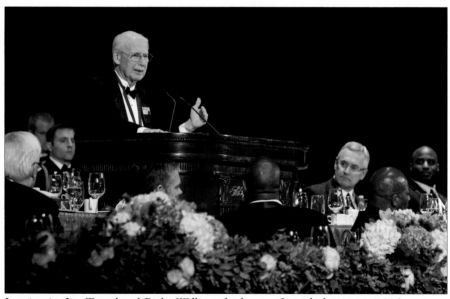

Luminaries Jim Tressel and Ricky Williams look on as I speak during my 2015 induction into the College Football Hall of Fame. It was an amazing honor.

The Foundation wall constructed in the Kansas State football indoor facility represents the players who were the true foundation of the greatest turnaround in college football history.

Our Kansas State indoor practice facility displays All-American players. Sean is third from the left.

Sharon and I stand in front of the Bill Snyder Pavilion at Missouri Western State. Being named for it is a great honor.

After I announced my retirement in 2018, my Kansas State family showed their appreciation for me. That's why I love the fine people of this community and school so much.

program. I had a history within the state of California both at the high school level and during my brief time under Coach McKay at USC, so the opportunity was intriguing. Peter and I were expected to talk after the Holiday Bowl. Although I was their top candidate, we never sat down for an interview. I told UCLA no.

The night before the Holiday Bowl, I grew emotional while speaking to the crowd of 20,000 loyal K-Staters at our pep rally. I had always been so proud of the sacrifices that our fans made to represent our school at bowl games, and it reiterated to me that I truly belonged at Kansas State. Our program had come a long way, but our work was far from finished. I was convinced that I needed to do what I had been hired to do at Kansas State. The university had been loyal to me, and I wanted to repay that loyalty.

Matt finished fifth in the country in passing efficiency. Chris Canty, a sophomore cornerback, earned consensus All-American honors and was a finalist for the Bronko Nagurski Award and the Jim Thorpe Award. Tim Colston was named Big 8 Defensive Player of the Year. Five players—Kevin Lockett, Percell Gaskins, Chuck Marlowe, Chris Canty, and Tim Colston— earned All-American honors. Four other players—Mitch, offensive tackle Chris Oltmanns, Dirk Ochs, and Joe Gordon—earned All-Big Eight honors.

It became paramount that our team displayed many of our 16 values during the Holiday Bowl after a very unfortunate incident occurred in the second quarter of the game. Matt suffered a neck injury following a helmet-to-helmet hit with a defender and after remaining down on the field for quite some time was taken to a nearby hospital. However, our players came together as a family and we owed it to each other to step up and upgrade our effort and performance level. That was always important, but it was particularly important when we lost one of our players. We handled adversity in a positive way. Brian Kavanagh came off the sideline to complete 18-of-24 passes for 242 yards and a school record-tying four touchdowns in a 54–21 victory and rightfully was named bowl MVP for his impressive performance.

In 1989, we lost 10 games in a season. Seven years later, we won 10 games in a season. At the time, I had not thought about our progress in that manner. Our 10–2 record was the best at Kansas State since 1910. We finished with our highest rankings in history—No. 7 in the Associated Press poll and No. 6 in the *USA Today*/CNN coaches poll. Our offense averaged a school-record 35.1 points per game. Our defense finished No. 1 in the country in allowing just 250.8 yards per game, which was the best mark by a Big 8 team since 1987. Our success was a tribute to that dynamic of daily improvement that we had preached and to the dedication of our players to improve every single day. A growth pattern had taken place and we had gone from one win to four wins to seven wins to nine wins to 10 wins. The proof was in the pudding, and it was easy to reflect upon all of the ways that daily improvement positively impacted our program. Kansas State, the first program in the history of college football to lose 500 games, was now recognized for something very different.

Kansas State joined Nebraska, Texas A&M, Ohio State, Florida, Florida State, and Penn State as the only schools in college football to win at least nine games in 1993, 1994, and 1995. I told our players: "Your accomplishments can be seen among the best in the country. Now remember the work required to attain our success and understand that it will require more work and continued improvement in order for us to improve upon our level of success moving forward."

Kansas State had become a nationally known program, and we had many positive aspects to promote. Consequently, we were able to enhance our recruiting across the country, build relationships, and visit the homes of many quality recruits who we felt had those intrinsic values that would make them a good fit for our program. When needed we pursued community college players who could provide immediate assistance to an area of need on our team. At the same time, we signed 50 high school players from 11 different states in the 1994, 1995, and 1996 recruiting classes. Over those three years, we signed 12 high school players from the state of Missouri, 11 from the state of Kansas, nine from Texas, seven from Florida, three from Colorado and Oklahoma, and one from Arizona, Illinois, Maryland, Nebraska, and Ohio. Our 1995 class featured seven high school players from the state of Florida, which represented the most players from a single state to sign with us over that three-year period.

During that time, the media began focusing more on our recruiting. Although my stance had always been not to spend excessive time recruiting five-star athletes, we did find talented players, and some of them were youngsters who just needed a chance and somebody to guide them. Many young men could walk out their front door, and their only possible role models were drug dealers and killers. Providing young men from undesirable environments a chance to pursue their academic interests and to learn the importance of personal values and how to set and achieve goals within the structure of our program was probably the most significant thing that we did at Kansas State. I had visited the homes of these young people. I had seen places without hope. We needed to rescue them. There were young people who were deemed to never have a chance in life. We brought some of them to our program. We promoted a value system and helped to teach them, guide them, and prepare them for life in an appropriate manner. It was meaningful to see these young people change the trajectory of their lives and consequently impact many other people in a positive way as well. We initiated a Black Leadership Academy at Kansas State to train and develop leaders from throughout the nation who could go back into the inner-city communities to guide and direct their local youth.

We endured some significant changes within our coaching staff between the 1994 and 1996 seasons. In all, we lost two offensive coordinators and a pair of co-defensive coordinators who were instrumental in the constant improvement of our program. Del Miller, the very first assistant coach who I hired at Kansas State, left his position as offensive coordinator and became the head coach at Southwest Missouri after the 1994 season. After serving as co-defensive coordinators for five years, Jim Leavitt was hired to become the first ever head coach at South Florida, and Bob Stoops was hired as defensive coordinator at the University of Florida following the 1995 season. Then Dana Dimel, who we had promoted to offensive coordinator after Del left, became head coach at Wyoming following the 1996 season.

Most coaches want to become head coaches, and I wanted to promote our coaches to become head coaches. I certainly didn't want to hold them back. I had mixed emotions because I hated to lose them, but I was happy to see them become head coaches. To lose both of our defensive coordinators in one year could have been a difficult change, but I rehired Bob Cope as our defensive coordinator and promoted defensive ends coach Mike Stoops to co-defensive coordinator. I also hired former linebacker Brent Venables as linebacker coach. Their experience in our program, enthusiasm, and compassion for young people enhanced the continuity within our program.

Cope had been our associate head coach and defensive coordinator in 1989 and 1990 and he returned to our program after spending two seasons as an assistant coach at USC and then three seasons at Baylor as a defensive backs coach, then defensive coordinator and assistant head coach. Bob and his wife Jimmie Ruth were very loyal people, and their children lived in Manhattan. Bob was diagnosed with cancer in September 1996 after he fell into a coma the week of our game against Nebraska. The prognosis was not good, as the cancer had spread to his bloodstream, brain, and lungs. Bob tried to continue to work, but I wouldn't allow it. He was simply too exhausted. He underwent radiation treatments and although Bob remained on our coaching staff, his last day at the football complex was October 1. The rest of our defensive staff—defensive line coach Mo Latimore, Stoops, and Venables—came together to fulfill Bob's duties for the remainder of the season. I asked Jimmie Ruth if I could pay for an airplane for them to go to Mexico for a treatment that wasn't available in the United States. They went down there for two weeks for the treatment. We just tried to do everything we could to try and get Bob through it. He passed away in August 1997 at 60 years of age.

In the midst of our changes on the coaching staff, we prepared for the greatest change since we had arrived: life as a member of the newly-formed Big 12 Conference.

On February 25, 1994, the Big 8 Conference formally invited four Southwest Conference schools—Baylor, Texas, Texas A&M, and Texas Tech— to join our eight conference members and form the Big 12 Conference. Without doing a significant amount of initial research, I was concerned. I liked the Big 8 and the teams that were in the conference. I wasn't alone. In speaking with many other Big 8 head coaches, it became clear that almost all of us initially opposed the idea of beginning a new conference. As far as Kansas State was concerned, we had steadily climbed toward the top of the Big 8 and had achieved a 55–36–1 record in eight seasons after the program had closed out the 1980s with a 4–50–1 mark. The addition of teams from the prominent Southwest Conference in essence meant that Kansas State was forced to almost start working its way toward the top all over again without even having taken a snap on the field. Those Southwest Conference programs would increase competition both on the field and in the recruiting realm. I had many questions. How would having a 12-team conference affect our non-conference schedule? Would the new conference eliminate most of our non-conference home games that allowed us to build a foundation each season? How would the new conference affect the number of home games we would play in a season?

I proposed that the Big 12 Conference be split into two six-team divisions, and that each Big 12 team play three non-conference games, five divisional games, and three cross-divisional games to satisfy an 11-game schedule. The two division champions would play in the Big 12 Championship Game, and the second-place team in each division would meet to decide the overall third-place finisher in the league. The Big 12 went in a different direction. We wrestled with the league's structure for quite some time.

The impact of the Big 12 was felt immediately. Seven Big 12 teams finished the 1995 season ranked in the top 25—the most of any conference in the country—with No. 1 Nebraska, No. 5 Colorado, No. 7 Kansas State, No. 9 Kansas, No. 14 Texas, No. 15 Texas A&M, and No. 23 Texas Tech. Again, I was concerned how the added competition within the new conference might affect our program.

The Big 12 Conference chose for Texas Tech to visit us for the inaugural Big 12 Conference game on August 31, 1996. Although I was pleased to play in the first Big 12 game, I was not enthusiastic that it would also be the first game of our entire season, and it would be against a conference team we knew very little about. Texas Tech was a special program and had finished no worse than second place during the final five years of the Southwest Conference, so we ran a greater risk of starting our season with a loss than in previous campaigns. As I said at the time, "We're leaping a mountain at the very beginning." The game would also draw a great deal of national attention, which consequently could create distractions for our players. However, the game excited our fans and our players to play in the first ever game in Big 12 Conference history. The game was significant for a multitude of reasons.

A certain level of confidence had developed within our entire program because of our consistent success in recent seasons. For the first time in our program's history, we entered a season nationally ranked at No. 21 in the AP poll. We were adjusting to some new personnel at certain spots, and it was a very busy time. In the past, we always had two weeks from the end of two-a-days to our first opponent, which allowed our players to absorb everything that they had learned over the course of practice. Playing in the first conference game so quickly made things a little more difficult.

We returned 13 starters, and I was confident about Brian Kavanagh as he entered his first season as our starting quarterback. He entered his senior season as our first quarterback to have four years in our offensive system and probably had a more astute knowledge of how we did things than any quarterback up to that point in time. Kevin Lockett had 145 catches for 2,150 yards and 20 touchdowns entering his senior season, but we would be without Eric Hickson, our top returning running back, who broke his leg in the spring game. Chris Canty, a consensus All-American, was going to split time at wide receiver and cornerback, but we would be without Joe Gordon half of the season due to injury. We were young up front, but we liked our top three linebackers—Travis Ochs, DeShawn Fogle, and redshirt freshman Mark Simoneau. Although it would be difficult to duplicate the defensive prowess that led to our No. 1 ranking in total defense in 1995, I felt good about our capabilities.

As it turned out, we needed every bit of our defense in a 21–14 win against Texas Tech. Although we led 21–3 with 10 minutes remaining in the game, we gave up a touchdown and a field goal down the stretch. The game was in question until we broke up a fourth-down pass at our goal line in the final seconds. Our crowd of 43,123 was loud and very supportive from beginning to end and made their presence felt during the nationally televised game. Our fans were always incredible but took things to another level over the course of the season, as we averaged 42,980 fans at our home games, which beat our previous record of 38,771 set during the 1995 season. We showed needed improvement in non-conference victories against Indiana State (59–3), Cincinnati (35–0), and Rice (34–7), which allowed us to gain some consistency in all areas and gave our reserves an opportunity to get onto the field. We struggled in a 39–3 loss against No. 6 Nebraska but responded in a positive way with a 35–10 win at Missouri.

One of the many challenges we faced during the first few years of the Big 12 Conference was gaining familiarity with our new league opponents. In 1996, we played against teams with which we had no previous experience and we traveled to unfamiliar cities, stayed in unfamiliar hotels, and played in unfamiliar stadiums. It became a constant process of trying to become familiar with the new conference teams, coaching staffs, players, schemes, and tendencies. Preparation during the out of season, spring, summer, and during each week of the season was always vital, but the necessity of making the most of every minute was particularly magnified when we played former Southwest Conference teams such as Texas A&M in College Station for the first time. Texas A&M had lost just twice at home in the 1990s, and R.C. Slocum was a very quality head coach who had won 80 percent of his games. The crowd of more than 64,000 with the 12th man and all of the traditions could make Kyle Field a daunting venue for any visiting team. Our players were highly motivated to defeat a team from the former Southwest Conference on their home turf. From the time we left the bus, I could sense that there was an extra little something going into the game. Our players wanted to show that they deserved the elite status that typically went to teams such as Texas A&M.

Texas A&M possessed one of the nation's top passing offenses, and we had the second-ranked pass defense in the country. Mario Smith tied the NCAA record with a 100-yard interception return at Missouri. We had made steady progress on defense with 21 sacks and 38 pass breakups during the first six games. We turned some early miscues into points and led 20–3 at halftime and then 23–10 late in the third quarter. Ultimately, we held Texas A&M to 151 passing yards in the game. We also forced two interceptions and recovered three fumbles. However, we committed some penalties and suffered a blocked punt, and that allowed Texas A&M to gain some momentum and pull to within three points. Just when the game suddenly appeared to be in doubt, Chris Canty chased down their receiver and stripped him of the football as he headed toward our end zone in the final seconds. Mark Simoneau recovered the ball at our 17-yard line, and we returned to

Manhattan with a 23–20 victory. Every road game was big. That we had the capacity to go into College Station, where visiting teams struggled, and return home successful in our mission spoke highly of our coaches, players, and support staff—our program.

It was so important to have a sense of loyalty to everyone in our program. Coaches and players were high profile, but there were so many people within the confines of our program that contributed to our success. Sometimes our players would not have been in a position to even walk onto the field if it wasn't for the many tasks that others performed behind the scenes. It was important to me that we recognized our secretaries, our doctors, our trainers, our managers and student managers, our equipment managers, our custodians, our training table employees, and others within the complex. We asked our players to write them thank you notes. We sent them Christmas cards. I made sure everyone in our football complex had the opportunity to take one trip with our team during the season so they might be recognized for their value to our program. I made sure those special guests flew in first class. Most people might think the head coach always sat in first class when flying with the team. I never sat in first class. I always sat in the row behind the first-class seats, and each assistant coach sat with his position group, so they were always accessible to their players. At some point during the season, every staff member sat in first class on a football trip.

After back-to-back road games, we returned home to play and led Oklahoma by 28 points in the fourth quarter before pulling out a 42–35 victory. Oklahoma played well at the end and didn't give up, but we let up. It was a great learning lesson for our players and coaches. More than halfway through our season, I could not think of another year where so many things had impacted our program. Some issues dealt with injuries because we lost both Eric Hickson and Martin Gramatica prior to the season and then lost several more players over the course of the season. Our defensive coaching staff shared duties among themselves when Bob Cope fell ill. We had a few issues with some players who believed that they had arrived. Our current players had not been with us when we went 1–10, so they had no idea everything that the players before them had experienced in order to build the foundation for our program and the present players. Now that

Kansas State had become regarded as somewhat of a prominent program in the country, a few players believed that they were pretty special since they were recruited into our program. That mind-set did not adhere with our 16 goals and consequently it was not a positive for their development or for the continuity of our program.

We beat Kansas 38–12 in Lawrence, which marked the first time since 1927 that a Kansas State senior class went undefeated in the Sunflower Showdown over the course of their careers. Brian threw a school-record four touchdown passes for the second week in a row. As I told our players afterward, "When the premise of our program is constant improvement, when we think along those lines and adhere to the principle that improvement never has to stop, these things can be achieved. It's not so much projecting our achievements but rather not being surprised when they arrive."

We improved to No. 9 in the AP poll and headed to play No. 6 Colorado in Boulder. Both teams were 8–1. It was the coldest game in my life. The temperature was about zero degrees, and the windchill dropped the temperatures to below zero on the field. I was pleased as our defense limited Colorado to two first-half touchdowns and kept them off the scoreboard the rest of the game. However, we only threatened to score one time during the game and were unable to move the ball past their 7-yard line, which sealed our fate. Consequently, in a game that we absolutely had to win in order to be considered for either the Fiesta Bowl, Orange Bowl, or Sugar Bowl, we left the field with a 12–0 defeat. It was incredibly disheartening. Through the years, the altitude in their stadium never affected our players, but something always seemed to hold us back because we rarely played well in Boulder. Following the game, we knew that our likely bowl destination would be the Cotton Bowl in Dallas and we virtually secured that spot with a 35–20 win against Iowa State on Senior Day. Our senior class became the first one in program history to win at least nine games every season in their careers.

On December 7, the Cotton Bowl officially invited us to play fifth-ranked Brigham Young on New Year's Day, which was our first New Year's Day bowl appearance. Our fans responded incredibly by purchasing 21,000 tickets the first day of ticket sales and then they purchased another 10,000 tickets over the next week. The Cotton Bowl was an ideal place for Kansas

State. Many of our largest alumni bases were located in the state of Texas, and Dallas was a relatively easy trip for our fans to travel to from the state of Kansas. As I said at the time, "We are bringing our home to Dallas." We had the three largest crowds in the history of college football to cross the state line to watch their team play, and that record began with our 45,000 fans that attended the Cotton Bowl.

However, hours after we accepted the Cotton Bowl invitation, one of our most-challenging nine-win seasons continued with an off-the-field incident that made national headlines. Chris Canty got himself into trouble and had to be disciplined. There was no doubt that Chris was one of the best defensive players in college football in 1995 and 1996. Chris was the first player in program history to be named a two-time first-team All-American by the Associated Press and he was the first player during our tenure to play both on offense and defense. He recorded 160 tackles, 14 interceptions, three forced fumbles, and two fumble recoveries over his three-year career while also returning 31 punts, seven kickoffs, and recording five catches as a wide receiver. He was one of the best multi-dimensional players in the country and had a swagger. But Chris paid the consequence for making a poor decision. Chris pulled his name from three major individual postseason awards—the Jim Thorpe Award, the Bronko Nagurski Award, and the Maxwell Award— causing the award committees to re-vote as Chris had a strong chance of winning the honors.

During our three previous bowl trips, we either practiced or played the bowl game on Christmas Day. This year, we allowed our players to be with their families on December 24 and 25. We reconvened at the football complex at 8:00 AM the following day and bussed to Manhattan Regional Airport to fly to Dallas. We had several good weeks of practice. We knew BYU quarterback Steve Sarkisian was the national leader in passing efficiency and had thrown for more than 4,000 yards and 33 touchdowns. But we also knew that we had one of the best pass defenses and cornerback combinations in the country in Joe Gordon and Chris, who could virtually shut down part of the field.

What do I remember most about the Cotton Bowl? In the final moments of his remarkable Kansas State career, Kevin caught a pass in the back of the end zone to win the game. However, officials ruled that Kevin was out of bounds, and we lost the game 19–15. Although a defender pushed Kevin as he caught the ball in the air, I still believe that Kevin got a toe inbounds in the back of the end zone. On our final possession, we drove the length of the field to the BYU 17-yard line, then Brian threw a perfectly placed ball that I believed Kevin caught over the defensive back for a touchdown. Instead, officials waived off the score.

Two plays later, a BYU player intercepted a pass at the 3-yard line with only seconds remaining in the game. I felt so badly for our players. Kevin was a very quality person. He wasn't a rah-rah guy but was a very good leader, always did the right thing, and represented the program extremely well. He finished his career with all of the receiving records—217 catches for 3,032 yards and 26 touchdowns—but you would never know it when speaking with him. Aaron Lockett, his brother, and Tyler Lockett, his son, demonstrated the same type of humility during their own remarkable careers at Kansas State.

It was an extremely difficult end to the Cotton Bowl. I really hurt for our players. Our players were nearly despondent over that loss. As a coach, I had been through difficult losses before, but I really had some anxiety for our players. I also felt so badly for our fans. Our fans were a part of our family. They traveled everywhere. They made a major statement throughout the entire season. Especially at the Cotton Bowl.

"More than anything, Coach Snyder brought discipline into my life. He takes a lot of pride in the little things and showed us that you can't accomplish a major goal unless you take care of the small things first. He cares deeply about his players, and, I mean, it is sincere with every one of them—from the All-Americans to the last guy on the depth chart."

—Jaime Mendez, Kansas State free safety, 1990–93

CHAPTER 10

PINOCCHIO

"I don't think anybody in college coaching has done what Bill Snyder has done. I broadcast for 14 years, and seven or eight of them were in college football, and no football coach did a better job of coaching football players than Bill Snyder. No football coach. No Coach of the Year. No national championship team. None of them. I saw him beat some teams that they had no business beating."

—Dick Vermeil, former Kansas City Chiefs head coach

The Electric Theater and Missouri Theater were located catty-corner from each other in downtown St. Joseph, Missouri. They were beautiful movie houses. Nobody quite makes them like that anymore. I watched many movies inside both theaters when I was a child. However, no film moved me quite like *Pinocchio*, which Disney released in 1940. I was 12 or 13 years old when I watched Pinocchio for the first time. I watched the movie three or four more times and I really enjoyed it for many different reasons.

Geppetto, an elderly woodcarver, carved a wooden puppet, whom he named Pinocchio. Geppetto loved Pinocchio very much and wished upon a star for Pinocchio to become a real human boy. A blue fairy brought Pinocchio to life and informed Pinocchio, who was still a puppet, that he must prove himself and display positive values in order to become a real live boy. Pinocchio journeyed out into the world, and his orneriness got him into trouble. Consequently, he battled through some adversity. In the end, Pinocchio demonstrated honesty, selflessness, and risked his own life while bravely rescuing Geppetto from death. The blue fairy concluded that

Pinocchio had learned strong values and rewarded Pinocchio by turning him into a real human boy.

I saw a little bit of myself in Pinocchio from beginning to end. I had the propensity to be ornery when I was younger, but my mother and so many other people invested themselves in providing guidance and direction and helped me to develop a stronger value system. Although I didn't necessarily face the same issues as Pinocchio, we both experienced attitudinal changes, and Pinocchio and I made a good deal of progress in strengthening our value system in life.

Geppetto was actually my favorite character in the movie. I admired Geppetto's desire to either have a child or someone he could mentor. Seeing Geppetto embrace Pinocchio with that desire to bring him to life brought a great deal of meaning to me. Geppetto taught Pinocchio a value system, which consequently helped Pinocchio make positive changes, and Pinocchio learned to have an affection for someone who cared so deeply about him. When Geppetto faced death as he was swallowed by the whale, the fact that Pinocchio sacrificed what could've been his life to save Geppetto indicated that Pinocchio had embraced the love and the values that Geppetto had provided for him. That equated to the love and values my mother and grandparents instilled into me. That's why I appreciated the movie so very much.

Geppetto had a passion for his craft and dearly wanted something special in his life, which was Pinocchio. As the story progressed, Geppetto transferred his wants to Pinocchio. That's what I passed along to my own children. That desire also manifested itself within the Kansas State program and other places where I coached over the course of my career. We wanted to help develop quality character and the capacity to create an environment in which young people could be successful in their lives. That is what Geppetto did for Pinocchio.

Pinocchio's learned values from Geppetto were important, as they were important to my children and to the young people in our program. The 16 Wildcat Goals for Success permeated Pinocchio's growth, and we wanted to bring those values to the young people in our program. Although some players already had a strong value system, we identified 16 goals as the foundation for individual development within our program.

Our first group of young players went through an awful lot. There had been a total lack of success. Players did not believe they were well-received by the outside world because they perceived themselves as losers, and it impacted several different areas of their lives. It hurt our players personally through their interaction with other people because people outside of the program probably never said so much as a positive comment to them. It also affected our players' capacity to be students. Many players left before and after we arrived, and many players experienced academic difficulty because they were too embarrassed to go to class. They had lost their desire to compete in the classroom as well as on the field. That caused harm. Some players made unhealthy choices while attempting to cope with their difficulties.

There were some similarities between our football program and Pinocchio. We gradually carved out our identity. The program was gradually coming to life. It wasn't something that just jumped up and said, "I've arrived." It was continued progress. There were ups and downs, but it continually grew. Everybody told me to run after we went 1–10 in our first year, but I believed our players had gradually improved throughout the course of the season. We weren't a finished product by any stretch of the imagination, but we made enough positive advancement that I believed we were on track to accomplish positive things. I certainly wanted to continue to be a part of it.

Back in the day, coaches took their players to a downtown movie the night before a game. Every night before a game, I instead rented movies and brought them into the football complex for our players. One of those nights, I'd have our players watch *Pinocchio*. When Geppetto carved out Pinocchio, it required time, effort, and care. Today, there's that prominence of instant self-gratification that exists with young people, and I don't totally fault them. I think parenting has to be able to make an attempt to manage that instead of allowing it to flourish. We always had ongoing dialogue about instant gratification and the detriment it can bring to any person, young or old, and how to best overcome it. The process involved establishing priorities regarding family, education, future, athletics, and everything significant in each person's life and then defining a plan to achieve success in those areas. Like Pinocchio, an individual must take gradual steps in his development.

Before each season, I had our players write down their priorities. Then I sat down in my office with each individual player, helped him to develop goals based upon his priorities, and then we established steps to reach his goals. Those steps were minor successes. My feeling was if he achieved one little step, he was a step closer, and in doing so, the young person could see success, and that tended to dilute that instant self-gratification. There was gratification in the fact that he accomplished one little step, and then he became motivated to pursue the next step and the next step.

On October 9, 1993, which was two days after my birthday, Tom Ross, one of my dearest friends who had introduced me to Sharon, traveled with his wife to watch our game against the University of Kansas. Afterward, Tom gifted me a large picture of Pinocchio and Geppetto and within the picture was also a small frame of film. It was an original negative cut from the first *Pinocchio* film.

In 1994, I received a special gift from my old high school friends, Gary Colvin, Bob Ross, and Jim Perry. They visited me in my office at the complex and presented me with a glass display case that contained a Geppetto figurine proudly holding the Pinocchio puppet by its strings. To have people I'd known since high school show their appreciation for something so dear to me was meaningful. It probably required quite a search to locate that piece of *Pinocchio* memorabilia. I kept the display on my desk for many years, and it sometimes served as a conversation piece. It gave me the opportunity to tell our visitors about Geppetto, his guidance to Pinocchio, how Geppetto turned around Pinocchio's life, and how meaningful that was to me. I have received so many Pinocchio gifts over the years. Some of the items are displayed in our home.

Years ago, I introduced my children to *Pinocchio*. I wanted my children to identify the meaningful aspects of the movie. I encouraged them to really see the meaning within the story instead of viewing it as just another cartoon movie. Afterward, I asked them to define for me the characteristics of Pinocchio and Geppetto and the impact one had on the other. I wanted to know how the story's meaning impacted them. It was like a school assignment.

Pinocchio came and went in movie theaters across the country. Disney re-released the movie a handful of times over the years, including in 1992 during our third year in Manhattan. I enjoyed the opportunity to watch *Pinocchio* inside a theater again. Then they sold Pinocchio on VHS tapes. I purchased every copy available in Manhattan and gave one to each of our children and to many other young people when our paths crossed. Years later, I bought everybody in our family *Pinocchio* on DVD. Soon I will purchase the movie for each of our grandchildren and great-grandchildren as well. More than 65 years have passed since I watched Pinocchio for the first time. The story and its meaning remain timeless.

"I didn't picture Coach Snyder doing anything other than coaching and watching film. I couldn't picture him doing anything else. He loved being around 'youngsters,' as he called them. He loved being around football. He loved taking notes on his digital voice recorder. He just loved being around the game and preparing kids to be young men. In medieval times there was Joe the Butcher or Dan the Fisherman. He was Bill the Coach. That was his thing, and he was one of the best to ever do it."

—Nick Leckey, Kansas State center, 2000–03

CHAPTER 11

MICHAEL BISHOP AND THE DUAL-THREAT QUARTERBACKS

"Bill Snyder was an incredible coach and he's one of them that I admired the most. He made Kansas State. It's not even possible to say Kansas State without acknowledging or mentioning Bill Snyder. I don't know whether they'd admit to it, or are even necessarily aware, but there are a lot of things Bill Snyder revolutionized in football, as far as the little things, organizing things, the way he analyzes and studies things. He was a notorious workaholic, but it's just the way he analyzes the game and looks at the game."

—Mike Leach, Mississippi State head coach

Michael Bishop stepped onto our football field for the first time in August 1997. He arrived on our seventh day of two-a-day practices. He had missed spring practice and summer workouts while completing community college coursework so he could be eligible to become a member of our program. In all reality, it was virtually impossible for a quarterback to arrive at Kansas State during the middle of two-a-day practices, jump into our offensive system with such little preparation time, and become our starting quarterback. But Michael did.

We all saw on film that Michael, a native of Willis, Texas, clearly possessed dual-threat talent. Michael also had a great deal of confidence while recording a 24–0 record with consecutive NCJAA National Championships at Blinn

(Texas) Junior College. At 6'1" and 205 pounds, Michael was a gifted runner (4.55 speed in the 40), athletic, and had an extremely strong arm. He was deceptive with the ball in his hands but yet a physical quarterback who could withstand getting tackled 30 times a game. Virtually every Division I-A program sought strictly passing quarterbacks, and few recruited running quarterbacks. Some programs believed Michael would be a better fit as a wide receiver or safety. Michael would've been a great running back as well. In high school, Michael also held responsibilities for kicking off, punting, and on defense.

However, Michael only wanted to play quarterback. I told Michael that he would have the opportunity to play quarterback at Kansas State. I envisioned that his blend of skills would be a great asset to our offense. He was our kind of quarterback.

From the first day we arrived at Kansas State University in 1989, we always looked for that quarterback who could run and throw the football. However, we didn't always have that quarterback who posed a running threat. Chad May was a very fine quarterback. He finished his career as a 1994 first-team All-American, and set Big 8 Conference passing records during his two seasons with us, but he was not a deceptive runner. Matt Miller, in his only year as a starter in 1995, set the school record for passing efficiency (157.3) in a single season and was a capable runner with 129 carries for 309 yards and eight touchdowns. Brian Kavanagh didn't possess that running ability but proved to be very effective while guiding us to double-digit wins with 20 passing touchdowns and just six interceptions in 1996.

Michael was simply different. He was perhaps the best pure athlete we ever had at quarterback. People compared him to Tommie Frazier at Nebraska, but Michael had a stronger arm. Shortly after Michael arrived, I took him off to the side in practice and said, "I just want to see how far you can throw it." Almost flat-footed, he threw it 70 yards in the air. After one practice, he threw the football 93 yards in front of his teammates. I always said that Michael could throw a football through a car wash without getting it wet. In fact, when Michael was with the New England Patriots a couple of years later, Tom Brady said that Michael had the strongest arm that he had ever seen. With Michael, we handcrafted the early gameplans as he continued to learn our system. If a play didn't pan out, he didn't bat an eye. He just took off and ran the ball and often had success doing it. He was like a sandlot player in that respect in his first year. He just made things happen. Sometimes Michael's penchant to improvise caused some of our coaches to hold their breath during a play, but often it resulted in a successful play, even though it wasn't executed as designed.

Sometimes our coaches looked at the sky over some of the things Michael did in practice, but they often ended up being successful plays, even though they were not executed as designed.

During his first game in a Kansas State uniform, Michael threw a school record-tying four touchdowns and amassed 270 total yards, including a 43-yard touchdown run, in a 47–7 victory at Northern Illinois. Actually, his performance was expected because we had an idea of his physical capabilities. Michael passed for 441 yards in one game and threw for more than 300 yards in three other contests. He rushed for 196 yards in one game and rushed for more than 100 yards three other times. Michael became the first Division I-A quarterback in history to record more than 1,500 passing yards and 500 rushing yards in each of his first two seasons. He also finished as runner-up to Ricky Williams for the 1998 Heisman Trophy.

We initiated several things on the offensive side of the ball that became prominent to many college football teams. Some head coaches had success and strongly believed in utilizing their own offensive system, but many coaches began to utilize the quarterback run game. Kansas State pioneered the quarterback running game in college football and in professional football. The zone-read and the "Wildcat" formation, which you hear announcers discuss during football games, also started with us. A lot of things happening in the football world today are gratifying because I feel confident those things were initiated at Kansas State.

The quarterback running game was far less complex than some believed. We simply added the word "quarterback" to all of our running play calls, and the quarterback would run that play instead of a running back. Runs designed for our running back or fullback were also designed for our quarterback. We nearly doubled the amount of running plays in our playbook by utilizing the quarterback to run each play that our other backs run. It was single-wing football.

One play was called "56-PopOut-QB-Draw." Michael was under center, faked the handoff to running back Eric Hickson, stepped back, and took a quick glance up field as if poised to pass the ball, and then took off. Or Michael faked an isolation play with the fullback leading and the running back trailing behind, dropped back, and threw a pop-out pass. When we ran Michael enough times, opposing defenses added an extra defender in the box, which was a positive because now we went to the passing game against man-to-man coverage and could locate the best matchup and throw the ball to that receiver.

The zone-read gave Michael an option to hand off the ball or keep it. We took every play that our running back ran and gave the quarterback the option to hand it off or keep the ball. We gave him a certain defender to read and left that defender unblocked. We gained a blocker, and they had a free man, but we ran the read or the option off of that defender. If that defender took the back, the quarterback kept the ball. If the free defender took the quarterback, the ball was given to the back. The quarterback running game with the read element fit in with our counter plays, isolation plays, power plays, and dive plays. Virtually every run play we had in our playbook became an option play (give or keep).

Bottom line was we ran the quarterback through our dual-threat concept whereas other teams weren't running their quarterbacks. That meant opposing defenses lacked experience and repetition in defending our style of offense because nobody used their quarterback in this manner. Defenses faced an uphill climb in defending us because they had no previous experience defending our type of offense.

People recognized the degree of success we had in utilizing the quarterback run game. Gradually, dual-threat quarterbacks around the country blossomed and flourished because of their ability to both run and throw and because of the additional pressure it placed upon defenses to defend them.

I was extremely proud of Michael when he won the 1998 Davey O'Brien Award and I was proud of the selection committee for making that decision. There were a lot of quarterbacks with gargantuan passing statistics, but Michael had the combination of both passing and rushing, so it was significant that he won the award. Michael passed for 2,844 yards and 23 touchdowns and just four interceptions and rushed for 748 yards and 14 touchdowns while taking Kansas State to its first undefeated regular season and achieving the No. 1 scoring offense in the nation. Michael was the first quarterback in Davey O'Brien Award history to throw for at least 1,500 yards and rush for 500 yards in a season. After Michael, six of the next 13 Davey O'Brien Award winners—Joe Hamilton, Eric Crouch, Vince Young, Tim Tebow, Cam Newton, and Robert Griffin III—were dual-threat quarterbacks.

Michael showed that running quarterbacks could flourish in major college football. Thus, Kansas State laid a blueprint for other teams to successfully utilize a dual-threat quarterback. Whereas once the dual-threat quarterback had gone overlooked unless he had a really dynamic throwing arm, high schools now put their best athlete at quarterback, and many of these quarterbacks were runners first and then passers. Eventually, they became proficient in both areas. In turn, this affected recruiting to a certain extent. Gradually, opponents on our schedule faced other offenses with a dual-threat quarterback, so consequently our opponents had already prepared for our style of offense by the time they faced us. We were no longer unique that week.

Over the years, a large number of coaches inquired about utilizing the dual-threat quarterback and asked to visit our program. During the summertime, one coach after another visited me and our coaches. Over time, the constant visitations from other coaches concerned me because I didn't want certain information to leave our football program and also because the visits took time away from our preparation for the upcoming season.

Prior to the 2001 season, Urban Meyer, a 36-year-old head coach at Bowling Green, spent one or two days with us at our football complex, learning about our quarterback running game. Of course, our coaching staff maintained certain restrictions while accommodating any coach because we didn't want to share everything, as it could come back to bite us, but Urban was a very bright young coach, and we likely weren't going to face his team. Of course, Urban eventually went on to the University of Florida and had a very successful dual-threat quarterback in Tim Tebow and he also used the quarterback running game at Ohio State University.

So much of our offense was based upon the capabilities of our quarterback. Some of our quarterbacks were more gifted at one aspect than the other, and those capabilities helped determine how much we utilized certain parts of the playbook. No matter who served as our quarterback, we could succeed while utilizing basically the same offense. Some quarterbacks simply operated at a little higher level than others, and consequently we had a more successful offense during that time.

Following the 1998 season, Jonathan Beasley became our starting quarterback. Jonathan wasn't as fast or athletic as Michael, but he could still run with the football. Jonathan's major strength was his knowledge of our offense and the opponent's defense. He was a coach on the field. Jonathan had a freer rein on utilizing audibles. He finished his Kansas State career with 4,642 passing yards and 965 rushing yards.

Ell Roberson arrived in our 1999 recruiting class as the highest-rated high school quarterback in our history. He was one of those high-profile quarterbacks who carried NFL aspirations. Obviously, Ell had physical capabilities, but his passion for the game was a part of his package and drew my attention. His first carry as a member of our team came on the opening play of our 2000 spring game and resulted in a 73-yard touchdown. Ell was a very confident young player, not unlike Michael, but he needed to play within the system. The more that Michael learned, retained, and utilized what the offense brought to him, the better his success. That was the same way with Ell. What became so prominent for Ell was the read-option game with Darren Sproles. Virtually every play, Ell could hand the ball to Darren or keep it. Those were special times to me.

Ell became the first quarterback in Big 12 Conference history to pass for 5,000 yards and rush for 2,500 more in a career. He tied Michael's record in winning 22 games as a starter and also captured All-American honors during a senior season in which he led our team to the 2003 Big 12 Championship.

I said at the time that I believed he was the toughest quarterback in the country that year.

We had a number of dual-threat quarterbacks who maybe didn't carry national attention and maybe didn't accumulate the numbers that others did, but they contributed significantly with the quarterback running game and the read-option game. That truly benefited our offense. Between 1997 and 2017, our quarterbacks rushed for at least 100 yards in 36 total games. Ten different quarterbacks rushed for at least 100 yards once in their careers: Michael, Ell, Allan Evridge, Alan Webb, Collin Klein, Daniel Sams, Jake Waters, Jesse Ertz, Joe Hubener, and Alex Delton. Ell rushed for a quarterback-record 228 yards against Nebraska in 2002, and seven other times, we had a quarterback rush for at least 150 yards in a game.

I had a checklist of items that I discussed with our quarterbacks either the night before or the day of every game. Each game was a little different. An opponent might present something that would require a different focus from our quarterback. Perhaps a defense jumped around and caused the quarterback to alter his mental approach, change the play, or recognize different keys, but we always had to keep our composure. I always stressed the significance of maintaining poise and moving onto the next snap. A quarterback had 10 teammates looking to him for leadership. He had to recognize and respond accordingly. It was his huddle, it was his team, and he was the guy to lead it and couldn't dwell on previous plays. Nobody has more things to pay attention to than a quarterback after he calls the play, but a quarterback sometimes allows the 35-second play clock to run out because he is looking at so many things. The day before the game when we visited the opponent's stadium, I pointed out the play and game clocks to our quarterbacks. I said, "Envision this clock tonight before you go to sleep." On gameday, they needed to be able to locate and see the 25- or 35-second clock immediately. Our quarterbacks always had to be cognizant of timeouts. We preferred to get into the last four minutes of a half with two or three timeouts if at all possible, but we also didn't want to put ourselves in harm's way because we needed to take a timeout and instead avoided doing so.

Our quarterbacks were expected to have good eyes and to throw the ball to our receiver and away from the defender. On running plays, our quarterbacks had to be cognizant of an area that we called the pocket, which is the far hip of the running back. He must place the ball into the lower portion of the stomach on the far hip and hold onto the ball until he was certain the running back possessed the ball. We expected our quarterbacks to ensure we had 11 players on the field before the snap. We had certain calls that might have been a little unique in terms of pre-snap shifting or certain types of gadgetry that we utilized in different games. The quarterbacks had to control that.

We had a different cadence for no-huddle situations and in our two-minute hurry-up offense. We might call two plays and not huddle between the two or call three plays and not huddle between any of them. We utilized the no-huddle offense in a variety of ways, and a different cadence was consistent with the no-huddle offense. We reminded our quarterbacks about the most significant audibles we planned for the running game and the passing game and why and when we would use them. Certain audibles were utilized against certain coverages and stunts by the defense.

We reminded our quarterbacks of "feet in cement." Our quarterback would go through his cadence, but the ball would never be snapped. We had "feet in cement timeout," which meant that if he went through his cadence and nobody jumped offside, then we called a timeout. Basically, we did "feet in cement" so opponents would feel the necessity to get lined up and thus reveal to us their defensive alignment. We also had "feet in cement, check with me," so we made sure we got to the line of scrimmage with plenty of time on the play clock, then we wouldn't snap it and wouldn't snap it, and then our quarterback could identify the defensive alignment and call an audible. We also had "feet in cement, dummy," and our quarterback would rise up and make a dummy audible, then we wouldn't snap it, and then he would rise up, make a live audible, and we would snap the ball and go through with the play.

Along with our quarterbacks, we reminded our wide receivers about various situations and procedures. Just as our quarterback made calls, our wide receivers could make a call to our quarterback to verify the coverages and potential blitzes. It was important for our quarterback to be observant when our wide receivers made such calls. For instance, if the defensive back lined up to the outside of our receiver, that might indicate that he was playing zone coverage, and our wide receiver called out "green" to identify that. If the defensive back lined up inside of our receiver, that might indicate either that he was going to blitz or play man-to-man coverage, and our wide receiver called out "red." When defenders lined up off of a wide receiver, it freed our wide receiver on short routes, and we reminded our quarterbacks that these plays were gifts and to check into them anytime the opportunity presented itself. Sometimes a defensive back did not line up over one of our wide receivers, so our receiver was basically uncovered. In this situation, our quarterback and wide receiver communicated through eye contact, and that eye contact indicated that our quarterback would hit our wide receiver on a quick "hot" route, which could result in good yardage. Anytime the ball was on the hash mark and the cornerback lined up on or inside the wide receiver to the short side of the field, more often than not he was going to come on a cornerback blitz, so we reminded our quarterbacks to remain alert. If the cornerback blitzed, our quarterback could rise up and throw the ball to the uncovered receiver.

We utilized all five wide receivers in our passing game and we had a five-man progression in virtually everything we did offensively if all five were able to get out on a route. If our running back didn't have to block, we checked him out and we reminded our quarterbacks that if necessary, they could lay the ball off to our running back to salvage the play. We always discussed "checking for keeps," where the quarterback kept the ball instead of handing off to the running back and ran the designed play. If the defense appeared vulnerable to our quarterback keeping the ball, we made sure we called more of those read-type plays. In the same regard, I reminded our quarterbacks to always carry out their fakes because it was important for the defense to pay attention to our quarterback, which then took pressure off of our running back. If the defense didn't honor our quarterback, then we called the plays that allowed him to keep the ball. When a defense presented a look that couldn't defend the zone-read, our quarterback could audible to that play.

Quarterback Jason Smargiasso didn't stay in the program very long, but he had the talent to be a running and throwing quarterback. Chad May wasn't a prolific running quarterback, but he was one of the most productive passers in Big 8 Conference history. Matt Miller was effective as a dual-threat quarterback. Jonathan Beasley was effective and knowledgeable. Dylan Meier threw the ball well, and though he didn't have all of the capabilities running the ball, he was still productive and started two years in our system. Alan Webb had dual-threat talents and was a one-year starter. Daniel Saus rushed for 199 yards against Baylor and was a gifted runner. Jake Waters set the school record for the most passing yards in a season (3,501) and could bring it down and run the ball. Jesse Ertz had two 150-yard rushing performances and was our starter for three years. Joe Hubener was long and lanky and had a 150-yard rushing game as well. Alex Delton rushed for a Kansas State bowl record 158 yards against UCLA in the 2017 Cactus Bowl, and Skylar Thompson also ran the ball well. Alex was more like a running back in terms of his running ability. Alex split time as a starter with Skylar Thompson as a talented runner.

Collin Klein finished his Kansas State career as the sixth quarterback in Big 12 history to pass for 4,000 yards and rush for 2,000 yards in a career. His 27 rushing touchdowns during his first season as a starter in 2011 tied the single-season Big 12 record and tied a national record for rushing touchdowns by a Division I-A quarterback. As a senior, Collin was a finalist for the 2012 Heisman Trophy.

But before Collin received any recognition, he was a redshirt freshman playing behind two upperclassmen quarterbacks in 2009. Although Collin never technically left the quarterback position and attended all of the position meetings, he asked if he could help the team in some capacity. We played him a little bit at wide receiver, and he caught six passes for 38 yards and one touchdown during the season. He was tall and could catch the ball, but he didn't necessarily make those fast cuts at the wide receiver position.

However, we saw that Collin could throw the ball and had the ability to run well enough and play physical enough to be considered a dual-threat quarterback. Carson Coffman, our starting quarterback, was injured for our ninth game of the 2010 season, so we gave Collin his first career start at quarterback on the road against the University of Texas. Collin rushed 25 times for 127 yards and two touchdowns while attempting just four passes in our 39–14 win against the Longhorns. He was an athletic and physical runner. Collin didn't have Michael's change-of-direction capabilities, but he was every bit as physical.

Collin reaffirmed our beliefs during an early-season road game at the University of Miami in 2011. He completed 12-of-18 passes for 133 yards and two touchdowns and rushed 22 times for 93 yards and one touchdown in a 28–24 win against the Hurricanes. He showed us what we knew all along. He was a mentally and physically tough individual. We wouldn't have won that ballgame at Miami without Collin's toughness. We just ran him over and over again. We figured if they couldn't stop Collin, there was no sense in stopping what worked in that or any game.

Collin's game continued to evolve. He gained a better understanding of the entirety of the offense, gained more confidence in his own capabilities, and understood what we wanted to accomplish at that position. His teammates learned to have great confidence in him and in his abilities, which was all a part of the process. What made Collin special was that he was a very bright individual and made it a point to have a great understanding of the offense. He was a quality leader, a team captain, and a great teammate. He was so very conscientious about the details of the game and became a vastly improved passer over his two seasons as a starter. Eventually, he knew all of the ins and outs of the offense. We opened up our audible game to him and gave him the opportunity to basically call plays from the field. We gave him the authority to change almost any play that came onto the field.

Collin tied Michael and Ell with a school-record 22 victories as a starter. He set eight school records and became the only quarterback from a Bowl Championship Series Automatic Qualifying school in the BCS era to rush for at least 20 touchdowns and pass for at least 10 touchdowns in multiple seasons.

The traits we looked for in a quarterback never varied over the years. We wanted a quarterback who could run and throw the football well, and a number of our quarterbacks possessed those capabilities. It was also significant that they were competitive, intelligent, and possessed leadership capabilities. The success of our quarterback running game was a great asset to our offense. The concept of the dual-threat quarterback and the quarterback running game was something we had in our playbook on the very first day.

"Other teams out there tried to run with their quarterback, but Coach Snyder took it to a whole different level. Coach Snyder was an offensive genius. He innovated an offense at Kansas State that nobody else was willing to do at that time. He assessed his talent, took a step back, and said, 'You know what? We're going to try this, and if we do it well, we're going to win a lot of games.' He started the quarterback run game. He took that big leap."

—Michael Bishop, Kansas State quarterback, 1997–98

CHAPTER 12

The First 11-Win Season

"Perhaps the highest compliment I can pay Bill Snyder is that he was unparalleled as a teacher of young men. The litany of Coach Snyder's former players who have gone on to great success as coaches and in other professions is a testament to the values they learned in his program at Kansas State. I always felt like Bill Snyder and his teams earned every yard, every victory, and every championship. The work ethic that Bill's mother instilled in him was unquestionably reflected in the personality of his football teams. Bill was always finding innovative new ways to give his teams an opportunity to win. What a lasting impact Bill Snyder made on college football and the coaching profession."

—Frank Beamer, former Virginia Tech head coach

We knew that we would enter the 1997 season without 14 starters from the previous season. Kevin Lockett finished his career as our all-time leader in all major receiving categories, Nyle Wiren was our all-time leader in sacks, and Brian Kavanagh had been amazing during his only season as starting quarterback. We would also miss our entire starting defensive secondary, which had been rated as the best unit in the country. Two-time All-American cornerback Chris Canty left after his junior year and was a first-round pick in the 1997 NFL Draft. Although we returned some players who had progressed fairly well at their positions, we lacked depth in some areas and genuinely needed to find players to fill immediate needs on both sides.

We addressed recruiting virtually every day. From the outset, each day we went around the meeting room, and each coach defined his needs for that particular recruiting cycle and who the prospects were at that time. We allotted scholarships for specific offensive and defensive positions in order to best address deficiencies. Each year, our coaching staff and graduate assistants watched film of between 600 and 800 recruits. That number quickly dwindled to between 80 and 100 total prospects that we ranked in order of priority. We identified between two and four prospects at each position as top-tier recruits. They were most crucial to watch in person, to visit in school and in their homes, and to invite to campus. We also built relationships with our second-tier and third-tier recruits through phone calls and written correspondence. We believed it was important to maintain dialogue with everybody virtually every day. Recruiting was a never-ending venture. Our coaches were sometimes in their office until midnight or beyond calling recruits on the West Coast. We covered the gamut in recruiting high schools and community colleges.

Although quality youngsters with strong value systems existed in high schools and community colleges, an unfair stigma surrounded community college players across the country. In the 1990s, most people within the realm of Division I-A college football perceived community college players as failures, players who had terrible grades, or who were bad people. Consequently, most Division I-A programs deemed community college players to be a risk due to their "problems." We had a different approach at Kansas State. We felt that a player's current station in life did not define him as a person. Instead, he was defined by what kind of person he was and his value system. There were good young people in high schools, good young people in community colleges, and good young people in Division I-A programs. We felt strongly that a community college player could provide immediate help because of his two years of upper-level football experience, and that he could flourish both as player and a person within the structure of our football program and our academic programs at Kansas State University. We did not recruit over our players with junior college recruits. We looked at them if there was a void at a position.

We signed a total of 286 players to scholarship between 1993 and 2005. That included 189 high school players and 101 transfer players. Ninety-five of those transfer players joined our program from community colleges. Many of those community college players came to us from the Jayhawk Conference, the powerhouse eight-team league that included Garden City, Hutchinson, Coffeyville, Butler, Highland, Dodge City, Fort Scott, and Independence. It was annually regarded as the premier community college conference in the country. We built strong relationships with the coaching staffs of each school. We had a distinct advantage due to our relationships and proximity to the Jayhawk Conference. Although a few Division I-A programs had begun to recruit Kansas community colleges, most Division I-A programs were hesitant due to the expense of private planes, which were necessary in order for these out-of-state schools to reach these smaller Kansas towns. Although we had never signed more than six community college players in a given year, we altered that trend dramatically in our 1997 signing class due to the vast array of talent within the Jayhawk Conference and how we believed those individuals could fit into our system and immediately contribute to our team. On February 5, 1997, we signed 15 high school players to scholarship and awarded scholarships to 12 community college players, including eight members of the Jayhawk Conference. It was believed to be among the largest collection of community college players in history to sign with a Division I-A program.

Our 12 community college players joined Kansas State with basically the same goals: they wanted to enhance their capabilities and contribute to our program as we strived to reach even greater success. We were one of just six Division I-A programs to win at least nine games in each of the past four seasons, we finished ranked in the top 20 in each of those four campaigns, and our 36–10–1 record over that span was third best in the Big 12 Conference, trailing only Nebraska (47–3) and Colorado (39–8–1). Although I never paid a great deal of attention to recruiting rankings, I was told that many people considered our signing class to be prominent nationally and regarded among the likes of Nebraska, Colorado, Texas, and Texas A&M for the first time. However, our players' steady development and their ability to positively contribute to our program was more important in our eyes.

We believed that we brought in many talented individuals, including several NJCAA All-Americans and many players who were considered to be among the top 100 community college players in the country. Michael Bishop was the second-rated community college quarterback in the country and went 24–0 at Blinn (Texas) Junior College with two NJCAA national championships. Offensive guard Brien Hanley was the second-rated community college offensive lineman out of Coffeyville Community College. Jeff Kelly was the top-rated community college linebacker out of Garden City Community College. Wide receiver Darnell McDonald and cornerback Cephus Scott were honorable mention NCJAA All-Americans out of Garden City Community College. Cornerback and kickoff returner Gerald Neasman was an honorable mention All-American out of Coffeyville Community College, and defensive tackle Nilijah McCoy was an honorable mention All-American out of Dodge City Community College.

Our recent success attracted many quality high school players as well. For the first time in history, we signed three *Parade* All-Americans in linebacker Ben Leber of Vermillion, South Dakota; defensive end Monty Beisel of Douglass, Kansas; and wide receiver Julius McMillan of Altus, Oklahoma. Additionally, running back Eric Gooden, defensive end DeVane Robinson, safety Milton Proctor, and defensive tackle Eric Everley were SuperPrep All-Americans. Cornerbacks Jerametrius Butler and Isaac Harvin were BlueChip All-Americans, and wide receiver Aaron Lockett was a PrepStar All-American.

Our 27-member signing class in 1997 became significant for various reasons, including its impact upon our overall scholarship count. We began with 47 players on scholarship in 1989 and over the course of seven years steadily built our total to 75 scholarship players. Now we had 83 total scholarship players, which was the closest we had ever been to reaching the NCAA limit of 85 scholarships for a Division I-A team.

This was another step forward. Four of our community college signees— Everett Burnett, Brien, Nilijah, and Keith Black—participated in spring practice and worked their way into the two-deep roster. The other eight reported with the rest of our newcomers on August 7. It did not take long before we recognized that we might be deeper than we had ever been and collectively every bit as talented. Michael started in all 12 games, and eight other community college signees earned starting spots over the course of the 1997 season. Michael earned Big 12 Conference Offensive Newcomer of the Year, and Jeff earned Big 12 Conference Defensive Newcomer of the Year. Jeff earned first-team All-Big 12 honors, Michael earned second-team

All-Big 12 honors, and Darnell and Gerald were honorable mention All-Big 12 selections.

However, before the season even began, I found several things very bothersome. I had hoped that the stress would somewhat ease as we worked our way through the process and became a prominent program, but I discovered that was not in my nature. Something always concerned me, including those little things that most people argued were too little to worry about. Nevertheless, I addressed every single item and detail and consequently had a more-than-full plate over the course of the season. Yet at the time, I believed it was all necessary. I flew to California one day, Texas the next day, and everywhere in between either recruiting, speaking at engagements, or attending events on behalf of Kansas State University. One of my daughters had a child, and another daughter began riding horses. We always tried to stay heavily invested in the lives of all of our children.

We continued to try and increase the salaries of our assistant coaches. I promoted Mark Mangino, our longest-tenured assistant coach, to running game coordinator in addition to his role as interior offensive line coach as he entered his seventh season. Jon Fabris had joined our staff in December 1996 as defensive ends coach. Mike Stoops entered his sixth year and his second year as defensive coordinator. In the meantime, we had discipline issues and behavioral issues concerning a few players, and I had to dismiss them. Over the course of the season, my relationship with the media grew strained. The media latched onto one thing and then another, and when they ran out of things to write negatively about, they wrote about how bad I was as a head coach. Some people wrote things that simply were inaccurate, but I did not want to argue with reporters and as always read very little of what was in print.

There was appropriate excitement regarding our program in the Manhattan community. We set our home attendance record by averaging 42,980 fans during the 1996 season and we sold out our 34,500 season tickets prior to the 1997 season. We were also fund-raising for a stadium expansion to accommodate between 50,000 and 60,000 fans. Our 37–5–1 home record was sixth best in the country in the 1990s. However, I cautioned our coaches and players to focus on the task at hand each day. In the grand scheme of the college football world, you are never too far from going 1–10 like the 1989 season with 13,000 people in the stadium. The status of the program could never be taken for granted. We had to be persistent. Anyone who entered my office saw a plaque on my desk titled "Persistence" with a valuable passage from former U.S. President Calvin Coolidge, which read: "Nothing in the world can take the place of persistence. Talent will not; nothing is more common than unsuccessful men with talent. Genius will not; unrewarded genius is almost a proverb. Education will not; the world is full of educated derelicts. Persistence and determination alone are omnipotent. The slogan 'Press On' has solved and always will solve the problems of the human race."

No position was more pressing than the quarterback spot. We headed into fall camp with a quarterback competition. Although Jonathan Beasley entered his sophomore season with eight games of experience, Michael just had that athletic ability, competitiveness, strong arm, and ability in the running game. Michael became our fourth different starting quarterback in five seasons and the least-experienced starting quarterback we had to that point. He was in our offensive system for less than a month and had to catch up quickly. Michael made adequate progress in our season opener at Northern Illinois. He passed for 172 yards and a school record-tying four touchdowns, rushed for 98 yards with a 43-yard touchdown run, and sat out the fourth quarter in our 47–7 victory. Yet he still had so much to improve upon. We generated 42 points and 383 yards of total offense in the first half on our way to the program's first road win in a season opener since 1975. Michael still had a lot of work ahead of him, but we believed that he was going to be okay. We also believed that he would hit some rough spots. As a team, we were not naïve to the fact that we possessed some ability and could be a better-than-decent team and perhaps a very good team.

Perhaps we suffered from a little bit of overconfidence. We led Ohio 23–0 in the third quarter before letting up and holding on for a 23–20 win in our home opener. Michael had a rough game, and we brought in Jonathan. We needed a 94-yard punt-return touchdown by Lamar Chapman and three field goals by Martin Gramatica of 52, 37, and 55 yards for the win. We had an honest assessment and evaluation after the game. We needed to take the proper steps to improve as a team. I believe we became better in our 58–0 win against Bowling Green. We had a school-record 638 total yards, including 439 yards on the ground, and we limited our opponent to just 56 yards of total offense in the game. Once again, the media criticized my scheduling, though it was important to me that we played early-season games that allowed us to build a foundation and possibly enable our second- and third-string players a chance to gain experience. Jonathan came into the game, gained some valuable repetitions, and attempted five passes while playing with our second- and third-string offensive linemen. Some teams might have kept their starters in the game and won 100–0. We did not. But their head coach refused to shake my hand after the game. I did not blame him, but I felt that it was important that we allowed Jonathan to gain some repetitions throwing the ball during his limited playing time.

During the week of our Big 12 Conference season opener at No. 3 Nebraska, a Nebraska assistant coach told the media that we practiced illegally. I called Tom Osborne. The coach apologized, and Tom told the media that in fact we were not conducting illegal practices. Nebraska was the standard in the Big 12, and we thought about the game virtually every day. I told the media that I was not frustrated that we had yet to defeat Nebraska, but it was hard to look past the fact that we had lost 28 consecutive games in the series. I believed that we had a good week of practice, and as usual, we practiced with simulated crowd noise, but Nebraska got on a roll and was difficult to stop. We trailed 41–12 heading into the fourth quarter and suffered a 56–26 loss. It was the most points we had allowed an opponent to score in five years. Michael grew very emotional on the sideline as the game progressed, and it was the first time of many that we witnessed his passionate competitive nature, which at times could be somewhat extreme.

However, I could empathize with Michael's frustration. After all, he had entered the game 27–1 as a starter. But Michael said some things that he should not have said to the media immediately afterward when he suggested that perhaps some of his teammates had quit during the game. Although he was a never-give-up guy, his remark was inappropriate. He apologized to the team on Monday. It was difficult to gauge if our team had shown weaknesses or if those deficiencies were just because we played Nebraska, but I had faith that we would be an angry team dedicated to overcoming that defeat. We had been resilient in the past, and I had reason to believe we would be resilient moving forward. It was not the first time we had faced disappointment and it likely would not be the last.

We had a good week of practice, and our players responded accordingly. Michael set the Big 12 record for rushing yards by a quarterback with 196 rushing yards on 14 carries and scored two touchdowns on the ground while throwing for another score in a 41–11 win against Missouri. One week later, we faced No. 14 Texas A&M, which ranked No. 1 nationally in scoring offense and No. 5 in rushing offense. We beat Texas A&M 36–17 and held the Aggies to 90 yards of total offense, including minus-35 rushing yards. It was the fewest total yards by a Texas A&M team in more than two decades. I was pleased with our offensive production given that Texas A&M had only allowed 43 points all season.

Michael went to the bench with an injured ankle during the game, and as always, our players surrounded our injured player as doctors performed their examination. We always did this in order to prevent the opposing coaches in the coaches' box from knowing the nature of our player's injury. Eventually we utilized a small tent. We intercepted the TV cameraman as he tried to poke his camera inside the huddle around Michael to reveal everything to the television audience. Of course, the cameraman objected to our protective nature. That argument wouldn't take place today because of the invention of the injury tent. Throughout my career, the media and even a few opposing head coaches criticized my decision not to discuss injuries. I did not discuss injuries the week prior to a game, the week after a game, and certainly not immediately after a game. My reasoning was simple: if everybody knew that Michael had a sprained right ankle, opponents could take advantage of that. We did not discuss injuries in order to protect our players. Michael returned the following week during a 26–7 win at Oklahoma, which gave us five straight wins over the Sooners for the first time in a series that began in 1908.

We felt good about Michael's progress and the strides made by our team. Our 248 rushing yards per game were on pace to set the school single-season record, and the 27 quarterback sacks by our defense ranked third in the country. We did not give Michael the keys to the offense. We called the plays for him, and if we changed the play, we did so from the sideline. When Michael went under center, he stepped out and looked at our sideline to see if we were changing the play. We pared down the offense during his first season to allow him to best utilize his talents. Even when he made a mistake, he often made a positive play out of it. He could turn the wrong way on a handoff and miss the running back, then run the play himself, and gain 10 or 20 yards. His recognition and growth within our system gradually improved as we went along.

Our defense deserved a lot of credit. We had been fortunate to have Bob Stoops and Jim Leavitt as defensive co-coordinators for several years. When they left, Bob's brother, Mike, served as our defensive coordinator. We finished No. 1, No. 16, and No. 4 in total defense between 1995 and 1997. We also finished No. 2, No. 11, and No. 6 in scoring defense over that span. We allowed fewer than 16 points and 300 total yards per game in each of those three seasons. The Stoops brothers—Ron Jr., Bobby, Mike, and Mark—all grew up in Youngstown, Ohio. Their father, Ron Sr., spent 30 years as defensive coordinator at Cardinal Mooney High School in Youngstown until his death in 1988. Three of the four sons—Bobby (Oklahoma), Mike (Arizona), and Mark (Kentucky) eventually became head coaches at the Division I-A level, and Ron Jr. became an assistant coach at Youngstown State. Bobby, Mike, and Mark all played for us at the University of Iowa. Bobby really fostered an aggressive-style defense for us at Kansas State, and Mike carried on many of Bobby's defensive schemes. We pressured the quarterback and played man-to-man, bump-and-run defense in the back end a fair amount of time. Our defenses took on the personality of Bobby and Jim and then maintained that same personality under Mike.

What I liked about Mike was that he was brash and wouldn't accept "almost" or "not too bad." With Mike, it was always: "get better." Mike was intense and could get awfully emotional while watching film in position meetings, coaching on the practice field, and when he sat in the coaches' box during games. When a defensive player on the sideline had to pick up the headset to receive instruction from Mike, the defensive player knew that he was in for it. We had to insulate the walls in the coaches' box because Mike's voice carried throughout the press box. That was humorous to a certain degree.

Our defense proved to be very prominent on a day in which we scored our fewest points all season in a 13–2 win at Texas Tech. The Texas Tech offense did not score a point and recorded just 117 yards in total offense with six first downs. I did not know how much more we could squeeze out of our defense than what we did in that game. It was one of those teaching moments for Michael, whose fourth-quarter interception marked our fourth turnover of the game and gave Texas Tech the ball at our 3-yard line. He completed 6-of-21 passes for 69 yards with one touchdown and three interceptions. Jonathan saw his most playing time of the season and put the game virtually out of reach with a 33-yard touchdown run in the final minutes of the game. Changing players because of a reason other than injury was difficult—and perhaps even more difficult for a quarterback—because everybody in the world knew it, and it could cause people to take sides and create drama. However, once in a while it became necessary. In that particular game, Michael was competitive as always, but Texas Tech had a very good defense, and it did not allow him to perform near his best.

I was cautious to make sure that our players were not too overhyped when we played the University of Kansas at home. Although we were favored by double digits, both No. 11 Kansas State (7–1) and Kansas (5–4) entered the contest in Manhattan with winning records for the second straight time. In 1995, we beat sixth-ranked Kansas 41–7, which was the highest-ranked opponent Kansas State had defeated in its history. It appeared that the rivalry was becoming a better quality rivalry given the recent success by both teams, which had not been the case in the previous decade. Our program had a 3–40–1 record between 1986 and 1989, and Kansas had a 9–34–1 record over that span. In the 1990s, we were 61–27–1 and were bowl eligible for a fifth straight season, and Kansas was 47–41–1 with two bowl appearances. This time we beat Kansas 48–16 and scored our most points ever in the Sunflower Showdown. Our five straight wins over Kansas marked our longest winning streak in the 95-year history of the series. Michael passed for 218 yards and three touchdowns, Gerald had a 99-yard kickoff-return touchdown and a 41-yard interception-return touchdown, and David Allen had a 70-yard punt-return touchdown.

For the third straight year, we moved into the top 10 in the Associated Press poll, but the week of preparation for our Senior Day game against Colorado was one of the most exhausting weeks of my life. I did not sleep the entire night before the game. There was just so much going on, and I was a worrier. My mind would not slow down. Although it had always been that way, it seemed to reach a different level, and I simply could not get certain things out of my mind. I did not think I was unlike most people. Whether we are awake or asleep, something is always on our mind. That's what our brain does. We wanted to beat Colorado so badly. The media made so much over the fact that our program was 0–11–1 against Colorado since 1984. Each of the previous two seasons, we had been ranked in the top 10 and lost to Colorado in 1995 (27–17) and 1996 (12–0). Our current No. 10 ranking kept us in the picture for an Alliance Bowl berth, but we still had to earn it. My exhausting week ended with a 37–20 win against Colorado. We led 30–6 heading into the fourth quarter. The Fiesta Bowl representatives were in attendance. It was a significant win because Colorado had been such a prominent program along with Nebraska and Oklahoma. Anytime we beat somebody for the first time, it was special. Now we just needed to beat Nebraska.

I was so proud of our 14-member senior class, which was the first senior class in our program's history to participate in a bowl game every year of their career. We established a new season attendance record with an average crowd of 43,091. Our ticket sales had improved by 5,000 percent since our arrival in 1989, and more than $5 million in Kansas State merchandise was sold in 1997, which ranked 18th nationally in collegiate sales. As the program became better, a sense of pride went along with that achievement, Jon Wefald said, as football was the front porch to the university. Consequently, our string of success put the program, university, community, and state in a different light. We could not go anywhere without seeing the Powercat logo license plates on the front of cars.

Shortly after our win over Colorado, Fiesta Bowl executive director John Junker indicated to me that we could likely be selected to play in the Fiesta

Bowl. Our players allowed us to have that opportunity when we finished out the regular season with a 28–3 win at Iowa State, which gave us 10 regular-season wins for the first time in history. Our seven-game conference winning streak was our longest in history as well. I believed that we were an appealing at-large team for the Fiesta Bowl due to our No. 9 ranking, our 10–1 record, and our fans' famous reputation for traveling to bowl games. My feelings heightened after Arizona's 28–16 upset victory against No. 12 Arizona State, which was considered to be the frontrunner for the Fiesta Bowl. The Fiesta Bowl joined the Orange Bowl and Sugar Bowl in the three-game Bowl Alliance, which had a $8.6 million payout for participating conferences. The Fiesta Bowl had the fourth and sixth picks in the selection order. The media believed that we would go to the Cotton Bowl because of our non-conference schedule. Fiesta Bowl executive director John Junker said, "In the last maybe eight to 10 years, I can think of two things that have lived up to their billing. They are Kansas State football and Michael Jordan."

On December 6, our coaches and players gathered in the Big 8 Room to watch the Alliance Bowl selection show on our TV. We had heavy snowfall that day in Manhattan. The Orange Bowl selected No. 2 Nebraska and No. 3 Tennessee, the Sugar Bowl selected No. 9 Ohio State and No. 4 Florida State, and the Fiesta Bowl selected No. 14 Syracuse and No. 10 Kansas State. Our game was scheduled for a 6:01 PM kickoff on December 31 at Sun Devil Stadium in Tempe, Arizona. We leapfrogged No. 5 UCLA, No. 6 Florida, and No. 7 North Carolina for a spot in an Alliance Bowl. We were deserving because our players earned their due. We belonged there.

Three days later, we attended a banquet in West Palm Beach, Florida, where Martin was named winner of the 1997 Lou Groza Award as the most outstanding kicker in college football. Martin also became just the fourth player in our program's history to be named an All-American by the Associated Press, joining punter Sean Snyder (1992), free safety Jaime Mendez (1993), and Chris (1995, 1996). Martin made 19-of-20 field-goal attempts, including all three attempts of 50-plus yards and he also made 37-of-38 extra-point attempts. He achieved these feats just one year after he blew out the knee in his kicking leg and had to miss the 1996 season. He received 48-of-67 first-place votes by the Groza Award committee. Martin was such a team-oriented guy, and the enthusiasm that he demonstrated enhanced the enthusiasm throughout the team, so he provided leadership without really doing anything other than being himself. He was a good young man from a nice family.

Our program experienced some inner turmoil over the next several weeks. First, it appeared that every college football program contacted our assistant coaches for potential jobs. Second, Max Urick, our athletic director, was in line to take another position. Then Arkansas athletic director Frank Broyles, who was inducted into the College Football Hall of Fame in 1983, offered me the Arkansas head coaching job. Although it was an appealing position, I had a sense of loyalty to our program, our players, our university, and our fans. At about the same time, Whitney, our youngest daughter, had an extensive oral surgery procedure, which weighed heavily on my mind. We had long, hard team practices. Our fans sold out our school's allotment of 21,000 Fiesta Bowl tickets in 10 days and were poised to purchase the unsold tickets from Syracuse's 13,500-ticket allotment. We paused practice one week as our players took their final exams. Our starting offensive and defensive players were consistent during the final four weeks of the regular season despite some players playing hurt down the stretch. As always, we initially focused our practice efforts on the development of our younger players before we delved into on-field game preparations. It was important that we were emotionally ready to play the game at just the right time and that our physical preparation and conditioning peaked at just the right time. That was difficult because of all of the time we had between the end of our regular season and the bowl game. We utilized our practice facility a majority of the time due to snowfall and inclement weather.

We flew into the Scottsdale Airport on Christmas Day and already faced adversity as we stepped off of our flight. Our equipment truck ran into inclement weather along its 1,100-mile drive west, so we spent our first day of preparation with no video equipment, no practice equipment, and no practice uniforms. There were so many concerns the week before the bowl game. No. 14 Syracuse was the Big East Conference champion and entered with a 9–3 record. It had won eight straight games after starting out the season with a 1–3 record. I believed Syracuse was playing as well as anybody in the country. Paul Pasqualoni was a very fine head coach who had won at least nine games in five of his seven seasons. Syracuse owned the longest streak in the nation by winning seven straight bowl games. At the same time, the media took note that the Fiesta Bowl was the first time we played a game at Sun Devil Stadium since our very first game—a 31–0 loss to Arizona State on September 9, 1989.

Of course, plenty of national attention surrounded the matchup between Michael and Syracuse quarterback Donovan McNabb, the Big East Offensive Player of the Year. McNabb had passed for 2,300 yards with 20 touchdowns and five interceptions and had rushed for nearly 400 yards with six touchdowns. Although we had one of the top five defenses in the country, we knew that we would have our hands full. Even though Michael had gained respect during the season, he always wanted more. Although Michael completed less than 45 percent of his passes, he had 1,557 passing yards with 13 touchdowns and eight interceptions, and his 566 rushing yards and nine touchdowns made him one of the more dynamic dual-threat quarterbacks in the country. Michael's competitiveness got him into hot water with me a time or two, but by the same token, that spirit behind his competitive nature was significant. If we had to correct anything in Michael's game, it was never his effort.

I awoke on December 31, the day of the Fiesta Bowl, still uncertain about the game, but I felt more confident and relaxed than I had felt all week. We were slight favorites and we felt strongly that we would have the home-field advantage. Upper New York had 18 inches of snow, and consequently several thousand Syracuse fans were unable to travel to the game. I hibernated inside our hotel for the most part during our bowl trips. When we were not at practice, I watched tape and prepared gameplans and practice schedules inside my hotel room. But I heard all of the stories about our fans.

They traveled in droves and did not go anywhere without their purple. Many Kansas State fans came from midwestern towns in the middle of the United States, and a majority of Kansas was Small Town, U.S.A. Many of these people perhaps did not have a lot of money, and they made the bowl trip their vacation and piled into a car and drove 1,000 miles, and we admired them so much for their loyalty and passion. Our fans cared so much about our school and our program. We witnessed that yet again when we left our locker room and jogged onto the field at Sun Devil Stadium. The official attendance was 69,367, and nearly 50,000 of those people were our fans. Kansas State set the record for the largest amount of fans to cross a state line to attend a game in the history of college football. Kansas State people always found a way, and I appreciated them so much for it. It was so very special and so meaningful to our players. We had a lot of dialogue about our fans prior to the game. We knew that we had to be the very best that we could be for our fans.

Our team went out and put together one of the most memorable victories in our program's history, a 35–18 win against Syracuse. We engineered three straight touchdown drives in the second quarter, and Michael completed a 77-yard touchdown pass to Darnell, which was the longest pass play in Fiesta Bowl history. We jumped out to a 21–3 lead. We led 21–15 at halftime after making some silly mistakes. We knew that Michael had to have a good game passing the football, and I was awfully pleased with his performance in the throwing game. His best passing game all season could not have come at a better time. It was important to understand that Michael only had been in our offensive system for four months. Nobody learned our system in four months. Nobody. Michael was named Offensive MVP of the bowl game after he completed a career-high 14 passes in 23 passing attempts for 317 yards and a school record-tying four touchdowns. He also rushed 15 times for 73 yards and a touchdown. Michael and Darnell really worked well together and they set or tied six Fiesta Bowl records. Darnell had seven catches for 206 yards and three touchdowns and seemed to make something close to an exceptional play every time he touched the ball.

Our defense held McNabb to 16-of-39 passing for 271 yards with two touchdowns, one interception, and one lost fumble. We led by 10 points with seven minutes remaining in the game when McNabb fumbled the ball at our 17-yard line. Travis Ochs, who intercepted a pass earlier in the game, was named the Defensive MVP after he recovered McNabb's fumble, and we marched down the field to put the game out of reach.

I stayed in the moment when I walked to midfield and shook hands with Coach Pasqualoni after our victory. At the time, I did not think about the fact that we had finished the season with an 11–1 record and I did not think about the fact that we had won more games than any team in the history of our program. I thought about our players, coaches, and fans. We truly won as a family. In the locker room, I told all of our coaches, players, and support staff how much I appreciated them, and how proud I was of them. Then I addressed where this victory could take us as a program and what it could mean for the future. That night, I wrote in my diary: "11–1 season. I should feel better."

"Coach was the same coach from Day One until the day I left. Everybody knows Manhattan isn't the easiest place to recruit, and to be able to compete with all of the top-of-the-line teams shows what kind of coach he is. I always viewed Coach Snyder as a father figure that you respect and do your best for. I couldn't ask for a better coach, a better person to mold me as a kid. When you're in college, you're a kid and become a man, and I owe all of that to Coach Snyder."

—Martin Gramatica, Kansas State kicker, 1994–98

CHAPTER 13

1998

"Bill Snyder will always be remembered as one of the greatest program builders college football has ever seen. What he did in turning around the fortunes at Kansas State is unprecedented, and his accomplishments are well-documented. But Coach Snyder's career extends well beyond that. The impact he's had on the enormous number of players and coaches who have played for or worked with him in his 50-plus years of coaching is immense. For me, he was a person I always looked up to and admired, a man I leaned on regularly for thoughts and advice, and he will always be a dear friend. I'm so lucky to have him in my life."

—Mack Brown, North Carolina head coach

The day after the Fiesta Bowl on New Year's Day, I flew to San Francisco to serve as the head coach of the West team in the 73rd annual East-West Shrine Bowl. My assistant coaches were Dave Rader of Tulsa and Tyrone Willingham of Stanford. We faced a very talented East team led by Tennessee head coach Phil Fulmer and assistant coaches Gary Barnett of Northwestern and Frank Beamer of Virginia Tech. Our West squad won 24–7. Todd Weiner and Kendyl Jacox, two of our very fine Kansas State offensive linemen, played on our West team. Todd and Kendyl blocked for West quarterback Scott Frost, who had just led Nebraska to a 42–17 win against Peyton Manning and Tennessee in the Orange Bowl. In the final year of the Bowl Alliance system, Nebraska was voted the 1997 national champion by the *USA Today/ ESPN* Coaches Poll while Michigan was voted 1997 national champion by the Associated Press.

The 1998 season began a new era of Division I-A football with the Bowl Championship Series, which by virtue of a formula derived from various computer rankings, would determine a bowl matchup between the No. 1 and No. 2 teams in the country. The Fiesta Bowl would host the inaugural BCS title game on January 4.

NFL coaches, front-office personnel, and scouts along with representatives from all different kinds of organizations attended the Shrine Bowl practices. Gil Brandt, who had served on the Dallas Cowboys staff for a number of years and was one of the main decision makers in selecting the *Playboy* All-American Team, approached me on the field after a practice. I was selected as *Playboy*'s Coach of the Year heading into the 1998 season, and *Playboy* was going to rank Kansas State as the No. 1 team in college football heading into the fall. I politely declined *Playboy*'s Coach of the Year honor for obvious reasons, but Gil asked me to reconsider my decision and accept the honor. After giving it some thought, I finally granted my approval and I attended the All-America photo shoot in May with Martin Gramatica, who was on the *Playboy* All-American team.

Ten years after we won one game during the entire season, we were recognized by a national publication as the No. 1 team in the country in the preseason. However, I did not give the recognition much thought. If anything, I worried that preseason recognition could cause our players to lose their focus and give into distractions. It was so important for everyone in our program to direct their attention to the next step and all of those many things that we needed to accomplish each day in order to perform to our full potential.

In the midst of our work during the offseason, a substantial number of coaches phoned me asking about the magic pill to turn around a program. I received messages and either responded or requested that they call back at a specific time due to the demands of our daily schedule. They were not extensive conversations, but I wanted to help coaches. At the same time, I wanted to keep some information to myself and our staff. Coaches are very definitive and precise and they all want to learn all of the ways to accomplish every existing possibility. That nature comes from teaching football techniques as much as anything. When I coached quarterbacks at the University of Iowa, Chuck Long commented that I worked with him for an hour, and we hadn't yet reached the point where he would release the ball. Coaches value the necessity for precision to an immense degree. When it comes to coaching aspects other than technique, I believe the same attention to detail and thoroughness carries over. That is significant. I told the coaches that there was no clear-cut road map. Each program was a little bit different, yet there exists many similarities. However, for so many reasons our situation at Kansas State was not close to anybody in college football—period. Nobody in the country built a program in the same manner that we built our program. Nobody. I did not receive a single phone call from a coach whose program had less than 50 percent of allowed scholarship players. I did not receive a single phone call from a coach whose program had lost 500 games in its history. I told the coaches that there was no comparing the plight and history of our program, so consequently our road map appeared vastly different than the road map for other programs.

I also received quite a few phone calls from college programs and NFL teams regarding potential head coaching positions. One NFL team—and for the life of me I never understood why—called me and said, "The contract is in the mail." That was the first thing they told me. Sure enough, an NFL contract showed up in my mailbox. I put that contract in a box somewhere. There were quite a number of offers, and so many of them were pure offers that began with an athletic director saying, "We'd like you to take this position." There were some attractive offers, but I did not allow myself to be lured.

My concern regarding the national attention surrounding our program greatly heightened one late night in February, when Michael Bishop was arrested following a fight in Aggieville. Although he was exonerated of any involvement, it did little to sway newspapers and sports networks across the nation from harping on Michael's initial arrest. To my understanding, no news source went back and amended its original report after Michael was cleared of any wrongdoing. I believe Michael was treated unfairly, and that concerned me a great deal for Michael, for people of his color, for the players in our program, and for the players interested in our program. However, I found Michael guilty of using poor judgement in putting himself into a situation in which he was around trouble late at night. For that reason, I punished him with early-morning running inside the stadium every weekday for several weeks.

One evening I was invited to a special ceremony in St. Joseph, Missouri. Mayor Larry Stobbs graciously declared March 24 as Bill Snyder Day, and the St. Joseph City Council presented me with the key to the city in front of my family, many high school classmates, and people around the community. My only regret was that my mother was not alive to enjoy the moment with me. She would have loved to have seen her son recognized in her town, where she was born and raised and where she had spent all except for a few years of her life. Had she been at the ceremony, she would have given me a hug and she would have told me that she was proud and happy. Then she probably would have asked me how I might further improve myself or what I hoped to accomplish next.

I said during the news conference immediately following the Fiesta Bowl that "there's more to come," and that was due in part to the fact that we returned 18 starters and both of our kickers from a team that won 11 games for the first time in program history. But there was no time for complacency. Prior to one meeting, I collected a stack of old national college football preseason magazines and read to our players the magazines' lofty predictions for prominent programs over the years—predictions that did not come close to fruition in part because players on those highly-regarded teams perhaps skipped steps and took their performance for granted. I reiterated over and over again that we must put in the effort, organization, and take the correct steps in order to reach our goals, or else our own program could suffer a similar unfortunate fate in the fall.

Did the 1998 season feature the best collection of talent we ever had in our program? In most cases, probably so. Yet it was so important for us to maintain that blue-collar approach that had brought us to such a level. We went back and reiterated to our players the process by which they had reached their success, we reiterated those Wildcat 16 Goals for Success, and we outlined the sacrifices that we made over the years in order to achieve positive results. That was the foundation for our program's success. If our players divorced themselves of that, then there would be trouble on the horizon.

We added several players in our recruiting class who eventually became very successful in our program in their own right, including incoming freshman cornerback Terence Newman, junior college transfer wide receiver Quincy Morgan, and running back Frank Murphy, who was the NCJAA Player of the Year. Frank came to us from Garden City Community College after he recorded 1,370 rushing yards on 210 carries and 26 touchdowns during the 1997 season. Frank had been teammates with Jeff Kelly, Darnell McDonald, and Cephus Scott at Garden City. Although Frank started out as our sixth-string running back as we began spring drills, he was an explosive player and set our all-time program record with a 4.21 40. In fact, Frank probably ran even faster than that when he was chased by defenders.

However, a very unfortunate situation transpired in late March when we discovered that Frank purchased a red 1985 BMW from a used car dealership in Garden City for $3,199.50. Our athletic director, Max Urick, did due diligence and immediately investigated the matter. Max also phoned the NCAA, which opened its own investigation as well. We ordered Frank to return the car when we determined a violation of NCAA rules. We also suspended Frank for the first four games of the 1998 season. The NCAA Division I Committee on Infractions found that a group of several boosters provided money to help Frank purchase the car. The NCAA ruled that Kansas State was not at fault. We took action and barred any person involved in violation from attending Kansas State events for five years. They also reimbursed our university a percentage of the cost required for us to investigate the matter. As a condition of Frank's reinstatement, he had to give the money to a charity. We also took away Frank's scholarship for the 1998 fall semester. It was important to me that I didn't share his discipline with the outside world, but the players knew that we levied heavy consequences for inappropriate conduct. Frank was a good guy. I liked Frank, he was a likable individual, and he had no idea he was violating any rules. That's why the car deal really pained me.

A record crowd of 12,120 attended our spring game. Fans waited in long lines for autographs from our players after the scrimmage. I remained on the field for several hours. I signed an autograph for every fan who wanted one as I always did and I thanked each one of them for their gracious support of our program. Our spring game raised $19,000 in ticket revenue, and we donated that to the Hale Library on campus, which had recently completed a major expansion and renovation. We donated our spring game ticket revenue for campus and community programs in need. Every year, our players voted for team captains at the end of spring drills and those captains were recognized prior to the opening kickoff of our spring game. Our team captains were running back Eric Hickson, offensive lineman Ryan Young, linebackers Travis Ochs, Mark Simoneau, and Jeff Kelly and Michael Bishop. Eric was an awfully fine running back. He was passionate and possessed verbal leadership. Ryan always handled his business very well. He set great examples through the quality of his performance and character. He was that big presence, that quiet guy who politely wrapped his arm around a teammate after a practice and said, "We can do better."

Travis was a very good solid person who promoted strong values to his teammates. He was an extremely hard worker, and his team was important to him. I don't believe that we ever had a player in our program who worked harder and as diligently sun up to sun down than Mark. One of my favorite stories about Mark was in team meetings. He sat in the front row on the first seat in the section farthest to the speaker's left. We always had our players sit up straight with both feet on the floor and eyes on the speaker. Mark always did what we asked him to do. If I spoke for two hours, Mark's eyes never left my lips. I could ask the team a question three days later, and Mark would quote verbatim everything that I had said. He always wanted to be the very best that he could possibly be and he became one of the finest players ever in our program. Jeff was outgoing, a hard worker who had talent and size to play his position, and I enjoyed him. Jeff was a verbal leader but usually spoke with a smile on his face. Although he could be quite humorous off of the field, Jeff was a fiery competitor on the field and he was a handful for offenses to handle. Michael just set the effort example. He was very vocal and he wanted everybody to work as hard as they could. He wasn't afraid to call anybody out, which was normally a positive quality within his leadership style.

During the summer, I had much dialogue with our assistant coaches regarding their potential pursuit of other coaching opportunities. I was concerned when our coaches were either being swayed to move or considering a move based upon their belief that Kansas State had reached its full possible potential. I addressed it. When a trusted source provided information to me regarding someone on our staff, we had discussions. I always wanted our coaches to take steps up in their careers, but I did not want coaches to spend part of their time thinking about another job at a time when we needed to heavily invest in our preparation for the season because keeping one eye upon any potential job openings distracted from their preparation. In coaching, there was so much to think about: so many people for whom we were responsible, so many people we could impact, so many things that could impact our program, and there were also things of which we had no control. Kansas State was not an empire, but we knew how empires were destroyed, and they were destroyed from within.

Prior to the season, we finalized details on a stadium expansion construction project to begin the week after our final home game. I always said that I wanted our teams to play in front of sold-out crowds and I did not want a stadium expansion that would create any empty seats. The original plan proposal included the addition of an upper deck on the east grandstands that would feature 31 suites and club level seating and the construction of an upper deck above the south end zone, which would be identical to the east and west sides and thus fully enclose the south end of the stadium. They said that it would increase our stadium's total capacity to 60,000 seats, and I did not want to increase the stadium to 60,000. We had not been assured that we would sell all of the tickets, and I wanted us to play in a packed stadium and I believed that expanding the stadium to 50,000 seats would enable us to do that. The $12.8 million east side expansion gave us a 50,000 capacity and was made possible by virtue of several generous high-dollar donors, who stepped forward in the midst of our program's success. It was all a part of the process and the passion of special people.

We had more than 70 players work out together over the summer in Manhattan. Rod Cole, who had served as our head strength and conditioning coach for nearly a decade, was so invaluable to our program. He and his staff worked long hours and developed a strength and toughness among our players. A man of great faith, Rod served a prominent role for various reasons, including leading our bible study and chapel services. Rod took great pride in developing our players each year, which was why I was so very happy for Rod when he earned 1998 National Strength and Conditioning Coach of the Year from the Pro Football Strength and Conditioning Coaches Society.

When we first arrived, Division I-A football consisted of 107 teams. Kansas State ranked at the bottom. Now we were a consensus top five team heading into our 10th season. Although I could appreciate the change, I also knew that our players could potentially read too deeply into the rankings. Preseason rankings did not impact me at all. The chemistry, expectations, and motivation differed from the previous season. Everything was different, so we had to help our players move in the right direction. Obviously, our players thought about Nebraska a great deal. Every writer at Big 12 Football Media Day asked our players about the Nebraska game on November 14 in Manhattan. Players discussed anything and everything. We didn't want them to think about certain things, but I'm sure they still thought about them. So many of our players proved to be mature and handle the external pressures, but some players got caught up in all of our recognition. I always favored setting high self-expectations, but we couldn't meet our own expectations without identifying how to get there and applying the necessary effort to reach those steps. However, our players understood Nebraska had been our program's nemesis throughout our tenure.

Our players knew Nebraska was our final hurdle. And it was time.

We beat Indiana State (66–0), Northern Illinois (73–7), Texas (48–7), Louisiana-Monroe (62–7), and No. 14 Colorado (16–9) to open the season, outscoring our first five opponents 265–30. In the closing seconds of the second quarter against Northern Illinois, we maneuvered the ball and took a loss on a play in order to get into position, and Martin made a 65-yard field goal, the longest field goal in NCAA history without use of a kicking tee. I just marveled over his field goal, and his celebrations were second to none. It was very special. Our defensive players knew that we had an opportunity to achieve a special feat the following week against Texas. It was easy every day in practice to motivate our players to play well against Ricky Williams, and they knew that he had the potential to embarrass any defense. Of course, Ricky went on to become the Division I-A all-time leading rusher with 6,279 yards, and we believed that if we were as strong of a defensive football team as we thought, we had to perform well against Ricky. We held him to 43 rushing yards on 25 carries. Although he finished with 75 rushing touchdowns in his career, Ricky did not reach the end zone against us.

Ricky and Michael both entered the season as Heisman Trophy candidates, but I did not think about whether the tide had shifted, and Michael had elevated himself above Ricky as the best player in college football. It wasn't in my nature to stir up controversy or begin a national campaign for a particular player. I deeply wanted Michael to win the Heisman Trophy, but I wanted *him* to do it—not me. So many universities campaigned for youngsters and tried to sway voters. I did not want Michael to win because somebody swayed a voter. I wanted Michael to sway all of the voters through his performance, which would make his achievements that much more meaningful. The team was most significant and the team had always been the foundation of our program. Our program was not about casting one player above all else.

We entered the Texas game as a 25-point favorite and left with a 41-point victory against Texas and first-year head coach Mack Brown, who took over in Austin after a successful tenure at North Carolina. Mack is a good person, and I liked the way that he coached. Of course, Mack went on to have a highly-successful career at Texas, but he was always very friendly and wasn't full of himself like some coaches can become when they experience a great deal of success. Mack and I just appreciated each other's plight regarding our programs and began communicating along that line until it built into a close relationship. We went 9–4 against the University of Texas during our tenure, which was significant given the fact that it was Texas, and that the Longhorns always had talented teams. I coached against friends far more than I ever wanted to over my career. I hated playing against friends and former coaches. It sometimes affected me. Mack, being a good friend, fit into that category. Mack and I still talk frequently.

What most struck me about our final non-conference game against Northeast Louisiana was not only that Michael gained a school-record 475 yards in total offense or that he passed for 441 yards and a school record-tying four touchdowns and no interceptions, but also that so many players contributed to his success. Michael completed a 97-yard pass to Aaron Lockett, which was the longest pass play in school history, but Aaron also had to catch and run with the ball. Our offensive line had to block for Michael, who was so good about engaging with his teammates and showing his appreciation for their efforts. Many other players through the years did exactly the same thing.

A few days ahead of our hard-fought victory at No. 14 Colorado, Michael perhaps went over the top in voicing his appreciation for a teammate. Michael told reporters that Frank Murphy, who was coming off of his four-game suspension, was going to score a touchdown the very first time that he touched the football. But Michael genuinely believed it. Really, what Michael tried to convey was that Frank was talented. Still, the media ran away with it, and Michael's words became a distraction, and I decided to give Michael a few weeks off from speaking to the media.

Our team continued to progress during victories against Oklahoma State (52–20), Iowa State (52–7), at Kansas (54–6), and at Baylor (49–6), but I did not let it be known to our players that I felt we were improving. I knew our coaches and players grew tired of hearing me find little things that were not exactly perfect following lopsided victories, but it was just in my nature, and they had become accustomed to it. Against Kansas, we posted the most-lopsided win in Sunflower Showdown history and were 8–0 for the first time in program history. Against Baylor, David Allen tied an NCAA record with his fourth punt-return touchdown of the season. This came after David had become the only player in NCAA history to record a punt-return touchdown in three consecutive games. David was enamored with being a punt returner. He believed that he would score every time that he touched the ball. The 10 other players on the punt-return team eagerly helped David to become a highly prominent player in college football. I encouraged him to applaud his teammates and give them the credit they deserved publicly. Even when David did not score, the resulting great field position was a testament to our emphasis on special teams. I was told that Kansas State focused on special teams more than any other program in the country, but we were also fortunate to have so many players who demonstrated such pride in contributing to our success in that particular arena.

Defensively, I believe that people would have been hard-pressed to find a better linebacking group in the country than Jeff Kelly, Mark Simoneau, and Travis Ochs during the 1998 season. Each was a Butkus Award candidate, and each was highly productive despite missing at least one game apiece over the course of the season. Jeff was a first-team All-American and Big 12 Defensive Player of the Year while collecting 87 tackles, including 23 tackles for a loss with six sacks, three interceptions, three forced fumbles, and two fumble recoveries. Mark was a second-team All-American and had a team-high 95 tackles, including nine tackles for a loss with 1½ sacks, two interceptions, two forced fumbles, and two fumble recoveries. Travis was an honorable mention All-Big 12 selection and finished fifth on the team with 51 tackles, including nine tackles for a loss with four sacks.

Shortly after our victory over Baylor, I became a little bit frightened. Ohio State had been ranked No. 1 in the *USA Today*/ESPN coaches poll during the first 10 weeks of the season, and we were ranked No. 2 heading into the weekend. At about the same time we won our game at Baylor, Ohio State suffered a 28–24 loss to Michigan State. That meant that on Sunday, November 8, 1998, Kansas State was ranked No. 1 in the *USA Today*/ESPN coaches poll for the first time in the history of college football. I was a little bit frightened because we had always been in a position to climb the ladder, and all of the sudden, we were at the top of the ladder, and consequently our role changed. Now we had to defend the top rung of the ladder. I told our coaches and players to be proud that we reached such an achievement but to understand how we got there and realize that unless we continued to progress that we would not be there very long. Staying there would be more difficult than getting there.

Six days later, we played Nebraska.

Legendary Kansas State men's basketball coach Jack Hartman passed away the day before we played Baylor, and I spent Monday morning of Nebraska week with the Hartman family at the funeral home. That afternoon, I became upset with our offense and our coaches during practice and I was concerned about our offense. I left the football complex after midnight and stopped on my way home to help an elderly woman whose car had broken down. On Tuesday morning, I attended Jack's funeral service at Ahearn Field House and then I addressed the media in the Big 8 Room at our highest-attended weekly news conference ever. The room was completely packed. Instead of going into the office at 6:00 AM on Wednesday, I woke up to sunshine for the first time in a year. On Thursday, the people from ESPN *College GameDay* and ABC Sports arrived, and distractions continued to mount. There were entirely too many people in my office. I was worried about Sean, who wore many hats in our program, and had added responsibilities thrust upon him during the week. I was concerned that Sean had too much on his plate. I helped some of our players with ticket problems, and Michael was concerned about whether he could find 19 tickets for his family. On Friday, Meredith and Shannon arrived in town.

Our program was in uncharted territory, and our players recognized that, which made it paramount that we remained consistent in every aspect throughout the week. Our preparation for Nebraska began in the summer as did our preparation for every opponent. Our coaches dedicated a portion of the summer to watch the film of every team, and our coaches prepared for each opponent as if it were a game week. During the summer we gave our players information similar to a weekly scouting report about each opponent along with that film work. We continued to collect information on each opponent over the course of the season. So each game week, we drew upon our preliminary summer information and the information collected over the course of the season and finalized our gameplan for that particular opponent. We always wanted to know the schemes that players believed could most benefit our team against an opponent.

Eleventh-ranked Nebraska entered with an 8–2 record after a 28–21 loss against Texas A&M and a 20–16 loss against Texas. Frank Solich served as an assistant coach under Tom Osborne for 19 years and was in his first season as head coach. Although Nebraska advanced to the national championship four of the previous five years, it lost twice in its first 10 games for the first time since 1992. Nebraska also averaged its fewest total yards per game (401.4) in 25 years, and Eric Crouch entered his fourth career start at quarterback as a redshirt freshman. But we also were well aware that we were undefeated each of the previous five times that we faced Nebraska and fell short in each of those games: 45–28, 17–6, 49–25, 39–3, and 56–26. Our players turned their high confidence into a valuable asset. They were not only confident, but they were also so highly motivated because we were in the best position ever to defeat Nebraska after our program had fallen short over the past 30 years. We led the country in scoring offense, scoring defense, total defense, pass efficiency defense, turnover margin, net punting, punt returns, and kickoff returns. Our players made beating Nebraska a greater motivation than the fact that we were the No. 1 ranked team in the country.

It was a madhouse on gameday. I learned that thousands of our fans waited outside of the stadium gates for several hours in the cold in order to be the first ones inside for ESPN *College GameDay*. Chris Fowler, Kirk Herbstreit, and Lee Corso were so very complimentary of Kansas State fans, and our crowd of 12,000 set the attendance record for their pregame college football show. I also learned that there had been 450 media requests for the game, and that representatives from the Fiesta Bowl, Orange Bowl, Sugar Bowl, Rose Bowl, and Cotton Bowl would be in attendance for the regionally televised 2:30 PM kickoff on ABC with Keith Jackson and Bob Griese. I did not know the economic impact of our Powercat logo filling TV screens across the country, but I later learned that every hotel room was filled in Manhattan, Junction City, Abilene, Salina, and that only a few hotel rooms were available in Topeka. Virtually every seat in every Manhattan pub and restaurant was standing room only, and Aggieville was packed long before noon.

As nighttime fell upon Manhattan shortly after 6:00 PM, thousands of fans climbed down from their seats and spilled onto the sidelines along the football field in the final seconds of our game. They waited and waited. When Jeff picked up a fumble and ran 23 yards into the end zone for the final touchdown, the fans ran onto the field only to be ordered back to the sideline. Three seconds still remained on the clock. Then finally the game was officially over, and the fans ran onto the field again, setting off a celebration unlike any I could remember in my career.

No. 1 Kansas State 40, No. 11 Nebraska 30.

A picture hangs above the desk in my home office. It is a photograph taken from the top of Bramlage Coliseum, which captures the scoreboard behind the north end zone, the goal posts in their final seconds of existence, and a flood of Kansas State fans that filled virtually every inch of turf on the football field. We had a record crowd of 44,298 inside the stadium. Our fans tore down the goal posts, and we were fortunate that they didn't tear down half of the stadium. I may have had tears in my eyes. I may have. I thought about all of these people who showed up, hoping and probably praying that this day would come. I thought about all of the people who saved up their money all year and made our bowl games their annual vacation. I thought about the man who drove all the way from western Kansas to meet me in the parking lot as I left our football facility at midnight a few days after the 1993 Cotton Bowl. Many of these people had been K-Staters for life. Thinking about those things allowed me to understand the importance of the Nebraska game, which served as a reward to our fans' loyalty and for caring so deeply about our program for so many years.

We had trailed 17–14 at halftime for the first time all season and we were tied 24–24 entering the fourth quarter. We led 27–24 and then trailed 30–27. Over the course of the game, we suffered five turnovers. Michael lost three fumbles and threw an interception. Each time that he returned to the sideline, I told him to just put everything that he had into the very next play and forget the previous mistakes. Michael entered the game 44–1 as a starting quarterback at any level and demonstrated composure down the stretch of the game. He completed 19-of-33 passes for 306 yards and two touchdowns and had 25 carries for 140 yards and two touchdowns. Trailing by three points and facing third down at the Nebraska 11-yard line, Michael rolled to his right, and all of the Nebraska defenders followed him, and then Michael looked left and found Darnell all alone in the end zone for the go-ahead score with five minutes, 25 seconds remaining. Darnell was not the first choice on the play. He was the second choice. But Michael looked for Darnell. The first read was the wide receiver lined up to the left side of the field. If that wide receiver was not open, then he dragged defenders to open the middle of the field for the second read, who was the crosser. Darnell, the crosser, lined up to the right side of the field, ran 10 yards up field, then cut, and ran right to left.

If the first read wasn't open, there was a good chance that the crosser would be open on the play. Michael went straight to his guy. Darnell came up to me before the game and said, "Coach, let me have it. You can count on me."

Darnell was good in almost every game that he played, but he was particularly impressive with 12 catches for 183 yards and two touchdowns against Nebraska.

The game wasn't over. We believed Nebraska would respond—and they did. But our defensive players were confident and determined to end the game. Nebraska faced fourth and 8 at our own 32-yard line when Crouch went back to pass, and Travis swiped and made contact with Crouch's facemask, sending Crouch spiraling to the ground. Although everybody contended that Travis should have been penalized for a facemask, more than 20 years later, I still believe that it was a call that could have gone either way. Our victory required one last defensive stand in the final seconds, and Joe Bob Clements forced Crouch to fumble the ball, and Jeff picked it up and ran into the end zone, setting off the celebration. It took quite some time for all of our players to squeeze past our fans and get off of the field. We had more people in our locker room than I normally allowed after a game. Senator Pat Roberts and Governor Bill Graves accompanied Jon Wefald. I kept my message somewhat brief because I wanted our players to have a little bit of time to enjoy the win, but I told them that we still had more to accomplish and that we could not allow the victory to pull us down. We needed to continue to work hard. We were the first team in Big 12 history to beat every team in the league since the league's inception in 1996, but we were still not where we wanted to be. It was not over. There was always more to come.

The media chastised me in the newspapers the following day for not allowing Michael to speak to reporters after the game. I allowed Michael a few moments with *Sports Illustrated*, and that was it. Looking back, the media's criticism was appropriate. I was not confident in the questions that the media at-large would ask Michael and how he might answer some of those questions. I apologized to our media on Tuesday during our weekly news conference.

If I had one characteristic, it was that I wasn't easily distracted, but I was distracted much of the next week. The media continued to criticize us despite our undefeated record, and I let that get to me during the week. We suffered the proverbial hangover during the final week of the regular season and trailed Missouri 13–10 at halftime before we pulled out a 31–25 victory in Columbia, Missouri, to win the Big 12 North Division and complete the first undefeated regular season in Kansas State history. After Kansas State went 3–40 in the four seasons prior to our arrival, we were now 76–27–1 in 10 seasons. We were also one of six programs in college football to win at least nine games in each of the past six seasons. We were also headed to the 1998 Big 12 Championship Game with a 19-game winning streak.

On Sunday, November 22, the day after our victory at Missouri, the University of Oklahoma fired John Blake as its head coach. Oklahoma was going to hire its third head coach in five years. A reliable source told me that Bobby Stoops, who had spent the previous three seasons as defensive coordinator under Steve Spurrier at Florida, was a finalist to take the Oklahoma job. On Monday, I told our assistant coaches to remain invested in our preparation for Texas A&M in the Big 12 Championship Game—even if they might consider another job after the season. I told them that we could address any potential movement within our staff at the appropriate time. During my weekly radio show on Thursday, one concerned caller mentioned that a couple of offensive assistant coaches could leave after the season. I contacted those coaches, and they said that they had not been contacted about other jobs. On Monday, November 30, our athletic director Max Urick alerted me that he heard that two of our assistant coaches—assistant head coach and defensive coordinator Mike Stoops and defensive run game coordinator and linebackers coach Brent Venables—were going to join Bobby at the University of Oklahoma. When Bobby was officially introduced as Oklahoma head coach the very next day on Tuesday, December 1, I had no doubt that Mike and Brent would join him. Again, at the time, I was very concerned about our preparation for Texas A&M. All I could do was encourage Mike and Brent to finish our preparation and stay invested in our team, and then they could move on.

We learned Michael was a finalist for the Heisman Trophy along with Ricky Williams, UCLA quarterback Cade McNown, and Kentucky quarterback Tim Couch, and the winner would be announced on December 12. David Allen was named a consensus All-American, and Michael Bishop, Jeff Kelly, Martin Gramatica, Mark Simoneau, Darnell McDonald, and Jarrod Cooper also earned All-American honors. I was fortunate to be named Paul "Bear" Bryant National Coach of the Year, Associated Press National Coach of the Year, Walter Camp National Coach of the Year, and Bobby Dodd National Coach of the Year, along with Big 12 Coach of the Year. It was the sixth time in nine years that I had been fortunate to be recognized as a league coach of the year.

Every seat was filled at our annual football program awards ceremony at McCain Auditorium, where each year we recognized the efforts of our players, our coaches, our support staff, and those individuals who were so very important to our program. That year, I announced a new award, the Joan Friederich Award, which would be given annually to honor the individual, who, through unselfishness, leadership, and commitment to Kansas State football, best represented the team concept.

However, the inner turmoil continued. On Tuesday of game week, I learned that one of our players inadvertently revealed to the media some details regarding our gameplan for Texas A&M, which put our coaching staff between a rock and a hard place. During my weekly radio show, callers continued to ask me about the impending departure of assistant coaches. On Friday, I was still concerned about our preparation as we left for St. Louis, Missouri, prior to our game on Saturday. With everything going on, I could never remember feeling this badly.

I truly did not understand the Bowl Championship Series rankings and I told the media as much during the week of the Big 12 Championship Game. Although I understood that there was a computer component, I did not understand the entirety of the ranking system or its nuances. Although we were ranked No. 1 in the *USA Today*/ESPN coaches poll and No. 2 in the Associated Press poll, we were ranked No. 3 in the BCS rankings with a score of 6.31. Tennessee ranked No. 1 in the BCS with a score of 4.99, and UCLA ranked No. 2 with a score of 5.03. Of course, we wanted to be one of the top two teams in the BCS to have the opportunity to play in the national championship game, but I emphasized to our players that the only thing we could attempt to control was the outcome of our game against Texas A&M. The same day that we played Texas A&M, Tennessee played Mississippi State in the Southeastern Conference title game, and UCLA brought its nation-leading, 20-game winning streak into Miami. Bottom line: we would play in the national championship game at the Fiesta Bowl if we beat Texas A&M, and either Tennessee or UCLA lost their game.

Our players appeared confident and focused as we did our walk-through at the Trans World Dome the night before the Big 12 Championship Game. We became familiar with the field and the location of the play clocks and scoreboards. We ensured that our bench and sideline were properly prepared for our arrival on Saturday and we retraced our steps from our locker room to our sideline to avoid any confusion. We tracked down the field operation staff and checked and double checked to ensure that all of our organizational questions were answered sufficiently. On gameday, Sean went upstairs and asked the game announcers not to announce the final score of other games over the stadium's public-address system during our game. We emphasized to them the importance that our coaches and players not hear that game's final result while our team was in the middle of playing our own game.

Tenth-ranked Texas A&M entered with a 10–2 record under R.C. Slocum. The Aggies ranked No. 4 in total defense and No. 95 in total offense. They suffered a 23–14 loss to No. 2 Florida State in their season opener and then won 10 straight games before a 26–24 loss at Texas on November 27. Texas A&M's starting quarterback Randy McCown suffered a broken collarbone against the Longhorns, meaning that we had to do due diligence in preparing for Branndon Stewart, a very capable senior quarterback that we faced in our 23–20 win in College Station in 1996. We ranked No. 1 in scoring offense and No. 2 in total defense. At the same time, at least three of our coaches were going to leave the program. Our players recognized that some of their coaches were going to leave them and were emotional about it. We entered the 2:30 PM kickoff at the Trans World Dome in St. Louis as a 16-point favorite.

We played well and led Texas A&M 17–3 in the second quarter. Michael completed all eight of his passing attempts and threw two touchdowns. Our defense kept the Aggies out of the end zone. Then at around 4:30 PM and with a few minutes remaining in the second quarter, the public-address announcer declared that, "Miami has just beaten No. 2 UCLA 49-45." More than 20 years later, I still remember that announcement clear as day. The reason why we insisted not to announce the score was to avoid distraction, and now it seemingly created a big distraction for our team. I often question whether the announcement was an excuse. I know what we did on the field. We led Texas A&M 27–12 heading into the fourth quarter. I later learned that across the country some of our fanbase stood in lines at pay phones waiting to speak with travel agents to book trips to Tempe, Arizona, for the Fiesta Bowl. Standing on the sideline, I feared the announcement could prompt some overconfidence among our players, causing them to lose focus.

I believe that was the case, and we made some mistakes. We led 27–19 with two minutes, 29 seconds remaining in the fourth quarter when Michael, who accounted for 442 total yards, ran up the middle for a first down at the Texas A&M 35-yard line. However, officials ruled that the ball squirted out, and Texas A&M recovered the fumble. I believed that Michael had possession of the ball as he hit the ground, but I knew it was a call that could go either way, and that time the call went against us. Texas A&M drove down the field and tied the score 27–27 on a touchdown pass and a two-point conversion with 65 seconds left. We committed 13 penalties in the game, including one that prevented Martin from attempting a 69-yard field goal in the final seconds. Instead, Michael had to throw a Hail Mary. Michael could throw the football 93 yards, but this time, he kind of short-armed it 54 yards. Everett Burnett came down with the ball at the 2-yard line as time ran out in the fourth quarter.

The teams traded field goals during the first overtime. We opened the second overtime with a field goal and a 33–30 lead. Then our defense had Texas A&M at third and 17 at the 32-yard line. Branndon completed a slant pass to Sirr Parker. And Parker ran. And he ran. The play broke to the outside, and he was in a position to outrun all our guys. He didn't have to get very far before I realized that he could go the distance. Then he dived into the pylon. It was a heartbreaking play. We had led by 15 points with less than three minutes to go in regulation. It was unlike anything any of us could ever imagine. Then came the eerie silence among our players on the field and everybody on our sideline. Our players were despondent. They couldn't move. It felt like a death. That's what I told the TV reporter on the field as I headed to our locker room. It felt like a death in the family, and that's exactly how I felt about it. Obviously, there was no comparison, but I did not deny my feelings. I cried in the locker room. I had not cried since my mother died.

I tried to be positive with our players. They suffered. I was suffering, and they suffered every bit as much as I did, but I did not want to say anything that might prompt even more misery than what was already there. In the end, I wanted to make sure that our players did not do anything to compound the dramatically negative situation, which could have been very easy to do.

I could not sleep that night. Then Sunday arrived. The nightmare only became worse. The final BCS standings were: 1. Tennessee, 2. Florida State, 3. Kansas State, 4. Ohio State, 5. UCLA. Tennessee and Florida State were headed to the Fiesta Bowl for the national championship. Then the Orange Bowl and Sugar Bowl did not invite us. The Orange Bowl invited Florida, which finished No. 8 in the BCS standings. The Sugar Bowl invited No. 4 Ohio State, the Big Ten co-champion. That meant that the No. 3 team in the BCS standings would play in a non-BCS bowl game. Then the top Big 12 bowls—the Cotton Bowl and the Holiday Bowl—did not select us, which I anticipated. Despite the fact that Texas was not ranked in the BCS standings and we had beaten Texas 48–7 earlier in the season, the Cotton Bowl selected the Longhorns. We discovered that the Holiday Bowl had already sold 10,000 tickets to Nebraska fans. I had been told ahead of our league title game that those two bowls had already selected their Big 12 participants because they had been certain that Kansas State would be in a BCS bowl and they needed to move on. They certainly moved on. We were selected to play 8–4 Purdue in the Alamo Bowl.

It was so disappointing to me that we were ranked No. 1, No. 2, and No. 3 in the polls and fell off the face of the Earth following a double-overtime loss. We had been passed over by many bowl games. I believed that the BCS system failed us in its first year. We had spent so many years teaching our young people that there are systems in our culture and in our society and that the system worked if we did things the right way, but it was evident that we could not trust this system. Months later, the BCS committee instituted what they referred to as the "Kansas State Rule," which assured that the No. 3 team in the final BCS standings would be invited to a BCS bowl game. Unfortunately, it took our 1998 Kansas State team to alter the criteria. I was upset, and it had nothing to do with playing Purdue. I spoke with our team for a long time. I believed that it was important for us to play in a bowl game. I cancelled our news conference and instead released a statement: "We are honored to have the opportunity to play in what is becoming a high-profile bowl. The Builders Square Alamo Bowl is in a great city and is played in a great facility. We'll be matched against a very strong and upcoming title contender in Purdue from the Big Ten."

Our players were still pained and angered. The first stage was dramatic disappointment, and then that gradually worked its way into anger. After I met with our players, I addressed all of our support staff and shared their pain as well. We had to hurt together and heal together. I tried to manage all of the emotions and everything going on within the program. Later, Mo Latimore, our longtime outstanding defensive line coach, entered my office and saw me sitting in my chair. He simply asked, "Coach, are you okay?" That was so heartwarming to me. Over the course of 48 hours, I tried to handle the emotions of so many people, but I had all of my own emotions as well and I just appreciated so much that somebody thought to ask me how I was doing at the end of a dramatically disappointing weekend.

Then Brent Venables told me for sure that he was going to join Bobby at Oklahoma, and Mike did the same. We had a game to prepare for. I let Mike go to Oklahoma and asked Brent to stay and coach in the Alamo Bowl. The media grabbed ahold of our coaching situation, and it became a focus heading into the bowl game. At the same time, our coaching staff was invested in recruiting, and there was concern that the departing coaches could impact our recruiting class, so that became an issue. As the weeks of bowl preparation wore on, we had to make some immediate decisions because now I had to try and hire assistant coaches. It was mind-wracking, and our young people were tremendously disappointed, and I hung onto that disappointment as well. I did not set a good example. It was extremely painful.

Michael was selected as the winner of the Davey O'Brien Award, which was given annually to the top quarterback in college football. I was deeply proud of Michael and all that he meant to our program. He completed 55.6 percent of his passes for 2,844 yards with 23 touchdowns and four interceptions. He had 177 carries for 748 yards and 14 touchdowns. He ranked sixth in the country with a pass efficiency rating of 159.6 and he ranked 10th in the country in averaging 299.93 total yards per game. He was the first recipient in Davey O'Brien Award history to throw for at least 1,500 yards and rush for 500 yards in a season. A few days later, Michael flew to New York City and finished as runner-up to Ricky for the 1998 Heisman Trophy.

As the days progressed, players who were usually resilient still had a difficult time moving forward. That became apparent. Then Mark Mangino, our assistant head coach and running game coordinator, informed me that he was leaving to join Bob, Mike, and Brent at Oklahoma. Mark had been with us for eight years. It was tough. With all due respect to Purdue, as we headed to San Antonio for the Alamo Bowl, I thought to myself, *This is not going to work. We're just not going to be able to handle this. It is going to take longer for us to get over everything.* I worried that our emotions would impact our bowl game. And our emotions had a significant impact on our performance. We suffered a 37–34 loss after Drew Brees threw a touchdown pass with 30 seconds left in the game. We were ready to go home.

I would like to think that the 1998 Kansas State football team was the best team in college football history not to play for a national championship. I would like to think that was the case. I just do not know for sure because I do not know the plight that faced other highly regarded teams over the years. All I know is that our 1998 Kansas State team was undefeated, the No. 1 team in the country, and on the doorstep of playing for the national championship—only to lose in two overtimes. During the season, we scored more points than anybody in the country, we had one of the top three defenses in the country, and we had the best punt-return team in the country. We had the best quarterback in the country, arguably the best linebacking trio in the country, and had the best punt returner and kicker in the country. We had our first undefeated regular season in history. But we still could have been better. We could have beaten Texas A&M.

"We knew exactly what they were going to run. Sirr Parker was going to run out of the backfield and motion out to the right with no receivers on that side. Texas A&M only ran one play from that formation, and we knew that from practice. I had a lot of freedom and wanted to jump out and run underneath that route, but it was difficult out of a three-technique. I always think about that play, knowing that they were going to run that play and not even thinking that the play was going to end the game and end our chance of playing for the national championship. I thought they might get a couple of yards, but for that play to decide the game? I was in shock. I couldn't believe how it ended."

—Darren Howard, Kansas State defensive end, 1996–99

CHAPTER 14

CONTINUING TO CLIMB

"Coach Snyder leaves an incredible legacy of success in many parts of college football and the coaching fraternity. He developed a program that hadn't had much success before he arrived into a program that year in and year out was as strong and respected as any out there. He sustained that over a long period of time. And he didn't do it just once; he did it twice. He has a long track record of coaches working under him who went on to head coaching positions and had their own success. I'll forever be grateful to Coach Snyder for the big opportunity he gave me as a young assistant to coach the secondary and then serve in a leadership position as a coordinator. Those seven years for me at Kansas State were as good as any that I've been a part of, and I learned a great deal about developing a program from being there."

—Bob Stoops, former Oklahoma head coach

Our fans journeyed in great, great numbers, braved the snowfall and ice, and spent many hours slowly white-knuckling their way southbound along nearly impassable Interstate-35 between Kansas and Dallas-Fort Worth. Purple filled the downtown district, purple filled the frigid lawn during our pep rally at the Starplex Amphitheatre, and approximately 35,000 Kansas State fans filled Cotton Bowl Stadium to cheer on our players in a 35–21 win against No. 21 Tennessee in the 2001 Cotton Bowl. In the last four seasons, we had beaten No. 14 Syracuse of the Big East Conference in the Fiesta Bowl, we had beaten Washington of the Pac-12 Conference in the Holiday Bowl, and we defeated a very fine Southeastern Conference team in Tennessee, which was two years removed from a national championship.

Our mission was always to be the toughest team on the field. To prepare for the Dallas-Fort Worth weather forecast, we spent a majority of our bowl preparation practicing outdoors in Manhattan and we did not allow weather to alter our gameplan for the bowl game. A majority of our players ran into Cotton Bowl Stadium without long sleeves while Tennessee players wore sweatshirts under their jerseys and parkas on their sideline. We sent a message, and I believe maintained a psychological edge throughout the game. Our 507 yards of total offense was the most allowed by Tennessee all season, and our option-oriented 297 rushing yards came against the third-ranked rush defense in the country. In his final career game, Jonathan Beasley passed for 210 yards and two touchdowns and rushed for 98 yards and one score to earn Offensive MVP. Running back Josh Scobey set a school bowl record with 147 rushing yards and two touchdowns. Quincy Morgan had seven catches for 145 yards and two touchdowns in his final game. Our defense entered ranked sixth in the country and allowed Tennessee to complete just seven passes while forcing three interceptions in the game. Tennessee head coach Phil Fulmer commented on our players' physical and tough-minded nature following the game when he said, "I thought they did a great job of executing and basically taking us out behind the woodshed and spanking us." Phil was a very talented football coach, and Tennessee entered the bowl on a seven-game winning streak, but our youngsters were well-prepared, confident, and executed our gameplan in an amazing way.

Although our gradual improvement contributed to a bowl victory that meant a great deal to so many people, I was most pleased for our 25 seniors, who accumulated a 44–7 record over the course of their careers while contributing to Kansas State teams that finished with 11–1, 11–2, 11–1, and 11–3 season records. Consequently, Kansas State joined Nebraska and Florida State as the only three programs in college football history to win at least 11 wins in four consecutive seasons. Over a four-year stretch, Nebraska and Tom Osborne recorded three undefeated seasons in 1994, 1995, and 1997 and twice finished No. 1 in the Associated Press poll. Florida State and Bobby Bowden finished ranked in the top five four straight years, including a undefeated season and No. 1 final ranking in 1999. Kansas State achieved its most victories in history over a four-year span and finished ranked in the top 10 each of those years. Obviously, we felt strongly about our success, but at the same time, at least one loss accompanied each of our 11-win seasons, so we were always a step short, and that left the door open for continued improvement. We never had a zero in the loss column. We always carried the potential to take another step.

Obviously, we were on track during the 1998 season up until the very end.

It required some time for us to turn the page on such an emotional chapter during our time in Manhattan. I believed that it was important for us all to get away, so I invested $50,000 and paid for our coaches and their wives to join Sharon and me along with several boosters on an Alaskan cruise after the 1998 season. Sharon and I had previously taken that cruise, and it was excellent. Fred Merrill Sr., who was a good friend and a great friend of the university, flew Sharon and me and Jon and Ruth Ann Wefald on his private plane to the cruise site to meet the others. During our cruise, we took helicopter trips to the top of mountainous glaciers that were otherwise unreachable. The scenery and sites were very beautiful. However, ample work laid ahead when we returned to Manhattan.

We were still trying to reach the top of our glacier.

Aside from losing 12 starters and 26 seniors following the 1998 season, we had to replace nearly half of the assistant coaches on our coaching staff. Mike Stoops, Brent Venables, and Mark Mangino had joined Bobby Stoops at Oklahoma. Jon Fabris, who had served as our defensive ends coach for two seasons, moved near his parents and took the same position at South Carolina. In January, I hired Phil Bennett to be our defensive coordinator and defensive secondary coach. Phil was a 21-year coaching veteran and came to us from Oklahoma, where he served as an assistant coach for one season after previously serving as defensive coordinator at Iowa State, Purdue, LSU, Texas A&M, and TCU. Bob Fello joined our staff as defensive ends coach, carried 23 years of coaching experience, and knew Phil very well having served with him on the same coaching staff at TCU. Jim Gush became our linebackers coach after leading Garden City Community College to three straight NJCAA Top 10 finishes. We promoted Matt Miller to tight ends coach after he served as student assistant in 1996 and as graduate assistant over the previous two seasons.

Mo Latimore entered the fifth season of his second tenure as defensive line coach, Greg Peterson entered his sixth season overall, including his third season as passing game coordinator, Ron Hudson entered his fifth season as offensive coordinator and quarterbacks coach, Sean Snyder entered his fifth season overall and his third as assistant athletics director/football operations, Michael Smith entered his fifth season overall and his third season as running backs coach, and offensive line coach Paul Dunn entered his second season with our program.

It was a tedious hiring process over the offseason, but I had gone through the process of hiring assistant coaches over the years. Still, it was a challenge to hire so many new coaches in the same offseason. Fortunately, Phil's familiarity with Bob Fello and Jim Gush did not make their hires too complex. It was a three-for-one hire, so to speak. It was always our goal to hire more than a good coach. We wanted people who had the same value system to guide and direct our players, we wanted to ensure Manhattan was the right fit for them and their families, and we wanted to explore job opportunities within the community for those wives who had been previously employed.

Over the previous eight seasons, we spent $14 million on facility renovations, and our program's budget steadily increased from $3.3 million to $5.9 million. We had exceeded our listed stadium capacity of 42,000 in 26 home games. The $12.8 million eastside stadium expansion, which would increase our seating capacity to 50,000, crept along during the summer. I could see the upper-level eastside stadium seating—along with the Powercat logo—upon our indoor practice facility from my bedroom. So the stadium and Powercat were the first things that I saw each morning.

Our $1 million Academic Learning Center entered its fourth season. We had $125,000 in new weight equipment, including six tons of free weights. Over the last six years, we graduated 77 of 96 (80 percent) seniors, and nine others were on pace to graduate through our Second Wind Program. When it came to gradual improvement in all facets of the program, the university, and the community, the proof was in the pudding. We headed toward the 1999 season among the most successful programs in the country over the previous five seasons, following Nebraska (57–6), Florida State (53–7–1), Florida (55–8–1), Tennessee (53–9), and Ohio State (52–11). Our 50–11 record was tied for sixth best with Penn State. Although I was pleased with our success, it took its toll, which had been ongoing from previous years. On more than one occasion in 1999, I contemplated that perhaps it should be my last year as head coach. Over time, so many things manifested themselves within the program, including players, coaches, and finances. A number of issues weighed on me every single day, and I tried to find solutions and not allow any issues to go by the wayside. Success allowed us to push certain things aside, but issues had steadily mounted over the course of several years.

Then shortly after 6:00 AM on August 11, Phil Bennett called me and delivered horrendous news. A brief early-morning thunderstorm had swept through Manhattan, and lightning struck Nancy, his 41-year-old wife, during her morning jog near their home, which was about a mile from our football complex. Phil was at Mercy Health Center across the street from our football stadium. Doctors worked to resuscitate Nancy in the emergency room. Sharon and I met Nancy earlier that summer shortly before she and Phil joined us on the Alaskan cruise. She was an absolutely wonderful lady and a devoted mother to 11-year-old Sam and eight-year-old Maddie. They had recently moved from Fort Worth, Texas to join Phil in Manhattan. Over the course of the next two weeks, I visited the hospital three or four times a day. Phil did not sleep, and I tried to comfort him. I told Phil to focus on Nancy and his children. Nancy remained on life support for 13 days and never regained consciousness. She passed away four days later on August 28. A funeral service was arranged in Manhattan, and another one was arranged in Alvarado, Texas, for all of Nancy's family and friends. I told Phil not to return to the office, but I realized before too long that Phil really needed coaching and football to keep his mind occupied following this horrible tragedy. We also realized that Phil needed to be around his children. We tried to combine the two, so we set up desks in our office so Sam and Maddie could do their homework after school and be around their father. Almost instantly all of our coaches began stopping by and visiting Sam and Maddie at their desks inside the complex. The arrangement seemed to help Phil and the children through many difficult months.

Nancy's death reiterated to all of us within our program that there were far more important things in life than football, beginning with family. We all felt very strongly for Phil and the children. Our defensive players wanted to perform at their very best level for Phil during his emotional first season with our program. Phil was a demanding coach similar to Bobby and Mike Stoops and Jim Leavitt before him. Phil was also a coach who genuinely cared about his players. He worked tirelessly to develop them and left no stone unturned in devising the optimal gameplan for each opponent. He hardly slept. We put together one of our best seasons defensively in our program's history. We finished ranked No. 2 in total defense, No. 3 in scoring defense, led the country in turnover margin, and recorded the best pass efficiency defense rating by a NCAA team since 1978.

We entered the 1999 season ranked No. 17 in the Associated Press poll. We finished the season ranked sixth, which was the highest season-ending ranking in our program's history. Although we battled through adversity, our players exemplified that never-give-up mentality. Six of our departed seniors from the 1998 team—Martin Gramatica, Jeff Kelly, Ryan Young, Michael Bishop, Justin Swift, and Darnell McDonald—were selected in the NFL draft. However, we felt strongly about many returning players such as Jonathan Beasley, Mark Simoneau, Darren Howard, Damion McIntosh, Lamar Chapman, Frank Murphy, Monty Beisel, Mario Fatafehi, Jarrod Cooper, Jerametrius Butler, Quincy Morgan, Jon McGraw, Ben Leber, Josh Scobey, and Aaron Lockett. Every year was different, so it became interesting to see how well the team gradually improved and grew together over the course of the next several months. Our players became a tight-knit group, did not point fingers, and went about handling their business in a workmanlike manner regardless of circumstance. After we beat Temple (40–0) and UTEP (40–7), we played from behind three times over the course of our next five games. We trailed 28–7 at halftime in our Big 12 Conference opener at Iowa State and came back to win 35–28 for the greatest comeback victory in a road game in our program's history. The following week, we trailed No. 15 Texas 14–6 and came back to win 35–17 in Austin, Texas. We won handily at Kansas (50–9) despite suffering a school-record 18 penalties in the game. Although we only led Utah State 19–0 heading into the fourth quarter, Joe Hall rushed for 143 of his career-high 195 yards in the second half and scored two touchdowns down the stretch of a 40–0 victory. We trailed Oklahoma State 21–0 and came back for a 44-21 win in Stillwater, Oklahoma, and that margin tied for our greatest comeback road win in history. After wins against Baylor (48–7) and Colorado (20–14), our 9–0 start to the season ended with a 41–15 loss at No. 7 Nebraska.

The Nebraska game on November 13, 1999 held special meaning, though it was not apparent on the scoreboard. It marked the 100th consecutive conference road game attended by Robert Lipson, a streak that began when Kansas State visited Kansas in Lawrence in the early 1970s. Robert stood on the sideline during our game at Nebraska. Robert was always around our program. He was a 49-year-old native of Liberty, New York, who originally came to Kansas State in the 1970s upon transferring from a junior college. Robert came to Kansas State when Vince Gibson was head coach, and Robert remained dedicated to the program through the coaching stints of Ellis Rainsberger, Jim Dickey, and Stan Parrish before we came to Manhattan. Over the years, Robert had grown into one of the most recognizable super fans in college football. Everybody at Kansas State knew Robert.

At about 5'6", Robert didn't stand out because of his size, but he was always recognizable to fans because of the large purple foam No. 1 finger and transistor radio that he carried so he could listen to the radio commentary. Robert always frequented tailgate parties outside of our stadium and was quick to discuss football with fellow Kansas State fans. Robert was a regular and a part of the Kansas State family. Fans always politely offered Robert a plate of their tailgate cuisine. But Robert did not stick around a single tailgate for too long. Robert had many more tailgate get-togethers to visit. Robert lived in a mobile home in Manhattan and worked as a salesman for Brown & Bigelow, which sold office supplies. I was never too sure that Robert's old Nissan truck would get him across town, much less make it to Boulder, Colorado, or Ames, Iowa, but he made it to every single game. Every time we stepped off of the bus outside of our hotel in a visiting city, Robert was already there holding the front door and waiting to greet us. From the time we arrived in Manhattan, we wanted to make Robert a part of our program. We brought him to practice, served him meals at our training table, and provided some financial assistance. We wanted him to feel good about having

Kansas State in his life. I told our players, "Who else do you know who would invest their livelihood and life in you?"

That struck a chord with our players, and they appreciated Robert a great deal. They always stopped to talk with Robert and shake hands after practice. I had Robert speak to our team on a number of occasions. He particularly had such a great passion for the Sunflower Showdown. Over the years, Robert's passion allowed him to reach other college football attendance milestones, but his 100th consecutive conference road game in Lincoln was special to him, and we wanted to recognize his achievement.

Six of our seven home games were above the 50,000 capacity, and a crowd of 51,235 supported our players during a 66–0 win against Missouri on Senior Day. It was the highest-attended Senior Day in Kansas State history. Lopsided games made me uncomfortable, and it quickly became evident that we were playing extremely well while Missouri struggled. We scored a school-record 35 points in the first quarter and scored our final points of the game with 16 minutes left to go in the most lopsided win in the 86-game series history. It also marked the most points our program had ever scored against a Big 8 or Big 12 opponent. I was pleased that the nature of the game afforded all of our seniors, regardless of their spot on the depth chart, a chance to see the field in front of their families. Our 22 consecutive home victories allowed us to conclude the 1990s with a 57–5–1 home record, and our .913 winning percentage ranked as fifth best in college football during the decade behind only Florida State (.974), Nebraska (.954), Florida (.934), and Texas A&M (.925). We finished the 1990s with 52 consecutive home wins against non-ranked opponents while our overall streak of 22 consecutive home wins was the second longest active home winning streak in the country. Nebraska had won 29 consecutive home games. For all of our success, ESPN recognized me as a College Football Coach of the Decade finalist, an honor that truly belonged to so many who had contributed to our program over the years.

Shortly after the conclusion of the regular season, David Allen, Jamie Rheem, Lamar Chapman, and Darren Howard, our all-time sack leader, were named All-Americans along with Mark Simoneau. It had been a particularly emotional Senior Day for Mark, a native of Smith Center, Kansas, who like so many of our in-state players, simply wanted a chance to play for the school that they had grown up following all of their lives. Mark was a quiet guy, but he was the most intense player to come through our program, and there was not a harder worker. I cannot think of anybody who had played any better at linebacker. Mark finished his senior season as a 1999 consensus All-American and as runner-up to the Butkus Award, which recognized the top linebacker in the country. A two-time All-American, Mark had a school-record 251 unassisted tackles, and his 400 total tackles ranked third all-time at Kansas State. Upon completion of his college career, Mark was drafted in the third round of the NFL draft and began an 11-year career with the Atlanta Falcons, Philadelphia Eagles, New Orleans Saints, and Kansas City Chiefs. Mark was voted into the College Football Hall of Fame in 2012.

I was concerned as the season went along that our players might believe that regardless of how we began the first half, we would automatically come back in the fourth quarter to win a game. We outscored our opponents 208–41 in the second half during the season, including 108–0 in the third quarter. Our season required one more comeback win in our 24–20 victory against Washington in the Holiday Bowl. Jonathan led a 20-play, 92-yard touchdown drive that consumed 10 minutes and resulted in the game-winning score with 5:58 left on the clock at Qualcomm Stadium.

The game, its finish, and the momentum produced from our positive results carried into the 2000 season. We returned 14 starters, including eight starters on offense. We had a fifth-year senior quarterback in Jonathan Beasley, a 1,000-yard receiver in Quincy Morgan, a record-setting pass-catcher in Aaron Lockett, All-Big 12 center Randall Cummins, and David Allen, a record-setting punt returner, who would also serve as our starting running back. We returned defensive ends Monty Beisel and Chris Johnson; defensive tackle Mario Fatefehi; linebacker Ben Leber; cornerbacks Jerametrius Butler and Dyshod Carter; and safety Jarrod Cooper, who each either earned All-American or All-Big 12 honors. We also returned Jamie Rheem, an All-American kicker who was runner-up for the 1999 Lou Groza Award.

However, nearly one year following the tragic death of Nancy Bennett, our program suffered another devastating loss when defensive lineman Anthony Bates died on July 31, 2000 from an undiagnosed heart condition called hypertrophic cardiomyopathy (HCM). Anthony was a 20 year old from Tempe, Arizona, and redshirted the 1999 season after transferring from Phoenix City Junior College. He was the only child of Sharon Bates, who launched the Anthony Bates Foundation in 2002. She has dedicated her life to speaking to groups and implementing heart screening efforts across the country to promote early detection for hidden heart ailments in young people. HCM is a genetic heart disease that attacks the heart muscle typically during the teenage years. The only way to detect HCM is through an echocardiogram of the heart. A person can live a normal life with early detection. Our program immediately embraced Sharon Bates' cause, and consequently we provided heart screenings for our players prior to each football season. There is no doubt in my mind that the tremendous efforts of Sharon Bates have saved many lives and have prevented parents from having to experience the loss of a child.

The earliest start to a season in our program's history came when we opened the 2000 season against the University of Iowa in the Eddie Robinson Classic at Kansas City's Arrowhead Stadium on August 26. We adjusted our summer practices accordingly. Although we seldom played non-conference games away from Manhattan and typically did not play a regular-season game against an opponent from a major conference, I had a great deal of respect for Eddie Robinson, and we graciously accepted the invitation to participate in a game that honored a great man in college football. Kirk Ferentz entered his second season as Iowa head coach. I had hired Kirk as our offensive line coach at Iowa in 1981 and I was pleased to see Iowa hire him as head coach, following Hayden Fry's retirement. Although I was pleased with our coaches and players during our 27–7 victory, I was not pleased that David had his NCAA-record eighth punt-return touchdown nullified by a questionable penalty and I was deeply concerned when David later suffered a sprained ankle that would cost him several games of his senior season.

We tried to make every week the same, get better, and stay as motivated as possible as we achieved a high degree of success in games against Louisiana Tech (54–10), Ball State (76–0), North Texas (55–10), Colorado (44–21), and Kansas (52–13). We outscored our first six opponents 308–61 and were ranked No. 2 in the country as we prepared to face No. 8 Oklahoma in Manhattan. The week started poorly. Sharon hit a deer with her car. Mack Brown and I spoke regularly, and Mack had incurred some struggles, so we addressed them on the phone. On Tuesday, the media began their parade of material, regarding the fact that we would face Bobby and Mike Stoops, Brent, and Mark on the opposite sideline for the first time. It was uncomfortable. So was the fact that Bobby, Mike, Brent, and Mark knew everything about our team and knew all of our audibles. We tried to make appropriate changes to many of our sideline signals during the week, but we were concerned that too many alterations over the course of the week could confuse our players. Toward the end of the week, rumors surfaced that we had sent spies to Norman, Oklahoma, which I resented, and I never did find out the rumor's origin.

So many aspects of the week could have presented distractions, including the fact that ESPN *College GameDay* had made Manhattan the epicenter of college football on Saturday. A total of 15,758 fans filled the lower east side of the stadium, which was an unofficial *GameDay* record. As kickoff neared, a sense of anxiety became evident among some of our players in our locker room. We ran onto the field in front of a stadium-record crowd of 53,011 and ran back into the locker room at halftime facing a 31–14 deficit. I believed that the fact that half of the Oklahoma coaching staff had previously been with our program affected the game to a certain degree, but we simply did not play well. We allowed Josh Heupel to throw for 374 yards and two touchdowns and we missed 17 tackles during the game. We scored 17 unanswered points during a 10-minute stretch in the second half and trailed 38–31 after Terence Newman returned a blocked punt 16 yards for a touchdown, but that was the last time we reached the end zone. Our 25-game home winning streak ended with a 41–31 loss.

Criticism steadily mounted over the next few weeks. Some of the media contended that Kansas State could not win a big game. After a win against Texas Tech (28–23), a loss at Texas A&M (26–10), and a win against Iowa State (56–10), our players appeared confident and had ample motivation as we prepared to face No. 4 Nebraska on Senior Night in Manhattan for the lead in the Big 12 North Division with one game remaining in the regular season. The bulletin board in our locker room became crowded during the week. Inside our players' lockers hung a red-colored sign that read: "41–15." That was the score of our loss to the Huskers in 1999.

Weeks later, someone made me a large photo taken from the south end zone of all of the Kansas State fans celebrating on the snowy field, as several fans tore down the goal post. The scoreboard located above our north end zone read: "29–28." Really, that's about all that needed to be said. Thousands of our fans from the stadium-record crowd of 53,811 remained inside the stadium long after the completion of the game, and I was so very happy for them to be able to celebrate another thrilling finish as we won back-to-back home games against Nebraska for the first time in our program's history. The snow began to fall with three minutes remaining in the game just before Quincy hauled in the game-winning 12-yard touchdown, which ranked among the shorter receptions in his career but arrived at the pinnacle moment in the game. Quincy's seven-catch, 199-yard, two-touchdown performance against Nebraska was the second best pass-catching performance in our program's history. Quincy finished his career as the first player in our program's history to record 1,000 receiving yards in back-to-back seasons. Our defense was phenomenal and held Eric Crouch to 2-of-13 passing for 39 yards and one interception and 42 rushing yards on 17 carries and one touchdown, which marked the lowest production by Crouch in his Heisman-Trophy-winning career. Crouch tried to salvage North Division title hopes with a fourth-down pass across the middle to Matt Davidson, but Dyshod Carter, our talented cornerback, knocked the ball away on the final defensive play of his career inside our stadium. Several of our players slid across the snowy field in celebration. Jarrod Cooper even made a snow angel.

As Jonathan made his way to the locker room after helping to lead our team to defeat its highest-ranked opponent in history, Coach Bennett, who engineered a tremendous defensive effort, high-fived a young girl wearing a purple No. 91 Anthony Bates jersey near the outside door to our complex. Then Phil stood quietly near the locker room door, staring up in the sky, as snowflakes covered his eyebrows, and tears filled his eyes. He thought about Nancy.

Although we clinched a berth in the Big 12 Championship Game for a second time in three years after a 28–24 win at Missouri, we likely suffered somewhat of an emotional hangover, which had concerned me throughout the week. We trailed 21–10 in the second quarter before we were able to seize control of the game. We allowed our players to return to their homes for Thanksgiving on Wednesday through Sunday. Our coaches and players needed the break after enduring the longest regular season in our program's history. Our coaches and players were in a unique position heading to face No. 1 Oklahoma in the Big 12 Championship Game at Arrowhead Stadium. We had never faced an opponent twice in a season. We practiced well leading up to the game and tried to make some adjustments based off of our first meeting against Oklahoma and we believed that it would be a good game. We took a 10–3 lead in the second quarter and were tied 10–10 at halftime. Oklahoma began first-half drives at our 27, 38, 17, and 28-yard line, but our defense held them to 10 points. We tied the score 17–17 when Aaron recorded a 58-yard punt-return touchdown in the third quarter. We played pretty decent against Heupel in holding the Heisman Trophy runner-up to just 202 passing yards and forcing him into three interceptions. But we allowed a couple key drives and found ourselves trailing 27–17 in the fourth quarter. Jonathan completed an 18-yard touchdown pass to Quincy with six seconds remaining in the game, but we fell short in a 27–24 loss.

Less than 12 hours later, we were invited to play in the Cotton Bowl. All we ever asked for from bowls with ties to the Big 12 Conference was to be placed where we deserved to go, and I was pleased and grateful for the Cotton Bowl honoring that. We had more than 15,000 Kansas State alumni in Texas, and half of those were in the Dallas-Fort Worth area. We were treated wonderfully during our stay prior to the 1997 Cotton Bowl and we felt strongly about the opportunity to play No. 21 Tennessee, a tradition-rich SEC program.

I was so very pleased for all of our coaches, players, and support staff for so many reasons after our 35–21 victory gave us an 11–3 final record. We finished ranked eighth, 10th, sixth, and ninth in the final Associated Press poll each of those four seasons and were ranked in the AP poll for 100 consecutive weeks. We joined Nebraska, Florida, and Florida State as the only programs to win at least nine games every season since 1993. We joined Nebraska, Michigan, Florida State, Tennessee, Florida, and Virginia Tech as the only teams to appear in a bowl game for an eighth straight season. Since the inception of the Big 12, our 34–6 conference record matched Nebraska as best in the league, and only Florida State (39–1 in the ACC) and Florida (35–5 in the SEC) had better conference records over that span.

We led the country with 549 total points over the course of the season and we ranked fourth in total defense and sixth in pass efficiency defense. We set 22 program records, including our 98.2 rushing yards allowed per game, which eclipsed our previous record of 98.3 rushing yards allowed per game during the 1998 season. Jamie Rheem was named runner-up for the Lou Groza Award for a second straight season. Aaron Lockett led the country in averaging 22.8 yards per punt return and became the third player in NCAA history to record a punt-return touchdown in consecutive games. Quincy Morgan, Mario Fatafehi, Randall Cummins, Aaron, and Jamie earned All-American honors. Derrick Yates was named Big 12 Defensive Newcomer of the Year, and Terry Pierce was named Big 12 Defensive Freshman of the Year.

Although Jonathan did not earn All-American recognition, he finished his career 21–4 as a starter and did everything well and was so consistent. He had the task of following Michael Bishop, and then a couple of years later Ell Roberson became a very prominent quarterback for our program. It was a tough duty. Jonathan spent a portion of his career injured and could not raise his arm above his head when we played at Nebraska in 1999. Jonathan quietly went about his work amid criticism by some fans. He finished fourth in program history with 4,642 passing yards and third with 33 touchdown passes. Jonathan was truly different from the others. Michael and Ell were explosive on the field, and both had explosive personalities whereas Jonathan, a mild-mannered young man, wasn't afraid to speak out in a leadership role and he wasn't going to jump up and down either. Some quarterbacks can have an unbelievable play and then have a tremendously negative play. Jonathan did not make a bunch of mistakes. Some would argue Jonathan wasn't a particularly explosive passer, but his 20.1 yards per completion finished second in the country behind Michael Vick. He had success because he made proper decisions on the field.

After Jonathan's graduation, we knew that we needed to find a quarterback who could step in and compete, potentially start, and at worst provide the depth necessary for the quarterback position. Already we had Ell, who arrived at Kansas State from Baytown, Texas, as one of the more highly-regarded dual-threat passers in the country in the Class of 1999. Ell gained limited experience his redshirt freshman season in 2000 and demonstrated that he would develop into a fine player once he learned the entirety of our offensive system. In an effort to fortify the quarterback situation, we signed Marc Dunn, who was the 2000 National Junior College Athletic Association Offensive Player of the Year after passing for 4,351 yards with 42 touchdowns and 17 interceptions at Ricks (Idaho) College.

Although we headed into the 2001 season with our coaching staff intact, we had to replace 12 starters along with a kicker and punter. We also had what was rated as the fourth-toughest schedule in Division I-A as eight of our 11 opponents on our 2001 schedule participated in a bowl game the previous season. And we opened the season at Southern California, as head coach Pete Carroll entered his first season after previously serving as head coach of the New England Patriots from 1997 to 1999. USC needed to fill a spot on its schedule, identified that we were available, and both schools agreed to a home-and-home series in 2001 and 2002. The series allowed us to play a game and gain some exposure on the West Coast and allowed our fans an opportunity to watch a non-conference game against a prominent opponent in Manhattan. As I knew long before I briefly served on John McKay's staff in 1965, the Coliseum was a storied structure, and I wanted our players to experience playing inside of it. My return to the stadium certainly brought back many memories. USC served as great motivation to our players through summer practice. Over the previous five seasons, we had been fortunate enough to beat Syracuse, Washington, Iowa, and Tennessee. We believed a regular-season trip to the West Coast would be something unique with the possibility of a major victory.

As the mystique of the Coliseum faded for our players, we continued to seek an identity. Ell completed just 7-of-16 passes for 26 yards and one interception in his first career start but also rushed for 119 yards on 21 carries. Our only touchdown was a product of center Nick Leckey recovering a fumble in the end zone. Our defense kept Carson Palmer out of the end zone, and we left with a 10–6 victory while holding USC to its fewest points in a home game since 1994. Our victory was the only time in a nine-year span that a non-conference opponent defeated USC in the Coliseum. As our players graciously recognized inside the locker room following the game, we had achieved our 100th victory since arriving in Manhattan, which was a special milestone, particularly to do so inside a legendary stadium where I held strong memories from my early coaching career. We had reached 100 victories faster than all except for 13 head coaches in the history of college football.

Three days later, I arrived at my office shortly after 6:00 AM, turned on my TV, and began my paperwork ahead of our usual coaching staff meeting at 8:00 AM. We never made it to our meeting. At 7:46 AM, a Boeing 767 aircraft flew into the North Tower of the World Trade Center in New York City. Seventeen minutes later, a second Boeing 767 aircraft flew into the South Tower of the World Trade Center. Thirty-four minutes later, a Boeing 757 aircraft flew into the side of the Pentagon. Twenty-six minutes later, a Boeing 757 aircraft crashed into a field in Pennsylvania. As our coaches and staff entered the complex, everybody just stood in silence in front of the large TV in our Big 8 Room and stared at the horrific images upon the screen, following the deadliest terrorist attack in human history. We were all emotionally empty. We were gutted.

Shortly after, Del Miller came into my office and told me that his son was diagnosed with cancer and given a 40 percent survival rate over the next five years. It was an absolutely horrible day. On Thursday, the Big 12 Conference announced the cancellation of all sporting events that weekend. Ultimately, we rescheduled our home game against Louisiana Tech for November 17. Following the official cancellation of our football game, I sent all of our coaches and players home. We attempted to practice on Saturday, but nobody was into it, and I assuredly wasn't into it. The September 11 tragedy hung in our minds. Throughout the year, so many things happened. I couldn't sleep—I never can sleep well—but I did not sleep as the death toll climbed. The American flag inside our stadium remained at half-staff for our game against New Mexico State on September 22. I delivered a message of togetherness and resiliency to our fans on the Jumbotron. Our players and coaches bowed their heads and held hands while standing along our sideline.

Our team and our crowd of 49,229 observed several moments of silence. A trumpeter from the Kansas State Marching Band broke formation, walked to the middle of the field, and played "Taps." It was the most emotional pregame we had ever experienced.

We scored on our first six possessions in a 64–0 victory. It was the 400th victory in the history of our program.

One week later, we began our worst losing streak since 1992.

The absurdity began shortly after 2:00 AM on September 29 when we awoke to some members of the University of Oklahoma Marching Band playing "Boomer Sooner" inside our hotel lobby. We had to meet for breakfast in four hours. No. 11 Kansas State at No. 3 Oklahoma was billed as the game of the week in college football for a second straight season, as evidenced by the ESPN *College GameDay* trucks parked near Memorial Stadium. Although we had an 11:00 AM kickoff, it felt like their crowd of 75,862 had not slept all night. They were among the angriest opposing fans that we had been around, which was likely a product of the coaching history between Kansas State and Oklahoma. In the first half, we allowed a touchdown off of a lost fumble, gave up a 63-yard touchdown pass, gave up an extended drive that resulted in a rushing touchdown, and fell for a fake punt that resulted in a score. We trailed 35–14 with seven minutes, 15 seconds remaining in the third quarter.

However, I was pleased with the fight demonstrated by our players. Although we entered the game leading the country with 308.5 rushing yards, Ell broke out with 257 passing yards and one touchdown to go along with 23 carries for 115 yards and two touchdowns. Ell brought us back and rushed for two touchdowns and completed a 57-yard touchdown pass to Ricky Lloyd with two minutes left in the game to make it a three-point game. We committed 17 penalties, including a questionable pass interference call that allowed Oklahoma to continue its drive and make a 33-yard field goal that proved to be the difference in the game. Ell's Hail Mary pass fell incomplete on the final play of the game, and we left with a 38–37 loss. Ell needed that game. He was a young man with a great deal of confidence, but he just hadn't yet played to his eventual capabilities. That performance gave him some confidence that he was getting closer to reaching his potential.

My concern heightened during our 16–6 loss against Colorado, which snapped our 58-game home winning streak against unranked opponents and gave us back-to-back losses for the first time since 1994. It became evident that our demise stemmed from our tremendous investment in preparation for the Oklahoma game. It was clear that we were unable to shake the memory of Oklahoma, and our players were exposed to a lot of positive comments about their performance, which may have caused some overconfidence the rest of the way. Ell scored our only touchdown with less than seven minutes remaining in the game, but we missed the extra point. We also missed a field goal, dropped a snap on a punt, and allowed a long punt return that resulted in a Colorado field goal. None of our players had ever lost two straight games. None of our players had been in this situation. I had been there before. I knew it would be important how our coaches and players responded. Afterward, we knew that Ell had suffered a severe ankle sprain and likely would miss multiple weeks.

I had not felt so badly after a game since the loss against Texas A&M in 1998. It seemed that everything was taking its toll. After the Colorado game, I thought very seriously about retirement for the first time.

Our losses piled up. In our 38–19 loss at Texas Tech, Mike Leach did a nice job with his Air Raid offense, as Kliff Kingsbury threw for 409 yards and four touchdowns against us during a difficult game in Lubbock, Texas. In his first-career start, Marc Dunn completed 16-of-40 passes for 197 yards with one touchdown and two interceptions. The Red Raiders captured their first Big 12 victory, and we dropped out of the Associated Press poll for the first time in 106 weeks. Then we suffered a 31–24 loss against Texas A&M, which gave us a four-game losing streak for the first time since 1992. It also marked the first time we had lost two straight home games since 1989.

Our program was full of issues. We hardly had enough healthy offensive linemen to conduct a practice and we continued to make costly mistakes on the field. We had lost our focus and were not adhering to the principle of striving to become better every day, which our program had been built upon. Some of our players displayed an attitude and behavior I had not been accustomed to seeing. Some players lost sight of the team element and had become selfish. In one single day, four different parents came into my office concerned that their sons were not playing enough. Some of our players felt like the season was lost, and that was evident in their lethargic practices. I also learned that some players were violating curfew. A few players ran into some difficulty in Aggieville. Unfortunately, issues of loyalty and trust within some of our coaching staff even began to surface, which pained me a great deal. I had learned that at least a few coaches were active in discussions with other programs during the season regarding potential jobs, which was atypical for a coach in any program to do during the season. We were on edge. We were unravelling in virtually every aspect. It was hard to see how we could dig ourselves out of the hole we had dug for ourselves. My doctor also informed me that I had to undergo hernia surgery after the season.

For the first time in my career, I sat down with Sharon and seriously discussed the possibility of retirement. My anxiety really wore me down prior to the KU game. I was certain that this would be my last year as head coach. I'm still not altogether certain how we pulled ourselves out of our tailspin, but after starting the season with a 2–4 record, we won four of our final five games. Our only loss at Nebraska (31–21) was a product of our own mistakes after we squandered a 14–13 lead at halftime. We outscored our other four opponents 146–19 with wins against Kansas (40–6), at Iowa State (42–3), Louisiana Tech (40–7), and Missouri (24–3). During one stretch, our defense went 156 minutes, 16 seconds without allowing a touchdown. Ell and Marc both played at quarterback in those games. Our run through the second half of the season qualified us for our ninth straight bowl game. The media attributed our late-season turnaround to a strong head coaching performance, to which I replied, "If it was a good coaching job, we wouldn't have lost four in a row."

I needed some time to reflect on those specific things that I might have considered differently and that could have altered the extent of our tailspin. But ultimately I was pleased with how our players responded. In the history of Kansas State football, only the 1911 team lost four consecutive games and still finished the regular season with a winning record. As we headed down the stretch of the season, it became evident that I would have to make some really hard decisions regarding a couple of our assistant coaches, which I had never had to do before at any level in my coaching career. From the outset,

I always believed that if our coaches did not perform well, it was on my shoulders. I felt it was my responsibility to teach them what I expected and how to achieve it. Although I never fired a single coach, I hinted to a couple of our coaches near the end of the season that perhaps they would be happier elsewhere. The 1998 and 2001 seasons were by far the most challenging seasons as it pertained to our coaching staff.

Phil was hired as SMU head coach on December 5 and left the program to begin his new duties. I immediately appointed Bob Fello and Jim Gush to replace him as we prepared to face No. 18 Syracuse in the Insight.com Bowl. Phil hired Bob as assistant head coach and Jim as defensive coordinator, and they joined him after the bowl game.

Syracuse had finished the regular season at 9–3 and had two top 25 wins. We were 6–5 and were a five-point favorite as we reached the December 30 kickoff at the open-roof Bank One Ballpark in Phoenix. It was a miserable game. We tried to find a spark with Ell, but we didn't move the ball. So we tried Marc Dunn but still didn't move the ball. Our two quarterbacks had both seen action in eight of our 11 games during the regular season and we ranked 111th in passing yardage. We switched quarterbacks six times in a 26–3 loss. I equated our quarterback situation to playing slot machines. We tried one for a while, and when nothing happened, we moved to the next one. We combined to complete 14-of-40 passes for 221 yards with two interceptions. We entered the game fifth nationally in averaging 257 rushing yards per game but recorded a season-low 33 yards on 34 carries in the game. Our only points came from Joe Rheem's 29-yard field goal in the first quarter before Syracuse scored the final 19 points in the game. I felt badly for our fans who traveled and had remained supportive during a difficult season. I was pleased for Ben Leber, Aaron Lockett, and Andy Eby, three seniors who earned All-American status during their final season. I was pleased for Josh Scobey, who finished his senior season with multiple school records, including 1,263 rushing yards, 114.8 rushing yards per game, and 31 career touchdowns.

However, we fell woefully short of our standard as coaches and players, and I was interested in finding out whether we still possessed that competitive spirit to put a disappointing season behind us and not allow it to happen again. After our bowl game, we defined that as a a horrible season and we needed to take the proper steps in order to avoid repeating it again. I wasn't necessarily a fan of looking back, but I knew there would be some relevance to doing so this time as we moved forward. Ultimately, I knew that I didn't want things to end this way. I knew that if I left that I would not be leaving the program in good enough shape to move forward.

I decided that I would return as head coach.

"Coach Snyder wasn't worried about being different or being hip. For him, it was always about what worked, and if it worked, we wouldn't change it, and if it didn't work, he'd find out how to make it work. He did that for so many years, then retired, then came back, and did that again, and he was very successful. Nothing changed. The schedules were the same, the meals were the same, and the pregame music was the same."

—David Allen, Kansas State running back, 1997–2000

CHAPTER 15

BUILDING A CHAMPION STEP BY STEP

"Bill Snyder has done the single greatest job of turning a football program around. No one has ever taken a program like this one and made it where it is now and stayed there. That is the difference."

—Lee Corso, ESPN

I believed the summer of 2002 was as important of a summer as we ever had up to that point in time. Coming off of our 6–6 record in 2001, I did not know the character of this squad. Our players and many of our coaches had not been in the position of having to respond to this degree of adversity that accompanied a season with many losses. Although a total of 18 points separated our team from nine wins, we did not take the necessary steps to get over the hump in several games, which fell back on me, our coaching staff, and the times that a player might have committed a critical mistake that contributed to our lack of success.

We set a school record with 257.7 rushing yards per game in 2001 and ranked third in total defense in allowing just 264.4 yards per game and yet we finished the 2001 season with our first non-winning season since 1992. We returned Ell Roberson and Marc Dunn, our two quarterbacks who each had completed less than half of their passes, and each had four touchdowns and eight interceptions during the 2001 season. We had sophomore running back Darren Sproles, who proved himself to be capable during his first season on the field. We had optimism for junior college transfer wide receiver

James Terry and Division I-A transfer fullback Travis Wilson. We returned All-American candidate Terry Pierce, Josh Buhl, and Bryan Hickman at linebacker. Defensive Newcomer of the Year Tank Reese returned at defensive tackle, and cornerback Terence Newman entered his senior year as a Jim Thorpe semifinalist.

Six days after the end of our 2001 season, I hired Bobby Elliott as our defensive coordinator and defensive secondary coach. Six days after I hired Bobby, I hired Bret Bielema as our co-defensive coordinator and linebackers coach. That meant over the course of eight seasons, we had six different individuals responsible for our defense—Bobby Stoops, Jim Leavitt, Mike Stoops, Phil Bennett, Bobby Elliott, and Bret Bielema. Bobby Elliott was a 25-year coaching veteran who had served the previous two seasons as associate head coach at Iowa State after having served as a defensive secondary coach for 12 years at the University of Iowa. He was the Iowa defensive coordinator in 1996–98 under Hayden Fry. Bobby had been diagnosed with a rare blood disease called polycythemia vera in the early 1990s, which had caused him some difficulty over the years and which ultimately caused his death at 64 years of age in 2017. He had served solely as the associate head coach his final two years at Iowa due to his disease, but he was a proficient defensive coach who wanted to resume his duties, and I wanted to give Bobby that chance. Bret was a 32-year-old former player at Iowa who was on the same team as Sean in 1988. Bret had spent 10 years at Iowa, first as a student assistant, then as a graduate assistant, and then as linebackers coach for six years. I felt strongly about Bret's capacity as a coach. He was a strong and demanding coach, which was what we needed following the previous season, and an adamant recruiter. He made sense for our coaching staff.

Despite our team struggles during the 2001 season, I felt strongly about our defense, which allowed just three touchdowns over the final five games of the regular season. Our defense returned several prominent players and featured a few new faces from a unit that ranked third in total defense (262.4 yards), seventh in scoring defense (16.3 points), 11th in rushing defense (a school-record 96.5 yards per game), and sixth in passing efficiency defense (95.9 rating). Despite the changeover in defensive coordinators, we were the only team in Division I-A to rank top five in total defense for five straight seasons. We finished ranked No. 4 in total defense in 1997, No. 3 in 1998, No. 2 in 1999, No. 4 in 2000, and No. 3 in 2001. Over the course of our practices and scrimmages, our defense was where we wanted it to be. We practiced well, played well, and had created some depth at virtually every position.

I probably approached several aspects of fall practice a little bit differently than some other coaches across the country, but I remained consistent in my beliefs. One such belief was my fall practice attire. To me, when it was hot, that was a great time to work out because of the various conditioning benefits for players. And it got hot in Manhattan. It wasn't unusual for our teams to play a couple of our non-conference home games in 100-degree temperatures each year. As July and August rolled around, without fail, many players complained about wearing all of their football gear and practicing in the heat. Whereas most coaches across the country were probably dressed in shorts and short-sleeved shirts, I always wanted our players to know that I was also making similar sacrifices and suffering through the heat with them. So I wore several layers of clothing, including a winter parka, on our practice field. Although my doctors were never fans of my clothing decision, it was important to me that our players recognized that I was sweating through a hot practice as well.

Six video cameras filmed each practice from fixed locations surrounding the field. This enabled me and the position coaches to watch every single movement by each of our players over the course of a practice. While viewing all of the practice film, I tape recorded notes about position groups and individual players to distribute to our coaches for discussion at our staff meetings. I always felt it was advantageous to carry a tape recorder at every practice. On the practice field, fundamentals and techniques were so detailed, and it could require 30 sentences to describe whether a player got into his stance perfectly. It would be impossible to adequately list all of the information I needed by taking written notes. I could speak much faster than I could write, so I used my voice recorder. That way I could speak and watch drills at the same time. After each practice, I transcribed my voice recorder and supplied our coaches with those notes to also discuss during our staff meetings.

One day during the second week of August, we always conducted what was called "Wildcat Day." The day began at 7:30 AM and concluded at 9:30 PM, and it entailed three practices and three meetings dedicated toward implementing all of our offense, defense, and special teams. No one changed clothes, and we ate lunch on the field. After our third practice, our players changed out of their uniforms, and we ate dinner, followed by our final meeting.

We also had another event called "Cat Day." Our strength and conditioning coaches utilized a numerical system to evaluate the performance of each player over the course of our out-of-season conditioning period. The two highest-graded players were selected as captains for Cat Day, and each captain alternated picks while drafting their teams. The two teams competed in eight to 10 events related to the out-of-season program to earn points. Every player had to compete in at least three events. The winning team enjoyed a steak dinner, and the losing team had extra running and hot dogs.

Our fall practice featured two scrimmages—one three-and-a-half hours in length and one two-and-a-half hours in length. We charted every throw in practice, every throw during seven-on-seven drills. Our two major scrimmages contributed 75 percent to our decision at quarterback. We determined that Marc demonstrated better accuracy and made the fewest number of mistakes and consequently would be our starting quarterback over Ell for the first game of the season. I emphasized to both quarterbacks that there was no guarantee that the depth chart would remain the same during the season.

Although Josh Scobey finished his senior season by rushing for the most yards (1,263) by any Kansas State player ever in a single season in 2001, the starting position at running back was not in question heading into 2002. In his first-career start, Darren Sproles rushed for 135 yards on 19 carries and scored a touchdown during our season-opening 48–3 victory against Western Kentucky. At 5'6" and 180 pounds, Darren demonstrated a capacity to run very well with the football while averaging 7.5 yards per carry on 28 rushing attempts and scoring one touchdown while playing in six games as a true freshman. However, the media pointed out Darren's size and questioned whether he might be durable enough to be a starting running back in a major conference. What people perhaps did not realize at the time was that Darren had spent his entire life proving people wrong.

As a youngster growing up in Olathe, Kansas, Darren was told that he was too small and then played entire games without being tackled during organized football games because he was too elusive and too good. The first time that Darren ever touched the football in an organized game, he ran 80 yards for a touchdown. He was nine. Darren continued to prove himself at Olathe North High School. Tyson Schwieger, one of our talented former wide receivers, served as an assistant coach at Olathe North, and notified us from the start to keep an eye on Darren. Matt Miller, who recruited the Kansas City area, called Darren and stayed in contact with him, his parents, and Olathe North head coach Gene Wier. I met Darren and his family for the first time after our 2000 spring game. His parents, Larry and Annette, were very fine people, and it was evident that they had instilled a strong value system into Darren. Although Darren had rushed for more than 2,034 yards and 22 touchdowns his junior season, we learned that his only other real correspondence had come from the University of Iowa and the University of Kansas because Darren preferred to attend a college close to home.

After our 2000 spring game, Darren and his family spent some time with Coach Miller in his office, and Darren indicated to him that he would like to play football at Kansas State. Matt accompanied Darren and his parents down the hall to my office, and we had a nice visit. I told Darren that our program was built upon young people who had been doubted and then developed into quality students and very fine players while adhering to our 16 Wildcat Goals for Success over the course of their four or five years in our program.

Darren made his presence known on our team almost immediately upon arrival prior to the 2001 season. He began his first day of practice as a running back on the scout-team offense and consistently beat our first-team defensive players. He had defensive players cramping up. At least once a practice, Darren ran the distance to the end zone. Darren competed with returning junior Danny Morris and Garden City Community College junior transfer Daniel Davis prior to the 2002 season. During one practice, we gave

Darren almost 20 straight handoffs against our starting defense. He proved his durability. So we were not surprised by Darren's success—even though everybody else seemed surprised by it.

In the 2002 season opener, Darren had 15 carries in the first half against Western Kentucky. I told Darren on the sideline, "They said you couldn't survive 20 carries, and you're going to get that in the first half." We ran Darren on virtually every play during the first couple of drives. I wanted to establish in everybody's minds what we already knew: Darren was a durable running back and could carry it as many times as required in a game. Darren's size was significant because defensive players could not see Darren behind our offensive linemen, and when he reached the second level of the defense, it was too late.

We outscored our first three non-conference opponents Western Kentucky (48–3), Louisiana Monroe (68–0), and Eastern Illinois (63–13) by a combined total of 179–16. Eastern Illinois had a very fine quarterback named Tony Romo, who we believed was one of the more under-appreciated quarterbacks in the country, but our defense held him to 23-of-35 passing for 169 yards with one touchdown and three interceptions. I was pleased to see Tony and Terence go on and help lead the Dallas Cowboys together for a number of years. One week after we faced Tony, who went on to be inducted into the College Football Hall of Fame in 2021, our defense had to prepare to face the University of Southern California quarterback Carson Palmer, who also enjoyed a very fine NFL career and joined Tony in the 2021 College Hall of Fame class.

It was during the 2002 season that the Kansas State football program unveiled the inaugural class for the Kansas State Football Ring of Honor. The names of Lynn Dickey, Steve Grogan, Jaime Mendez, Sean Snyder, Gary Spani, and Veryl Switzer were permanently affixed to the east side upper deck during a halftime ceremony. We set high standards to be eligible for this honor. The player had to be a Kansas State graduate who had been out of school for at least five years, possess quality character, and be a first-team All-American. In 2008, we honored David Allen, Martin Gramatica, Terence, and Mark Simoneau. In 2015, we honored Michael Bishop, Jordy Nelson, Clarence Scott, and Darren.

USC was ranked No. 11 when it visited us for our final non-conference game. We entered the game ranked No. 25, which made this one of the few top 25 matchups that weekend. It was our first home game in 14 years against a ranked non-conference opponent. We were mindful of our narrow 10–6 victory the previous season in the Coliseum and how we forced Palmer to fumble the football on the final possession to secure the win. We led the country with 59.7 points and 414.7 total yards per game, but USC had the country's top-ranked defense and was a very talented offensive team with track speed in wide receivers Kareem Kelly and Mike Williams and running back Sultan McCullough. Terence was eager for the matchup against Kelly, who was one of the premier pass catchers in the country. He had reportedly told the Los Angeles media that Terence wasn't good enough to play in the Pac-10. It turned out that Terence had the last word in the game. Although Terence held Kelly to just three catches for 42 yards, he also contributed to a momentum-changing play on special teams just before halftime that elicited perhaps the loudest cheers in our stadium's history. USC scored a touchdown to cut our lead to 10–6, but defensive end Henry Bryant blocked the extra-point attempt, and Terence picked up the football and zig-zagged 90 yards behind some excellent blocking for a two-point blocked kick return with 32 seconds remaining until halftime. Our crowd of 49,276 was tremendous, and afterward Pete Carroll said it was the most intimidating crowd USC had played in front of during his tenure.

After a scoreless first quarter, we decided to substitute Ell for Marc to try and gain an offensive spark, and Ell stepped up in a significant way. He completed 10-of-15 passes for 134 yards and one touchdown and rushed for 70 yards on 23 carries and one touchdown. It became clear that Ell had good chemistry engineering our zone-read with Darren, who had 20 carries for 78 yards and one touchdown. Afterward, Coach Carroll said, "How many times did he make something happen when we had him?"

Palmer was a four-year starter and finished the 2002 season with 3,942 passing yards, 33 touchdowns, and 10 interceptions while winning the Heisman Trophy, but our defense recorded nine pass breakups and two sacks and held him to the worst performance of his senior season. He completed just 18-of-47 passes for 186 yards and one touchdown and was penalized for intentional grounding. We led 27–6 early in the fourth quarter before USC responded with two touchdowns, but our defense held USC on fourth and 15 at our 38-yard line with 25 seconds remaining in the game to preserve a 27–20 victory.

We jumped from No. 25 to No. 13 in the rankings but showed that we could not handle our success the following weekend at Colorado, as we allowed 483 total yards and three touchdowns of 70-plus yards in a 35–31 loss in Boulder, Colorado. However, our players prepared themselves during the course of the next week to play as well as they could, and consequently we beat Oklahoma State 44–9 while recording 499 total yards and forcing four interceptions. The win did not come without some major concern regarding our kicking game. We had three extra-point attempts blocked, which we knew could come back to bite us down the road. Our inclination proved accurate. A matchup between No. 17 Kansas State and No. 8 Texas was decided in heartbreaking fashion at home. Trailing 17–14, we drove to the Texas 18-yard line in the final seconds, but they blocked our 36-yard field-goal attempt just before time expired, and we lost the game. We could have thrown the fade or the slant instead of attempting the field goal, so that was an unsuccessful decision on my part.

We followed the process, we became better, and we became more productive after the two losses at Colorado and against No. 8 Texas by a total of seven points. It was important that we were able to bounce back after the previous season. The important thing was not the dips in the road but how we responded, and we got into a better rhythm and maintained the proper approach as coaches and players to prepare ourselves. Consequently, we went on one of the most prominent five-game stretches by any Big 12 Conference team. We beat Baylor (44–10), Kansas (64–0), No. 21 Iowa State (58–7), Nebraska (49–13), and Missouri (38–0), outscoring five very fine teams a combined 253–30. Over the stretch, we captured the most lopsided victory in Sunflower Showdown history, we claimed our most lopsided victory against a nationally-ranked team (Iowa State) in program history, we recorded our largest victory ever against Nebraska while handing them their worst loss in a game since 1968, and our shutout win at Missouri marked the first time the Tigers hadn't scored a single point in 34 games. Collectively, we won our final five Big 12 games by an average score of 50–6. I believed at the time that it was the best that we had played during our time in the program.

At the same time, it became evident that Ell and Darren had become the top ground-gaining tandem in our program's history. Ell completed 52 percent of his passes for 1,580 yards and seven touchdowns and four interceptions but was arguably even more dangerous carrying the football. Ell finished third in single-season history in total offense (2,612 yards), sixth in single-season history in rushing yards (1,032), fourth in rushing touchdowns (16), and was the third fastest to reach 1,000 rushing yards (196 carries). Against Nebraska, he set single-play, single-game, and single-season records for rushing yards by a Kansas State quarterback, as he recorded 228 rushing yards on 29 carries with three touchdowns. His 91-yard rush was the longest by a Kansas State player since 1948. He probably played as well as any quarterback in the country over the final four games while averaging 178.3 yards passing and 105.8 yards rushing per contest.

Darren, who virtually everybody outside of our program counted out prior to the season, set eight program records during his first year as a starter. He set a single-season record with 1,465 rushing yards, he was the fastest to reach 1,000 rushing yards in a season (159 carries), he finished second in program history with 17 rushing touchdowns, and he finished his sophomore season with nine consecutive 100-yard rushing performances and averaged 124.9 rushing yards per game against Big 12 opponents. Darren's 6.18 yards per carry ranked fourth in the country behind Heisman Trophy candidates Larry Johnson of Penn State (7.70), Quentin Griffin of Oklahoma (6.56), and Willis McGahee of Miami (6.22). On one play against USC, Darren took a pitch five yards behind the line of scrimmage, and three defenders surrounded him within a five-yard radius. Darren spun 360 degrees, the defenders ran into each other, and Darren was off. That highlight opened ESPN's *SportsCenter* later that night. Over the course of the season, Darren also had nine receptions, four kickoff returns, and 15 punt returns for a program-record 1,800 all-purpose yards. Ell and Darren each rushed for 100 yards against Nebraska and Colorado. They shared our Offensive MVP award after the season.

Our Defensive MVP was an easy choice. Shortly after the conclusion of the regular season, Terence earned consensus All-American honors and stood on stage at the ESPN College Football Awards Show at Disney World to accept the Jim Thorpe Award given annually to the top defensive back in the country. I was so very proud of all of Terence's accomplishments and the way that he always carried himself during his time in our program and during his Pro Bowl career in the NFL. Terence was a native of Salina, Kansas, and was one of those lightly recruited in-state players who we believed possessed all of those qualities we sought in a player for our program. Terence came from a single-parent household, which I could obviously appreciate. Wanda Newman, his mother, was a wonderful lady and did a tremendous job raising him. Terence wasn't particularly big physically in high school. He was 5'4" and 110 pounds as a freshman at Salina Central High School. But Terence always had track speed and he developed into a 5'11", 185-pound cornerback with a 4.26 40 speed and a 41½-inch vertical leap during his time in our program. His 10.22 mark in the 100-meter dash set a Kansas State record and qualified him for the 2001 Big 12 Outdoor Championship, where he earned the title of "Big 12 Fastest Man" by winning the event with a time of 10.29—a title that he successfully defended in 2002. Terence's body exuded confidence, and he played as a cornerback, return specialist, and wide receiver. He hoped opposing quarterbacks threw the ball in his direction.

Terence's 54 tackles his senior season were more than Charles Woodson (44) posted his final year at Michigan in 1997 and Deion Sanders (37) had as a senior at Florida State in 1988. Terence's five interceptions and 16 pass breakups were also more than either player recorded during their final seasons. Terence's average of 28.5 yards on kickoff returns and 14.9 yards on punt returns also exceeded the marks by Tim Brown (19.8 and 11.7) during his 1987 Heisman Trophy season. Although Terence was named Big 12 Defensive Player of the Year, he was also capable of quality performance on offense as a receiver and on special teams as a return man. During our early-season game against Louisiana Monroe, Terence caught a 51-yard over-the-shoulder touchdown pass on the first play that he was inserted on offense for his first-career reception. He scored another touchdown on a 40-yard punt return. One week later against Eastern Illinois, he returned a kickoff 95 yards for a touchdown. Against Missouri, he had a 71-yard punt-return touchdown. Terence always worked and was so invested in getting everything that he could out of every play, every practice, and every game.

Terence was rewarded for his hard work when he was selected by the Cowboys with the fifth selection overall in the 2003 NFL Draft. Terence was the highest drafted Kansas State player since Veryl Switzer was selected by the Green Bay Packers with the fourth pick in the 1954 NFL Draft. Kansas State had 27 players taken in the NFL draft between 1999 and 2003, which were the most by a Big 12 program over that span. Our players who went on to join NFL teams over the years all had one thing in common: they were motivated to improve every single day. As of 2003, we had 37 players on NFL preseason rosters, which ranked only behind Nebraska (42) and Colorado (40) among Big 12 programs.

Our defensive players worked to match Terence's intensity and effort on the field. Our linebackers—juniors Terry Pierce, Josh Buhl, and Bryan Hickman—provided ideal playmaking ability and leadership. Josh led our team in tackles (135) with Terry (110) and Bryan (79) behind him. They were all from around the same area in Texas and knew each other extremely well. Terry was a physical match for the position and ran well. Josh was the smaller of the three, but he was quicker and a hard hitter. Bryan was a mixture of both players and a good tackler. Our efforts enabled us to have another successful season defensively. We finished No. 1 in the country in scoring defense (11.8), No. 2 in total defense (249.0), No. 2 in rushing defense (69.5), and No. 3 in passing efficiency defense (91.7). We were the only program in the country to rank in the top five in total defense in each of the previous six seasons.

Our offense ranked among the best during our time in the program. We were No. 2 in the country in scoring offense (44.9), No. 15 in total offense (423.4), No. 5 in rushing offense (264.5), and No. 7 in passing efficiency (147.0). We set the program record with 3,433 rushing yards and led the country with 53 rushing touchdowns. Our average victory margin (33.0) led the country despite playing against eight opponents that played in a bowl game. Our 79 touchdowns tied Boise State for most in the country.

Terence, Darren, and Nick Leckey each earned All-American honors, and I was grateful to be named Big 12 Conference Coach of the Year, which was our fifth conference coach of the year honor since we began our program. We finished second in the Big 12 North Division by virtue of our loss to Colorado, which consequently took our fate out of our hands. Once again, we addressed the necessity to continue making daily improvement as we sought to finish our season in a special way. Jon Wefald, Tim Weiser, and I flew to Miami on December 3 and made a pitch to the Orange Bowl committee prior to the announcement of the Bowl Championship Series game pairings. Kansas State had a 10–2 record and had climbed two spots to No. 8 in the BCS standings ahead of Texas and one spot behind Oklahoma. Seven points separated us from an undefeated regular season. We joined Florida State and Nebraska as the only programs in college football history to win 11 games in four consecutive seasons and we had three of the largest crowds in college football history ever to cross the state line to attend a bowl game. We assured the Orange Bowl that we could bring 25,000 to the January 2 game at Pro Player Stadium. On selection day, we were not invited and instead headed to the Holiday Bowl to face Arizona State, which was 8–5 and had lost three of its last four games.

Our players read the newspapers, so they knew we were 18-point favorites. As much as I addressed that the predictions meant nothing and cautioned them not to take a team for granted, we went out, laid an egg and trailed 20–7 in the second quarter. Terence was superb with a career-high 10 tackles, a career-high three catches for 47 yards, and two rushes for 26 yards. We fought back to tie the score 27–27 with six minutes, 41 seconds remaining in the game. On our final drive, Ell used his legs and his arm to take us to the Arizona State 10-yard line. Then when we absolutely needed Ell to make a play, he fired a pass across the middle to wide receiver Derrick Evans with 1:15 left, which lifted us to a 34–27 victory. When it was all on the line, Ell was very special. He was excellent mentally, threw the ball well, ran the ball well, and was there when we needed him.

The season was rewarding for our fans. Our players were only here for four or five years, but our fans were always with us year in and year out through the good and the not-so-good. We experienced a dip in 2001 and we responded in a very positive way in 2002, and our fans responded famously as always. We had generated momentum, but we wanted to prove during the 2003 season that our fans' confidence was warranted. I believe that we did that.

The 2003 season was perhaps my hardest season, and I really contemplated retirement. Although I was in the second year of a contract that ran through 2007, I truly believed this would be it. I was 63 years old and in my 15th season as Kansas State head coach and I was uncertain that I could do the position justice any longer. We had experienced difficult seasons for a variety of different reasons, but 2003 was perhaps the hardest season for me. We had ongoing internal issues such as coaches speaking about jobs with other schools. We had discipline issues, behavioral issues, and eligibility issues involving our players. We had six different players arrested during the summer and thus dismissed several players from our program. The issues preyed on me daily. Distractions mushroomed, required our attention, and consumed time that was designated for football. Each little incident took away from things that we wanted to be doing to help the program. The issues did not go away immediately over the course of the season. The issues required great effort to process. Despite our success, when we stepped away from the field, all of the issues flooded back. Our success did not remedy our issues. We were a better football team than we deserved to be.

In July, I played nine holes of golf with Jim Colbert and I went away to St. Louis with Sharon and Whitney for a weekend horseshow. Otherwise, I was in the office. Our coaching staff took two weeks of vacation each summer, but it was always a complex time preparing for any season and it required diligent work and my full attention. Del Miller returned to our staff as offensive coordinator. We entered the season ranked No. 6 in the Associated Press poll and No. 5 in the ESPN/*USA Today* coaches poll, which represented our highest ranking ever heading into a season. We entered the season with Ell and Darren garnering preseason attention as possible Heisman Trophy candidates. We returned 12 starters. We also opened our season against Cal in the Black Coaches Association Classic at Arrowhead Stadium on August 23, which meant we began practice earlier than usual. Our first practice was July 29, and I felt it was important for me to be at practice to help our coaches and players prepare for the season, so I did not attend the Big 12 Football Media Day event in Kansas City on July 31 and instead remained in Manhattan for practice and appeared in front of reporters via a video teleconference. Although it wasn't the popular decision at the time, I felt it was a necessary one given the early start to our season.

As with almost every summer, our season schedule remained a topic among the media. After we played two Division I-AA teams in Western Kentucky and Eastern Illinois in 2002, we had a Division I-A opponent back out of our game in 2003 and consequently had to find another non-conference opponent. When we were unable to find a Division I-A team to visit Manhattan, we settled on a Division I-AA squad, so we would play both Massachusetts and McNeese State in the fall. Later, we accepted the offer to play California in the BCA Classic because it was an opportunity for our fans to watch two major-conference programs inside an NFL stadium that was a two-hour drive from Manhattan and because of the strength of schedule element that was prominent in the eyes of the BCS committee. However, I contended all along that all that we had to do was win our games, and the schedule strength would not matter. The BCA Classic was an exempt game by the NCAA, which meant we would play a 13-game schedule with the capacity to play two additional games with the Big 12 Championship Game and a bowl game. I did not see that as a great obstacle. Our players were eager to start the season.

On our first play of the season, Darren ran for a 53-yard gain. On the second play, Ell pitched the ball to Darren on an option play, and he ran around four defenders for a five-yard touchdown. Although we were 27-point favorites against California, we kept them in the game and gave up 440 total yards. However, Ell passed for 205 yards and three touchdowns and rushed for 145 yards, Darren rushed for a career-high 175 yards and one touchdown, and James Terry had four catches for 116 yards and one touchdown in a 42–28 victory.

In the midst of our first four non-conference games against California, Troy State (41–5), McNeese State (55–14), and Massachusetts (38–7), we battled some adversity. Darren injured his left leg against Troy State and was helped to the locker room, but he returned and played against

McNeese State. Ell fractured a bone in his left non-throwing hand against McNeese State and did not dress against Massachusetts. Although Ell wore his uniform, we decided not to play him in our final non-conference game against Marshall because we believed there was too much risk involved in playing him. Although we were admittedly limited in our playbook with backup quarterback Jeff Schwinn as our starter, our team perhaps saw that we were favored by 19 points and consequently took Marshall lightly. We committed four turnovers, trailed 16–10 at halftime, and faced fourth and goal from the 6-yard line with less than 20 seconds remaining in the game. We had a pass go off of our wide receiver's hands in the end zone and we suffered a 27–20 loss. It snapped our 10-game winning streak and marked our first home loss to a non-conference opponent since 1989. I do not believe that we played a worse game during our time in the program than we did against Marshall. It was an absolutely miserable game. Even with Ell's return to the field, we started our Big 12 season with back-to-back losses at No. 13 Texas (24–20) and at Oklahoma State (38–34). That gave us three straight losses by a combined 15 points. Those games showed our players how close we were but took us back to the foundation of the process of the program. If we showed daily improvement, we would return to the win column. For now, we were out of the national rankings.

However, we finished our regular season on a six-game winning streak against Colorado (49–20), Kansas (42–6), Baylor (38–10), Iowa State (45–0), at No. 18 Nebraska (38–9), and against Missouri (24–14). Against Colorado, Ell passed for 242 yards and three touchdowns and added 49 rushing yards to become the first player in program history to reach 6,000 total yards in a career. Against Kansas, we won a Sunflower Showdown-record 11th consecutive series victory while outscoring KU 450–97 over that stretch. Against Baylor, Darren recorded 308 all-purpose yards, the most by a Kansas State player in a game since 1969. Against Iowa State, Darren had a career-high 201 rushing yards on 19 carries with three touchdowns of 23, 70, and 32 yards during our first shutout victory against the Cyclones since 1970. We allowed one touchdown over a stretch of 16 quarters, which was perhaps our best such stretch on defense during our time in the program.

It was difficult for me to maintain my focus the week leading up to Nebraska. Meredith, my daughter, gave birth to Gavin, her first child. Joe Paterno was a good friend, and he was in the midst of a 3–9 record for his worst season ever at Penn State, so I was awfully concerned and spent time talking with him. Then prior to our game, a Kansas State student was killed in an automobile accident on the way to Lincoln, Nebraska. No. 18 Nebraska was 8–2 overall and 4–2 in the Big 12, and we were 8–3 overall and 4–2 in the Big 12. The winner would likely represent the North Division and face No. 1 Oklahoma in the Big 12 Championship Game. Ell and Nebraska quarterback Jammal Lord exchanged dialogue through the media during the week, which only escalated when Ell and Jammal spoke heatedly back and forth at midfield prior to the coin toss. Ell stood up for our team, pretty much saying, "You've dominated Kansas State here for years, but this is not the same Kansas State team, and we're here to prove it."

Our players fed off of Ell's energy, and it carried onto the field. Ell passed for 313 yards and two touchdowns and added 90 rushing yards while Darren had 140 rushing yards. Our offense had a season-high 561 yards, the most allowed by Nebraska all season. Nebraska entered ranked fifth in the country in averaging 241.6 rushing yards per game, and we held them to 195 rushing yards. Nebraska finished with 293 total yards, including just 77 yards in the second half, while committing four turnovers. Jammal completed 8-of-26 passes for 98 yards and two interceptions while rushing for 88 yards.

Our 38–9 victory marked the worst home loss for Nebraska in 45 years. After the game, our players jogged to the southwest corner of Tom Osborne Field and applauded the Kansas State Marching Band and the 4,000 purple-clad fans in that section of the stadium. Unfortunately, my strong emotions from our program's first victory in Lincoln in 35 years quickly became diluted when Nebraska defensive coordinator Bo Pelini came down from the coaches' box, rushed toward me on the field, and shouted vulgarities at me. I had left Darren in the game until he was able to continue his streak of 100-yard rushing games. Nebraska fans sent me cards apologizing for Pelini's actions, and the Nebraska athletic director phoned me as well. To beat a team where we had lost for a long period of time was special. Our program had lost the previous 17 times in Lincoln by an average of 34 points. We had taken that next step, which was one of many steps we needed to accomplish. I was happy for our players and our fans.

Although our 24–14 win against Missouri earned us our third outright North Division title in six years and thus added another item to our trophy case, the game was special because our players were motivated to perform well for the 29 seniors in their final home game and because Darren recorded a single-game record 273 rushing yards and two touchdowns. After our senior ceremony inside of the complex following the game, I returned to my office to begin preparations for undefeated Oklahoma. We had two weeks to prepare for the team that many called the greatest team in college football history.

Over the course of the next two weeks, we emphasized to our players that we could not forget that we reached this spot by virtue of playing sound football, executing in all areas, and improving each day. We also drew upon a few things from our playbooks that we had not used over the course of the season. Oklahoma was a two-touchdown favorite, but our players felt strongly that we could win the game and they were motivated by the fact that everyone in the country doubted them. They carried no fear whatsoever. They carried an appropriate confidence level, they had prepared well, and they believed that they had the capabilities to be successful. In our locker room at Arrowhead Stadium, we emphasized that each snap in the game takes about six seconds, and we might play 40 snaps on offense and on defense in a half, which means that we play a total of 240 seconds each half. Our question to our players was simply: how could we not give our best effort for those four total minutes?

As was our custom, we dimmed the lights, and our coaches and players watched a motivational video created by Scott Eilert, our director of video services and senior video coordinator who has won multiple national and Big 12 awards and was inducted into the Collegiate Sports Video Association Hall of Fame in 2017. A 1991 Kansas State graduate, Scott played a vital role in the success of our program. I normally did not need motivation, but Scott's motivational videos elevated my own emotion, and our players always looked forward to his video prior to each game. Scott is very talented.

Oklahoma had won 17 of its last 18 games against nationally ranked opponents and had not lost a bowl game or a conference championship game in five years. Oklahoma had scored in double digits in 64 straight games. During the 2003 season, Oklahoma scored at least 50 points in seven games and outscored Big 12 opponents by an average score of 52–11. Oklahoma trailed a total of six minutes during the season. It had outscored opponents 212–29 in the second quarter. Oklahoma ranked No. 1 in the country in scoring offense, passing efficiency offense, total defense, and passing efficiency defense and ranked No. 3 in scoring defense. Consensus All-American Jason White passed for 3,446 yards and 40 touchdowns and six interceptions, and six other Oklahoma players were named All-Americans as well.

Early in the fourth quarter, more than half of the sellout crowd of 79,451 donned in crimson had left the stadium. At 10:50 PM, all that remained were our Kansas State fans and the final few minutes of our 35–7 victory, which gave us our first conference championship since 1934, our first ever victory over a top-ranked team, and 11 victories for the sixth time in seven seasons. We snapped Oklahoma's 14-game winning streak by handing them their worst loss in five seasons. We gained 519 total yards against a top-ranked defense that allowed just 233.7 yards per game. We allowed seven points against a team that averaged 48 points per game. We forced two interceptions against a quarterback who had thrown just six all season. Ell completed 10-of-17 passes for 227 yards and a Big 12 Championship Game record four touchdowns, and Darren had a Big 12 Championship Game-record 235 rushing yards, which marked the most ever gained by a single player against Oklahoma. Darren also had three catches for 88 yards and one touchdown, which came on a 60-yard, catch-and-run touchdown that gave us a 21–7 lead heading into halftime. His 345 all-purpose yards were the most in program history. Linebacker Ted Sims returned an interception 27 yards for a touchdown to cap what many considered to be among the greatest upsets in college football history.

Immediately after the game in an emotional response to Darren's performance, I encouraged Heisman Trophy voters across the country to remember his name while I visited with ABC sideline reporter Jack Arute on the field. Darren epitomized everything that I felt so strongly about.

He was a wonderful, humble young person and did nothing to promote himself. I always wanted our players to earn their accolades on their own, but I believed that he was deserving of any award that he could receive and I also believed that he had been overlooked, as much as anything, because he played at Kansas State. Darren had the 10th most rushing yards in Division I-A history and was the first player to reach 2,000 all-purpose yards. However, it turned out that Darren was not invited to New York City as a finalist for the Heisman Trophy that following week. He finished fifth in the final voting.

It was always important to enjoy the moment after a win. However, the night did not feel complete. Del was with his wife Jan, and they were with their son, Troy, at an Iowa City hospital. Troy had been diagnosed with a rare transitional cell cancer in September 2001. The cancer began in his kidney and spread to his lymph nodes. We provided transportation for Del and his family to the Mayo Clinic. The cancer went into remission for about a year after treatment. But the cancer returned. Del needed to be with his son during his battle. Troy passed away in June 2004.

On the field, many of our players in their white road uniforms swung their helmets in celebration and shouted, "We shocked the world!" Fiesta Bowl chairman Leon Levitt shook Tim Weiser's hand and pinned his lapel with a Fiesta Bowl badge to commemorate our program's first berth in a Bowl Championship Series bowl game. Less than 24 hours later, it was formally announced that No. 8 Kansas State would play No. 7 Ohio State in the Fiesta Bowl on January 2. Our players had ample time before their next game, so they could expand their enjoyment a little bit longer, but as coaches we had to move onto the next thing. For me, that entailed returning to my office, where all of the previous issues within our program remained, and many of them were still embedded in my mind. They simply would not go away. Although many people considered the victory to be the most significant in our program's history, my happiness over our win was very, very short-lived. I flew back with our daughter Whitney and Jon Wefald on the school plane. As good as the victory was supposed to feel, I still felt somewhat unfulfilled remembering the 1998 Big 12 Championship Game against Texas A&M.

That loss still lingered. It had taken its toll.

Although we set multiple marks during our victory against Oklahoma, I was most pleased with how our players had battled back from adversity during the season. We won our final seven games by an average of four touchdowns and set 42 program records over the course of the season. Our average margin of victory in our last 22 wins was 35.1 points. We joined Nebraska (1993–99) as the only teams in college football history to win at least 11 games in six of seven seasons. Our 49–15 record in Big 12 Conference games since the league's inception was best in conference history. We were one of six programs in the country to advance to 11 straight bowl games. We joined Oklahoma as the only two teams in the country to rank in the top 10 in scoring offense and scoring defense. We finished ranked in the top 15 in total defense in eight of nine seasons and were also the only program in the country to rank in the top six in total defense in each of the previous seven seasons.

Josh Buhl had a program-record 184 tackles, James Terry had a program-record 1,232 receiving yards, and Darren Sproles had a program-record 1,986 rushing yards. Nick Leckey, Darren, Josh, James, and Ell Roberson all earned All-American honors.

I was particularly pleased with how Ell Roberson led our team and developed as a quarterback over his five years in our program. Ell had been considered the most highly regarded high school quarterback to ever sign with Kansas State and steadily grew. He entered his final season with physical traits—a 4.49 40-yard dash and a 385-pound bench press—that established quarterback position records for our program. He became the first quarterback in Big 12 history to pass for 5,000 yards and rush for 2,500 in a career and tied Michael Bishop by winning 22 career games. Ell finished third in Big 12 history with 7,917 total yards and became the only player in program history to finish top three in passing touchdowns (37) and rushing touchdowns (40). During his senior season, he helped us to defeat No. 18 Nebraska and No. 1 Oklahoma by a combined score of 73–16, and neither game was played in Manhattan.

I was interested to see how our team would respond after we were selected to our first Bowl Championship Series game in history. However, a phone call awakened me in the early morning hours of New Year's Day.

A player had violated our team curfew and had apparently been involved in a matter that demanded our attention. I opted not to send him back to Manhattan or suspend him for the Fiesta Bowl because it seemed merely a token consequence and I never wanted to punish our entire program and fanbase for the actions of one individual. But I believed the price of his irresponsibility deserved to be far greater than a single game and ultimately revoked his scholarship. A few days after our 35–28 loss to Ohio State in the Fiesta Bowl, I wrote a letter to Kansas State fans. They deserved a better ending to an otherwise successful season.

"I want to thank Bill Snyder for giving me the opportunity to be a student-athlete and grow as a person at Kansas State. I owe him a lot personally because of everything that he did in helping me become a man during my time in school. He was able to change the perception of Kansas State by turning it into a winner. In the future, when people think about Kansas State, they will think about Bill Snyder."

—Terence Newman, Kansas State cornerback, 1998–2002

CHAPTER 16

Handwritten Notes
with Meaning

"Coach Snyder is a true legend in this game. It's been amazing to watch the turnaround at Kansas State, and he was certainly the catalyst for that. To get to compete against him and to get to know him a little bit here over the last couple of years was a great honor. I'll always remember the handwritten notes I received from him after every single game we played, kind of a personal touch I always felt from him. I very much appreciate what he did for Kansas State, this league, and college football."

—Lincoln Riley, Oklahoma head coach

In this day and age, we all get into a hurry. When we do so, we might overlook some things that are significant in life and that are significant to others. I always admired my mother. She had beautiful handwriting and always took the time to write letters. Maybe that influenced my passion to do the same. People do special things in their lives, and it's significant that they are recognized for their achievements. I have a great appreciation for their accomplishments. In my small way, I recognize those people by writing notes. I want them to know someone appreciates them.

I'm not altogether certain when I began writing handwritten notes. These days, we have access in a heartbeat through texting, emails, Facebook, and Twitter, but I believe handwritten notes are more meaningful. Even if I can recognize someone in person, I write a note. I want people to know my thoughts are sincere, genuine, and that I appreciate their accomplishments and have taken the time to put it on paper. I want them to know that I'm invested in their achievement. Putting thoughts on paper is my preferred method of correspondence.

I don't write notes just to write notes. There is always a purpose of recognizing a special occasion. I still write a great deal of notes today. As a head football coach, all of the issues within our football program required my attention, but I took time each day to write notes. Some days I wrote two or three notes; other days I wrote many more. Often, my notes had nothing to do with football. Joan Friederich and Teresa Williams researched newspapers and other sources to find people within the Manhattan community and Kansas State University who achieved something very positive in their lives. However, I've sent notes to locations throughout the world and to people who are going through a hard time or deserve recognition. I wrote notes—and still do—to congratulate people who won awards, faculty members who were recognized or were issued grants for research projects, and retirees who had been significantly invested in the university or community and had brought success to their venture. A lot of the people I did not know. I admired what they accomplished and I wanted them to know it.

Over the years, I've written notes to federal government officials who have positively impacted the state of Kansas and who have promoted issues concerning the farming population, which is so dear to our state. Every senator is not from a farm state, and consequently they don't always support certain issues, but I have recognized senators when they did vote positively on a topic that could impact the people in the state of Kansas. I've written notes to our Kansas senators and governors. I've written notes to organizations, including people in the National Football Foundation, which continues to do special things and has been significant in its realm in highlighting college football across the nation, and I've written to the NCAA, which has done amazing things for college athletes and college athletics. Many of the notes are directed to people who have illnesses, deaths in the family, injuries, or unfortunate circumstances in their lives.

Early on during our time at Kansas State, I designed stationary and note cards. Our stationary featured a large, lightly visible Powercat logo centered on the page. I ensured that the Powercat logo was prominent on the front of the note card. We designed note cards for different occasions, including birthday cards, congratulatory cards, wedding cards, and sympathy cards, etc., I put a great deal of thought into the printed message featured in each card. I always added a handwritten message in every card I sent as well.

Even though I often verbally applauded our players when they achieved an accomplishment, I wrote them notes and put them in their lockers, so that they knew that I appreciated them enough that I was willing to take the time to put my feelings on paper.

We always had a birthday list that contained the birthdays of everybody—players, coaches, and their families—in our program. I always sent a birthday card to everybody in our program and for the birthdays of their family members to let them know that they're thought of on their special day. An assistant coach, trainer, or secretary might have a young child, and I wanted that child to know he or she was in my thoughts.

I send a letter twice a year to each of our former players who are identified as a "Golden Cat." I also sent letters to former players who had not yet received their bachelor's degree at Kansas State, encouraging them to return and earn their degree through our Second Wind program. Years ago, we had a young man in our football program from my hometown of St. Joseph, Missouri, and he left without earning his degree. I continued to call and send him letters. He called me one day and said, "I did it."

I said, "You did what?"

He said, "I got my degree."

I said, "Stay on the line." I walked to our academic office in the complex to verify his achievement because he had told me for the past 25 years that he would get his degree. It turned out that after all of this time he had indeed received his degree. I returned to my phone and spoke with him for a while, then I wrote him a congratulatory note. Now as a 50 year old, what would be the impact of receiving a degree for him? The impact was that he did it, he could say that he did it, and that he made it important to his life as well.

I cannot recall the most memorable cards or letters that I've written through the years. What has always been most memorable to me is someone going through a difficult time or when somebody has done something in a very successful and special manner. I've written college football coaches across the country and I have probably written most of the coaches that have come through our conference at one time or another to recognize achievements—perhaps an upset win—or to let them know my appreciation for their positive impact within their community or the game of football.

I always wrote opposing football players—win or lose—to let them know that I appreciated their performance in the ballgame. I sent a card to Patrick Mahomes II a few years ago after we defeated Texas Tech. He was such a competitive young guy. I wanted him to know that I appreciated his competitive nature and his never-give-up approach toward the ballgame. Other times, an opposing player might commit a costly mistake in a ballgame, and that's a hard thing because it was visible to everybody, including the TV audience. I don't believe one snap of a football game defines the game's outcome because there are too many events that take place within a ballgame. However, a young person can very readily believe that he cost his team the ballgame. I send a card to that player, emphasizing that the good Lord has helped him through difficulties in his past, and the good Lord will do so again and to keep forging ahead, and the successes will come.

The perception existed that I disliked the media, but sometimes when a writer wrote or did something unique, special, or good, I would send him or her a note. I never hated the media.

I always send condolence cards when a really negative event occurs in somebody's life, perhaps a death in the family. People might be in a time of pain and need people to embrace them. Maybe I'm not physically there, but I let them know that I'm thinking about them. Sometimes I write to people with a terminal illness. Those are the most difficult to write. My hope is that if I send an appropriate message, a positive message, that they might be able to forget their grief for a moment.

I run through hundreds of purple pens every year writing notes. My print appears diagonally on my notes and letters because I'm left-handed, and I find it easier to write across my body. I probably began this writing style in elementary school. We sat in those wood desks with the arm that flapped over, and there were only right-handed desks, so I had to reach across the desk in order to write. I receive comments on my writing style all of the time. My angst comes in the fact that purple ink fades. Somebody on social media might share one of the notes I wrote, and the writing has faded to a light red color over the years. I don't want my writing to fade, but I want to keep using purple ink.

I've always appreciated people who have sent notes to me. I hang on to letters and emails from people, who for some unknown reason, thank me for what I do. The letters and notes are all special because somebody took the time out of their day to sit down, think about what they wanted to express, then put their thoughts to paper. Then they spent money on a stamp and took the time to walk to their mailbox. And many are people I've never met in my life.

Over the years, I have accumulated enough boxes of correspondence from people to fill an entire room. In particular, I was so grateful for the outpouring of correspondence I received over the course of my cancer treatment in 2017. That people cared enough to sit down and pen a note is so meaningful to me, and it was especially meaningful during that period of time in my life. Each of those handwritten cards—and I read all of them—were significant and meant a tremendous amount to me. It took a substantial amount of time for me to write everybody back. Initially, I let the letters pile up, then I answered them along with the other letters as they were delivered.

The number of letters and notes that I write continues to vary by the day, but it remains important to me that I take a few minutes to let people understand that I recognize and admire their achievements or empathize with their difficulties in life. I think people appreciate that. And I appreciate people.

"Coach Snyder valued people over performance. There was no person too small or too insignificant for Coach. Me, for example. As a backup kicker for five years, only playing two plays my entire career, Coach still made time for me. I was not getting letters from him based on my ability to perform, but simply because he wanted to acknowledge the personal wins in my own life as Dillon."

—Dillon Wilson, Kansas State kicker, 2012–15

CHAPTER 17

STEPPING DOWN

"Coach Snyder's leadership will continue to serve as an incredible example to others. He and Sharon have had a huge impact on the community and on the kids whose lives they have touched. Most impressive to me, beyond his undisputable role in football, is that he truly cares about college students. I don't know many other coaches who can be found front and center at other sporting events, supporting their university teams. It's evident Coach Snyder cares about not only the school and the students, but the entire community. That's the mark of a great leader."

—Kathleen Sebelius, former Kansas governor

Every time that I believed I might step down, the thought dissipated. The workload as a head coach was never ending, and I quickly moved on with preparations for the next season. I never identified an end spot for my coaching career. However, the end of the 2003 season coupled with challenging seasons in 2004 and 2005 left me worn down and mentally exhausted. In 2003, when we became just the second program in college football history to win at least 11 games in six of seven seasons, we emphasized to our players the daily work that was necessary to reach that degree of success. Many of our key players graduated after the 2003 season, and many of our players in 2004 lived off of the Kansas State name. Consequently, we lacked the appropriate attitude, failed to utilize our 16 Wildcat Goals for Success, and did not play to our potential during a 4–7 campaign. It marked our first losing season since 1992.

I believed we were determined to take the necessary steps in order to improve our performance the following year. Instead in 2005, we won only one of our first seven Big 12 Conference games, a 12–3 victory against Kansas, and suffered narrow losses to Texas A&M (30–28), Colorado (23–20), and at Nebraska (27–25). Our penchant for falling short in very winnable games tremendously impacted our season's outcome. Our setback in Lincoln, Nebraska, guaranteed back-to-back losing seasons for the first time since 1989 and 1990. Unlike our first two seasons, when we made many errors but still made headway, that was not the case in 2004 and 2005. There was a large list of issues within our program, and that led to those unsuccessful seasons. I was more concerned about our players maintaining an appropriate attitude and effort level than I was about the result upon the scoreboard. Our effort simply wasn't consistent like it was in previous years. The role of a head coach was to get all of the oars rowing together in the same direction. That had been a challenging task in many previous seasons, and it had become even more so after the 2003 Big 12 Championship Game. It was extremely taxing.

About one month after the end of the 2004 season, I told athletic director Tim Weiser that I was ready to resign. I was frustrated with many things. We talked several times about whether I should step down. Some people believed that it was time. I said on my first day at Kansas State that I did not want a contract and that if there came a point in time when I should not coach, we would not have a problem and I would step away. After giving the matter more thought, I told Tim that I would return for the 2005 season. Then as the months progressed, I got to the point where I finally said, "It's time."

On Sunday, November 13, 2005, one day after we suffered our fifth straight defeat with a two-point loss at Nebraska, I told Sharon and Sean that I was going to retire. Sean shared some of my pains regarding many of the issues and problems within our program. I believed that my decision pained Sean both as a son and as a member of our program. Sean told me that he did not want me to retire, but he understood my reasoning and he wanted me to do what made me comfortable. Sharon knew it was time. Later in the day, I met with Jon Wefald, Bob Krause, and Tim at Jon's house on the Kansas State campus. It wasn't a particularly long conversation. I said, "I think we all know why we're here. It's time." They understood my thoughts, but they just wanted to make sure I was certain about my decision.

My reasoning was predicated upon everything going on within our football program more so than it was about wins and losses. It might have been easier to step away had we come off a highly successful season because there was an innate desire to make things right after an unsuccessful one. That made it difficult. Mental frustration made me contemplate retirement in the past. This time was different. So many aspects of the coaching profession impacted my family over my 17 years as Kansas State head coach. We had achieved six 11-win seasons, 11 winning seasons, four Big 12 North Division titles, and three appearances in the Big 12 Championship Game, and one conference title, but my family had suffered over time. That was my biggest concern. It had also become painful for them to read the criticism about me in the newspapers after we lost a game. I hated to leave our program after a losing season, but I did not want to put my family through any more. I just tried to do what was best for them and the program.

Every year, I thought about stepping down. Our program was in the midst of a transition after the 2003 season that helped shape the course of the 2004 and 2005 seasons. For all of the success that we achieved over the previous 11 bowl seasons, we headed toward the 2004 season and faced many challenges and unknowns. At 34 years old, Bret Bielema had served as co-defensive coordinator for defenses that ranked No. 2 and No. 6 in the nation and he aspired to move up. Barry Alvarez hired Bret as defensive coordinator at Wisconsin. Barry had coached Bret at the University of Iowa, so it was a good fit. Staff turnover was always possible for a variety of reasons, so I always had a No. 1, No. 2, and No. 3 choice in the event that a coach left for a job at another program. I hired Chris Cosh from South Carolina as our linebackers coach and I promoted Joe Bob Clements from graduate assistant to defensive ends coach and recruiting coordinator. I felt that Joe Bob would be a strong asset to our staff in a full-time capacity and I always believed that he would have an awfully successful career.

February 18 turned out to be a key date. That was when the Kansas State athletic department agreed to play Fresno State in a two-for-one series beginning with a game on September 11 in Manhattan. We would travel to

Fresno, California, in 2007, and Fresno State would play again in Manhattan in 2008. Texas Tech, Oklahoma State, and Colorado State had exercised buyout clauses to avoid playing in Fresno. Our buyout was in the high six figures, which meant we were tied to the series. I wasn't very excited about the series, but it carried additional recruiting possibilities in California. As the 2004 season unfolded, the non-conference game against Fresno State became memorable for all of the wrong reasons.

We headed toward the spring tasked with replacing a plethora of talent. On offense, we lost All-Americans Ell Roberson, Nick Leckey, and James Terry along with All-Big 12 selections Ryan Lilja and Travis Wilson after the 2003 season. On defense, we lost All-American Josh Buhl along with All-Big 12 selections Bryan Hickman, Justin Montgomery, Andrew Shull, Rashad Washington, Randy Jordan, and Thomas Houchin. We also lost kicker Jared Brite and long snapper Mike Wilson.

Days before the January 15 deadline for underclassmen to declare for the 2004 NFL Draft, Darren Sproles came into my office and told me that he would return for his senior season. As we had done with each of our players when they contemplated leaving early for the NFL, we did due diligence, gathering the facts regarding Darren's NFL prospects. I let him make his decision and then shared my feelings with him. I believed that Darren made the appropriate choice to return because I believed he still had not yet played to his full capacity despite recording the 10th most rushing yards (1,986) in NCAA history during his junior season. Although he had been a proven punt returner during his sophomore and junior seasons, he did not fully develop his talent as a kickoff returner until his senior season—a skill that paid dividends as his 63 kickoff returns during his 2005 rookie season ranked fourth in the NFL. If there was a part of Darren's game that needed improvement, he always worked diligently to become his best in that area. Darren said that he wanted to earn his college degree in speech pathology. It was a promise that he made to his mother. I've always admired his passion for his family.

Annette Sproles was a strong woman. At 41 years old, she was surrounded by her family in Olathe, Kansas, on April 25 when she passed away from cancer. Larry Sproles said that many people did not know of his wife's illness.

She never said a word. The cancer started in her colon, then moved to her liver, lungs, and finally her brain. Darren cancelled a spring break trip to Florida with his teammates to be with his mother. He fetched groceries. They talked late into the night. When she felt down, he made her laugh. Many of the 22 brothers and sisters between Larry and Annette traveled from four different states to be near her. Darren held Annette's hand and assured her that he would take care of his little brother, 14-year-old Terence.

Three hundred people packed the pews and stood in the aisles, 200 more filled the lower fellowship hall, and others stood along the stone steps outside of the west entrance to the Second Baptist Church of Olathe for Annette's funeral service at 11:00 AM on April 29. We knew Annette and Larry and knew that family was important in Darren's life. We could see the teachings of Darren's family and what his mother meant to his maturity. She was very important to his growing up and his value system. I spoke at funeral services many times, but speaking at Annette's funeral was painful because of the pain Darren and his family experienced as she went to be with the Lord. She felt very strongly about Darren's education. We held Darren out of spring practice and invited Terence to spend time with Darren on the sideline during our spring game. They were still healing emotionally and they needed each other.

Although we had never singled out a player on our football media guide cover, our sports information staff approached me in the spring and felt strongly about putting Darren on the cover. Although it took much convincing anytime I was asked to break from consistency in any arena, I said, "Go ahead." But it still wasn't an easy decision. It was the first time that we had a player who entered a season as a legitimate Heisman Trophy candidate. As always, I wanted Darren to earn the award based on his performance, not based upon a gesture to sway the voters. Our sports information department also designed a website, DarrenSproles43.com, that allowed Kansas State fans and national media a chance to see Darren's highlights from each game during the season. As I said at Big 12 Media Day, "You're not going to receive a jack-in-the-box in the mail that has a Darren Sproles pop up." Yet the hype surrounding Darren continued into the preseason. Darren handled the attention as well as anybody could. He said that he just wanted to win games.

I did not know how our team would respond when we were predicted to finish first in the Big 12 North Division in the Big 12 preseason poll. I shared publicly that the capability was there, but we had to invest ourselves in the manner that most everyone through the previous years had invested themselves in order to achieve success. There was a big if as to whether our current players would follow suit.

Not all of them did.

It took just two games for us to knock ourselves out of the national rankings. Darren had a program-record 42 carries for 221 yards and one touchdown, and we needed all of his ability in a 27–13 win against Division I-AA Western Kentucky. We had sophomore Dylan Meier and sophomore transfer Allen Webb at quarterback. Dylan threw the ball well, and Allen was a talented runner, so there was a combination of skills, and they played about equal time over the course of the season. It was always a difficult task playing two quarterbacks. Most coaches advised against it. However, I believed this was the fairest approach as they both deserved to be starters. They perhaps were not the same type of quarterbacks that we had in the past, but they contributed together at near the same level as some of the previous quarterbacks. Our belief was that to choose one over the other would cause us to cut our offensive production in half, and utilizing both allowed us to use the total package effectively. We attempted to balance it out so that both quarterbacks could pass and run, but we played to their strengths as much as possible. It wasn't enough.

We were a two-touchdown favorite when we faced Fresno State on September 11. In my 16 years, we had never had a football team that just got beat up as badly as we did in a 45–21 loss in front of our home crowd of 46,468 and a national TV audience. We allowed Fresno State to beat its highest-ranked team ever on the road and to score its most points ever against a major-conference team. We allowed our most points against a non-conference opponent in 13 years. Dylan injured his right shoulder in the season opener, and Allen struggled considerably in his first career start. He did not complete a pass until less than 10 minutes remained in the game.

Due to our abundance of three-and-outs, we were unable to utilize Darren. His 11 carries for 37 yards marked his lowest output since his freshman season. I always remembered losses more so than wins. We weren't into that game and I will forever regret our preparation and performance. We were ranked No. 12 and had high expectations. Many people within our program believed that we had won before and thus would win again and did not make the total investment to achieve the desired success. We needed to get back to where we had to scrap and dig, play above and beyond our individual capabilities, and carry emotion while working to achieve positive results but not become overconfident. We could not afford to carry the belief that winning would just happen without us doing anything to earn the victory. That's not the way life works and certainly not what had brought previous successes to our program.

Darren put together the top rushing performance in program history with 38 carries for 292 yards and one touchdown in 40–20 win against Louisiana-Lafayette, but we opened the Big 12 schedule with a 42–30 loss to Texas A&M. However, the true test of how we would respond arrived a few weeks later in Lawrence. Our 31–28 loss to Kansas ended our 11-game winning streak in the series. Dylan threw an 86-yard touchdown pass to Tony Madison to give us a 21–17 lead with 13 minutes remaining in the game, but we allowed two touchdowns in the final five minutes. After the game, I emphasized to our players how close we were based upon the narrow defeat. It was in our hands. I shared with them that we were all invested in the loss. I accepted the responsibility for making bad choices that contributed to the poor preparation and performance. I told our players that we were committed to correcting our mistakes as a coaching staff and I asked our players to do exactly the same thing.

Our record dropped to 2–4 after a 31–21 loss against No. 2 Oklahoma, but we responded the following week with a 45–21 win against Nebraska. We kept the identity of the starting quarterback a secret until Dylan put on a headset, and Allen jogged onto the field. Allen rushed 34 times for 147 yards and four touchdowns while leading us to score three unanswered touchdowns to win the game. Although the victory showed that the players and coaches were becoming more invested and taking some positive steps,

I was concerned that we might fall into the mind-set that we were going to roll through the rest of our games because we beat Nebraska. All of a sudden, we were back at the beginning with individuals believing that we had arrived again. Not learning from one's mistakes is a major shortcoming in life and in football.

The losses mounted. Texas Tech was an amazing team under Mike Leach and the Air Raid offense, which was relatively new to the Big 12 Conference, and our defense could not slow them down in a 35–25 loss. We overcame a 21-point deficit in a 35–24 win at Missouri but quickly came down to Earth again. Joel Klatt threw a 64-yard touchdown pass with five seconds remaining, and we suffered a 38–31 loss at Colorado. We were there for 59 minutes and 55 seconds and then all of the sudden we weren't there in the final five seconds of the game. We had some painful losses. This one eliminated us from the chance to go to a bowl game for the first time since 1992.

It was disheartening. Darren always accepted responsibility and he accepted more responsibility than necessary his senior season. Darren needed help, and all 11 players had to play together. It didn't happen and he couldn't do it on his own. Darren and I had a great deal of trust in each other. He heavily bought into our value system. When I had a Zoom call with Darren on January 11, 2021, to tell him that he had been voted into the 2021 College Football Hall of Fame class, he stated that he continued to live by our values and goals. He is a very humble young man, and I admire that a great deal. I believe he felt strongly that he could talk to me about anything. Darren said that he grew up so much when he was at Kansas State, but he was special before he came to Manhattan through the tremendous guidance of his family.

Darren set 23 school records during his Kansas State career and owned virtually every career, single-season, and single-game mark for both rushing and all-purpose yards. His 4,979 career rushing yards ranked 11th all time in college football history. His 6,812 all-purpose yards ranked sixth. He established school records with 48 career touchdowns and 45 rushing touchdowns. He recorded 24 career 100-yard rushing performances and surpassed 200 rushing yards five times in his 45-game career. He led the nation with a school-record 1,986 rushing yards along with 2,735 all-purpose yards and became the first running back in school history to earn first-team All-American honors by the Associated Press in 2003. In the final game of his career, Darren rushed for 167 yards on 21 carries and scored one touchdown during a 37–23 loss to Iowa State on Senior Day. We led 23–9 early in the fourth quarter and then we allowed 28 unanswered points, including three touchdowns in the final three minutes. It was our worst unraveling in any game during my first 16 years as head coach. Our 4–7 record was our program's worst since 1989.

In the locker room, I told our players what they could anticipate and expect from me and the program and reiterated what our program was really all about. I did not think that some of them understood what our program expected of them and advised them to do some soul searching. I told them if they were unwilling to work at it, it would be best for all if they didn't come back. We had to get back to basics and perhaps to a greater degree than ever before. I wanted young men who wanted to be a part of something that they helped make special, so there was an investment on their part. When we first arrived at Kansas State, we had a small number of young men, and some were leaving because they had never been invested in those kinds of work habits. I wanted to go back to that testing ground. How badly did they really want it? I didn't want to drive players away. But it was important to identify those players who were there for the right reasons and the ones who chose not to give their full effort.

On January 18, 2005, we began our winter conditioning program inside the indoor practice facility at 6:45 AM. Trash cans were located around the facility for players to utilize if necessary. After a string of tardiness among some players, we moved the start of workouts to 6:00 AM. We announced that each late-arriving player would cause workouts to begin five minutes earlier. The final workout on March 29 began at 5:45 AM. The message was that we wanted players who were responsible and accountable, which was the exact requirement on the football field. The bottom line: we needed to be invested. Our winter workouts were not a form of punishment. We couldn't say, "You went 4–7 so we're punishing you with early workouts."

That simply would not work. But our players quickly realized that's how we built the program beginning in 1989, and this is what was required, and they had to realize there were consequences for poor effort. We were responsible for our own performance. If we didn't perform appropriately, we lost. During a meeting, I asked, "Who isn't bothered by losing? Raise your hand." Of course, nobody raised their hand.

Upon watching videotape of our younger players in practice over the course of the past year, I brought a pair of redshirt sophomores from the state of Kansas into my office during the spring. Jordy Nelson was a walk-on defensive back from nearby Riley, Kansas, who was a member of our scout squad in 2004. Wide receiver Marcus Watts was a former grayshirt from Hays, Kansas, and emerged as our special teams MVP in 2004. At the time, neither of them had yet been on the field in their respective roles. But in observing them in practice, I felt that Marcus had the skills and mentality to be a better defensive secondary player and that Jordy had the skills to be a better wide receiver. I told them, "This is my suggestion, and I want you to go home and think about whether or not you want to change positions."

They said, "We don't need to think about it. If you think that switching positions is best then that's what we'll do."

It turned out to be a positive change for Jordy and Marcus. Jordy finished his career in 2007 as the only wide receiver to earn consensus All-American recognition in Kansas State history while establishing nine school records. Marcus emerged as a two-time All-Big 12 free safety who recorded 160 total tackles, including two sacks to go along with eight tackles for a loss and four interceptions over the course of three seasons.

Jordy admitted that he had never played wide receiver in his life, but he was eager to learn the whole playbook. During his first five games at wide receiver, he became the first player in Kansas State history to catch a touchdown in five straight games. Jordy was a good-sized target at 6'3" and 210 pounds and a very fine athlete with a 4.51 time in the 40. He possessed impressive movement skills, change-of-direction ability, and excellent hands. He was also a physical player, so he could out-finesse or out-physical defensive backs.

There are various types of attention that can accompany being a head coach at a prominent program. In May of 2005, I was surprised to learn that my name and our school had been mentioned in a Hollywood movie. During a scene in *The Longest Yard*, Adam Sandler's character mentioned "Coach Snyder" while referencing Kansas State—a movie line that I learned did not go unnoticed by audiences at Seth Child Cinema in Manhattan.

We gradually gained some confidence while winning all three of our non-conference games against Florida International (35–21), at Marshall (21–19), and against North Texas (54–7). I always remember the game at Marshall in Huntington, West Virginia, for two reasons. Justin McKinney intercepted a pass at our 21-yard line with 2.8 seconds remaining to secure our win, and the circuit board on the wall behind our sideline at Joan C. Edwards Stadium shorted out in the second half, rendering all 12 headsets worn by our coaching staff useless, and the game officials would not delay the game until they were repaired, which forced me to use Sean's cellphone in order to communicate with our coaches in the press box. I was not an electrical engineer, but I was angered by it. We opened the Big 12 with a 41–23 loss at Oklahoma, which scored the first 26 points while playing without All-American running back Adrian Peterson. We could feel our players say, "Here we go again." Actually, the attitude that was prevalent could have been: *maybe we aren't as good as the previous Kansas State teams.* We had issues with team personnel, but attitude also played a major part in our deficiencies. The game was marred by an explosion during the second quarter when a device was detonated in a courtyard area outside of Memorial Stadium, which caused one fatality. I was unaware of the explosion until we went to our bus after the game.

Although we failed to score 20 points for the first time in three years, we somehow survived to defeat Kansas 12–3. We were outgained 282–182 and committed 12 penalties, but our defense stopped Kansas six times in our territory, recovered three fumbles, blocked a field goal, and recorded a safety. Allan Evridge threw an eight-yard touchdown to Jordy in the fourth quarter, which marked the only time either team reached the end zone.

We won just one more time during our final six games.

No. 13 Texas Tech led the nation with 52 points and 433 passing yards per game under Leach's Air Raid offensive attack, and the Red Raiders handled us 59–20 while we allowed a school-record 669 passing yards and five touchdowns and gave up our most points in a game since 1990. We played well in several games down the stretch and still came up short in the aforementioned losses to Texas A&M, Colorado, and Nebraska. We were not eligible for a bowl game in back-to-back seasons for the first time since 1990 and 1991. I could say it's human nature to become acclimated to the previous many years, but all that did was confirm my expectations. My expectations were always extremely high, and that never changed. It wasn't about the scores as much as the performance level. I labored under the assumption that if we did it the way it should be done, we would succeed. When we weren't doing things as well as necessary, we couldn't be surprised with the negative results. Did we make the effort to be the best we could be across the board? We suffered from that void. In our 11 losses in the Big 12 between the 2004 and 2005 seasons, four defeats were by seven or fewer points, and three were decided by 12 or fewer points.

I had a gnawing feeling of: *how can I change this?* The feelings about retirement began a week or two before our game in Lincoln. And it was painful. We had won before with lesser talent. However, we ranked either at the bottom or near the bottom of the Big 12 in total offense and rushing offense, punt returns, turnover margin, and penalties. I knew things were going wrong with this group. I wasn't certain I could get it corrected. That wasn't a good place to be. Everything had caught up to us. When we returned from Lincoln, my feeling was simply enough is enough. On Sunday, I told Sean of my decision to retire. Then I told Tim, Bob, and Jon at the president's home. I believed that it made sense to wait until after our final game against Missouri to make an announcement to eliminate distraction. They didn't believe that it would be possible for the news to remain a secret that long. So after Monday's practice, I told our coaches and players to go into the locker room. It was an emotional time when I informed them that I was going to retire after our final game of the season. For years, it was normally taken for granted that I would be back. Through the years, players graduated and moved on, and assistant coaches left, but I always occupied that corner office in the complex. Our players were mature and understood the nature of coaching at this level. My announcement seemed to surprise some of our players, and it might not have been that much of a surprise to others. However, it was an announcement that most people anticipated could come at any point in time. Still, there were some emotional moments with players and coaches alike inside our meeting room. On Tuesday morning, we issued a news release for an afternoon news conference.

Hayden Fry phoned me on Tuesday morning. Later, after talking to him, I took the podium to explain to the media and the wonderful and supportive Kansas State people why I decided it was best for the university, for myself, and my family for me to retire. I appreciated Hayden's call and his concern for me. During those years with Hayden at the University of Iowa, I never quite understood why he did some of the things that he did. Being a younger fellow at the time, I thought that I had all of the answers. When I got to sit in the chair as a head coach, I realized at the time that Hayden knew a heck of a lot more than I did about what was going on. I learned while sitting in that chair that if I did not have a crisis on hand, I needed to grab a cup of coffee and hang on because a crisis was coming, and several certainly arrived over the years.

I was greeted by a standing-room-only crowd of longtime Kansas State employees and many dear friends as I entered the team meeting room for my news conference. Sharon, Sean, Wanda, Shannon, Ross, and Whitney sat in the front row. I blew them kisses, took a deep breath, and then I began to speak. "The question is why, and the answer to me is really simple," I said. "Kansas State has been very good to Bill Snyder and to our family and to our football program. I appreciate this university and this community a great deal. I think for everybody there is a right time, and it's normally pretty difficult to define when that right time is. To me, this is the right time."

We still had a game to play. That's what I repeated to our coaches and players during the week. After my news conference, I hugged my family, returned to my office, and kept my door closed as much as possible on Wednesday, Thursday, and Friday to eliminate distractions. As I parked in the spot labeled "Head Coach" one more time early Saturday morning, a large group of Kansas State fans standing on the grassy fields on the other side of Kimball Avenue cheered as I exited my car and made my way up the steps of the Vanier Football Complex. A sign along a fence read: "THANKS COACH." It was me who was thankful. Seventeen years. I had been blessed. Big 12 Commissioner Kevin Weiberg visited me in my office. He asked me if I believed that I was making the right decision. Players normally didn't dedicate games to their coaches, but I believed a part of their motivation to do so was to see me go out with a win. It was important to me that our 22 seniors went out with a win as well.

During a brief ceremony prior to kickoff, Kansas State—by a proclamation of the Kansas Board of Regents—officially renamed KSU Stadium as Bill Snyder Family Stadium. Tim had initially phoned and said that they wanted to rename the stadium. He said they wanted to rename it "Bill Snyder Stadium." I told Tim that I wasn't sure that they should do that, and he told me it was already decided by the Board of Regents. I called him the next day and said, "I will consent to it if you name it 'Bill Snyder Family Stadium,'" in honor of my immediate family and their investment in my life but also for the Kansas State family and our fans who had been such a great part of it.

My mind was hazy during the game. Afterward, I told the media, "If there was any good coaching today, it wasn't me. I was just there." I was emotionally drained. It had been a long week. We came back from a 14-point second-half deficit to beat Missouri 36–28. Jordy caught the final touchdown pass of the game, and linebacker Brandon Archer intercepted a Brad Smith pass and raced 45 yards down the Missouri sideline for the final score with one minute, 23 seconds remaining in the game. Our crowd of 46,309 responded to the play with some of the loudest cheers in stadium history. It was a dramatic finish to my 205th career game at the university and the football program that carried so many special memories.

What I did not anticipate was Jordy and senior offensive lineman Jeromey Clary hoisting me upon their shoulders after the game and carrying me off of the field for the final time. I still have a big photo of that scene in my home office. I had a big smile on my face. I had never been one to allow that sort of thing to happen, but I appreciated the gesture a great deal. It was a memorable win. I told our players that I appreciated them for their caring, for their work and effort in winning the last one. I told them that we would meet on Monday and discuss the future and the efforts necessary in order to get our program back on track.

I doubt a day passed that I didn't wake up with football on my mind. I questioned myself, *Was it the right thing?* I never found an answer, but I questioned myself. About two weeks later, I revisited Wefald, Weiser, and Krause. I told them I had experienced some uncertainty with my original decision. We discussed it. Jon said, "Let's move on." I had two thoughts. Jon was probably right, and I always said that if somebody wanted me to move on, I'd move on. They were doing what they thought was best for me. I just had some uncertainty. It became hard for me to snap my fingers and bring closure to the emotions that had accompanied such a strong investment over the course of years. I wondered how long it would take for me to be at ease with myself. And with my decision.

"Coach Snyder is the greatest coach to ever turn around a football program. The things that he did nobody else has done. Before I went to college, everybody told me that I wouldn't make it. Coach Snyder told me that I would make it, and he believed in me. As a player, there were times when you thought it was too hard, but you never gave up. When we won the 2003 Big 12 Championship, it felt like we won the Super Bowl."

—Darren Sproles, Kansas State running back, 2001–04

CHAPTER 18

THE IMPORTANCE
OF MENTORSHIP

"I'll tell you something Bill always did. When he retired the first time, he would write me and tell me to stay in coaching. He always encouraged me. I was so glad when I saw him get back into coaching. His legacy will be that he was one of the most successful coaches ever, and he did it honestly. Bill is a wonderful man."

—Bobby Bowden, former Florida State head coach

Mentorship became important to me from a very early age. Without knowing the meaning of the word, many people gave me guidance and direction at various stages of my life. So many people served as great mentors to me. Obviously, mentorship started with my mother. Some people might say that's just parenting, but my belief is that parenting and mentoring can be one and the same. My grandparents were also strong mentors to me. When others recognized my mother had her hands full while working long hours as a single parent, they stepped in to provide mentorship. Through the years, so many people, coaches, administrators, teachers, and teammates have provided me with guidance and direction and have supported me through my life. Many of them have passed. However, my mother still mentors me. Certain situations come up in my life, and I immediately fall back on my mother's direction, which she provided for me many years ago.

People contribute to my life without even knowing it. I've met so many people in my role as a football coach. People don't say, "Coach, you should do this," but you come in contact with some people and develop relationships, and things come up in conversation that I relate to and put into my life as well.

Soon after we arrived in Manhattan, we visited the Kansas State College of Education and we were approved to teach a one-hour credit course, which I volunteered to teach. It served as a part of our head start program for incoming football players. The course focused on the importance of academics and developing a value system and served as an introduction to our football program. It was a great opportunity for me to engage with our incoming players to discuss many issues outside of football and to listen to speakers who I invited from all across the university and Manhattan community. We also developed a mentoring program for all of our players. Just as we developed a head start program, we also developed a transition program to help indoctrinate our players into life after football and how to be a good husband, a good father, and a good employee. We invited businessmen and businesswomen from all over the state. We had an introduction period followed by a meal with speakers, and these individuals paired off with our players to serve as mentors, and the relationships grew. Although the program meant a lot to our players, I always felt that it also carried an even greater meaning for the people serving as mentors. Players heard me talk about values and life, but after a while, I probably sounded like a parent, and the players drifted toward thinking, *Yeah, I know Coach is right, but I don't want to hear that anymore.* This program was beneficial in that aspect.

Most of the time, when we think about mentorship, we think about an individual receiving guidance and the value that mentorship creates for that individual. We developed a program for our players to serve as mentors in the Manhattan community, and they really took it to heart. Here were young men in a reasonably small community who participated in football at Kansas State University and to whom young people looked up. We told our players, "You have a great platform as student-athletes to mentor young people and to help guide and direct them in a positive direction, and we need to take advantage of that opportunity."

I believed that the capacity for our players to serve as mentors would benefit the youth and families in the community while also helping our players extend themselves—sometimes without even knowing it, which would benefit their own value system and personal well-being.

Our players visited local schools to counsel and mentor young people. They spoke to students and adopted a student to be a mentee. I communicated with the Manhattan superintendent and all of the principals in and around Manhattan. I asked them to identify those students in need in their schools who could use guidance. Even though everyone could utilize mentoring in a variety of ways, I asked permission for each of these needy and troubled students to pair up with our players. It developed into an amazing mentoring program. Every once in a while, we saw an article featuring one of our players and the young person they mentored. It just had such an impact on all of the young people, and virtually every single one of them profited from their relationship with one of our players. In fact, every one of them went on to high school and graduated, which was somewhat unique. Our players volunteered for Big Brothers and the Boys & Girls Club of Manhattan. I invited our players to bring their mentees to our football practice and let them be introduced to the other players.

One such child was a 12 year old named Kaiden Schroeder. Shortly after our 2012 football season, Ryan Mueller, a former walk-on from Leawood, Kansas, who later became one of our team captains, visited Kaiden at Children's Mercy Hospital in Kansas City. Kaiden had been diagnosed with acute lymphocytic leukemia a few years prior and had undergone a bone marrow transplant. Ryan gave him a No. 44 Kansas State football jersey, and many of our players sent him handwritten notes. Each player on our team really embraced him. Ryan became friends with Kaiden and then served as his mentor. Ryan approached me prior to the 2014 spring game and asked a favor. He wanted to know if we could give Kaiden an opportunity to be involved with a play during the spring game. So Kaiden came into the game for one play, ran for a 30-yard touchdown, and all of our players carried him off the field. It was extremely meaningful to that young guy. I was certainly in favor of it. It created great enthusiasm throughout the stadium.

It has been amazing to see the growth within the realm of leadership and mentorship across Kansas State University. In 1997, the Kansas Board of Regents approved Leadership Studies as a minor. Dr. Susan M. Scott served as the director, and Dr. Robert Shoop served as professor and senior scholar with an operating budget of less than $5,000. Robert approached me about his desire to collaborate on a textbook that could be utilized in his introduction to leadership concepts class. *Leadership Lessons from Bill Snyder* was published in September 1998, and the curriculum basically taught the same intrinsic values and leadership concepts that we shared with our football team every year. Then in 2017, I collaborated with Jefferson Knapp and illustrator Tim Ladwig on a children's book, *Take It from Me*, which was a 32-page illustrated family book that highlighted our 16 Wildcat Goals for Success. It was my hope that parents and guardians read the book with their children, which allowed them to mentor and expound upon many of the messages that we shared within the text.

Although I had spent many years serving as a mentor to my children and to the young people in our programs—first as a high school coach and then as a college coach—my involvement in mentorship assumed a more prominent role after my first retirement following the 2005 season. Kansas Governor Kathleen Sebelius appointed me to develop an organization to promote mentoring throughout the state of Kansas. This is how we initiated Kansas Mentors. We launched the state-funded mentoring program in 2006 to connect existing mentoring programs with one another and to serve as a resource center for communities wishing to start a program. I learned many small communities simply lacked funding necessary to sustain mentoring programs. Eventually, we had more than 250 mentoring programs in the 105 counties within the state of Kansas.

Kansas Mentors was well-received. The organization gained media interest, which helped a great deal in spreading the message, and people paid attention in part because we served as strong advocates. I wanted to have an impact beyond the game of football. Many families weren't aware of how to identify local mentoring opportunities for their children. A parent might not look at a Boys & Girls Club or other entities as mentoring organizations. I wanted to see one-on-one communication and relationships grow in an effort for one individual to promote a value system to another young person. While servicing mentor programs across the state, it became apparent we could promote in-school mentoring in virtually every school district, which could be very meaningful. I sent letters to the superintendent of every school district within the state of Kansas to promote mentoring programs within their districts. My belief was that every teacher within a school could become a mentor to several youth, and upperclassmen could become mentors to young people in the community, and community members could mentor within their schools. There was a great learning experience and responsibility for high school juniors and seniors mentoring eighth graders or freshmen. Mentors grow through mentoring, which is of great value to those who are involved with it. We strived to get 100 percent of Kansas schools invested in mentoring either in being mentored or serving as a mentor to others. It was quite a challenge, but it was meaningful to do. My goal wasn't to diminish the involvement of local mentoring organizations but rather to advance their efforts while other youngsters were mentored through the school system. The combination of the two entities would hopefully address every youngster in the state.

Kansas Mentors became a member of the national organization MENTOR: The National Mentoring Partnership. MENTOR recognized Kansas Mentors for its positive impact within the state of Kansas. In January 2015, I was fortunate to be recognized for my passion for mentorship when I was awarded the 2015 Excellence in Mentoring Award by MENTOR in a special ceremony in Washington, D.C. It was probably one of the most rewarding honors I've ever received. I've always viewed my role in life as a mentor and a teacher. People said I was in the coaching field, and I'd venture to say I was in the mentoring field with some attachments to it. If anything I did was worthwhile, it was the mentoring aspect within my role as a football coach. You could say "Mentor Nick Saban" just as easily as you could say "Coach Nick Saban" dependent upon how you viewed the position of head coach.

I believe leadership and mentoring for the most part is one and the same. When Governor Sebelius initiated the Wichita-based Kansas Leadership Center, the active CEO was Kansas Congressman Ed O'Malley, who had headed an effort to name K-177 "Bill Snyder Highway." I was asked to serve on the leadership center's board of directors. The leadership center's mission was to offer leadership development programs to foster stronger, healthier, and more prosperous communities within the state. We wanted communities to be self-sustaining and embrace a variety of programs, many of them new programs, for the betterment of the community. Once again, it was mentoring, as the Kansas Leadership Center mentored the leadership in each of the communities within the state.

Communities either thrive or fail to thrive based upon their leadership, particularly in smaller communities. We've seen an awful lot of smaller communities in the Midwest lose considerable population, which is unfortunate, because there's something to be said for small town, midwestern-valued communities. I always saw it as something really special given the opportunity to travel into so many small communities. The life in a small town can be truly desirable. It brings real and unique meaning to family and to people caring about people.

In 2014, the Staley School of Leadership Studies at Kansas State University approached me with a proposal. Since Kansas State began the leadership studies interdisciplinary minor in 1997, the school has grown with more than 1,000 students enrolled in the leadership studies minor and more than 2,500 students enrolled in its programs and courses. Starting in 2015, the School of Leadership Studies wanted to implement a values-centered program focused on developing foresight, initiative, and desire to enhance community leadership, which would be comprised of a 40-member class of students entering their final year of undergraduate studies. They would name it the "Snyder Leadership Legacy Fellows Program."

Part of the Snyder Leadership Legacy Fellows Program allowed students within the fellowship program to connect with mentors to explore the transition from student to professional life. Each fall, the Snyder Fellows mentored youth activities through the Manhattan Parks and Recreation Department. So Snyder Fellows were mentored and served as mentors. It's the foundation for an outgrowth of mentoring. I tried to promote the capacity to leave Kansas State upon graduation and provide leadership within a community and to help develop leadership in that community in many different ways. I always felt that was important. I address the students in the program in a variety of different ways. The Snyder Leadership Legacy Fellows

Program entered in its seventh year in 2021, which meant more than 240 students over that span invested a great deal in mentoring and leadership and carried that growth into many communities. The program continues to blossom. Following graduation ceremonies each year, I receive notes from the members of the Snyder Leadership Legacy Fellows Program, expressing their appreciation and enthusiasm for the program.

I believe there is hope for any generation. We all need the right guidance and direction, and everybody is looking for it. What becomes significant is identifying those people who possess the capabilities of mentoring and are willing to provide that kind of help. It's so easy for a parent to say, "My child doesn't need mentoring. I'll mentor my child. I'll guide and direct and teach him." However, the human nature aspect of a young person promotes the thought of becoming less attentive to a parent than to someone else. That's one reason why mentoring is significant in a young person's life.

It is my hope that every youngster in the state of Kansas might be matched up with a mentor. Although we normally perceive mentorship as working with young people, it becomes important to remember that mentorship serves any age group. We can have a mentor at any age. I certainly have.

"Coach Snyder always preached about having a good value system. It really does help you not only on the field but off the field in understanding how handling situations in life. If you have a core value system and you have that consistent mind-set, you're going to be successful. Coach Snyder taught me how to be a man. Without him I wouldn't be where I am today."

—Cody Whitehair, Kansas State offensive lineman, 2012–15

CHAPTER 19

THE RETURN

"Bill Snyder leaves, then Kansas State struggles, then he comes back, and resurrects it again. He maximized players' potential, and they had toughness and discipline. Every year, his teams were among the least penalized, and his special teams were always an X factor and always good. He covered all the little details. He is a Hall of Famer and one of the greatest coaches of all time."

—David Pollack, ESPN

Virtually every night, I had crazy dreams. Often my dreams centered around the theme that I tried to go someplace but could never reach my destination, though the exact details, like most dreams, escaped me when I awoke. Upon reflection, the dreams about me trying to get somewhere carried significant meaning. It proved difficult to process all of the thoughts that raced through my mind each day. To say that it took some time to adjust to life without coaching football was a vast understatement. At 66 years of age, I was beginning a new journey along an unfamiliar path. One day I felt one way. The next day I felt another way. All of the thoughts seemed to run in cycles, and it continued to be that way for the first several months of retirement.

The 22 days between my announcement to Jon Wefald, Tim Weiser, and Bob Krause that I was going to retire and the search for the next Kansas State head coach proved to be a busy one. Gary Patterson, a Kansas State alum and TCU head coach, signed a contract extension through 2012 and was out of the equation to come to Kansas State. Jim Leavitt was in his ninth season as South Florida head coach and obviously knew our program. Jim was also the fourth lowest paid head coach among 66 schools in the

Bowl Championship Conference. Phil Bennett, who left our coaching staff following the 2001 season to become head coach at Southern Methodist, had just completed his fourth season, and he was a name to ponder given his familiarity with our program. Dana Dimel, whom we hired on our original staff in 1989, served as head coach at Wyoming and Houston in recent years and expressed an interest in the head coaching position. Dana, as did many, felt that an individual already familiar with our program was best suited to be head coach. Del Miller, the first assistant coach I ever hired at Kansas State, was very passionate about the possibility of leading our program, having been at Kansas State for more than a decade. Del also believed that elevating a current coach on staff to head coach would ease the transition.

I felt strongly all along that the new head coach should have a Kansas State background.

On Wednesday, November 30, Tim, Bob, and associate athletic director Jim Epps flew to Charlottesville, Virginia, and conducted their first interview with Ron Prince, a 36-year-old offensive coordinator at Virginia. They were impressed by him during their interview. The following morning, they all flew into Topeka to meet with me and Jon. I met Ron for the first time in a hotel room at the Capitol Plaza Hotel. Ron had grown up in Junction City, Kansas, and he seemed to have a working knowledge of what football was all about from a fundamental and X's and O's standpoint. I was still interested in someone who had a Kansas State background. Sean, Jim, Phil, Dana, and Del were my list of top candidates.

I didn't recommend Sean for the head coaching position based solely upon the fact that he was my son. Sean had done so much for Kansas State football over the years and held countless positions not just in name but in function within our program. I didn't believe that there was anybody in the country who ever carried as many responsibilities as Sean did. He coached special teams, served as director of operations, and his on-field coaching experience coupled with his hands-on, day-to-day interaction with everyone within our program was an ideal fit for a head coach. However, they weren't going to hire Sean as head coach. I believed that if they weren't going to hire Sean, they probably felt that it would be inappropriate to hire any of the other candidates on my list that had current or past coaching experience in our program.

After Jon and I spoke with Ron, he left the hotel room. Jon and Tim wanted to offer Ron the head coaching job when they brought him back into the room. I still held out for someone else. I asked, "Would you allow me to make one last phone call for someone you could interview?" I called Jim, who told me that he couldn't pursue the Kansas State job because earlier that week he had signed an extension at South Florida through the 2012 season. Jon and Tim called Ron back into the hotel room, and they offered him the position.

Kansas State hired Ron as head coach on December 4.

In the meantime, many of our former coaches and staff members elicited my help as they sought to gain employment at another college football program. Many of our recently graduated players asked me to call potential employers. A couple of our former players who were athletic directors called for advice. I had no trouble staying occupied and I truly wanted to help. I felt bad for coaches in particular who most likely would lose their jobs at Kansas State. That was the main reason I stayed as head coach for so long. Also, Kansas City Chiefs head coach Herm Edwards invited me to spend some time with him. One day I talked football with Oregon State head coach Mike Riley and the next day I talked football with Mike Leach or Mack Brown. And so on. My time was occupied.

Here's something I learned about myself rather quickly: I was not good at not being busy. I wanted to be involved, I wanted to help others, I wanted to help the right causes and did so in various ways. I spoke at dozens of engagements in and around the state of Kansas and the country. In one month, I spoke at the National Blue Key Convention, the American Farm Bureau Federation Young Farmers & Ranchers, the Associated General Contractors Convention, and the Dillons Lecture Series. I spoke at state, regional, and national coaching conventions. I rode in parades. I attended a North Texas reunion in Denton, Texas, and I was able to spend some time with many of our former players and coaches from our era. I spent some time with Warren and Mary Lynn Staley, two great K-Staters who were in the initial stages of putting together plans for the construction of the Leadership

Studies Building on our campus. I met and had lunch with the Prince of Saudi Arabia before he delivered a Landon Lecture at McCain Auditorium. I flew to Palm Beach, Florida, to visit my good friend, Tom Ross, who had introduced me to Sharon many years ago in Iowa. We rented a cabin at Lake of the Ozarks for a week-long vacation with all of our family. At home, I walked the treadmill for an hour each day. Sharon and I enjoyed attending productions at the Columbian Theatre in Wamego, Kansas. But most of all, I just enjoyed spending time with our family.

Joe Paterno told me that I would get awfully sick and tired of watching Little League games, but I enjoyed every one of them. We traveled to watch grandsons Matt and Tate play in their football, baseball, and basketball games and to watch granddaughter Katheryn play softball. Daughters Shannon and Meredith moved to Manhattan, and Meredith finished her degree at Kansas State University. So for many months, all five children lived in Manhattan. We were able to watch Sydney, our granddaughter, compete in gymnastics and perform in Washington Dance Studio recitals at McCain Auditorium. Nearly every day, we had one or two of our grandchildren's events on our calendar. Whitney, our youngest daughter, was a member of the Kansas State equestrian team, earned English MVP honors, and eventually earned All-American honors on a program that ranked fifth in the nation. When she was nine, Whitney rode for the first time at Horse Crazy Day Camp and she was hooked. She became an English rider and navigated horses over three- and four-foot-plus barriers in equestrian competitions. Eventually we bought her a horse. Competitions took her to many states. At age 15, she placed ninth in the 2001 national finals. I enjoyed Whitney's competitiveness and I was so proud of her as I was all of our children. During my retirement, we started the Bill Snyder Family Scholarship—one for football and one for equestrian—in honor of our children who had participated in each sport while obtaining their degrees at Kansas State. The equestrian scholarship now goes to a female athlete regardless of sport.

On January 9, 2006, I sat with the family of Kansas Governor Kathleen Sebelius for her 2006 State of the State Address in the House Chamber in the Capitol Building in Topeka. Governor Sebelius formally recognized me as chairman of a new state-sponsored mentoring program for children called Kansas Mentors. The initiative allowed us to define existing mentoring programs in the state, define the areas they cover, help them financially, and recruit volunteer mentors for youth. Every Kansas child deserves someone he or she can look up to and learn from outside of the household. We formed an advisory board consisting of representatives of different mentoring associations across the state. I spent a lot of time making contacts with schools and encouraging them to develop mentoring programs. Then in 2007, Kathleen initiated the Wichita-based Kansas Leadership Center under the guidance of Kansas Congressman Ed O'Malley. I was asked to serve on the leadership center's board of directors. The leadership center's mission was to offer leadership development programs to foster stronger, healthier, and more prosperous communities within the state. I attended numerous state legislature and congressional meetings in Topeka. On those days, I sometimes met my good friend Max Falkenstien for lunch. Governor Sebelius gave me an office down the hall from her office in the state capitol, which I very much appreciated and used frequently.

In addition to serving as chairman of the Kansas Mentors Council and the Kansas Leadership Council, I served on the board of directors for the Kansas Leadership Center, the Natural History Museum at Prairiefire in Kansas City, and the Kansas Sports Hall of Fame. I served on the Terry C. Johnson Cancer Research Advisory Council, the Manhattan Community Foundation Board of Trustees, and the KSU Foundation Board of Trustees. I was also honorary co-chairman of the Kansas Masonic Partnership for Life, along with several other boards. I helped fund-raising efforts for the Marianna Kistler Beach Museum of Art, Hale Library, and the Kansas State University Johnson Cancer Research Center. I wanted to impact each of those positions and thus spent a great deal of time trying to do so.

A few days after Governor Sebelius graciously appointed me to serve as chairman of Kansas Mentors, I traveled to be inducted into the Missouri Sports Hall of Fame in Springfield, Missouri. I was honored to be inducted in the same class with Gary Spani, who was the first consensus All-American at Kansas State and a member of the Kansas City Chiefs Hall of Fame; legendary manager Tony La Russa; and St. Louis Cardinals great and Hall of Famer Lou Brock. But most of all, I was deeply proud, humbled, and honored to be inducted into the Missouri Sports Hall of Fame alongside Dr. Norris Patterson, who allowed me to join the William Jewell College football team in 1959 and who remained one of the most prominent people in my life. Dr. Patterson finished his 18-year career as William Jewell head coach with a 134–33–10 record and led his teams to 13 conference titles and national runner-up five times. He also touched thousands of lives, including mine.

In June, I was inducted into the Kansas Sports Hall of Fame alongside Charlie Richard, my roommate and teammate at William Jewell College. Charlie, who passed away in 1994, had a positive impact upon my life and he was inducted posthumously after compiling a 123–28–1 record during a 14-year career as head coach at Baker University. It truly was amazing to be surrounded by so many people who were so prominent in my life. Virtually all of my family was in attendance for the ceremony at John Q. Hammons Plaza in Wichita, along with Jack and Donna Vanier, Bob Krause, and Ernie and Bonnie Barrett. Max was my presenter and he said some very nice words before I took the podium. I shared with the crowd exactly what I had shared with our players over a 44-year career, including the previous 17 years at Kansas State: surround yourselves with people who could truly make a difference in your life and who genuinely want to make your life better. I closed my brief speech with one final thought: "Seventeen years ago, when I arrived in Manhattan for the first time, the media asked me, 'Why did you come to Kansas State?' And I said, 'I came to Kansas State because of the people.' And that is why we are going to stay in Kansas—because of people like yourselves across the state of Kansas who have been so very nice to our family over all of these years."

During my retirement, I engaged with people from virtually every university within the state of Kansas. I believed it was important for people to be tremendously proud to be from the state of Kansas.

On the morning of September 20, I was joined by my family; Governor Sebelius; Kansas secretary of transportation Deb Miller; and state representatives Lee Tafanelli, Sydney Carlin, Tom Hawk; and Ed O'Malley at Bosco Plaza on the Kansas State campus for the official dedication of Bill Snyder Highway. Our family gathered behind the large brown street sign with "Bill Snyder Highway" printed in white. One street sign would be erected north of Manhattan just to the north of the entrance to the Tuttle Creek Visitor's Center, and another street sign would be located just north of the Geary/Riley County line south of Manhattan on K-177. Ed, a Kansas State alumnus who introduced the bill to the state legislature to rename the highway, was very gracious. He said, "I wish every piece of legislation was as easy to pass as the Coach Snyder Highway legislation."

I jokingly added, "There was one dissenting vote: a KU graduate. I sent her a note, and she apologized. I said that both schools were awfully good, so she didn't have anything to be ashamed of."

At the highway dedication, I said that I would sign the first traffic ticket given on K-177, which was met with laughter and applause.

For hundreds of thousands of K-Staters, regardless of current residence, taking the Exit 313 ramp and driving the nine-mile stretch along K-177 toward Manhattan was like coming home. Three miles south of Manhattan on K-177 was Scenic Overlook, a popular roadside stop. Scenic Overlook offers a breathtaking view of the 8,600-acre tallgrass Konza Prairie Biological Station located in the Flint Hills and jointly owned by the Nature Conservatory and Kansas State University. Flint Hills harbors some of the last native tallgrass prairieland in the United States. Further down the highway, the white iconic "K" and "S" letters on K-Hill come into view.

The Manhattan community and the state of Kansas had truly drawn together over the previous 17 years. The K-177 highway tied it all together. It was not Bill Snyder. It was my family, all of our coaches, all of our players, all of our support staff, and all of our phenomenal fanbase. In the 1990s, K-177 increased from a two-lane highway to a four-lane highway, which symbolized the progress made by Kansas State University and our football program. The growth and energy within the Manhattan community was amazing during that time. K-Staters played a big part in why K-177 had to increase from two lanes to four. Between 1989 and 2006, enrollment increased from around 17,000 to about 23,000 at Kansas State University, and the campus featured nearly two million square feet of new construction. The city of Manhattan grew from about 37,000 people to more than 53,000. Annual retail sales increased from about $400 million to nearly $1 billion. Private donations to Kansas State increased from less than $6 million to nearly $100 million per year. Our attendance at home football games increased from 13,000 to more than 50,000. The number of hotels and hotel rooms nearly tripled in and around surrounding communities. I was told that a home football weekend generated more than $1 million in economic revenue for the Manhattan community. So it was a real honor for somebody to name a highway in my honor, knowing that the highway would likely be there for years and years. Being with my family and knowing that they had such an investment was memorable to me as were countless special friends who over the years had contributed to the overall growth of Kansas State University.

The Kansas State people had been wonderful for many years, but their feelings toward our men's basketball program appeared to become enhanced with the hiring of Bob Huggins as head coach in March 2006. Ernie Barrett and I enjoyed attending basketball practice, and Sharon and I enjoyed watching the basketball games at Bramlage Coliseum. Bob had an impressive presence about him, and his players played hard, a characteristic that remained prominent within the program when Frank Martin was promoted from associate head coach to head coach the following season after Bob accepted the head coaching position at West Virginia, his alma mater. As Sharon and I made our way to our seats in the arena prior to a Monday night game between Kansas State and Texas Tech on January 8, 2007, we passed the Texas Tech basketball team as it jogged toward its locker room. Bobby Knight stopped me, shook my hand, and said, "You did the best job ever. Even God couldn't have done what you did."

In early 2007, we scored a victory for the Kansas Sports Hall of Fame. Ted Hayes served as Kansas Sports Hall of Fame director for 22 years until he retired in 2013. The Kansas Sports Hall of Fame moved from Lawrence to Abilene in 1991 but closed its doors in 2002 due to a lack of funding. The Hall of Fame reopened in Wichita's Old Town entertainment district in 2005, following a $1.2 million fund-raising campaign and now occupies the historic Wichita Boathouse along the Arkansas River. When the Hall of Fame moved to Wichita, it needed financial help in order to remain open. I went to Topeka and spent some time with the Committee on Ways and Means, and Senate Bill No. 79 materialized out of our discussions. The State of Kansas legislature established in the state treasury the Kansas Sports Hall of Fame fund. Bill No. 79 called for three installments of $500,000 in state funding for the Kansas Sports Hall of Fame in 2007, 2008, and 2009. Ted truly was the face of the Hall of Fame and was a great athletics historian. He did a wonderful job maintaining the Hall of Fame despite its financial challenges over the years.

One of the most disheartening moments during my retirement arrived on January 28, 2007. Kansas State finished 7–6 in Coach Prince's first season. One month after the season, disruption hit the program, and several individuals were fired from their positions. That included Jim "Shorty" Kleinau. Shorty graduated from Oklahoma State in 1977 and had served as equipment manager for the Kansas State football program since 1979. Shorty (28 years), Joan Friederich (36 years), and building manager Lyle Hasenbank (35 years) were fixtures within our program and were truly invaluable to our success. Shorty had been the longest active equipment manager in the Big 12 Conference and had established the "cradle of equipment managers" in grooming six former student-managers into prominent roles either at the college or NFL level. Shorty had a loving wife, Debbie, and his life revolved around our football program. Shorty helped start our Kansas State Golden Cats program that served to involve and inform former players about the present football program. Every year, we honored one of our players with the Jim "Shorty" Kleinau Award, which was given to the player who best represented loyalty, hard work, commitment, and dedication to a common cause. Shorty truly was one of the most loyal individuals I had ever known. Sean, who served as associate athletic director for football operations, was tasked with informing Shorty that he had been fired from Prince's football staff. It broke Sean's heart. It greatly upset Shorty, and he called and asked me if I would visit him in his home. We spoke for three hours. It was hard. Fortunately, we were able to help Shorty continue his career at Oklahoma State. Their athletic department was very gracious in making arrangements for him to be on staff.

I maintained an office in the football complex, and Joan continued to assist me along with the present coaching staff. Prince was always gracious to me. His mother passed away in 2007, so we talked. I could empathize as my mother passed away when I was Kansas State head coach. But mostly I didn't want to be in the way, so I went to my office when nobody was in the building, did my work, and left notes for Joan on her desk.

After seven years as athletic director, Tim left to become the deputy commissioner of the Big 12 Conference in February 2008. Jon appointed Bob and Jim to jointly occupy the athletic director position. I respected Tim as it pertained to the coach-athletic director relationship, and we have since become good friends over the years. In May, Jon told me that he was going to retire at the end of the 2008–09 academic year. Obviously, Jon was a very good friend, and his absence would leave a void in so many ways. Kansas State ranked first among all 500 public universities with 124 Rhodes, Marshall, Truman, Goldwater, and Udall Scholarships between 1986 and 2008. Private givings rose to $100 million, and overall research funding rose to $220 million. Kansas State ranked second among land-grant universities in national professor awards. However, Jon also knew the value of football. When our football program began to take off in the 1990s, Jon saw to a greater degree the impact that Kansas State football had upon the university, community, and state. Jon came to practices and spoke numerous times to our teams. He gave luncheons for recruits during their official visits. He showed that Kansas State cared about its student-athletes along with all of the young people at the university. Once a year, Jon even put on a jersey and played touch football with our team inside our stadium. Jon was the quarterback. For both teams.

An interesting opportunity arrived prior to the 2008 season. Tom Osborne, along with many other prominent former college football head coaches, had been selected to serve as voting members for the Legends Poll, which was really an interesting concept. Each week, the organizers provided the coaches with DVDs to watch and evaluate what we deemed to be the top 25 teams in the nation. Each coach was assigned different teams, and they discussed each team during a weekly conference call. The Legends Poll appeared each week in *The Sporting News* and over the course of a few years included voting members such as Bobby Bowden, Hayden Fry, Bo Schembechler, Frank Broyles, John Cooper, Terry Donahue, Vince Dooley, LaVell Edwards, Bobby Ross, R.C. Slocum, and Gene Stallings. When Tom became Nebraska athletic director prior to the 2008 season, he asked me to replace him in the group. I wanted to do it right, so I spent a significant amount of time watching tape. I tried to embrace the entirety of my assigned teams from all standpoints and compared one team to the other. Having never really paid attention to all of those teams during my coaching career, it was a different yet enjoyable experience. I didn't have a great deal of knowledge about many of the teams, so it required a great deal of diligence. I enjoyed hearing the assessments by each coach. From a coaching standpoint, I saw certain facets within some offenses, defenses, and special teams that would have had potential to work schematically within our system when I was at Kansas State. I certainly started out serving on the Legends Poll carrying no projection about my future.

I did not know Kansas State was going to fire Coach Prince, but I knew that Jon believed that it was important to see positive steps during the 2008 season. Kansas State won its first two non-conference games and then suffered a 38–29 loss during a Wednesday night nationally televised game at Louisville. Jon and Jim Colbert apparently had dialogue. Colbert told me, "Jon wants you to come back." Then Jon asked me, "Would you be interested?" I told him that Kansas State still had a head coach and that I did not want to cause a disruption. I told Jon that I was not interested. I continued to process our conversation over the next few months. I spoke with Sharon. I spoke with our children. They all said, "If you're happy, stay retired; if you want to still coach, do it."

Yet I was comfortable and enjoying life. It was enjoyable to help others and spend more time with my family. I listed the positives and negatives of returning as head coach. It stayed on my mind. Sometimes, the answer in my heart was yes, and other times, it was no. When I retired, my family expressed sadness for me because being a head coach had been my identity for so many years, and they believed that I desired to coach and did not want to see me unhappy. So there was a conflict: they wanted to see me around more, and yet their preference was that I was happy. I began receiving a lot of input from other people, and rumors ran thick through the Kansas State fanbase. On November 1, Pat Roberts, Jon, myself, and others sat in the visitors' suite at Memorial Stadium and watched a 52–21 loss to Kansas in Lawrence. Kansas State had not beaten Kansas in three seasons, and it was disheartening to our fanbase and our administration. At the same time, our average home football attendance (45,190) was at its lowest since we expanded the stadium to 50,000 prior to the 1999 season. People said to me, "Come back." That's what Kansas State people seemed to want, and I became convinced that was how I could help them.

Bob announced the firing of Prince four days after the loss at Kansas and with three games remaining in the 2008 season. Later in the week, Jon asked me again if I would consider coming back. I told him that I was giving it some thought. Coach Paterno, who turned 82 on December 21, won the Big Ten title and said that he would continue coaching at Penn State in 2009. Coach Bowden was 79 years old and was in his 33rd season as head coach at Florida State. They had both been surprised that I had retired in the first place.

On Sunday, November 23, I told my family that I would return as head coach. They were amazing. They wanted me to do what I wanted to do. I spoke with Meredith on the phone. She said, "Yes, I'm crying tears of happiness." Sean began unpacking the boxes that contained my playbooks and staff manuals. Then I called Jon and informed him of my decision. I called Joan, Pat, Jim, the Barretts, and several others. My only regret was that I did not have time to reach out to everyone who was important to me before news broke of my return as head coach at Kansas State. By 9:50 PM, ESPN had a story on its website.

Fourteen hours later, I wore my dark suit and yellow tie, stood behind a familiar podium, and shared some familiar thoughts with many familiar faces during my re-introduction news conference in the Legend's Room at Bramlage Coliseum. I looked around the room and said, "You're probably wondering why in the devil I want to do this again."

I shared that we would care about the young people in our program. I shared that we would try to unite the Kansas State family again and that we would try to get back to the Kansas State way. The Kansas State family, to a degree, was in flux. I wanted to help. The waves had gotten high, and the water became a little rough, and the Kansas State family had been riding the waves. I wanted to be able to smooth the waters. Kansas State University was unique and Kansas State people were—and continue to be—truly special. Kansas State people were blue-collar, roll-up-your-sleeves, hard-working, lunch-pail type of people, and I fit into this kind of environment. I did not know how many games we would win, but I knew that we would quickly meet with our players, build a coaching staff, and begin the process of trying to become a little bit better every day. It was the only way I knew. I felt a responsibility to the Kansas State people to smooth the waters. We needed to get back to being a family, a caring family, a family that embraced people and cared about its people and cared about doing the right things. The question by some was whether I could relate with today's young people.

My answer was: "When I meet with our players, they are probably going to think that very question. I don't know whether they will ask it or not, but they will certainly think along those lines. I am going to answer the question before it is asked. My answer would be: if you care, I can relate to you. If you will work hard, I can relate to you. If you want to do right and be a good person, I can relate to you. If you care about academics and try to be the best student you can be, I can relate to you. If you want to do some things that are contrary to that, then I would probably have a hard time relating to you. That is the approach right now. That is what I feel. If you really care about the young people that you have, then you care about all those things that are hard. It is hard with my own family, but they know those things. They know the intrinsic values are so significant and important to me and that they should be important to them as well. They know that I don't bend along those lines."

After the news conference, I hugged all of our family members, who were seated in the front row, then I shook hands with so many people from all different arenas within the university who graciously welcomed me back, and then I went into my office. I had agreed to a five-year contract with a total compensation that would grow to $1.85 million per year. But it had never been about the money, and I never wanted a contract. I received 470 emails and text messages that day. I began making phone calls to potential assistant coaches. I called Del. I called Dana. In one week, our coaching staff was three-fourths complete.

On December 2, we loaded up the school plane for a six-stop whirlwind Catbacker reunion of sorts with Kansas State people across the state. We started at Garden City at 8:00 AM, were on the ground in Wichita at 10:00

AM, moved on to Kansas City by 11:45 AM, reached Topeka by 1:30 PM, landed in Salina by 3:00 PM, and then met gatherers in the team room at the Vanier Complex at 4:30 PM. Seeing Kansas State people always impacted me. They always showed their affection and appreciation and were very gracious people, and it had nothing to do with football. However, I saw that I was doing something that pleased them. I thought about farming communities. They worked the same kind of hours I did and they did it to feed the world. It was a hard life. If a hard rain came, everything they invested for six months sometimes went for naught. There was pain in their lives. Like football coaches, they dealt with uncertainty all of the time. To see some joy on their faces and to see something that made them happy and to feel a part of that was a pretty special feeling for me.

Thirteen hours after we began our journey across the state of Kansas, I stood in our team meeting room surrounded by Kansas State people and closed with a few important thoughts: "Let me tell you once again: you're the heart and soul of Kansas State University, and I thank you so very, very much for all that you have done in the past and all that you will do. I wouldn't ask you for a nickel. I ask you to come to our ballgames with your families. Bring your friends, support these guys. Boo me, support them, and we'll work at it. Somehow, someway, we'll try to get this thing so that it really works in the way that you were accustomed to it working. Thank you very much."

Then I went into my office. I had a dozen phone calls to make and enough paperwork to last me until summer. My goal was to get home by midnight. I missed that goal.

Our coaching staff materialized by the second week of December. It featured seven individuals who had been a part of our program in previous years with defensive line coach Mo Latimore (26 years), associate head coach Sean (15), co-offensive coordinators Del (13) and Dana (12), wide receivers coach Michael Smith (13), defensive ends coach Joe Bob Clements (8), and co-defensive coordinator Chris Cosh (three). We brought in co-defensive coordinator Vic Koenning from Clemson and offensive line coach Charlie Dickey from Utah and retained Ricky Rahne from the previous staff to coach tight ends. Our coaching staff featured 205 total years of experience.

With the February 4 national Signing Day less than two months away, our coaching staff worked diligently to become reacquainted with high school and community college coaches across the state of Kansas. They all remembered how we had always made the state of Kansas so important to our program and they welcomed our return. Our coaching staff was on the road virtually every day to Colorado, California, Arizona, Mississippi, Florida, Missouri, Texas, Oklahoma, Illinois, Louisiana, Georgia, and, of course, throughout the state of Kansas. It required time to become fully indoctrinated in what had taken place, what had been done, who was out there, and what they were all about. It was a monumental task and required much time to get everything into place. We believed that we identified some talented youngsters and projected how they might further develop in our program. Several recruits remembered the Kansas State of the past and were excited about the possibility of helping the program become successful again. On national Signing Day, I stated, "Ask me in four years, and I'll have a better idea regarding the success of this signing class."

Although the national recruiting services contended that we had the worst signing class in the Big 12 Conference, we strongly felt otherwise. We signed numerous young people who left a mark on our program by the time they finished their eligibility including: running back Daniel Thomas, safety Ty Zimmerman, fullback Braden Wilson, junior college transfer defensive end Meshak Williams, wide receiver Tramaine Thompson, right end Travis Tannahill, linebacker Blake Slaughter, offensive tackle Cornelius Lucas, safety Emmanuel Lamur, and running back John Hubert. Each of these young men played a significant role in our success.

Kirk Schulz was hired as president of Kansas State University on February 11 and officially started his seven-year tenure on June 15. Kirk had served as dean of engineering and vice president for research and economic development at Mississippi State. We didn't have that casual interaction like Jon and I had, which I understood. Kirk also had many university-wide issues that required his attention. Kirk felt that his job was to hire an athletic director, and the athletic director's job was to work with the coaches while Kirk tended to other arenas of the university. Kirk's first major decision as incoming president arrived when he hired John Currie as athletic director on

May 14. John had worked for several years as an administrator within the Tennessee athletic department.

John was a very business-oriented individual and wasn't somebody that I felt like I could sit down with for coffee. Our relationship was professional over the course of his seven years in Manhattan. I was uncomfortable with some of the elements that John wanted to alter in the player-oriented programs that we had utilized for years within our football program. I was concerned about the salaries of our assistant coaches. Structurally, John reassigned the duties of some of our staff, including Sean. Whereas Sean had answered to me for years upon years, John altered the internal structure, which meant that Sean now reported to John instead of to me. John altered our program to a certain degree through a variety of changes. John later told me that he made some positive changes in his professional life after leaving Kansas State. We have spoken on a few occasions since he left Kansas State. However, during my initial meeting with John, he informed me that he was going to change some things within my contract, and I was not pleased with all of the changes. I told him, as I had told the other administrators, "I don't need a contract."

Within our football program, we had to learn to shield ourselves from those things over which we had no control. That included our finances in 2008. Although the Kansas State athletic budget was now at $42 million, it would likely show a $2 million deficit due to declining donations, which put on hold renovations to our football stadium. To me, the answer to all of the problems was for us to do everything that we could in order to become an improved football team. It was basically the same process as in 1989. My anxiety was centered around: can we rebuild the process? Can we begin the process of improving our players, our coaching staff, and the program? There were a variety of ways to do things, and we did things somewhat differently than the previous staff. Sometimes change was harder for some than others. Everybody had to become acclimated to the necessary changes.

I sat down and spoke with every player on our team individually. I wanted to get to know these new young people in our program and learn about their families, their academic and career goals, and their values. People asked me if young people were different than they were in 1989. I didn't think there was too much of a difference. An air of instant self-gratification permeated virtually all segments of our society, but we couldn't paint all young people with such a broad brush. Each one had his own strengths and weaknesses. We all did. When we gained a feel for what was truly significant in their lives and their sensitivity toward school, football, life, and personal well-being, we found a plethora of similarities to our previous players over the years.

Although we inherited 17 starters, including seven on offense, eight on defense, and two on special teams, I remained uncertain about how well we could get things back to the way they had been for years and years. Even though many of our coaches were already well-versed with the program, we had to bring a team of players, a coaching staff, and a support staff together. We worked diligently to get everybody on the same page, so it wasn't totally unlike 1989 in that respect. However, we headed into the 2009 season in vastly different standing than we did in 1989. Kansas State had finished 7–6, 5–7, and 5–7 over the course of the three seasons during my retirement, so at least returning players had experienced success to a certain degree. Kansas State had won one game in three seasons prior to our arrival in 1989 when we started at rock bottom. We developed our program upon strong core values and those 16 Wildcat Goals for Success. That wouldn't change. And we would also go back to our traditional uniforms that everybody in the nation identified as Kansas State football.

Everybody had opinions. The media had become consumed with printing mostly opinion as opposed to simply writing the news as it happened. Somebody told me that Tom Dienhart, a national college football writer for Rivals.com, said, "Resurrecting Bill Snyder is hardly the answer to what ails Kansas State. I don't care if he's tanned, rested, and ready after a three-year sabbatical. At 69, Snyder is not the answer to the Wildcats' problems." There were other doubters as well. Some things we simply couldn't avoid. Our players read the newspapers and websites. Somebody was always prone to comment on a critical story so-and-so wrote. I had put a disclaimer on newspaper clippings long ago and learned not to read them during the season.

However, I was aware that a majority of people outside of the Kansas State family and our program carried low expectations for our team. We were picked to finish fifth out of six teams in the Big 12 North Division for the 2009 season. In our final game that year, we were playing Nebraska on national television for the right to represent the North Division in the Big 12 Championship Game.

"I was never a star player and wasn't a big factor my last two years after two heart operations, but Coach Snyder honored me with the toughness award my senior year, and he told me that no matter the fight he knew I would be in the corner swinging. He taught me to be both mentally and physically tougher than my opponent or any situation in life. I'm forever grateful to Coach for instilling that trait into me. To this day, every time I get to see Coach, he welcomes me with arms wide open."

—Kaleb Drinkgern, Kansas State offensive tackle, 2008–11

CHAPTER 20

BUILDING ANOTHER CHAMPION

"The respect that I have for Coach Snyder and his ability to build a program and sustain it is second to none. You can tell his fingerprints are all over the Kansas State program because it has sustained success over the long haul, and I think that's my admiration for what he's built and how he's done it. It's amazing how successful he was for such a long period of time. He is giant in our profession."

—Matt Campbell, Iowa State head coach

We turned off the lights inside our locker room shortly before 7:00 PM on December 1, 2012. This had always been one of the final segments of our pregame routine. For the next few moments, we sat in silence and we visualized success. We believed that visualizing positive results along with the objectives for the game—envisioning what you had to execute and seeing yourself doing it successfully—was always important, but it was perhaps even more so on this particular night. Fourteen days had passed since we had suffered a 52–24 loss at Baylor in Waco, Texas, which ended our perfect season after 10 consecutive wins and consequently cost us a chance to possibly play for a national championship. That was behind us. Our final regular-season game against No. 23 Texas in front of our fans on Senior Night demanded our full focus. We sat in darkness for a few moments and envisioned success. We believed that if we played focused, performed to our capabilities, and stuck together as a family, we would end the night victorious and reach a special accomplishment in the form of the 2012 Big 12 Championship title. We had a marking on the floor to our locker room entryway. It simply read, "CROSS THE LINE." When we crossed the line, nothing else mattered except how we played over the course of the next 60 minutes. The phrase "CROSS THE LINE" meant to all of us—players, coaches, and staff—don't cross that line to the battlefield if you haven't invested everything in preparation for the game and weren't willing to give it everything you had.

As was the case every season, we did not envision winning 10 or 11 games. We always said that we had the capabilities of being a successful football team and cautioned our players that just because we had attained a degree of success the previous season did not guarantee our success the next season. We had to go back to the beginning, and it began with our 16 Wildcat Goals for Success. Within the scope of those 16 goals lies the true keys to a great season: a genuine commitment to unity, unselfishness, team effort, and attitude centered on what was best for the team, how to deal with success, and how to overcome failures.

Our climb began when we returned prior to the 2009 season, and we incurred some setbacks along the way. We were building and climbing the ladder again. We weren't nearly in the position we had been in when we first arrived in 1989. These players had experienced some degree of success, so we were on much more stable ground. But it was a process to get our new players in the program to gain an understanding of our system within the program itself and to reacclimate those players who had previously been with us to our system. It required time to accomplish those tasks.

From our 6–6 record in 2009 to our 7–6 record in 2010, we gradually became a better and a closer football program. In 2009, we took our first two opponents for granted and consequently won narrowly against Massachusetts (21–17) and lost at Louisiana Lafayette (17–15). We appeared unprepared in losses at UCLA (23–9) and at Texas Tech (66–14). And yet after our loss to the Red Raiders, we turned around one week later and beat a very good Texas A&M team 62–14, which marked our most points scored and largest margin of victory in a Big 12 Conference game since 2002. It also marked the greatest scoring differential over the course of two games in Big 12 Conference history. In our final game of the season, we played Nebraska for the right to represent the North Division in the Big 12 Championship Game. It reiterated to us that we had control over our level of performance and over our successes and failures. It wasn't about which team had the most five-star players but which team's players were better prepared, best motivated, and played the best and hardest together as a true family. It wasn't about talent but rather about caring enough, commitment, focus, discipline, execution, and togetherness. We talked so much about spirit, finishing, starting the game strong, and leadership. We demonstrated each of those virtues at times but not nearly consistently enough in order to sustain success and lost to a very good Nebraska team 17–3.

We made incremental growth during the 2010 season and started strong with four straight victories, including a 31–22 win against UCLA in the season opener. But we took our performance for granted and were embarrassed by No. 7 Nebraska (48–13) at home. After we won in impressive fashion at Kansas (59–7) while scoring the second most points by either team in Sunflower Showdown history, we lost four of our final six conference games and we needed the fourth quarter to win at North Texas (49–41) to have a winning season and qualify for a bowl game.

Running back Daniel Thomas, who accounted for nearly 40 percent of the total touches and 40 percent of our total offensive yards during his All-American senior season, recorded perhaps the finest game of his career with a career-high 269 rushing yards on 36 carries and two touchdowns at North Texas. Daniel had success taking the direct snap out of the Wildcat formation several times during the season and in particular during that game. At 6'2" and 235 pounds, Daniel was a tough and physical running back from Hillard, Florida, who had come to us from Northwest Mississippi Community College and fit well in our system. Daniel was very quiet and friendly and he was a strong runner and had good movement and good speed for his size. Daniel recorded 1,265 rushing yards and 11 touchdowns to earn 2009 Big 12 Offensive Newcomer of the Year and improved to rank eighth nationally with 1,585 yards and 19 touchdowns to earn second-team All-American honors his senior season. He finished ranked in the top three in nine different statistical categories in our program's history and was a prominent part of our success during his two seasons.

We finished the 2010 season with our most victories (seven) since 2003 and were invited to play Syracuse in the inaugural Pinstripe Bowl at Yankee

Stadium in Bronx, New York. It was the first NCAA bowl game in the Bronx since the 1962 Gotham Bowl. I grew up a New York Yankees fan and had watched Mickey Mantle and other greats play minor league baseball games in St. Joseph, Missouri. I always had strong feelings about the Yankees. Today, I still have a case with six baseballs signed more than 50 years ago by Yankees greats. I have an autographed Mickey Mantle jersey along with large autographed photos of Mantle and Roger Maris. The transportation logistics to and from the stadium were less than desirable due to traffic, but I was fine playing a football game inside such an historic venue. I believed it would be a memorable experience. As it turned out, that was a vast understatement.

Just 28 seconds into the bowl game, Daniel broke off a 51-yard run for a touchdown, marking the quickest touchdown that we had ever scored in a bowl game. Sadly, all anybody on our sideline will ever remember was the highly controversial penalty flag for excessive celebration that took us out of the extra-point and two-point range to tie the game. One of our top wide receivers, who was playing in his final game, caught a 30-yard touchdown to bring us to within 36–34 with one minute, 13 seconds remaining in the fourth quarter. Shortly after crossing the goal line, he dropped the ball, raised his right arm, and quickly gave a military-style salute toward the Kansas State fans seated behind the back of the end zone. He said that he saluted out of respect for his teammates and our fans. However, he received a 15-yard unsportsmanlike conduct penalty for his gesture. That meant the line of scrimmage for our point-after attempt moved from the 3-yard line to the 18. Of course, we had to go for a two-point conversion attempt to try and tie the score. Our pass fell incomplete, and Syracuse ran out the clock. Our players were devastated after the game. Everybody was upset. I was upset. I was upset with the call. I rewatched the tape over and over again and still to this day conclude that the salute was not meant to taunt our opponent. It was meant for and directed to his teammates and fans. In the locker room, I reiterated that we couldn't fault one instance because we had so many opportunities to win the game. Any of us could have made a play to win the game. The outcome of the game was not the fault of a single individual. Afterward, I refused to discuss the penalty with the media, though I had plenty that I could have said about it.

One of my smartest hires arrived prior to the 2010 season when Chris Dawson, a veteran of more than 20 years in the field of strength training, joined our staff as director of strength and conditioning. Chris had previously earned the National Collegiate Strength and Conditioning Coach of the Year Award and trained more than 30 players who had been selected in the NFL draft. Chris had a major impact on our program. We shared the same philosophies and were proponents of not only developing strength, but also developing disciplined, physical athletes who possessed the necessary endurance to sustain their performance level through all four quarters. Chris was a hard worker who carried high expectations for himself, his staff, and our players. He was great with players but at the same time held them accountable.

The 2010 season featured a pair of tragedies that far exceeded the game of football. On March 24, Elijah Alexander, a 1991 team captain who was a part of "The Foundation" of our program, died of multiple myeloma, a bone marrow cancer. He was just 39 years old. On April 19, I received a phone call. Dylan Meier, one of our team leaders and a starting quarterback toward the end of our first tenure, passed away after he fell from the top of a trail while hiking in Arkansas' Ozark National Forest with his parents and two brothers. Dylan, a native of Pittsburg, Kansas, was the first Kansas native to start at quarterback for us. He meant so much to so many people for so many different reasons. More than 1,000 people attended his funeral. Dylan was just 26 years old. He had been full of life, always well-liked by his teammates, and was a kind soul with many interests outside of football. Had he been around today, he would've already toured the world twice and would've been on every ocean liner and climbed every mountain. He had such an amazing life ahead of him. His death was very painful for his family and for our football family. The news of Elijah and Dylan's deaths was tremendously painful for me and those associated with our program.

Shortly after, the Big 12 Conference also effectively lost some of its family. For about 15 months, rumors circulated regarding conference realignment. Although there had been grudges and feuding between a few schools, nothing became official until June 11, 2010. That's the day that the regents for the University of Nebraska voted unanimously to join and begin competition as a member of the Big Ten Conference in the 2011 season. Soon after, Colorado announced its departure for what became the Pac-12. Texas A&M followed suit and announced on August 31, 2011 that it would join the Southeastern Conference in 2012. Missouri announced on November 6 that it would also join the SEC in 2012. All of the talk was out there. There was dialogue that other Big 12 teams could possibly leave, the Big 12 might dissolve, and Kansas State, Iowa State, Kansas, and Baylor might have to relocate to perhaps the Mountain West or Big East.

The actual desire of some Big 12 schools to switch conferences might have been overstated in some cases. The schools that left probably felt that there was some instability within the conference and felt that moving to another conference would benefit them. I publicly stated from the outset that I believed that the schools that chose to leave had made a mistake. I heard from many Nebraska fans who suggested otherwise. Certainly, Nebraska's decision to leave was neither positive for the Big 12 nor for its program. At least, I didn't believe it was. When we were the Big 8, we had the No. 1, No. 2, and No. 3 teams in the nation almost every year in Nebraska, Colorado, and Oklahoma. Since its inception in 1996, the Big 12 had proven itself as one of the very top conferences in the country.

I believe collegiate athletics has become primarily about dollars and cents. *USA Today* reported that $2.9 billion was generated by the Power Five conferences for the 2019 fiscal year, and the University of Texas ranked No. 1 nationally in generating more than $223 million in total revenue while the University of Oklahoma ranked eighth at $163 million in 2018–19. In July of 2021, Texas and Oklahoma notified the Big 12 they intended to leave the league after the Big 12 media rights deal expires on June 30, 2025, at which time they are scheduled to join the Southeastern Conference. That would give the SEC the first 16-team super-conference in college athletics. Schools depart the Big 12, and things change, but we've seen it all before. Will our conference be the same? No, and I understand that, but Kansas State University will play football games, and our fans will still be among the most passionate fans in America. Each time there has been a change within the conference, Kansas State has landed on its feet just fine. I don't see a reason why Kansas State can't do the same this time around.

When Colorado, Missouri, Nebraska, and Texas A&M left the Big 12, it was difficult for the league. Everybody in our conference had to think, *What do we do if another school pulls the plug?* Everybody also had different opinions about which schools they would invite to the Big 12. The Big 12 became a 10-member conference in 2011. In 2012 TCU and West Virginia replaced Texas A&M and Missouri in the conference. I believed that the Big 12 should have added four schools because 12 teams was the appropriate number for our conference and because it also fit Kansas State to have two six-team divisions and a conference championship game. I was not in favor of the elimination of the Big 12 Championship Game between 2011 and 2016.

Throughout the realignment discussion, we knew that we just needed to focus on our own football program. We couldn't allow rumors to disrupt our preparation for the 2011 season. A lot can change in college football coaching. I was saddened when Bobby Bowden was forced to leave Florida State after all that he meant to that university, the state, and the football program. Over a 33-year career, Bobby won two national titles, 12 Atlantic Coast Conference championships, and finished 14 consecutive seasons ranked in the top five in the final Associated Press poll. Bobby coached his final game at age 80 in the 2010 Gator Bowl. He finished with a 377–129–4 overall record. His absence left a void in college football. As I entered my 20th season at Kansas State in 2011, only my good friends Joe Paterno (46 years) and Frank Beamer (25 years) had spent more years as a head coach at their current Power-Five conference school. There were 120 Football Bowl Subdivision head coaches in the country. Entering the fall, they had served as a head coach at their current school for an average of 4.2 years, and 88 head coaches had spent fewer than five years at their current program. Only 16 head coaches headed into the 2011 season with double-digit years of experience at their current school. Four of those head coaches were in the Big 12: Mack Brown (13 years), Bob Stoops (12), Gary Pinkel (10), and myself. The Big 12 had more active head coaches with double-digit tenures than the Pac-12 (one), the SEC (one), and the Big East (one) combined.

One thing remained consistent since we arrived in Manhattan in 1989: the desperate need in our society for young people to develop strong values, to learn how to work hard, to develop strong self-discipline, to make commitments, to develop and live by what became our 16 Wildcat Goals for Success, and to accept responsibility for doing things the appropriate way. All of those values remained the same. Had there been a difference over the years in the acceptance of those values? Yes, there had been a dramatic difference. Some people might have believed that the intrinsic values were not important. However, those values were the spine of our program. Our desire was always for our players to develop and carry those intrinsic values throughout their lives after leaving Kansas State.

The value of family was always important to us. We began to use the slogan "FAMILY" shortly after we arrived, and the university eventually adopted "FAMILY" as its slogan as well. The family concept was crucial to our program in 1989 simply because there were very few behind us. It took a while for that to grow. We just lacked the support. Family wasn't just about 100 players in a locker room. Everybody within our program was a part of that family. That's why I asked our players to stop in and say "Good morning" or "Good afternoon" to Joan Friederich, Teresa Williams, and others in our office. I always explained to our players that our task would be infinitely more difficult without these people within our program. That family extended into our stadium as 13,000 fans grew into 50,000. When we played baseball at 12 years old, most of us had family in the stands. When our players went onto the field to play, they had family in the stands, and it wasn't just immediate family—it was everybody there. There was a reason why we renamed it Bill Snyder Family Stadium. It was because so many people, including our fans, were a part of that; they were a part of our family.

Shortly after the 2011 season began, we enhanced our concept of "FAMILY" even more prominently in the form of the black capital letters "FAMILY" painted across a block of wood that our players proudly carried onto the field before each game. Before long, Kansas State students began bringing their own "FAMILY" block of wood to our games, and eventually dozens of students began showing off their own blocks of wood bearing one of our 16 goals to the TV cameras during our games. Our block of wood began in the hands of Mitch Holthus as he stood inside the ballroom at the Manhattan Holiday Inn a couple of weeks before we beat Texas A&M 53–50 in four overtimes during the longest game in Big 12 history. Mitch is a passionate K-Stater and a very good friend. He is known across the country as a Hall of Fame announcer, who is entering his 27ᵗʰ season as Voice of the Kansas City Chiefs in 2021, but Mitch got his start by serving as Voice of the Wildcats at Kansas State for 13 years. He always became very animated and brought out a lot of emotions when he spoke to our players. That night in the hotel ballroom, our players wore their customary purple warmups and surrounded Mitch, as he detailed the theme—bring the wood—and emphasized the importance of doing everything "the Kansas State way." "You should thank God every day because this is a place where you learn how to build—how to build your lives, how to build your careers, and how to build your souls," Mitch said. "When you signed with this school, your life changed because you came to a place where you get to earn it. When you play at a place like this and play for a man like that, it changes your life. If you study scripture, Moses only parted the Red Sea once. Coach is doing it twice. When you play for a man like that and at a place like this, you learn how to do it right because you learn how to build. I love this 2011 team more than I have loved any team in a long time because you're one of the old-school Kansas State teams. You're doing it the Kansas State way."

Mitch presented one block of wood to a team member representing each class—senior safety Tysyn Hartman, junior quarterback Collin Klein, sophomore linebacker Tre Walker, and freshman center B.J. Finney, and he gave one block of wood to Michael Smith, who represented the coaching staff. Each of the individuals who received a block of wood was directed to write their individual goals and team goals on the block of wood, keeping one side of the block blank. At our team meeting on Monday, each of those players would present their block of wood to another team member in their class who they felt best "brought the wood" during our most recent game. Our players continued to pass along the block of wood within each class throughout the season. At the end of the season, each class wrote down everything that they had accomplished as a class on the side of the wood block that remained blank. It was an effective team building exercise. It was about developing and strengthening our family. Family was more than a word. It permeated the Kansas State family throughout the nation. It certainly served as the backbone of our team.

Prior to each game, we gave our players the opportunity to earn the prestigious honor of carrying the FAMILY block of wood onto the field. We always had announced weekly awards to recognize the achievements of players in our program, and this particular item, which served as a trophy of sorts, further enhanced our players' desire to succeed both on and off the field. Based upon a point system derived from classroom achievements, behavior, attitude, and on-field performance in the previous game, players earned the distinction of carrying the FAMILY block of wood, the American flag, the Fort Riley flag, the state of Kansas flag, and the Powercat flag. We wanted to carry those flags out of the locker room each game to recognize our country, state, university, and Fort Riley. It carried a sense of honor among our players and staff.

Over our time at Kansas State, we invited numerous people to address our team. Sean had become good friends with Eric Stonestreet, a 1996 Kansas State alumnus who had won an Emmy Award for Outstanding Supporting Actor in a Comedy Series in 2010 (he won the award again in 2012) for his role on ABC's *Modern Family*. Eric spoke to our team on the field after a practice early in the 2011 season and he shared his love for Kansas State and for our football program. Eric grew up in Kansas City, Kansas, and his parents, Vince and Anne, raised him with a strong value system. Our players benefitted from hearing Eric share his journey, which actually began when he auditioned for a small role in a play at Kansas State and then turned it into a highly successful career because of his passion, perseverance, and commitment to his craft. Eric reiterated the importance of goal-setting with our players and he made a positive impact upon them. For him to be so famous, he was humble and he enjoyed talking to our players. Over the years, Eric returned to Kansas State to attend football games when his schedule permitted and he enjoyed speaking to fans at many of our bowl pep rallies. I'm unsure if there are many actors or public figures in the country who are more passionate about their alma mater than Eric. It seemed like whenever he was on a TV talk show, he always found a way to mention Kansas State during the conversation. He is a down-to-Earth guy and a good friend.

At the start of the 2011 season, we were picked eighth in the Big 12 preseason poll with a first-year full-time starter at quarterback in Collin.

We were a lightly regarded team in a talented conference. We carried ample motivation as a family.

We demonstrated our togetherness as a family numerous times during the season, but perhaps no stronger than when our defense stopped the University of Miami inside our 2-yard line on four straight plays to secure a 28–24 win at Sun Life Stadium in Coral Gables, Florida. On the road, with the game on the line, and with our backs to the wall as Miami faced first and goal from the 2, our defense collectively executed one of the most remarkable goal-line stands in college football history. Tre tackled quarterback Jacory Harris just short of the goal line on fourth down with 49 seconds remaining in the game. If there is one thing that draws people together better than that feat, I have yet to see it. Those 11 guys on the field had come together as one—period. There was a photo of Collin in the Cat Pack, jogging off of the field arm in arm with his teammates, and Collin's teammates appeared to be helping hold him up as we came off of the field. Collin had bloody elbows, blood and dirt on his jersey, and truly epitomized why Kirk Herbstreit ranked him as the No. 1 throwback player in college football. Collin completed 12-of-18 passes for 133 yards and two touchdowns and he ran aggressively with 22 carries for 93 yards and one score. He simply refused to be beaten. We entered as 12-point underdogs and we refused to lose. After the game, we had a feeling that this was a special win, but we knew that we had ample room for improvement.

The following week, we faced No. 15 Baylor, which had a very fine quarterback in Robert Griffin III and averaged 594 total yards while scoring 50, 48, and 56 points in its first three games. We knew that Arthur Brown had talent, but he demonstrated his athleticism while intercepting a pass and chasing down Griffin a few times in our 36–35 win at home. Arthur was the Michael Bishop of our defense. He had the skill and ability but had to learn our defensive system. We turned him loose and he continued to grow, becoming an outstanding player. Arthur and younger brother Bryce Brown, along with Chris Harper, had been highly touted high school prospects in Wichita. Arthur (Miami), Bryce (Tennessee), and Chris (Oregon) all wanted to attend out-of-state, high-profile programs and discovered that it wasn't all that they believed it would be. All of them contacted me and wanted to come home and play at Kansas State. They had to work their way up the ladder, but they earned their way. Arthur was Big 12 Defensive Newcomer of the Year and then Big 12 Defensive Player of the Year, recording 100 tackles his first year and 101 tackles the next, becoming a first-team All-American linebacker and NFL draft pick. Bryce was a skilled running back and became an NFL draft pick. Chris finished ninth all time in receptions (123), 10th in career receiving yards (1,734), and seventh in career receiving touchdowns (12), and also was an NFL draft pick.

Our victories at Miami and against No. 17 Baylor moved us to No. 20 in the AP poll for the first time since 2004. We were taking steps, and the national ranking was tangible evidence of our improvement. The fact that we were picked as the underdog in nine of our games during the season provided an abundance of spirit, and we rallied around that underdog identity. Being the underdog had been the nature of Kansas State football. We had to be special to compete each week under those circumstances and fight above it all. A feeling of insult lingered in our players' minds. We started 7–0 for the first time since 1999 and won four straight times as the underdog. By the end of the season, we were near the top of college football in single-digit victories. We won eight games by three, four, one, seven, seven, three, four, and seven points. Odds simply suggested that a team would be prone to lose one or more of those. We overcame back-to-back losses against No. 11 Oklahoma (58–17) and at No. 3 Oklahoma State (52–45) and outlasted Texas A&M 53–50 in four overtimes. To me, it was one of the greatest games of our time. We showed perseverance and fight. We didn't give in. I told our players in the locker room, "Had it gone 15 overtimes, I'm confident we would have played equally as hard in every one of those overtimes, and we would have persevered in the end."

The togetherness was demonstrated in the photo of Collin's fifth rushing touchdown—a one-yard score when he plunged through the offensive line and into the end zone to end the game. There were a mountain of our players, and then there was Collin on his elbows with the ball across the goal line. We truly won together.

Picked during the 2011 preseason as the eighth best team in the Big 12, we finished with a 10–3 record, ascended to No. 8 in the final BCS standings, and finished second place in the conference behind Oklahoma State. We were the only team in the top 15 of the final BCS standings that didn't receive a single vote in either of the two major polls at the start of the season. That team, which doubters believed entered with marginal talent and was expected to struggle mightily in the meat of the conference season, played deeper into January than any team in Kansas State history and finished ranked at No. 16 in the final AP poll. With the word "family" goes the word "trust," and that's what our players learned to do. They learned to have great faith and great trust in each other, and that led to that family environment for which they took such great pride.

We earned a team award for our achievements. That was the vernacular I used in addressing our team as I shared honors for Big 12 Coach of the Year, Woody Hayes National Coach of the Year, and the Associated Press National Coach of the Year with our coaches, support staff, and players. When we had returned in 2009, there was a feeling that we could move forward. People in our program believed, they bought in, and they wanted to be a part of something special. They wanted to succeed and they were hungry for success. In 1989, we had 13,000 fans that felt that hunger. We came back a second time, and our fans wanted to experience it again. The hunger had never left. Now our program was recognizable again, and people could easily say it was one of the better programs in the country. For it to happen once, to make that climb, it enhanced expectations and recognition when we returned that if we put all of the right pieces together, it could happen—again.

Every year is different. I expressed that to our team numerous times as we prepared for the 2012 season. We returned 17 starters, including eight on offense, six on defense, and three specialists. It included Collin, who earned first-team All-Big 12 honors as an all-purpose player and tied an FBS quarterback record by rushing for 27 touchdowns in 2011. It included Tyler Lockett, who earned 2011 Big 12 Offensive Freshman of the Year honors and first-team Walter Camp All-American honors while setting the Big 12 and Kansas State record in averaging a nation-leading 35.2 yards per kickoff return. It included Arthur, who earned 2011 Big 12 Defensive Newcomer of the Year honors as his 100 tackles were the most by a player since 2006. It also included cornerback Nigel Malone, who earned second-team Walter

Camp All-American honors after he recorded seven interceptions, which tied for third most in the country.

Although we were picked sixth in the Big 12 preseason poll, we felt strongly about the potential for our team if we could eliminate distractions and remain focused one day at a time. Our players responded favorably, and consequently we were able to achieve a 10–0 record for our second best start in program history. But it wasn't as much about the win-loss record as it was about the climb we made to reach our first ever No. 1 ranking in the BCS standings. Our conference opener at No. 6 Oklahoma was a true test as we entered as a 15-point underdog against a program that had won 78 of its last 81 home games and was 14–0 against top 25 opponents in Norman, Oklahoma, since 1999. We had not won in Norman since 1997 and we had never beaten a team ranked this high on the road. We gained momentum early when linebacker Justin Tuggle caused Oklahoma quarterback Landry Jones to fumble the football, and linebacker Jarell Childs caught the ball off a bounce and rolled into the end zone for a 7–3 lead. Collin's five-yard touchdown run with 13:16 remaining in the game gave us the lead for good at 17–13. The crowd of 85,276, the eighth largest gathering ever to watch a game in a stadium where the Sooners' mystique seemed infallible, largely fell silent—aside from a patch of purple that roared in excitement over the twist of fate at Memorial Stadium.

We were underdogs once again during our second Big 12 road game when we visited West Virginia in Morgantown, West Virginia, for the first time. We were ranked No. 4 in the BCS standings behind Alabama, Florida, and Oregon yet had to remain focused. We knew Dana Holgorsen was a talented coach with a talented staff, Geno Smith was a very fine quarterback, and West Virginia was picked to finish second in the Big 12 during its first season in the conference. We also knew that West Virginia carried a reputation for very active and demonstrative fans at 60,000-capacity Milan Puskar Stadium. I called around to many different coaches to discuss their experiences playing at West Virginia, and everybody told me their fans were rowdy and loud. The meeting between No. 4 Kansas State and No. 17 West Virginia was billed as the national game of the week, and the media focused on the matchup between Collin and Geno, who were both considered Heisman Trophy candidates. Energy ran thick inside the stadium. However, we had the good fortunate of somewhat quieting the stadium. Collin threw for a career-high 323 yards and three touchdowns and ran for four touchdowns during our 55–14 win against the Mountaineers. I was pleased with our preparation and execution as we scored on our first eight possessions, including seven touchdowns. We held Geno to 143 passing yards and one touchdown and two interceptions. By the time Collin threw his final 20-yard touchdown to Tyler late in the third quarter, it became easy to see our Kansas State fans. Our fans had taken over a virtually empty stadium.

We held TCU to its fewest points ever in a home game under Gary Patterson in a 23–10 victory on November 10, which marked our 10th straight victory. Two days later, we rose to No. 1 in the BCS standings followed by No. 2 Oregon, No. 3 Notre Dame, and No. 4 Alabama. During our first team meeting of the week, we addressed the attention from outside of our program, corrected our mistakes from watching videotape, and broke for a nice dinner. On Tuesday, Collin was greeted with a surprise while speaking to 500 children at a Manhattan elementary school. He was presented with a plaque as one of 22 members of the Allstate AFCA Good Works Team, which recognized his community service efforts in the Manhattan community. On Thursday, Collin was featured on the cover of *Sports Illustrated*, and the headline read in all caps: "27 THINGS YOU NEED TO KNOW ABOUT THE BEST PLAYER ON THE NATION'S BEST TEAM." Collin was considered by many as the favorite to win the Heisman Trophy. Throughout the season, I had no doubt that Collin would handle any attention appropriately. Collin was a mature, humble young man who handled positive recognition in the right way and projected his acclaim to his teammates.

I couldn't point to anything in particular, but I was concerned during the course of the week prior to our game at Baylor. We were perhaps a little bit more matter of fact than I preferred, but we remained diligent in our preparation. Phil Bennett was now Baylor's defensive coordinator. That also concerned me. But we were a disciplined group, led the nation in both turnover margin and fewest penalties, and held nine of our first 10 opponents to fewer than 25 points. Then everything came crashing down. Our 52–24 loss with one game remaining knocked us off the top spot for a possible berth in the national championship game. Our players and coaches were in utter disbelief. They were devastated. I told our players that I didn't have them prepared well enough for the game. It was a difficult game to accept.

Two weeks later, we sat silently in darkness inside our locker room shortly before 7:00 PM and prior to our ceremonial Senior Night player introductions. In a few moments, a crowd of 50,912 would cheer for each of our 27 seniors as their names were announced and they joined their families on the football field. But at the moment, all of our preparation, soul searching, determination, and commitment had brought us to this point of sitting in darkness, envisioning positive results. When the locker room lights came on, I offered some parting words: "Family! Let's be a family tonight! Let's do it for the seniors and let's do it for every single guy in this room. All right men, it's time to go. Let's get this done."

Shortly before 11:00 PM, the song "We Are The Champions" rang out across our stadium, fans raced onto the field, players dumped a bucket of ice water over the back of my windbreaker, and I hugged my friend Mack Brown near midfield after our 42–28 win against No. 23 Texas. We captured a share of the 2012 Big 12 Championship with Oklahoma but secured our conference's automatic Bowl Championship Series bowl berth by virtue of our tiebreaking win against Oklahoma. Although we were one of just nine BCS programs to win at least 10 games in each of the past two seasons, one fact perhaps best illustrated our climb: in going from six wins (in 2009) to seven wins (in 2010) to 10 wins (in 2011) to 11 wins (in 2012), we were the only program in the AP poll to improve upon its win total in each of the past four seasons. It was a feat in Big 12 history shared only by Oklahoma, which improved upon its win total each year between 1997 and 2000.

Immediately following the game, Collin Klein, Arthur Brown, B.J. Finney, Ty Zimmerman, and Tre Walker joined me on a podium to hoist the Big 12 Championship trophy during a brief ceremony on the field. I spoke to our fans on a microphone: "You represent what it says up there on the stadium. We talk about family, and you're a big, big part of it."

We entered our first BCS bowl game ranked No. 5 in the BCS standings and set to face No. 4 Oregon in the 2013 Fiesta Bowl on January 3 at University of Phoenix Stadium in Glendale, Arizona. The crowd of 70,242 featured an estimated 40,000 Kansas State fans, which tied for the second largest Kansas State contingency in bowl game history. Following our 35–17 loss against Oregon, I addressed our players in the locker room. I thanked them for their hard work and I reminded them that no one outside of our program expected us to win the Big 12 title and represent our conference in a BCS bowl game. Our 27 seniors finished their careers with 34 victories, which represented the most victories by a senior class since the 2003 senior class won 39 career games. Our 11–2 record represented one of the greatest seasons in our program's history. We had been fortunate to win 11 games in six previous seasons. All of those seasons were special. However, no one outside of our program predicted that we would come close to winning 11 games in 2012.

Although we long carried the national stigma of being a team without stars, Collin finished third for the Heisman Trophy. Collin finished with a 22–6 record as a starting quarterback to tie Michael and Ell Roberson for the most career wins. He also finished an impressive career ranked in the top five in 26 different game, season, and career statistical categories. In addition, six of our players earned All-American honors: Arthur, Ty, Anthony Cantele, Tyler, Nigel, and Travis Tannahill. We also had the most players in the conference earn first-team All-Big 12 honors by the league's coaches and first-team honors by the AP. When I was named 2012 Bobby Dodd National Coach of the Year and Big 12 Coach of the Year, I told our team that the awards weren't about Bill Snyder. They were about something greater.

They were about family.

"The consistency, hard work, and leadership that Coach Snyder provides for us is pretty special. To pick one or two things that totally define Coach Snyder would cut it short. The competitive drive can consume a person, and they might lose sight of what's really important, but that isn't the case with Coach Snyder. Nobody wants to win more than he does, but his balance with how much he cares about people while still wanting to win is pretty amazing, and I greatly admire it."

—Collin Klein, Kansas State quarterback, 2009–12

CHAPTER 21

THE CLOSE OF
ANOTHER CHAPTER

"Bill Snyder has been such a fixture in college football and has meant so much to me. I've been so honored and proud to be able to compete against him, be in our Big 12 meetings with him, and see him around. He's had such an impact on our sport and our profession. He's meant so much to everyone in the Big 12 and in college football. His legacy has been written and will live on for a long, long time."

—Dana Holgorsen, University of Houston head coach

Moments after the 2012 Heisman Trophy ceremony in New York City on Saturday, December 8, 2012, Collin Klein, one of three finalists for the top honor in college football, took a moment out of one of the most prominent nights in his life to graciously try and help sustain the success of our football program. Collin got on the phone with a junior college quarterback named Jake Waters. Jake earned 2012 National Junior College Offensive Player of the Year honors while leading undefeated Iowa Western Community College to its first national title. In his sophomore season, Jake broke Cam Newton's NJCAA completion percentage record (73 percent) while passing for 3,501 yards and 39 touchdowns to just three interceptions. Although Alabama and Texas showed late interest in Jake, he had narrowed his list of possible Football Bowl Subdivision destinations to Penn State and Kansas State. Jake had arrived in Manhattan on Friday, the day before Collin talked to him from the Heisman Trophy ceremony.

Tyler Lockett, who had built a relationship with Jake over the course of the previous few months, served as Jake's host during his official recruiting visit that weekend. Collin and Tyler were always positive ambassadors for our program, and I believe that they had gained Jake's trust.

Jake was going to announce his decision that following Thursday, so Del Miller, our co-offensive coordinator and quarterbacks coach, drove three hours to visit Jake and his parents at their home in Council Bluffs, Iowa, on Wednesday night. Obviously, we were pleased that Jake ultimately chose to join our program. We had a strong history with quarterbacks, and many of them had gained national acclaim. Although Jake was a dynamic and accurate passer, we believed that he possessed the capacity to become a complete run-pass quarterback in our system. Jake became the first junior college transfer since Michael Bishop in 1997 to enter our program and immediately start at quarterback and he gradually flourished into a very fine leader and talented player. Jake finished his two-year Kansas State career ranked No. 1 all time in total offense per game (260.2 yards), passing efficiency (155.62 rating), and completion percentage (64.1 percent) and ranked No. 2 all time in passing yards (5,970) and touchdown passes (40) in our program's history.

At a time when we basically reconstructed our depth chart following the departure of 27 seniors after the 2012 season, our program's facilities underwent construction as well. It began with the implosion of the Dev Nelson press box on December 15, 2012. The five-story press box featured 22 suites and served us well since its construction in 1993 and yet over a span of nearly 20 years had gradually become one of the smallest and least modern press boxes in the Big 12 Conference. That changed with the West Stadium Center, which ran the length of the football field and featured 250,000 square feet at a cost of $90 million. The West Stadium Center was built by a joint venture of Mortenson Construction Company and GE Johnson Construction Company, which was owned by K-State alum Jim Johnson. It included 41 suites, 35 loge boxes, and 750 club seats; an upgraded media, broadcast, and operations level providing enhanced television and technology capacities; a university lounge and event space; a student-athlete performance cafeteria center; and the Hall of Honor, which recognized many of the outstanding players in our program's history. Workers moved the last of the furniture into the West Stadium Center just a few days before we opened the 2013 season at home against North Dakota State.

Hours before our season opener on August 30, I joined Sharon, our five children and their spouses, all of our grandchildren, and many dear friends outside of the main entrance to the West Stadium Center for a brief ceremony. The Kansas State athletic department pulled the sheet off of a 12-feet tall bronze statue of myself. The statue captured me posed with my left hand on my hip while wearing a windbreaker, turtleneck, khakis, and Nike Cortez shoes while holding a felt-tip pen and my notepad in my right hand. Sharon and the children had worked behind the scenes with the sculptor, who completed the 1,800-pound statue in six months. More than one year had passed since Tim Weiser first approached me about the athletic department's desire to construct the statue, and I originally requested that my wife and all five of my children stand alongside me on the statue. As a compromise, the base of the statue featured bronzed handprints of each of my immediate family members. I was humbled that our athletic department had felt strongly about constructing such a monument that would greet Kansas State people as they entered Bill Snyder Family Stadium.

Prior to the 2013 season, I also signed a five-year contract extension through the 2017 season, which included a clause that I could retire at any time without penalty. We had won 170 total games, which ranked fourth among all FBS coaches, and our winning percentage (.833) over the previous two seasons ranked fourth among Power-Five conference programs behind Alabama (.916), Oregon (.880), and LSU (.880). National publications referred to me as a "wizard" and "silver-haired fox," but there was no magic or secret formula to our success during our first tenure or during our second tenure. Our success was a product of commitment and hard work by so many people. Athlon Sports ranked the top head coaches this way: 1. Nick Saban, Alabama (159–55–1 in 17 years), 2. Urban Meyer, Ohio State (116–23 in 11 years), and 3. Bill Snyder (170–85–1 in 21 years). I appreciated being included in such esteemed company. At 73 years of age, I was the oldest active head coach in major college football, which wasn't as significant to me as it perhaps was to others. Although I was in good health, I understood that many young perspective players might invest their future upon my decision to remain as head coach. I wasn't naive to the fact that other football programs probably called attention to my age when they recruited against us for prospective players. I believed that some young people hesitated to join our program due to my own uncertainty regarding how much longer I would be on the sideline. I always told the truth to our recruits, and sometimes my honesty came back to affect our recruiting.

Hours after the statue unveiling, we went out and suffered a 24–21 loss to North Dakota State, the defending FCS national champion. We entered the game with 56 wins in our last 58 home non-conference games and left the field with the first season-opening loss by our staff since 1989. North Dakota State appeared highly motivated, and we appeared unmotivated and we perhaps took our performance for granted. Afterward, I accepted the responsibility of not having our team properly prepared for the game.

It proved to be one of several early setbacks. We began the season at 2–4 and opened the Big 12 schedule with three straight defeats—at Texas (31–21), at No. 21 Oklahoma State (33–29), and against No. 15 Baylor (35–25)—for the first time since 2004. Along with our inconsistent start to the season arrived a quandary at quarterback. For the first time in our program's history, we had a quarterback pass for 1,000 yards and another quarterback rush for 500 yards in a season, and they accomplished this feat after only six games. Jake had 1,036 passing yards and four touchdowns and five interceptions and he had 151 rushing yards and two touchdowns. Sophomore Daniel Sams rushed for 118 yards and one touchdown at Oklahoma State, and his three-touchdown, 199-yard rushing performance against Baylor marked the second most rushing yards ever by a Kansas State quarterback.

Whether Jake or Daniel took the snaps, our capacity for offensive success began with our offensive line, which carried an identity centered around physical play up front under offensive line coach Charlie Dickey. Charlie joined our initial coaching staff in 2009, and his responsibilities grew to include run game coordinator in 2016 and co-offensive coordinator in 2018. During Charlie's 10 seasons on our staff, our offensive linemen earned three All-American honors and 23 All-Big 12 honors, including 11 first-team selections. Charlie was the best offensive line coach that any offensive lineman in the country could be around. He taught good technique, and our offensive linemen believed in him. They were invested in the program and wanted to succeed. Charlie was such a hard worker and did everything the right way and was very demanding. He knew how to be demanding and productive at the same time. He built a strong relationship with his players, and they all respected him and knew that he demanded their best each and every day. Charlie was very beneficial for our program. Our offensive line enhanced our improvement in 2013 behind five returning starters in left tackle Cornelius Lucas, left guard Cody Whitehair, center B.J. Finney, right guard Keenan Taylor, and right tackle Tavon Rooks. Four reached the NFL as rookies—Cornelius (with the 2014 Detroit Lions), Cody (with the 2016 Chicago Bears), B.J. (with the 2015 Pittsburgh Steelers), and Tavon (with the 2014 New Orleans Saints). They opened lanes for senior running back John Hubert to gain 1,000 rushing yards and for Daniel to run for 800 yards as well and gave Jake time in the pocket to utilize his capabilities in the passing game.

Meanwhile, the on-field chemistry between Jake and Tyler evolved over the course of the season. After Tyler had career highs with 13 catches for 237 yards in the Big 12 opener at Texas, he exceeded that performance with 12 catches for 278 yards and three touchdowns against Oklahoma. Tyler finished his junior season with seven 100-yard receiving performances. We all hoped and expected that Jake and Tyler would enhance their chemistry during their two years together. They were players who really cared and improved their capabilities within the team confines. Both were gifted. Tyler ran quite well and gained many of his yards after making the catch, and Jake had a nice touch in delivering the ball downfield. One day after practice, I looked out my office window and saw that Jake and Tyler had remained on the field for extra practice and to perfect their timing and execution on various routes. That became a daily event.

After our 2–4 start to the season, we had a come-together meeting centered around our team's discipline and on identifying specific issues and their impact upon our collective performance. We did an extremely poor job of coaching early in the season and consequently did not play to our capabilities and fell short in winnable games. We had to accept the responsibility to become a more disciplined team and to have an understanding for how our quarterbacks could impact our team in a positive way. We had to come together or go home. Our players chose to not give up and commit to that daily improvement, which they had gotten away from.

We won six of our final seven games to finish with an 8–5 record and capped it with a 31–14 victory against Michigan in the 2013 Buffalo Wild Wings Bowl. It proved to be the greatest mid-season turnaround by a team in Big 12 Conference history. Our players possessed ample motivation and a strong desire to beat a traditional powerhouse like Michigan, and we had the best final week of bowl practice that I could remember. Then we went out in the game and scored on our first three possessions—all touchdown passes from Jake to Tyler—while our defense surrendered its fewest points in a bowl game in 19 years.

I was happy for all 26 seniors who were able to finish their careers with a memorable victory and I was pleased that senior safety Ty Zimmerman, the quarterback of our defense, could be a part of it. Ty came to us from Junction City, Kansas, as a quarterback. He finished his career joining Jaime Mendez as the only safeties in our program's history to earn All-American honors in two seasons and as the only player in our program's history to earn all-conference honors in four consecutive seasons. He handled his success just like Jaime did by going to work focused every day, providing leadership, and making plays on the field. Ty wasn't heavily recruited, but we believed that he had good range, ran reasonably well, and had a great attitude. He finished third all time with 13 career interceptions. However, Ty had to overcome adversity during his final two seasons. First, Ty injured his left fibula late in the 2012 season. Then he injured his right fibula late in the 2013 season. Ty was cleared to play in the bowl game, and for him to have the opportunity to finish his career on the field was extremely important to him.

However, when defensive end Ryan Mueller chased me 15 yards down the sideline and poured a Gatorade bucket full of water over my head with 2:25 remaining in the game, it was perhaps a little bit less than appropriate. Although I knew Ryan's gesture had good intentions, I just believed that it was a premature celebration. After the game, I said, "I saw the water bucket coming, but I'm too old to get out of the way."

I was pleased for our players and fans that we were able to finish our season in a positive way. But inside, my distaste for the overall state of college football grew. Less than an hour before our bowl game, my good friend Mack Brown brought an end to his 16-year career at the University of Texas when he coached his final game in the Alamo Bowl. Mack was awfully close to longtime university president Bill Powers and athletic director DeLoss Dodds, but DeLoss announced his retirement in October after three decades at the helm. In November, Texas hired Steve Patterson as its new athletic director. On December 14, Mack announced a surprise resignation. Mack led Texas to the 2005 national championship and he guided Texas to back-to-back 11-win seasons, nine consecutive 10-win seasons, and 10 consecutive nine-win seasons for the first time in history. He had a 158–48 record and was 98–33 in Big 12 games. He had one losing season at 5–7 in 2010 but went 8–5, 9–4, and 8–5 with three bowl games in his final three seasons.

Apparently, the university administration succumbed to pressure from high-dollar boosters, which was a big surprise for Mack, and he agreed to resign. It reinforced my belief that college football was getting way out of whack. It was a high-dollar business, and we head coaches made too much money, and a majority of head coaches could never win enough games to keep everyone happy. Mack had tremendous success, but boosters were upset because he didn't win a national championship every year. Boosters put millions of dollars into college football programs, but the boosters are not completely at fault. The college football system is at fault. It's our college football system that creates such an environment. I told Mack that he shouldn't stay in a program that didn't appreciate him. I knew Mack would land on his feet. He became a successful college football TV studio analyst, then went back to North Carolina as head coach. Mack coached North Carolina for 10 seasons prior to his 16-year tenure at Texas. He and his wife still owned a home in North Carolina. I knew it would be the perfect fit for him. Prior to Mack's return to North Carolina, the program had won just five games in 2017 and 2018. Mack won 15 games during his first two seasons in 2019 and 2020 and led North Carolina to a bowl game both years.

My feelings about the state of college football continued to decline heading toward the 2014 season, and I shared some of my thoughts publicly during a summer news conference. I believed that college athletics, football in particular, had changed dramatically over the years. We had sold out. We had become all about dollars and cents. The concept of college football no longer had any bearing on the quality of person or the quality of students. It irritated me that Mack lost his job after a career of positively impacting the young men in their program. A university could have a great institution and provide a great education but have a poor football team and consequently the university would be lightly regarded. Meanwhile, the popular national perception existed that if a university had a successful football program, then it was a great university regardless of the academic successes. College is supposed to be about education. That doesn't demean college football itself. Fans and players enjoy college football, and it's a game that allows young people to learn so much about life skills and build a value system, but our current society has made college football bigger than what it should be within the realm of higher education, which is truly unfortunate.

I had strong feelings about all of our athletic programs at Kansas State, but my family particularly invested themselves in football and equestrian. Whitney, our daughter, earned All-American honors while competing on the nationally ranked equestrian team between 2006 and 2009, and each year our family had extended an athletic scholarship to a member of the equestrian program. We now provide yearly scholarship aid to a female student-athlete and a football student-athlete. We loved what riding horses had done for Whitney growing up and all of the young ladies on the team, and so many of them came to Kansas State because of their love for horses and equestrian. The fact that the equestrian team had 90 members each year made the program ideal from a Title IX perspective. So we were surprised and pained when our athletic department announced in October 2014 that it would drop equestrian as one of its 16 sponsored sports in 2016. The week of our athletic department's announcement, the equestrian team moved to No. 3 in the National Collegiate Equestrian Association rankings, which represented the highest ranking in our equestrian program's history. Dropping equestrian made absolutely no sense to me, but John believed that it was the appropriate move and he said that finances factored into the decision. I offered to fund the equestrian program myself and I knew that I could acquire the proper financial help to sustain the program. I can't say that the decision to end the equestrian program didn't strain our relationship, but John did what he believed was in the best interest of the athletic department. The decision just made no sense to me.

I always tried to do what was in the best interest of my family, my friends, and Kansas State University, but it turned out that my desire to support a very good friend conflicted with the interests of our university and somewhat created a stir across the state of Kansas. In late October, I took a moment to sit down and discuss the many fine attributes of Senator Pat Roberts in front of a video camera. Portions of my comments appeared in a statewide television re-election campaign commercial prior to the November election. I was unaware that Kansas State employees were forbidden from supporting a friend on camera. I didn't know the guidelines. We all vote. I didn't see why any Kansas State professor couldn't say that he supported a good friend running for an office. I didn't believe there was an issue. Sue Peterson, our director of governmental relations, and John contacted me on behalf of the president regarding the interview, and I publicly apologized for the situation at a news conference.

I also heard from the Big 12 Conference on a separate matter. The Big 12 took issue with my gameday attire. John notified me that the Big 12 would no longer allow me to wear my customary bowl game windbreakers on the sideline. I kept windbreakers from several of our bowl games, and each windbreaker featured a patch that recognized that particular bowl game. I always grabbed one of those windbreakers out of my locker without paying attention to what it said on it to wear on gameday. The Big 12 was concerned that I promoted some bowls that were no longer affiliated with the conference. I understood their reasoning, but I had worn my windbreakers for years without any objection.

I always wanted to feel comfortable on the practice field and on the sideline and I kept my attire and routine consistent. I wore the Nike Cortez shoe from the very beginning. I simply liked the shoe, and it was comfortable. When I learned that Nike might discontinue the Cortez shoe, I had Nike send me several pairs to last me many years. I still have half a dozen pairs that I never wore. Through the years, many people began to identify myself with the Nike Cortez shoe. I didn't try to make a fashion statement. It was all about comfort and consistency, and I just wore whatever was conveniently available.

For me, consistency also included my diet and exercise habits. In order to make the most of every minute, I tried to walk the treadmill in my office between five and seven days per week while watching videotape. I sometimes never missed a single day over a three-week span. That routine remains consistent today at my home. My doctors were never fans of my eating habits because I ate one meal per day, and it was usually late at night after I had left the office. Sharon loved to cook and is a very good cook. For years she prepared a plate for me and left it in the refrigerator each night for me to reheat and eat before bed. During the 2014 season, somebody spotted me at the Taco Bell drive-thru on Claflin Drive late one night, which became a newspaper story. Although I didn't visit Taco Bell nine times per week, I did go through the drive-thru sometimes because not too many drive-thrus were open at midnight. My order was always consistent as well. I kept it simple: tacos and burritos.

Every aspect of our program centered on consistency. We had a 56-item checklist that we referred to when we addressed our players in the locker room prior to each game. We emphasized playing hard every snap; fundamentals; eliminating turnovers, penalties, and busts; making big plays; taking pride in individual and collective performance; winning the line of scrimmage, winning the fourth quarter, and winning the kicking game; what this particular game means to our seniors; outhitting and being tougher than our opponent; maintaining focus, intensity, and concentration; remembering our team goals and what we have yet to achieve; what records we could achieve during this particular game; our current standing for a bowl game; our record in home games; why we still haven't gained respect; preseason magazine predictions; bulletin-board material from our opponent and media comments during the week; dedicating this particular game to someone; getting the crowd into the game; playing smart; leadership; winning individual battles; visualizing success; playing with great effort, emotion, and execution; playing as a family; and never giving up. I didn't address every item, but those that seemed most applicable for that game.

Our pregame routine on the field remained consistent for more than 20 years. Our players practiced our pregame routine prior to each season as we familiarized our new players with our tradition. We wanted to ensure that all of our players properly executed each period of our pregame routine. One facet of our pregame routine became particularly popular among our Kansas State fans. Some people referred to our collection of pregame songs as "Snyder Music." The process of creating our original list of songs began soon after our arrival at Kansas State and officially debuted in the 1993 season. Whenever I heard a song that delivered a motivational or inspirational message within its lyrics, I asked Scott Eilert, our video director, to add that particular song to our growing music collection, which we played over the speakers in our football stadium prior to each game and during the week of practice. Most of the songs on our playlist and the order of each song remained consistent over the years. The timing and duration of each song was significant, as the songs corresponded with a particular segment of our on-field pregame activities:

Kansas State Football Pregame Music Playlist

Song	Band	Duration
"Beautiful Day"	U2	4:06
"Lay Your Hands on Me"	Bon Jovi	5:58
"The Secret of My Success"	Night Ranger	3:47
"Unbelievable"	EMF	3:30
"Where the Streets Have No Name"	U2	4:46
"Right Now"	Van Halen	5:21
"Welcome to the Jungle"	Guns N' Roses	4:31
"Thunderstruck"	AC/DC	4:52
"New Sensation"	INXS	3:39
"All Fired Up"	Pat Benatar	4:08
"We Ready"	Archie Eversole	2:39
"We Will Rock You"	Queen	2:02
"Eye of the Tiger"	Survivor	4:07
"Livin' on a Prayer"	Bon Jovi	4:11
"Even Better Than the Real Thing"	U2	3:42
"Days Like These"	Asia	4:06
"One Vision"	Queen	4:02
"Stand Up (for the Champions)"	Right Said Fred	3:12
"Proud of the House We Built"	Brooks & Dunn	3:47

We instituted many things that evolved into traditions such as "FAMILY" and pregame music, but we also took such great pride in so many other aspects of our program. One of those areas was our Kansas State walk-on tradition. Although we offered Tate Snyder, my grandson, a scholarship when he arrived in 2010, both of my sons began their Kansas State careers as non-scholarship players. Sean walked on and earned the starting job at punter and became a 1992 consensus All-American. Ross transferred from Butler County Community College and walked on as a running back in 1997. We obviously loved our players, but these were special individuals as well as my children. Yet I was harder on them than I was with anybody else in our program because I didn't want anyone inside of our locker room to think that my children received special treatment. I wanted all of our players to realize that my children had to earn their way as well. I was told that it was the first time in college football history that a head coach had a son on his coaching staff while also coaching his grandson, which was special for me and our family.

Our walk-on program began from the very outset because we only had 47 players on scholarship. A majority of our non-scholarship players were Kansas natives who just wanted an opportunity to develop as players and people within our program. I carried a special appreciation for the plight of walk-on players, as I began my own college football career long ago as a walk-on. We researched both scholarship and non-scholarship prospects thoroughly in order to identify their value system, work habits, and passion and commitment to become the best student, player, and person that they could be in our program and after graduation. We spoke with parents, siblings, grandparents, principals, counselors, teachers, head coaches, assistant coaches, secretaries, and custodians about every young person that we pursued. We wanted prospects that would be committed to climbing the ladder and who possessed an appropriate skill level as well. We followed prospects in all of their competitive endeavors. Whereas many major colleges were focused on signing a finished product, we rarely pursued the five-star athletes. Most of our prospects, walk-ons in particular, had neither received a great deal of attention from major colleges nor had reached their full potential. As coaches, we projected how they might develop and could potentially contribute during their time in our program.

We never had a top 10 recruiting class, but we still proved ourselves to be national contenders. I often questioned the validity in categorizing one prospect as a three-star and one as a four-star. I knew that I couldn't distinguish the two just by their on-field performance. But I thought that I knew a lot about value systems and the capacity to improve. To me, it wasn't about the rankings of signees that came into our program but how well they developed over their time at Kansas State. If they committed to daily improvement and if they did all of the things necessary to become a better person, a better student, a better player, and a better family person every single day, then they likely experienced positive things at Kansas State that they could carry on into their lives. The growth of our players didn't surprise me. If players invested themselves appropriately and adhered to the process, then they became better. When players sustained their growth over four or five years, they became very productive players and contributed heavily to the program's success.

I walked off of the practice field with a player during an in-season practice shortly after our arrival at Kansas State. He was a walk-on fourth teamer who had played in our previous game. He said, "Coach, I just want to thank you for giving me an opportunity to be a part of this program and to have the opportunity to get on the field." He said that he had previously never played in a college football game. He told me, "We walk-ons had never been recognized in such a way. Before you were here, the non-scholarship players dressed in a separate locker room and wore hand-me-down equipment. Now we feel like we belong."

We always ensured that all of our players were treated equally. We always addressed scholarship and non-scholarship players the same way in our meetings and on the field. Walk-ons perhaps carried a special built-in motivation because they knew that we would give them an opportunity if they worked hard and fully committed themselves to the steps necessary in order to achieve daily improvement. During my pair of tenures, 40 walk-ons became starters in our program. Six walk-ons went to play in the NFL—Sean, Michael Smith, Rock Cartwright, B.J., Jon McGraw, and Jordy Nelson. Eight walk-ons earned All-American honors, and 18 walk-ons earned all-conference honors during their careers at Kansas State.

Our 2014 team was unique due to the fact that four of our eight team captains were former walk-ons, including All-Big 12 linebacker Jonathan Truman, All-American defensive end Ryan Mueller, and defensive back Weston Hiebert, and B.J. Finney, an All-American center. It was believed to be the largest number of former walk-ons to serve as team captains in our program's history. They provided excellent leadership for us along with fellow team captains Tyler Lockett, Jake Waters, Dante Barnett, and Curry Sexton. We continually had more walk-on players earn scholarships than any other program in the country.

The season was unique for another reason as well, as Andre Coleman came in to replace Michael Smith as wide receivers coach when Michael left to join Bret Bielema at Arkansas. Collin Klein also joined our program as assistant director of recruiting and defensive quality control coach. Collin left briefly to serve as quarterbacks coach at Northern Iowa in 2016 before returning to our staff as quarterbacks coach the following year. We promoted Collin to co-offensive coordinator and quarterbacks coach and promoted Andre Coleman to offensive coordinator in 2018. We had eight former Kansas State players on our staff in 2014, including Sean, Andre, Collin, Dana Dimel, Mo Latimore, Blake Seiler, Zach Hanson, and Ben Kall.

On the field, it was in our hands to be a 10- or 11-win team in 2014. When Daniel chose to transfer to McNeese State during the offseason, it put the ball firmly in the hands of Jake, and we began our season with a 7–1 record. Our lone loss over that stretch was a 20–14 defeat to No. 5 Auburn. Our other key game during the first half of the season was at No. 11 Oklahoma. It was interesting because over the summer I had been with Bobby Stoops at the Country Stampede annual music festival near Manhattan. Bobby introduced me to his friend, Toby Keith, an Oklahoma native and big Oklahoma football supporter. We went into Toby's tour bus and visited for a while. Toby seemed like a really nice guy. I felt strongly about our chances heading into Norman, Oklahoma, and we came out with a 31–30 victory, becoming the first program since 1999 to defeat the University of Oklahoma two times in Norman. Barry Switzer called me and asked if I would swing by his house in Norman after the game. He said that he would be standing outside to greet the bus. Barry had been very gracious over the years and made the comment, "He's not the coach of the year. He's not the coach of the decade. He's the coach of the century."

I was humbled by his comments toward me because they came from an individual who was probably as prominent as any coach in the country during the century. Barry always said what was on his mind, so I knew his words were sincere. On our way to the airport after our victory over Oklahoma, I directed our team busses toward Barry's house. Sure enough, Barry stood in his front lawn with a big drink in his hand and saluted us.

What delighted me as much as our win were the words the airline stewardess said over the intercom as we descended to Manhattan Regional Airport. She said, "I just want you to know that you are by far the most polite group of young men who have ever flown with us." Her words meant a lot, and they were words I had heard several times. It goes back to our 16 Wildcat Goals for Success and the value system that we instilled into our players. It's a part of being a good person. It's why we have our players take the time to write a quick thank you note to the hotel housekeeper who serviced their room for their hard work every time we stay in a hotel. At the end of the day, each housekeeper might have 50 or more thank you notes. It was important that they realized how much we appreciated their service.

One week after defeating Oklahoma, we beat Texas 23–0, which marked our first shutout in history against the Longhorns and our first shutout against a Big 12 team since 2003. Our student section chanted, "We own Texas!" after we won for the sixth time in the last seven games against the Longhorns, which was an impressive stretch for any team in the country against the University of Texas.

I was pleased with the progression of our players over the course of the season. One of the top playmakers proved to be Curry Sexton, a senior wide receiver who had come to us from Abilene, Kansas, as a grayshirt. Over his first three seasons, Curry had 50 catches for 564 yards. He finished his senior season with 79 catches for 1,059 yards and five touchdowns. At a time when we needed someone to step up to take some of the pressure off of Tyler, Curry stepped up in a prominent way. He finished with the third most receptions by a player ever in a single season, trailing only Jordy and Tyler.

By the end of the regular season, we were ranked No. 9, but we suffered a 38-27 loss at No. 5 Baylor. That meant that our three losses during the regular season were against No. 5 Auburn, at No. 6 TCU, and at No. 5 Baylor. However, I was particularly concerned after our loss at Baylor because we as coaches didn't utilize many of the plays that we had invested many hours practicing all week. I met with our coaches on Sunday after the game and shared with them that it was highly important for all of us to be on the same page. We needed to truly improve our performances as coaches. I believed there was some unrest among our coaches, but it all came down to responsibility and accountability. I was never going to fire anyone, but it was my responsibility to ensure that we all handled our responsibilities as coaches in an appropriate fashion.

When we met as a staff prior to our game against No. 14 UCLA in the Alamo Bowl, I was concerned that there was an overconfidence that would affect our performance on the field, perhaps an assumption that certain things would or might not take place. We trailed 31-6 at halftime. I counted 28 points that we left on the field. We had 25,000 Kansas State fans at the game and were being beaten so badly. When we went into the locker room at halftime, I wrote two words on the dry-erase board: "YOUR CHOICE." I told our team at halftime that ESPN announcers had called one particular bowl team "quitters" earlier in the day. We had to decide if we wanted to be recognized as quitters. I told our players that if they weren't prepared to fight to take off their uniform and stay in the locker room. We came back and fell just short in a 40-35 loss in the Alamodome. I was so very proud of how they responded in the second half.

Fittingly, our final score of the 2014 season was a 29-yard touchdown pass from Jake to Tyler with 1:21 left in the game. It marked the 178th time that Jake had completed a pass to Tyler in their two years together. It made them the top quarterback-wide receiver duo in our program's history.

Tyler, a consensus All-American, recorded an Alamo Bowl-record 13 catches for 164 yards and two touchdowns while also amassing an Alamo Bowl-record 249 all-purpose yards. He finished with 106 catches for 1,515 yards and 11 touchdowns to trail only Jordy for the best season by a pass catcher in school history. Tyler finished No. 1 all time with 249 receptions for 3,710 yards and 29 touchdowns, passing each of the previous records established by his father Kevin Lockett during the 1990s. Tyler finished third in Big 12 history with 6,586 all-purpose yards and averaged a remarkable 17.3 yards on 380 career touches.

What the Lockett family did on the football field went without saying. It is an amazing family. We talk about intrinsic values and people who represent those 16 Wildcat Goals for Success, and the Locketts did just that. All of them had outstanding character, academic success, and did things the right way.

Starting with Kevin (1993–96), then younger brother Aaron (1998–2001), and then onto Tyler (2011–14), the Locketts were all All-Americans and were a part of 114 of 187 career victories by end of the 2014 season. The Locketts were a part of four of our seven 11-win seasons, played in a total of 12 bowl games, and Kevin (1997 Kansas City Chiefs), Aaron (2002 Tampa Bay Buccaneers), and Tyler (2015 Seattle Seahawks) all were drafted by NFL teams. The Lockett family combined for 603 catches, 9,142 receiving yards, and 69 receiving touchdowns at Kansas State. They collectively averaged 15.2 yards every time they caught a football. In all, they combined to produce 13,655 all-purpose yards during their time in our program.

I knew John and Beatrice Lockett, Kevin and Aaron's parents, well, and they are magnificent people. It was never difficult for me to understand why Kevin, Aaron, and Tyler were already such fine people when they arrived at Kansas State and why they remain that way to this day. They were raised so well. They were quality young men in every aspect.

The 2014 season marked the end of a chapter in so many ways.

"There's really no way to describe Coach Snyder's impact on my life, but it can almost all be tied to the Wildcat Goals he created his first year. His treatment of walk-on players was also really powerful. Before Coach Snyder, walk-on players had separate locker rooms, had to share lockers, and had to use outdated equipment. When Coach Snyder arrived, any new player to the program couldn't tell the difference between walk-on and scholarship players because Coach Snyder treated us all the same. We were one family with one goal, and that was to turn around the program."

—Joe Boone, Kansas State linebacker, 1988–91

CHAPTER 22

COACHING PHILOSOPHIES

"One of the great honors of my career has been the opportunity to share the field with Coach Snyder on two occasions. I will forever remember after losing to K-State in 2017 that I received a note from coach encouraging me and our team. He is the epitome of class, dignity, and doing things the right way. I hope in some small way I can continue carry on his legacy by coaching and winning the right way."

—Matt Rhule, Carolina Panthers head coach

Coaches are in a very precarious profession. People judge us in terms of wins and losses. That goes with our position. Coaching can be uncomfortable in that respect, particularly when a team loses. However, I believe that, even though people judge us in terms of wins and losses, success and a lack of success come in many different forms, and the result on the scoreboard doesn't necessarily define our success. If we truly have a genuine interest in young people, if we care about their intrinsic values and principles, then we in our own right will have a successful program because we're directing young people to understand what it takes to be successful in all areas of life, have the desire to do so, and do the right things. There is sometimes a fine line between winning and losing, but guiding a program based upon principles and values is paramount. When young people become receptive to the idea of making daily improvement in all areas of their lives and fully investing themselves in the process of improving a little bit more each day, they enhance their chances of experiencing collective success each week. Over time, the virtue of consistent growth can elevate a program.

When we arrived at Kansas State University prior to the 1989 season, I was cognizant of the fact that no person on any university campus was better compensated than the head football coach. If I was a faculty member, I understandably would have said, "Why is he making that kind of money when I'm a professor making between $30,000 to $50,000 per year and have to share an office?" One of our initial efforts entailed educating our faculty about our football program and our commitment to shaping the lives of young people on and off the football field with education being at the top of the list. Kansas State University had nine different colleges (College of Agriculture; College of Architecture, Planning, and Design; College of Arts and Sciences; College of Business Administration; College of Education; College of Engineering; College of Health and Human Sciences; Kansas State Polytechnic; and College of Veterinary Medicine), and I asked each of our assistant coaches to serve as our liaison with each college. Our assistant coaches and I reached out to the dean, assistant dean, and faculty members within each college and remained in contact with each college throughout each year, including the summer. We shared information about our football program while also gaining an education about each college. Our program built relationships within our academic community and gained their support. I personally dealt with any issues or concerns between academics and our program. I sent a state-of-the-program letter to all of our faculty several times per year and detailed all of our many program-oriented activities geared toward the overall development of our young people. We stressed the importance of academic performance to every person in our program. We enriched their college experience by implementing various programs dedicated toward helping the Manhattan community. Our faculty had not previously been aware that our players went into the community and visited retirement homes, hospitals, and worked with children within the community. Our VIP "Very Important Person" program allowed our players to serve as big brothers to at-risk youth. We taught the children the principles and values of our program, brought them into the Vanier Football Complex, provided them with positive direction, and emphasized the importance of education.

I invited different faculty members from each college to watch football games with their families inside our stadium suite. That was special to them.

I invited a college dean to be a guest on each of my weekly television shows because I felt strongly about promoting education. This platform allowed each dean the opportunity to educate our viewers about the many positive virtues within their academic programs. I hoped that the appearance by these deans might spark an interest in high schoolers and parents as they consider an academic concentration within our university. I believed that our efforts enabled us to build the strongest relationship between a football program and university faculty in the country.

Our assistant coaches also built strong bonds with the parents of our young people. Our assistant coaches called the parents of every player in their position group once per month during the entire calendar year. I also contacted the parents by phone, mail, and in person. Over the years, I received numerous phone calls and correspondence from parents who expressed gratitude for our diligence in maintaining constant communication. We sometimes visited the home of a recruit whose older brother played football at a different major college. When we sat down and promised the recruit's parents that we would continually call and update them on their son's performance on and off the field, often the parents said, "We are so glad you will call us each month. We've kind of lost contact with our oldest son. Nobody from that football program ever calls us."

People always asked me, "What do you do after football season?" My answer was always the same: I worked just as hard as I did during the season. Between August and January, I was normally in my office 16 to 18 hours per day, seven days a week. And when I wasn't traveling during the offseason, I was in my office navigating a to-do list that could stretch into the ensuing offseason. I believed that maintaining my work habits and adhering to a consistent daily schedule allowed me to set an example for our assistant coaches and our players. I always encouraged our assistant coaches to not only accept responsibilities, but to also seek out additional responsibilities. I was fortunate to be around many assistant coaches who shared good ideas and demonstrated the capacity to make an incredibly positive impact upon our program. I believed that success was predicated upon the collective efforts of all of our assistant coaches and our support staff, and it was an all-encompassing, around-the-clock process throughout the year.

So often as coaches, we can fall prey to narrowing our focus solely to the X's and O's of football. When I served as an assistant coach, I consumed myself with X's and O's, fundamentals, and taught our players to be the best that they could be in all areas of their lives. However, I lacked the concept of seeing the global picture within the program. I learned from experience that a coaching staff must invest itself in more than the X's and O's in order to achieve success. Our assistant coaches and support staff at Kansas State held myriad responsibilities. When I was a walk-on freshman football player at the University of Missouri many years ago, nearly every program in the country did not have strength coaches or academic advisors. Over my tenure as a head coach, I witnessed the growth of football programs across the country, including our own. At the start of the 2018 season, Kansas State had 10 athletic department senior staff members, 29 football support staff members, 12 members of the Kansas State athletics communications office, and the list seemingly went on. For many years it seemed as though we had nearly as many support staff personnel as we had football players on our roster.

As a head coach, it was always important to expect and demand the completion of each given task. When I levied a responsibility upon a staff member, I made sure that he or she fulfilled that responsibility. Although it was a rarity, I knew that I must prepare myself to assume the responsibility if the staff member didn't properly invest himself in his duties. It was always paramount for our coaches and support staff to accept responsibility and be held accountable. Many people always accepted responsibility for a win, and that was human nature. Human nature also suggested that many people would deflect the blame following a loss. If we were unsuccessful in a game, I went into my postgame news conference and publicly took responsibility for the defeat. However, behind closed doors in our very next staff meeting, I outlined our deficiencies and I evaluated the performance of our assistant coaches as well as their position groups. I ensured that everyone on our coaching staff understood where we stood, the ways in which we needed to improve, and how we would go about achieving that necessary improvement and eliminating weaknesses. Early in the week following each game and after opponents had a chance to evaluate the videotape of their game against our team, I always asked the opposing head coach if he would share his evaluation of our team to ensure that we hadn't missed something within the evaluation of ourselves.

When it came to preparation, scouting an opponent, and studying tendencies, I quickly accumulated stacks of paper 12 inches high that detailed all of an opponent's tendencies, schemes, and personnel evaluations. I had binders upon binders of material stacked on my desk and filed in bookshelves, but it was well-organized. I told our coaches that we would stick to our offensive and defensive systems, and if we found new schemes that met our needs and our personnel, we massaged the system to accommodate adjustments. However, we had to identify our priorities and those things that gave us the best opportunity for victory. We believed that a program and a player could become proficient in any area when it became an emphasis. If we wanted to be a good option football team, we knew that we had to put an emphasis on executing option football and consequently we became a proficient option football team and recorded the top two season rushing totals in program history in back-to-back seasons while leading the country in scoring offense. We always emphasized defense and consequently we were the only program in the country to rank in the top six in total defense over a seven-year span. We always emphasized special teams, and consequently Kansas State recorded the most non-offensive touchdowns in the country between 1999 and 2018, and a majority of those touchdowns were a product of our precision and discipline while blocking for our kickoff returners and punt returners.

When I was a 31-year-old head coach at Foothill High School in Santa Ana, California, I suggested to our coaches that we should have the answer to every challenge. We could outwork and out-scheme our opponents. We installed an offense in which our quarterback went to the line of scrimmage to audible to the perfect play against the opponent's defensive formation. It was a great idea, but our quarterback frequently checked into the wrong plays in practice. I said, "When this happens, you check to this play."

However, I made a youthful error by not properly grooming our quarterback to shoulder such a responsibility through repetitions in practice. Consequently, he wasn't well-prepared, and we didn't perform well and lost our first game. I knew we needed to emphasize the proper operation at the line of scrimmage prior to each play, but I didn't make it important enough each day in practice. Therefore, though I believed it was a crucial segment to our offensive capabilities, in actuality we weren't committed to it. I learned that when something was significant, then I had to make it truly important. It was a valuable lesson early in my coaching career.

Whether I was a high school coach, an assistant coach at a small college, an assistant coach at a major college, or the head coach of a major college, it was always important that our players knew that we genuinely cared about their best interest as young men and students. Sometimes, that was a hard sell. I could stand in front of our players in a meeting and say, "I care about you," but we also had to show that we cared about them. In many programs across the country, it was amazing how assistant coaches always wanted to be the good guys. They wanted to put their arm around their player and tell him that he loved him to death. And that's not all bad. However, it was always important for coaches to discipline their players, and that started from the top down. Coddling players was wrong and inappropriate for them. It was important that we built relationships with our players, disciplined our players, and made them accountable to the program and to each other. They had to demonstrate accountability to their coaches and teammates and they had to hold their teammates accountable as well. I believed that if we didn't instill discipline into our players, we would do them a disservice and we would not live up to our duties as coaches. We could do that through a sincere, caring relationship.

We always shared with our players that we had control over our level of performance and over our successes and/or failures. It wasn't about who had the best players but about whose players were best prepared, best motivated, and played the best and hardest together as a true family. It's not about the talent but more so caring enough, commitment, focus, discipline, and togetherness. We talked so much about spirit, starting, finishing, leadership, and the necessity to demonstrate consistency in each of those areas in order to achieve success each week. When we failed, I never told our players, "You failed." I always said, "We failed," which included myself, our coaches, and players. Our successes were also a product of the contributions by all of us, players and coaches alike.

We believed that a commitment to our team goals fostered success. Within the scope of our 16 Wildcat Goals for Success were the true keys to achieving positive results each season. That included a genuine commitment to unity, unselfishness, team effort, and attitude centered on a team-first approach, along with learning how to deal with success and how to overcome failures. We never wanted anyone to say, "The Wildcats did not play with spirit and heart." We shared that each individual could and should contribute to the team's spirit and enthusiasm, and practicing and playing as hard as possible also fell into that same category. Each of us had total control over our attitude. We shared with our players that if they practiced hard; played hard; played with passion, emotion, and spirit; believed in themselves and their coaches and never gave up, they would achieve success. However, we could take nothing for granted and had to commit ourselves to improvement and great effort. Conversely, if we looked back or if we looked for someone to blame, we were looking in the wrong direction. However, it was always important to learn from our past mistakes, make an honest self-assessment, and define a new direction as an individual and as a team.

In our initial meeting with our team prior to each season, we spent some time sharing with them how our program was built and why it was truly important to accept the principles and 16 team goals, which were truly the foundation of the program. It was a strong and solid foundation. We shared with our players that Kansas State football had been around for a century and had more losses than any program in college football history when we arrived prior to the 1989 season. We shared how the program began to climb and achieved a tradition of being recognized as one of the top programs in the country. It was important for our players to understand that while they did not build the tradition, they were each in a position to build upon it. Before each season, we asked our players to consider the following:

1. We are one of only two programs in the history of college football to win 11 games in four consecutive seasons and in six of seven consecutive seasons.
2. We won or tied for the Big 12 North Division Championship four years.

3. We won two Big 12 Championships.
4. We were one winnable game away from playing for a national championship in two different years.
5. There is still room at the top.

We also asked our players to invest time and consider the following questions:

1. Will we take this season for granted?
2. Will we learn from our mistakes of past seasons?
3. Will we have the competitive spirit and be as hungry as the top Kansas State teams in history, which achieved well beyond the expectations of the football world?
4. Will we care enough to overcome the adversity that some other teams could not?
5. Will we totally unite, become totally unselfish, and care enough to accept without complaint the sacrifices necessary to become champions?
6. Will we commit ourselves individually and collectively to finding a way to improve each and every day?
7. Will we work and play as hard as possible, believe in ourselves, care about our team, refuse to give up, and always compete with great spirit and passion until the end?
8. Will we develop the true family relationship again?

We felt that as a program became better and achieved more success, more people might want and/or feel that they deserved more credit. Those individuals often became selfish and pulled away from the team concept, thus creating an atmosphere in which the team began a downward spiral, and success could not happen. We understood that the desire for individual success was perfectly natural but emphasized that in a team sport individual success came through team success. If the team succeeded, players would succeed and be rewarded. Therefore, by being unselfish and being committed

314 Bill Snyder: My Football Life and the Rest of the Story

to a team attitude, our players were preparing for their success, which would come because we were successful as a team and as a family.

Consistency was always in my nature. My mother instilled that trait into me at a young age. It was important for young people to become acclimated to consistency. We as coaches can say things, but do we demonstrate it? My vision of consistency didn't address whether or not an individual made changes, but it was important to gain a level of consistency in all areas of our lives. It wasn't about showing up 10 minutes late one day, showing up on time the next day, and showing up five minutes late the day after. It wasn't about going to class sometimes. It was about teaching young people to conduct their lives with consistency, which in turn allowed others to anticipate, expect, and trust them in all areas of their lives. I truly believe that our players trusted our process. Did players always want to do it that way? Did they always want to work hard? No, but there was never any doubt because we were consistent. Consistency was always a very positive characteristic.

Coaches talk about winning the day. I don't believe anyone used that phrase when we arrived at Kansas State. We believed that it was important to stay focused on right now. Whereas most coaches perhaps promoted going 1–0 and winning the game, which was fine, we felt it was important to take that philosophy one step further. It was about being 1–0 every minute of every hour of every day or every week. Win the moment. From Day One, it was about going 1–0 in this meeting. In practice, it was about running this drill and that drill to perfection, then doing it again. How much was going 1–0 a part of the greatest turnaround in college football history? It certainly had its impact. It's about consistently winning the moment. We didn't just say it, but we did it and then we assessed it, so there was always an evaluation, which in turn promoted accountability among our players. It wasn't about winning and losing but rather it was about being the best we could be at every moment.

Here are some additional thoughts I shared with our coaches and players:

- Family and faith are <u>most</u> important.
- Do right.
- Serve others and those less fortunate.
- Eliminate vanity.

- Maintain an hour-by-hour daily schedule and a written to-do list.
- Be open to change—if it's the right change at the right time.

We always talked to our young people about making decisions. This was always our philosophy: we would make decisions that were in the very best interest of our football program, and sometimes that decision wouldn't be in the best interest of an individual player. I always encouraged our assistant coaches to grasp the global perspective of a decision within our program. As assistant coaches, they understood that the head coach at some point made decisions that weren't popular, but those decisions were in the best interest of the entire program. And we always asked that the players make decisions in their lives based on this question: if I choose to do this, will it help me become a better person, a better student, and/or a better player?

When I made a decision, I always asked myself, *What are my priorities?* I ensured that I made a decision based upon those priorities while ensuring that my decision was in the best interest of our program. Before every decision I made, I asked myself, *Will this decision improve our program?* If the answer was yes, then we executed that decision. Our assistant coaches and our players fully knew that when I made a decision, I made that particular decision for a good reason and for them and that it was well thought-out.

I was always a big believer in the process. I was always a big believer in plans. I was always a big believer in sticking to my process to achieve goals. The more quality repetition, the better the result. So often young people make decisions without sticking to a process. If we did one thing at Kansas State University, we instilled into young people a process by which they made decisions long after graduation. Young people didn't want to hear, "You've got to make the right decision." Young people didn't want to hear a lecture on knowing right from wrong because they had spent the first 18 years of their life learning the difference between the two before they arrived in our program. However, young people needed a process by which they made decisions for themselves, and we hoped that they ultimately would make the right decisions.

Our players learned that most decisions had no or little significance on their lives, a few decisions moderately impacted their lives, and a very few decisions dramatically impacted the rest of their lives. We encouraged our young people to take 10 seconds out of their lives and ask themselves, *If I do this, will it align with my priorities? Will it help me achieve my goals?* We told our players—outside of their faith and family—that becoming the best person, best student, and best athlete were their top priorities. If their decisions helped them to achieve those goals, then we encouraged them to act on their decision with the greatest possible enthusiasm. As coaches and leaders, it was important that we gave our players a process by which they could make positive life choices. They knew that they were responsible for their decisions and they learned to spend a few moments to process the possible consequences of their choice.

When we knew that our players grasped the philosophies and the process involved in building toward individual and collective growth, we knew that we had accomplished something really, really special.

Team Emphasis

1. Play to Your Strengths.
   (Show us.)
2. Improve at Your Weaknesses as Well as Your Strengths.
   (Know what they are.)
3. Contribute to the Spirit of This Team.
   (Emotion—enthusiasm—don't wait for someone else. Display it.)
4. Promote Toughness.
   (Be tough—throw yourself around—no fear—can take a hit.)
5. Never Give In (Practice or Games).
   (Once makes it easier to do again.)
6. Be a Playmaker.
   (Be a go-to-guy—want the title.)
7. Focus on Great Execution.
   (Team—be where you're supposed to be—doing what you're supposed to be doing every snap.)
8. Focus on Your Physical Needs.
   (Weight gain/loss/strength/speed/quickness)
9. Attitude—Consistent
   (Not based on a good day or bad day.)

10. Provide Leadership.
    (Encourage and help others. Don't allow any teammate to do anything, which will hurt our team.)

Team Gameday Goals

1. Be the **TOUGHEST**, **MOST PHYSICAL**, and **MOST SPIRITED** team on the field.
2. Maintain total focus and concentration for four quarters.
3. **NEVER, NEVER**, ever give up.
4. Win the fourth quarter and the first five minutes of the first and third quarter.
5. Win the kicking game.
6. Allow no turnovers, no penalties, and no missed assignments.
7. Play great defense.
8. Start and finish every snap and every quarter better than your opponent.
9. Win your matchup.
10. **WIN!!!**

"Coach Snyder was one of the most consistent people I have ever been around. He was that way as a coach and person, but more importantly, the program was run in a consistent manner as well. That provided everyone within the opportunity to understand their role and embrace it, then carry it out to the best of their ability. Everyone knew the schedule, you knew what practice was going to be like, you even knew what meals you were going to eat. The program was a well-oiled machine. That was the only way to do it. There was no other option."

—Zach Hanson, Kansas State offensive tackle, 2009–11

CHAPTER 23

COLLEGE FOOTBALL
HALL OF FAME

"Coach Snyder has always been one of the people in this game that I have respected the most as a competitor on the field and now covering him from the booth. However, it is his character, integrity, and class as a man that I continue to admire and cherish. College football is indebted to one of the greatest coaches in its history for his unwavering commitment to excellence and his steadfast belief in team and family."

—Joel Klatt, FOX Sports Analyst

On January 9, 2015, Sharon and I traveled to the Renaissance Dallas Hotel and attended a news conference that formally announced the 2015 National Football Foundation College Football Hall of Fame Class. Former Ohio State head coach Jim Tressel and I were selected for the Hall of Fame class along with 15 former first team All-Americans. We would be formally inducted into the Hall of Fame at the 58th National Football Foundation Annual Awards dinner on December 8 at the Waldorf Astoria in New York City. Former All-Americans Brian Bosworth (1984–86 Oklahoma), Bob Breunig (1972–74 Arizona State), and Lincoln Kennedy (1989–92 Washington) joined me at the news conference in Dallas to share our appreciation for the honor. Three days later, Jim and I would walk to midfield and participate in the ceremonial coin toss at the College Football Playoff National Championship between No. 2 Oregon and No. 4 Ohio State at AT&T Stadium.

Rece Davis of ESPN served as master of ceremonies at the Hall of Fame announcement news conference and he was very kind in his comments. He called our turnaround at Kansas State University "perhaps the greatest coaching job of our generation." Shortly after, I shared some comments and I took the opportunity to recognize my family, who made so many sacrifices while they supported me during my 23 years as Kansas State head football coach. I thanked Sharon, Sean, Shannon, Meredith, and Ross. When Rece opened the floor for questions from the audience, Sharon requested the microphone. "I just have one question," she said. "Bill is very good at math, and I used to be a math teacher. However, I need to remind him that we have five children." Laughter filled the ballroom. I quickly realized that I had neglected to mention Whitney, our youngest daughter with the rest of our family. My mistake sparked some light-hearted national attention.

Over the years, I had been inducted into the Kansas Sports Hall of Fame and Missouri Sports Hall of Fame along with several others. The inclusion into any Hall of Fame is meaningful, but the College Football Hall of Fame symbolized the highest achievement by a coach or player in the country. Walter Camp became a member of the first College Football Hall of Fame class in 1951. Over the next 64 years, another 202 coaches entered the Hall of Fame. I was just the fourth coach to be inducted while still actively leading a program, humbly sharing the distinction with Bobby Bowden (2006), John Gagliardi (2006), and Joe Paterno (2007). Hall of Fame eligibility for coaches began three years after retirement or immediately following retirement if he was at least 70 years of age. However, active coaches were eligible at 75 years of age—provided that he had been a head coach for a minimum of 10 years and had coached at least 100 games with a .600 winning percentage. I was 75 years old, I had coached in 282 games, and I owned a 187–94–1 record with a .665 winning percentage, so I met the criteria for the National Football Foundation to place me on the Hall of Fame ballot.

During the middle of our 2015 season, I half-jokingly suggested that they might reconsider my induction. After we won our first three games, we lost six straight, which marked our longest losing streak since 1989. Eight players on our two-deep depth chart missed a combined 24 games during perhaps our most injury-plagued stretch ever. We didn't win a game in 63 days, and it took a toll on our team. I began to question my role as head coach and considered how my performance aligned with my own high standards. We encountered some discipline and accountability issues, and I elected to suspend the scholarships of a few players due to their judgement errors off of the field. We dealt with concerns across the board. We always identified our flaws and worked toward correcting them each week, but I remained concerned over the myriad of inconsistencies that hindered our on-field performance.

For whatever reason and perhaps it was just the nature of the beast, I always seemed to quickly move on from a victory and spend several more hours scrutinizing videotape following a loss. However, the constant desire for improvement had always been a major part of our program's foundation. Following each game—win or lose—I went into my office and began the process of determining our faults. Why did a certain error occur? How did the error occur? Then I spent time identifying ways that we could correct the error. It was a lengthy process but also a necessity so we could begin the week by working toward eliminating our mistakes before preparing for our next opponent.

My 76th birthday arrived in the midst of our struggle. Although I always enjoyed sending birthday cards to other people, I never placed a great deal of emphasis on my own birthday. The stacks of birthday cards upon Joan Friederich's desk and a birthday cake with a single candle separated October 7 from the other days of the year, yet the structure of my day never deviated from any other 24-hour period during football season. On this particular birthday, Sydney, my granddaughter, made a surprise delivery of biscuits and gravy to my office. Jim Colbert stopped in for a while, and many dear friends and former players called with birthday wishes. That evening, Kansas State fans called in during my weekly coach's radio show and also wished me happy birthday, which was unnecessary but genuinely appreciated. Over the next week, I sent thank you notes to everyone who took the time to mail me a birthday card. Every year, I put my birthday cards into a large box, then I placed that box on top of identical boxes in a room in our home. I kept every piece of written correspondence addressed to me, whether it be good, bad, or indifferent.

Our players showed grit and demonstrated that never-give-up approach that was so prevalent in our past successful teams, and consequently, we finished the regular season with a 6–6 record to become just the third team in the country since 1980 to endure a six-game losing streak and still become bowl eligible. We also became the first team in Big 12 Conference history to stave off bowl elimination in three straight games.

On Sunday, December 6, the day after our bowl-clinching 24–23 win against West Virginia, I chartered a plane for $60,000 and flew our 30-member traveling party to New York City. We had Sharon and her father; Sean, Shannon, Meredith, Ross, and Whitney; our eight grandchildren—Sydney, Katherine, Tate, Matthew, Alexis, Gavin, Kadin, and Tylin; and our great grandchild, D.J. We also brought several dear friends with us on the plane. For as honored as I was to be a member of the College Football Hall of Fame induction class, I was equally honored that I could share the experience with many people who were so very important in my life. I had a media teleconference as soon as we arrived at the Waldorf Astoria. That evening Bob Krause and Marty Vanier sponsored a very nice dinner for our family and many people who were with our program from the very beginning: Steve Miller, Jon and Ruth Ann Wefald, Jack and Donna Vanier, Ernie and Bonnie Barrett, Carl and Mary Ice, Allen Renz and Amy Button Renz, and Lee Borck and Jackie Hartman Borck were among those in attendance.

On Monday, the Big 12 Conference held a reception inside the hotel prior to our more intimate evening cocktail function hosted by Kansas State University. Over the span of a few hours, I was able to visit with many dear friends, coaches who I had previously served under or worked beside during my career, and former players in our program. Among the list of attendees were: Senator Pat Roberts, Senator Jerry Moran, the Wefalds, the Vaniers, Bob Krause, the Barretts, the Ices, the Borcks, the Renzs, Mack Brown, Tom and Nancy Osborne, Jim Colbert, Bob Ross, Donnie Duncan, Max Falkenstien, Hayden Fry, Barry Alvarez, Kirk Ferentz, Bobby Stoops, Jim Leavitt, Mark Mangino, Mike Stoops, Dana Dimel, Michael Smith, Phil Bennett, Bret Bielema, Bob Stanley, Frank Hernandez, Al Jones, Gary Spani (2002 College Football Hall of Fame inductee), and Mark Simoneau (2012 College Football Hall of Fame inductee).

Honestly, it was a little bit overwhelming. I normally didn't show much emotion, but I had to back away from tears from time to time. Looking around the room conjured memories of each person. I grew emotional seeing my family and how proud they were and I reflected upon how major a role they played in every success because of their sacrifices over the years. Throughout the evening, I found myself thinking about history more than at any time before because I couldn't take a step without seeing people who were so heavily invested in Kansas State University and our football program. I thought about all of the great people that I met at the University of Iowa. I thought about those dear friends who had been proud K-Staters long before 1989 and remained supportive throughout the previous unsuccessful years of the Kansas State football program and who were so instrumental in the construction of the program, the facilities, and everything that went along with it.

I thought about Sean, who had more responsibilities within our program than any other assistant coach in the country and who had always been by my side. I thought about Ross and Tate, who also had played on our team, and I thought about the fact that all of our children and grandchildren had either graduated or were in the process of earning their degree from Kansas State. I was proud of our former players who were in attendance and I was proud of our past and current assistant coaches and perhaps even more so for those who had been given the opportunity to serve as head coaches, including Bobby Stoops (Oklahoma), Jim Leavitt (South Florida), Mark Mangino (Kansas), Mike Stoops (Arizona), Phil Bennett (SMU), Dana Dimel (Wyoming and Houston), Eric Wolford (Youngstown State), Manny Matsakis (Emporia State, Texas State, and Bethany), Del Miller (Missouri State), and Bret Bielema (Wisconsin, Arkansas, and Illinois). Our coaching tree featured a prominent group of individuals, including several who basically started at Kansas State and who were gracious in sharing with me how their time in our program helped to influence their coaching philosophies and teaching of young men. I never enjoyed coaching against our former coaches, and in less than a month, we would face an Arkansas team with Bret and Michael on the opposite sideline, so they knew how we prepared and they had prolific insight into our offense, defense, and special teams, which concerned me a great deal heading toward the Liberty Bowl.

At times, I just looked around the room at everyone. I wondered when the significance of this trip and everything that it entailed for many different reasons would eventually sink in.

Bob Ross, who made the trip and was one of my best friends from St. Joseph, Missouri, told me that the mayor of St. Joseph had declared Tuesday "Coach Bill Snyder Recognition Day." It meant a great deal to me, as my mother and grandparents had remained there for so many years, and I always enjoyed going back and seeing the remarkable community and the wonderful people who truly impacted my life. I thought about my high school coaches, elementary school teachers, and so many other people and I appreciated them all. Mostly, I thought about my mother.

Although I very much enjoyed Monday evening's event, I never fully relaxed. Half of my mind was still back in Manhattan. One of our players had been arrested for an alcohol-related offense, and I spent a portion of the day dealing with that issue. I had received a phone call from a prominent player at the University of Oklahoma who wanted to transfer to Kansas State and that same day I received a phone call from a prominent Kansas State player who wished to transfer to another school. Meanwhile, our assistant coaches and players were two days into our initial preparation for the bowl game.

About one month before we arrived in New York City, National Football Foundation President and CEO Steve Hatchell, who I had known for a number of years, asked me to speak at the induction ceremony on behalf of the 17-member Hall of Fame class. Coach Tressel had a tremendous coaching record and he was a second-generation inductee, as his father, Lee Tressel, was inducted in 1996, so I was honored by Steve's invitation. I had delivered thousands of speeches over the previous four decades, but this was a different arena. The people in the audience were every bit as successful and talented as the individuals on the stage, and I knew that I had to do right by them. I also knew that it was important to express the sense of gratitude felt by all of the inductees and to convey our overall appreciation to the National Football Foundation, the College Football Hall of Fame, and to all of the many people, past and present, who had played a prominent role in helping us to achieve such a great honor. I spent some time writing an outline and then practiced the speech aloud to familiarize myself with enunciating each of the words.

I tucked my speech outline in the inner pocket of my tuxedo jacket as Sharon and I headed out of our hotel room to meet all of our family. All of the men in our family wore tuxedos, the women wore beautiful evening gowns, and we posed for a wonderful photo at the foot of the stairs at the Waldorf Astoria. A group of Kansas State fans, many dressed in purple, greeted us at the door to the ballroom. I spent some time visiting with them because they played a significant role in this special evening as well. Had our stadium attendance remained at 13,000, as it was when we first arrived at Kansas State, there wouldn't have been a Hall of Fame head coach. Before heading into the ballroom, I hugged each of my family members.

Facing the audience of more than 2,000 people, the inductees sat on a stage that included four rows of long dinner tables trimmed in greenery with gray and white linens. I occupied the fourth chair to the right of the podium. I sat between Ricky Williams and Coach Tressel. As we finished dinner, the lights above the audience dimmed, illuminating the seated inductees and Hall of Fame dignitaries on the stage, and ballroom chatter softened to a whisper. Then I was called to the podium and I shared some thoughts:

> Without saying a great deal about what we've accomplished, it is an amazing honor for each and every one of us on the dais tonight. My congratulations to every award winner this evening. As you can all see, amazing people—not just from an athletic standpoint but from a value system—character and those things that we all believe when we say football matters, that it instills in each and every one of us and so many of you out in the crowd, virtually all of you who have experienced what that value system truly is.
>
> On behalf of all the award winners up here, I certainly want to thank the National Football Foundation for the opportunity for each and every one of us to be here and certainly to Steve Hatchell, who

has been a long-standing advocate of what is really right about the game of college football.

As we venture through the evening and on into the future and having heard virtually every one of the players speak this morning at a press conference, it became very evident that all of us have the same feelings. That is, yes, we are humbled and honored, but we also recognize what so many other people have meant to our successes. This has been an opportunity to express our gratitude and our thanks and our love and our caring to those people who have meant so much to each of us and have given us the opportunity to have a degree of success that each and every one of us will cherish for the rest of our lives and the opportunity to be here this evening and express that.

I've been blessed myself and I think every inductee feels the same way to have a family that genuinely cares, a family that is invested in what we have done, a family that has created a tremendous amount of sacrifice on their own part on behalf of each and every one of us.

I've been blessed to have an amazing family. Virtually every one of them is here tonight. We have five children and eight grandchildren and a great grandchild, and every single one of them made the trip to New York City. I wouldn't have come without them in all honesty because of what they have meant to me in my life and the sacrifices they have made. I think everybody up here can express exactly the same thing.

I appreciate what Condoleezza Rice, the NFF Gold Medal Recipient, had to say. When you look around and see the people here and the people that have been recognized this evening, this isn't just about the game. It isn't about what takes place between the white lines all the time. It's about the benefits and the foundation that it creates for the lives of so many young people across the world. I think everybody has been invested in that. We have an amazing gratitude for those people who have made and created the opportunity for each of us to be here. I think of all the wonderful players that we have certainly had in the programs I've been in and I think all of the people up here, the players, have a great appreciation for those other teammates that provided them the opportunity to have success on the football field and off the field and a great gratitude to all the coaches we have been surrounded by throughout or lives. The amazing administrations, the faculty, the students, the fans…it just goes on and on.

There's so many people in each and every program and probably every young athlete in here—not so young anymore—but the athletes up here, you've all been in the training room and gotten taped, and somebody cared for you. There are so many people who are so heavily invested in what this game is all about.

At the end of the day, it is about a value system that allows young people to have great successes in their lives. I have such an appreciation for this foundation because it is about that. When they promote football, it matters in such an amazing way when you think of all the young people we've been around that had very little to begin with, those that came from a background that they were destined for failure, and they became successful individuals because of the game, what it stands for, and the value system it created for so many people.

I thank the foundation, I thank all of you here. There are so many of you out there that represent exactly that, so many coaches in the audience who do exactly that. Yes, it's important to be successful on the field and it's important to win, but the real value of the game of football is what it does to help create an environment in which young people can become successful in their lives, in all ventures of their lives. You've all had a part in that. Thank you so very much.

When they presented me with the ceremonial College Football Hall of Fame plaque, the inscription easily could have read, "Bill Snyder and Family" and it could have gone on and listed everyone who had been so valuable in our program. They would have assuredly needed a bigger plaque. The honor just reiterated the fact to me once again that we needed so many special people to achieve special things. Before we arrived, Kansas State had four winning seasons in a span of 56 years, eight seasons without one victory, seven seasons with one victory, and eight seasons with two victories. During one 10-year stretch, Kansas State had a 9–82–3 record, and during another 10-year stretch, it went 14–84. Kansas State was unable to win a single game in the two seasons prior to 1989. Then we won one game. Our players began to believe. Then we recorded five wins, seven wins, five wins, nine wins, nine wins, 10 wins, and nine wins. Then we became just the second program in college football history to win 11 games in four straight seasons and six times in a seven-year span. We couldn't have achieved our success without special people.

The 2015 season was unique in that many remarkable coaches retired. On October 12, Steve Spurrier announced his immediate resignation from South Carolina six games into the season after putting together a 228–89–2 record over his 25-year career. Just three days later, Jerry Kill announced his immediate resignation due to health concerns from epilepsy after going 152–99 in 22 years, including the last five at Minnesota. On November 1, Frank Beamer announced his retirement from Virginia Tech after the season. Frank was the winningest active coach in the Football Bowl Subdivision with a 238–121–2 record over 29 years at Virginia Tech. Then on November 13, Gary Pinkel announced his resignation from Missouri after the season. Gary had a 191–110–3 record in 25 years, including the last 15 years at Missouri. Steve, Frank, and Gary each were the all-time winningest coach at their school. Between Steve, Frank, Gary, and Jerry, a total of 809 victories and 101 years of head coaching experience walked away from the game in 2015 and left a void in college football.

Although I had signed my five-year contract extension in 2013 with the idea that "I'm going to be back," I was the oldest active head coach in the country and I knew that my standing remained in question prior to each season due to the fact that I wasn't able to say, "I'm definitely going to be back." During those times when I might begin to ponder life without coaching football, I'd begun to think about so many other things, and life would never be the same if I left. I'd go back and forth and then I'd be back in the chair again. I wasn't in coaching to reach the Hall of Fame, so it wasn't a career-ending event. We were on the verge of reaching our 25th season and 200th career victory, which were each significant milestones, but I didn't consider milestones whenever I contemplated retirement. The things that kept me coming back were the same—family, fans, helping young men lay their foundation for a successful life after football, and the fact that as a head coach, a lot of people counted on me. To walk out of my office for good would be like a father leaving his family at home and never returning again. I wanted to remain at home with my family.

"Coach Snyder brought a tremendous sense of pride to Kansas State in how he turned around the football program, how he accomplished so much for the university and the state of Kansas, and in how he touched so many lives outside of football. People constantly align themselves with him and follow his leadership style and how he brings integrity to everything that he does."

—Jon McGraw, Kansas State safety, 1998–2001

CHAPTER 24

BEATING CANCER

"Bill Snyder has possibly done more with less than anyone in college football history. His ability to find and develop players while molding a family and a team is legendary. He is Kansas State. But more important is the love and appreciation I have for him as a man—from the heartfelt, personal letters he would send to opponents to the loving way he helped his first gay player navigate coming out publicly in 2017. His acceptance and love is everything to me and to this young man. Family first, team first always. We have often compared cancer notes and walked this road together the last several years. He has encouraged me, and I hope I have encouraged him. I simply love this man. He is everything right about college football but more importantly, humankind."

—Holly Rowe, ESPN

Two hundred.

Honestly, the constant weekly cycle of evaluating our performance from the previous week and preparing for our next opponent left little or no time to contemplate any milestone achievements—and that was never our primary focus. From the beginning, we felt that every game and every win was significant, and the amount of time that we invested into our daily preparation so that we could have the opportunity for success in the next game never wavered. So when we took the field to play the University of Kansas on November 26, 2016, my anxieties weren't directed toward reaching 200 career victories as much as they were focused on beating KU.

After our 34–19 win, Big 12 Conference Commissioner Bob Bowlsby joined us on the field and he made a brief presentation to recognize the

200-win milestone. All of my family was able to attend the game, which made the day even more special. Then for the second time in my career, our players carried me off of the field. Only 25 other coaches had ever reached 200 victories at the Football Bowl Subdivision level, and only Joe Paterno, LaVell Edwards, Tom Osborne, Chris Ault, and Vince Dooley had achieved the milestone while coaching exclusively at one school.

Inside the locker room, Kansas Governor Sam Brownback congratulated our players and coaching staff and he presented our team with the Governor's Cup Trophy. We had been fortunate to defeat the University of Kansas in all eight of our games since I returned to the sideline and in 20 of the last 21 meetings as a coaching staff. This time I shared with the media my displeasure that we led 34–9 and suffered a few costly mistakes in the fourth quarter, which made it a closer score. At our annual senior reception event inside the Vanier Family Football Complex, I shared our appreciation for the commitment by our senior players over the course of their careers and I expressed our gratitude to the families for allowing their sons to be a part of our program.

Shortly after, I sat down with Voice of the Wildcats, Wyatt Thompson, to film my weekly television show. Starting with Mitch Holthus, then Greg Sharpe, and Wyatt, we were fortunate to have some of the best play-by-play announcers in the sportscasting business over the years at Kansas State. Each had been honored as Kansas Sportscaster of the Year at least twice. Stan Weber, who had been with us since the beginning, was as fine of a color analyst as there was for a team in college football. They were all great ambassadors for our program.

Instead of going back to my office to review the videotape of our performance in the game, I went home to spend the evening with all of our family. Then I took a couple of our grandchildren bowling.

The eight months leading up to the milestone achievement proved to be dramatic for various reasons. In March, our school president left to become president at Washington State University. As the Kansas Board of Regents and Kansas State University began to explore potential candidates for president, I already had one name in mind: General Richard B. Myers. Dick was born in Kansas City, graduated from Kansas State in 1965, and had been a member of the Air Force ROTC on campus. His distinguished 40-year career in the Air Force culminated in his promotion to Chairman of the Joint Chiefs of Staff in 2001. Dick served as the principal military advisor to President George W. Bush until he retired in 2005. I felt it was significant to have somebody in charge who understood the uniqueness of Kansas State University, who understood our people, who cherished our university's history, and who likely wouldn't attempt to alter the culture of what had made our university special for so many years. Dick was a prominent national figure, and I felt that his presence as a K-Stater would return a sense of calmness to our campus. I told one Board of Regent member: "The Board needs to hire Dick Myers as the next president."

She replied, "Do you think he would be interested? We had not considered him."

I asked Dick if he would consider this opportunity. He initially was uncertain, but eventually told me that he might be interested, and I shared that with board members. He was named interim university president in April and became the permanent president in November.

We always had our "Unity Sharing" team-building exercise in which players shared personal stories with their teammates. These were pretty heavy and very personal topics—things you probably wouldn't normally share with anybody other than your family and closest friends. What transpired was that sense of unity, that friendship, and that trust for each other, along with that willingness to share privileged information because you trusted that your teammates would handle it appropriately. Prior to the 2016 season, sophomore Scott Frantz, our starting left tackle, told his teammates that he was gay.

Scott first came to my office to share this information with me privately. I suggested that he might want to share it with his teammates. He indicated that he would and later that day after practice volunteered to speak and shared his status with his teammates.

Scott was one of the first known college football players in the country to openly share such information. It was really an amazing experience. I was confident that our players would receive Scott's words in a very positive way—and they did just that. It was emotional. They cheered for their teammate and his courage. Everyone was very receptive to Scott, and his sexual orientation didn't change one thing about how his teammates felt about him. Our players grew tighter. Holly Rowe, a dear friend, came to Manhattan and shared Scott's story on ESPN's *SportsCenter*, as Scott hoped to reach others across the country who were in a similar situation. That hit home with me.

I met Jerry Kill for the first time a few months prior to the 2016 season. Although our paths had not previously crossed, I had great respect for Jerry from his time as head coach at Minnesota before he retired due to health-related issues. The Kansas State athletic director hired Jerry as associate athletic director for administration. In doing so, Jerry assumed a role on the senior departmental staff and served as "chief administrator for the football program," which struck me as somewhat peculiar. We had never had such a position, and Sean handled the administrative duties for our program.

A couple of months following his arrival, Jerry visited my office. Jerry was a very honest, straightforward, and open individual. It appeared that he had been put into an uncomfortable situation. Jerry outlined to me the expectations that were placed upon him. He said, "I'm on your side, Coach. I've never been in a football program, including my own, that has this level of efficiency and organization." Jerry left to become offensive coordinator at Rutgers immediately after the season.

We won five of our final six regular-season games to finish the regular season with an 8–4 record and earn an opportunity to play Texas A&M in the 2016 Texas Bowl. We joined Georgia Tech and USC as the only teams in the country to start out the season with a 3–3 record and finish with at least eight victories. We had the opportunity to win in the fourth quarter but came up short in losses against West Virginia (17–16) and No. 22 Oklahoma State (43–37). I was pleased with the resiliency of our team over the course of the season, but as was the case in 2016, our setbacks during the first six games were concerning.

I flew to New York City the day after the bowl announcement to attend the 2016 College Football Hall of Fame induction ceremony. I had fought a persistent sore throat for several weeks. During the return flight to Manhattan, I made a frightful discovery.

I felt a lump on the right side of my neck.

On December 9, I visited Dr. Keith Wright, my longtime physician. His concern prompted a biopsy. Three days later, I sat alone in Dr. Benjamin Pease's office in Manhattan. Dr. Pease, a neck tumor specialist, explained that my biopsy report revealed cancer in a lymph gland. It is a day I will never forget. Throat cancer. I was told that I had a 60 to 70 percent chance to live five years at that time. Other than Meredith's accident and my mother's death, it was the worst day of my life.

What would this mean for my family? What could I do? How could I deal with this? Where would I receive treatments? What if they didn't work? I had so many questions and concerns. My mind went in all different directions. I tried to process the diagnosis throughout the day and I finally shared the news with Sharon that evening. I told Sean that as our associate head coach he needed to prepare to take over the program if necessary. Sharon and Sean were emotional, but I told them that it was important that nobody else knew about the situation. At the time, I wasn't even sure that I should have told them. I was selfish because I neither wanted a distraction prior to the bowl game nor wanted to put the rest of our family in agony.

The day after my cancer diagnosis, Sean I and traveled to NRG Stadium in Houston for a site visit, which was customary prior to any bowl game. Then I visited the nearby MD Anderson Cancer Center. Their doctors coordinated a treatment plan with the University of Kansas Medical Center under the guidance of Dr. Douglas A. Girod, who is now the chancellor at the University of Kansas. This partnership between MD Anderson and KU Med enabled me to travel to Kansas City for my chemotherapy treatments and radiation treatments over the course of six weeks. The fact that MRI scans failed to locate the initial cancer cell remained the greatest concern, as it opened the possibility for the cancer to return. They planned surgery for early January to remove the neck tumor, a spot on the back of my throat, and a spot on my tongue.

Following our 33–28 win against Texas A&M in the Texas Bowl, I asked all of our family to come to our hotel suite. I informed them of my throat cancer. It was a very difficult night. My final diary entry for 2016 read: "I don't know what 2017 holds, but I do know that we have the most wonderful family ever. Our children are amazing. I love each member of our family in a heartfelt way. A lot of successes come my way but none without my family. No one has been better supported."

I called President Myers a few days after my surgery and told him that I had throat cancer. The athletic director pushed for me to step down. I discovered that he already had an individual in place to become the next head coach. I asked President Myers to inform the athletic director that I intended to return for the 2017 season. Shortly after I spoke with President Myers, I told our coaches and players about my cancer during a meeting at the Vanier Family Football Complex. I wanted to go about my business and do everything that I could for my family and for our football program. I knew that staying actively involved would help me for many different reasons. I had plenty to do in my office. I was going to coach unless I hurt my family, hurt the program, or hurt myself.

My six-week treatment schedule consisted of radiation five times per week and chemotherapy once per week. On alternate evenings, I left my office and drove two hours to KU Med for a radiation treatment. I stayed overnight, received another radiation treatment the following morning, and then drove back to my office. I was still in my office seven days per week. I just had difficulty speaking and swallowing for several weeks following surgery. Sometimes I brought my paperwork home. I just had difficulty speaking and swallowing for several weeks following surgery. The doctors gave me a feeding tube for nourishment. They put me on a water-only diet and said that following the completion of my treatment schedule I could resume drinking coffee as long as it was in moderation. That was never how I drank my coffee.

In February, somebody apparently spotted me at KU Med. Internet rumors began to circulate. People across the state of Kansas grew concerned about my health. On February 13, we released a public statement that revealed my cancer diagnosis. Fatigue took its toll and became more pronounced as the weeks wore on. My weight dropped from 160 to just below 130 pounds. I was on the field for most of our spring practices but watched some of them from the press box. Media speculation and rumors shifted toward the future of our program. One theory suggested that I was going to corner Kansas

State into hiring Sean as head coach. Those theorists were unaware that a few years prior the athletic director eliminated the language in my contract that enabled me to name my successor. I felt that even if I was to step down just one week before the start of the season, the athletic director would find his own guy.

Del Miller, the very first coach I hired on our staff in 1989, told me in February that he wanted to retire. His announcement surprised me. He had been an integral part of our program for many years spread out over the course of a couple of different tenures. Del had a great family with his wife Jan and sons, Todd, Troy, and Tad, and he would be missed.

Amid the cancer treatments, the fatigue, spring football, and the persistent rumors regarding my future, I encountered another situation. I learned that for an undetermined period of time the athletic director had been calling our players and some of our assistant coaches into his office. He apparently had been asking them to critique our program and my job as head coach. Although I certainly supported our players' right to share their feelings, I took issue with the manner by which the conversations were facilitated. It was the veil of secrecy that surrounded these conversations with members of our program that most angered me.

I never claimed that I was an easy head coach for whom to work. I always required a great deal from our assistant coaches, and the expectations were perhaps higher than many assistant coaches expected when they joined our staff. Over the years, I had seen many of our coaches climb the ladder and accept more prominent positions at other schools and I encouraged them to do so. I always extended a hand whenever a former assistant coach needed a letter of recommendation or asked me to place a call to another head coach regarding a job opening. I had seen so many of our assistant coaches elevate themselves to expanded roles within our program as well.

As a coaching staff, we experienced more inner turmoil during this period than we perhaps ever had during our time at Kansas State. Coaches butted heads. Coaches took sides. Things got a little bit heavy. We had 10-plus competitive coaches together inside a meeting room. They each shared their feelings and ideas in an effort to positively impact the program or our performance on the football field. Conflicting ideas are a part of the profession, but outside of the meeting room, it created a lack of loyalty and staff separation. Whenever a coach voiced his issues—good, bad, or indifferent—among the rest of our staff inside the meeting room, a sense of loyalty went along with that particular action. Whenever a coach shared his issues elsewhere, he had failed to follow Rule No. 1 in our coaching staff manual: "Do not share staff or team information outside of our staff." It became evident that we had more loyalty issues within our coaching staff than I could remember.

Over the years, people suggested that my loyalty toward our assistant coaches was one of my flaws because I had never fired an assistant coach. For the first time in my career, I had no choice but to release a member of our coaching staff following the 2016 season.

The athletic director left for Tennessee in late February 2017, and the search for his replacement began immediately. Eventually, I was asked to talk to the two finalists for the athletic director position. One of the finalists, Gene Taylor, was deputy athletic director at the University of Iowa, so I called Kirk Ferentz and spoke with him and a few other people within the Iowa athletic department. Each of them provided positive feedback regarding Gene's capabilities. Then I spoke with Gene, offered my recommendation for him, and Gene was hired as athletic director. Through the years, people asked me if I had ever considered serving jointly as both the athletic director and head football coach. I knew some head football coaches who had done so, but after about one minute of contemplation, I moved onto other things. I already had plenty on my plate and had never ever had a desire to serve in that position.

I completed my treatments in early March and was on the sideline for our spring game on April 22. I had begun to eat meals, and our dietician staff led by Scott Trausch graciously brought me weight-gain shakes daily. My weight slowly increased to between 145 to 150 pounds, but it was a process. Over the course of the previous couple of months, I had received boxes upon boxes of cards and well wishes from all corners of the country. I still have every one of those cards. Some of the notes nearly brought me to tears. People were truly wonderful in supporting me throughout my cancer treatments. I went through many purple pens while writing thank you notes to everyone. I answered every letter. I always do.

I loved my family. I loved the Kansas State people. I loved coaching football and wanted to keep doing it. None of that changed over the course of my journey through cancer. The journey also reaffirmed that I was a creature of habit, I was not good about giving up, and consequently I realized that I had probably made what I did for a living so important that it created a degree of imbalance in my life. I learned that my routine over the years—the long hours, the one-meal-a-day diet, not enough fluids, not enough sleep, and too much coffee—had perhaps impacted my health and that if left unchanged could lead to negative consequences. Although I had always walked on the treadmill in my office while watching videotape, I also began riding a stationary bike in my office 30 minutes per day and I did sets of 30 repetitions with light weights. When the weather was favorable, I also swam at home. My daily routine now consists of one hour on the treadmill while performing 100-plus repetitions per six exercises (a total of 600 reps) with 12 ½-pound weights. On certain days, I also swim.

Four months after my cancer announcement elicited some national attention, the media shared some thoughts about me again. This time they focused on one of my coaching philosophies. We had a freshman in our program who failed to follow our program regulations, and his behavior led to off-the-field issues that impacted his role on our team. In June, he wanted to transfer to another school. I had always said that a player was free to leave our program, but I wasn't going to release him from his scholarship because a part of the developmental process as a person and a player was to honor a commitment and not give up. So although he could choose to quit and attend another school, he would not be eligible to receive financial aid in his first year.

Critics suggested that I needed to release the player from his commitment to our program. I felt that would be a disservice to that player. Many players, who failed to follow certain regulations within our program and suffered consequences due to their infractions, responded favorably and became productive members of our teams over the years, thus learning great life lessons. I felt that this individual could follow suit. The national spotlight on this particular situation intensified to the point that I feared it could cause a distraction to the other young people in our program. So we opted to release the player from his scholarship, and he went on his way.

Sixteen months later, the NCAA transfer portal officially debuted, prompting a new era of college football, which I feel unfortunately caters toward this age of instant self-gratification. It could create a horrible environment for coaches for several different reasons. First, if a young player doesn't see the field because he is behind a second- or third-year player who is more developed within the program, that young player can simply pack up and leave. What message is the portal sending to players? Second, a prominent part of being a coach is asking players to work hard, focus on their schoolwork, conduct themselves like gentlemen, and strive to improve every single day. When players fail to adhere to guidelines, coaches have a responsibility to carry out consequences. Today, there is no recourse for inappropriate behavior. A player can enter the portal rather than accept the consequences of inappropriate decisions.

I seldom raised my voice and I never talked down to a player, but now if players don't cherish the fact that a head coach or an assistant coach is trying to improve them as people or as players, those players can get into their cars, and nobody will hear from them again. Consequently, many coaches now walk on their tiptoes, which tempers the development process. If a player says, "Coach, if you discipline me, I'm walking out of that door," who has control? Then if other players side with that player and other players side with the head coach, suddenly the program experiences division, disorientation, and consequently is likely headed toward failure.

Today, we see the instant self-gratification mentality begin early. Some young people have become participants of a social media-driven culture in which the number of scholarship offers and the publicity derived from those scholarship offers becomes more important than really identifying the university that best suits their needs in all aspects of life. Certain adults get into the ears of some of these players early and tell them that they're special and that they're the next big thing, so they grow up carrying a false sense of entitlement. Then after they take their recruiting trips and head off to college, they find themselves at the bottom of the pecking order. But wait—everyone told him that he was the next big thing. What does he do if he isn't on the field 30 snaps per game during his freshman year? Did those coaches or the same adults back home instill into that young person the value of hard work, discipline, development, and commitment, or will that young person spend his time sulking and fall behind his teammates? Will he listen to his college coaches and progress in their system so that he may better develop his capabilities and eventually see the field? Or will he decide to leave?

There are many young people who utilize the NCAA transfer portal for various reasons, but the sheer number of transfers in this short span since the system began amazes me, as it does most coaches. The direction college athletics and college football are headed is really concerning. The legislation is concerning and it appears that it might only continue. I would fight it. I would be outspoken. If college athletics continues in this direction, it isn't inappropriate to speculate that we could see a negative impact on many athletic programs in our country.

Universities and colleges were founded upon educating young people, but today so much of the college environment revolves around college athletics, primarily the revenue-generating sports, which are led by football. In 2021 the college athletics world embarked upon its most significant change in history, as legislation within state laws and NCAA rules allow student-athletes to financially profit from their name, image, and likeness (NIL). There's a great deal of uncertainty regarding where this new NIL era is headed and the state of amateurism rules, and as of summer of 2021, not every state had yet put NIL laws into place. I believe the NIL has been approached inappropriately. I'm not opposed to student-athletes receiving increased funding, but not in this manner. Consider by the time at least a few freshmen student-athletes finish their first two semesters, they potentially will have garnered more money than all of their college professors might combine to make in four full years. Just think about that. The NIL era will change everything. Virtually nothing will ever be the same again. College athletics have always promoted unity, teammates caring for teammates, and bringing young people together. Now if a quarterback is making $1 million and his offensive linemen have no money in their pockets—could some disharmony arise within the locker room? In my eyes, the NIL totally opposes the intent of college athletics. I could certainly envision and feel comfortable with each university providing an equal amount of additional funding to each of their athletes, thus eliminating inequity, jealousy, and selfishness, and allow them to have more time to focus on their education.

Prior to the 2017 season, national college football writer Bill Connelly of SBNation.com wrote, "Bill Snyder is nearing a second Hall of Fame-worthy career at Kansas State." It referenced that Kansas State went 17–20 in our three years away from the sideline. Then between 2009 and 2016, we posted six, seven, 10, 11, eight, nine, six, and nine wins. But early in the 2017 season, we were ranked 18th in the country when we visited Vanderbilt, and our 14–7 loss marked just the third time in the previous 93 games that we failed to score at least 10 points. Once again, we finished the first half of the regular season with a 3–3 record. It was the third consecutive year that we were at or below .500 heading into the second half of the season and yet we then went 5–2 in the remaining games to finish the season 8–5.

One of our football program's proudest moments each season arrived when we had the opportunity to recognize the soldiers who served our country at home and abroad. We honored their service annually on Fort Riley Day. Prior to the game, soldiers addressed our players inside the locker room. Our team captains then carried the Iron Rangers and Big Red One flags out of the locker room. We allocated reserved seating to the soldiers from various units at Fort Riley. The First Infantry Division participated in the coin toss and performed pushups alongside Willie Wildcat following each Kansas State score. Our partner unit, the First Battalion, 28th Infantry, Fourth Infantry Brigade Combat Team, First Infantry Division, known as the "Black Lions," celebrated each Kansas State touchdown with a volley of cannon fire. The First Infantry Division Band played with the Kansas State marching band before the game and during the halftime show.

Our football program enjoyed a one-of-a-kind partnership with the units at Fort Riley, which involved a wider-reaching plan started by U.S. Army Lieutenant Colonel Arthur DeGroat. One day, our players traveled to Fort Riley for physical training with the soldiers, and then another day the soldiers worked out with our players on our football field. The Football Writers Association of America recognized our football program's unique partnership with Fort Riley by presenting us with the 2017 Armed Forces

Merit Award, which was very gracious and a tribute to Fort Riley opening its doors and allowing our players a glimpse into the life of the soldiers who serve and protect our freedom.

Although we fought through some difficulties during the 2017 season, Kansas State continued to excel in one area that had long been a trademark of our program: special teams. For the second time in three years, Sean was named National Special Teams Coach of the Year. In 2017, we ranked No. 1 in the country in the ESPN special teams efficiency rating and finished in the top 15 in special teams efficiency for the fifth time in seven years. Since Sean earned the official title of special teams coach prior to the 2011 season, our players accumulated nine first- or second-team All-American honors on special teams, and we either set or tied eight team records and 20 individual records. In 2017, second-team All-American D.J. Reed ranked second in both punt return average (14.9 yards) and kickoff return average (34.2 yards). Kicker Matthew McCrane earned first-team All-Big 12 honors while finishing his career No. 1 all-time in field-goal accuracy (86.4 percent), extra-point accuracy (99.3 percent), career field goals (57), consecutive field goals made (16), and consecutive extra points made (105). Matthew was the sixth most accurate kicker in NCAA history.

We faced several questions, and the quarterback position became a weekly concern, but we finished our regular season with an 8–5 record. In his first full season on our staff as quarterbacks coach, Collin Klein did a good job of instilling that next-man-up mentality into our signal-callers, which was necessary given the fact senior Jesse Ertz, sophomore Alex Delton, and redshirt freshman Skylar Thompson each started several games. Ertz ended his career with a leg injury early in the season. Then Delton became the starter before he struggled with concussions. Thompson, the third-string redshirt freshman, helped to guide us to an overtime victory at Texas Tech (42–35) and a victory at No. 10 Oklahoma State (45–40). When Thompson was ineffective early in the 2017 Cactus Bowl, Delton came off the sideline to earn Cactus Bowl Offensive MVP honors, as he completed 7-of-10 passes for 52 yards and one touchdown and rushed 20 times for 158 yards and three touchdowns in a 35–17 win against UCLA. It was our most-lopsided postseason victory since the 1995 Holiday Bowl.

All of my family joined us on the field for the postgame bowl trophy presentation. Then my entire family posed for a photo on a football field covered in celebratory confetti. I was glad that all of our family was able attend the bowl game if for some reason I did not return as head coach. The cancer treatments—coupled with the inner turmoil within our program—had drained me.

One media report in particular late in the season caught my attention. The story claimed that Jim Leavitt had reached a verbal agreement with Kansas State officials to become head coach for the 2018 season and the report further claimed that I had prevented the deal from coming to fruition due to my desire for Sean to become head coach. Furthermore, the report claimed that Kansas State officials had guaranteed Jim $3 million if he wasn't named our head coach by January 1, 2018.

I had spoken with Jim because I knew that his name was being thrown around as a possible successor. Jim was completing his first season as Oregon defensive coordinator. He told me, "Oregon wants me to sign a new contract."

I told him, "You might want to have them put into your contract the clause that you would be exempt from any financial penalty if you left to become head coach at Kansas State." I told Jim that I was certainly a fan of his, but I was a major fan of Sean as well. My top two preferred successors for head coach had always been Sean and then Jim. I was certainly in favor of Jim taking the position of head coach if he was selected for the job at Kansas State, but I also shared with him that I wasn't yet prepared to retire. To my knowledge, the purported $3 million deal between Jim and our administration was erroneous. I trusted President Myers and Gene. They told me that the story was untrue.

One week after we completed our season, I informed my family and then our administration and team that I would return as head coach for a 27th season. As I maintained every year, I would stay as head coach if I remained in good health, continued to make a positive impact upon the young people in our program, and was still wanted by our fans and our administration. Kansas State responded by giving me a new five-year contract to run through the 2022 season.

"When I think of Coach Snyder it's hard not to immediately think of his attention to detail, unrelenting work ethic, and unyielding discipline, but I don't think that he receives enough credit for how he taught us to be leaders. All great leaders must possess the power of observation to truly understand the best course of action. He had a stoic demeanor in practice, watching, observing, and whispering notes into his recorder. He knew what was best for the team because he felt it—he absorbed it. He taught me that leaders must have the capacity to shut their mouths and listen, to be present, and to observe. So to use one of his favorite words, I appreciate Coach Snyder for leading by example and showing us how to be tough, self-confident leaders."

—Ben Leber, Kansas State linebacker, 1998–2001

CHAPTER 25

FINAL STEPDOWN

"We came to Kansas State because of the people, stayed because of the people, and returned because of the people, and that remains unchanged."

—Bill Snyder

January 17, 2018 is still tremendously painful for our entire family. I speak with each of my children virtually every day. Given Sean's array of responsibilities within our football program as associate head coach, special teams coordinator, and director of football operations, our conversations were more frequent. It was not alarming when Sean called me as I sat inside of my office shortly after 1:00 PM. Not in a million years could I have predicted the words that came from Sean's mouth. "Matthew is dead."

"Where are you?" I asked.

"I'm at his house."

"I'll be right there."

Sean loves each of his children dearly, but he and Matthew were particularly close. Matthew was a 22 year old with a great smile, a caring nature, and always seemed to carry a positive outlook. A few miles from my office, Sean discovered that Matthew had taken his own life inside of his home.

Tragic. Unreal. Our emotions are still raw. It feels like it happened yesterday. Matthew's passing left a huge hole in the hearts of our family. The days, weeks, and months drew out as our family processed our emotions. We loved Matthew and we will always miss him. It is impossible to know what each day may bring.

Prior to the 2018 season, we perhaps experienced more movement within our coaching staff than any other year. For the first time, we had two new coordinators as wide receivers coach Andre Coleman took over as offensive coordinator, and linebackers coach Blake Seiler took over as defensive coordinator. Offensive line coach Charlie Dickey and quarterbacks coach Collin Klein served as co-offensive coordinators. Brian Norwood joined our staff as co-defensive coordinator and defensive secondary coach. Eric Hickson joined our staff as running backs coach, and Zach Hanson joined as tight ends coach.

We returned 14 starters, including 12 who started in at least half of the games the previous season. However, we felt that we needed leadership to surface over the course of the offseason and, consequently, for the first time we opted not to select the team captains by our spring football game. Instead, we decided to wait until fall practices began, hoping more players might embrace a leadership role in the summer while striving to be voted captains prior to the season. All-American senior offensive tackle Dalton Risner became just the fifth player to be a three-time captain in our program. Junior quarterback Alex Delton became our other team captain while seven other players assumed co-captain roles.

One of our departed 2017 team captains, cornerback D.J. Reed, was selected by the San Francisco 49ers in the 2018 NFL Draft. Our program had experienced many positive trends over the years, but our Big 12-leading streak with at least one Kansas State player taken in 25 straight NFL drafts tied for the 12th longest streak in the country. As evidenced by the 137 Kansas State players who went to the NFL either as draft picks or free agents over the course of both my tenures, the number of recruiting stars next to player's name coming out of high school or junior college didn't define the capacity for our young people to develop and elevate themselves to the professional level, and many of our players had extended NFL careers.

On May 13, I flew to Scott City, Kansas, to speak at a Catbacker event and shared that we needed to show vast improvement from where we finished spring practice. On May 23, I visited KU Med for a follow-up appointment and then I spoke at a Catbacker event at the Sedgwick County Zoo in Wichita. I shared that the 16 Wildcat Goals for Success and the virtue of persistence helped me over the course of my battle with cancer and I encouraged the Kansas State people to try and utilize those values in every aspect of their lives. I shared with Catbacker groups in Topeka and Manhattan my displeasure that we had initiated a trend of starting slow in the season (4–3 in 2016 and 3–4 in 2017) but that I had been impressed with how our teams had bounced back in the second half of those seasons (5–1 in 2016 and 5–1 in 2017).

Our team began summer workouts on June 4. For five days, our players trained under the guidance of members of the Navy SEALs between 5:00 AM and 9:00 AM in what was called "The Program," which emphasized team building, commitment, toughness, accountability, and discipline. It was regarded as the best leadership development and team building program in the country. Director of strength and conditioning Chris Dawson shared positive reports following our team's week in The Program.

I experienced a different type of workout at Big 12 Conference football media days at the Ford Center in Frisco, Texas. At 78 years old and with 27 years of coaching experience, I was the oldest active and longest tenured head football coach in the country and I kept a pretty brisk pace while walking up and down corridors, speaking with personalities from FOX and ESPN, and receiving warm greetings from so many individuals I had known over the years. Many of them wrote me cards during my cancer treatments. I felt energized. I nursed a cup of coffee while walking to each destination at the media day event and shared my favorable health status numerous times with different inquirers. One reporter asked, "Is retirement a topic of daily conversation?"

I replied, "Only when I get around you guys. Then it's a topic of conversation. I've got a six-year-old great-grandchild that I want to coach. So that'll tell you."

The reporter followed, "How old will that make you then?"

I said, "206."

I enjoyed seeing our fellow Big 12 head coaches seated around the same room. For a moment, it took me back to the start of the Big 12 Conference, when Spike Dykes and I shook hands prior to the inaugural conference football game on August 31, 1996 in Manhattan. Since then, I had shaken hands with 44 different Big 12 head coaches. Although all 10 head coaches in our conference returned from the 2017 season, we were a relatively young collection of coaches. Half of them had coached at their current school for fewer than four years. I embarked upon the 10ᵗʰ season of my second tenure as one of two head coaches in college football history to have two different tenures at one school and record at least 70 wins each time—136 wins between 1989–2005 and 74 wins between 2009–17. We went 53–27 against Big 12 opponents during the first 10 years of the conference (1996–2005) and we were 48–31 against conference opponents entering the 10ᵗʰ year of our second stint.

Interestingly, since 2009, only 11 schools in the country maintained the same head coach. Of those, only Nick Saban, Dabo Swinney, Mike Gundy, and myself had been fortunate to win at least six games each year over that nine-year span. We had been fortunate enough to win 74 games for an average of 8.1 wins per year, made eight straight bowl appearances (the third longest streak in the Big 12), captured one Big 12 Championship, and had finished at least fourth place in our conference in five of the last seven years.

Every year was different. We started out the 2018 season with a 2–1 record and went into a tailspin. We lost five of our next six games, including a painful 51–14 defeat at No. 8 Oklahoma. Afterward, someone asked me, "How do you go about redirecting the ship?"

I replied, "I'm uncertain if the ship has been in this condition before."

Late that night, I wrote in my diary: "Worst feeling that I can remember."

I stayed up most of the night and evaluated the videotape of the game. On Sunday, I wrote Lincoln Riley a congratulatory note and then I addressed myriad issues with our coaching staff. I was angry. I felt horrible about the way that we prepared for the game. Too often in college football on-field execution becomes the scapegoat. In actuality, seldom does execution fall solely on the players' shoulders. Execution also takes place in a coach's office and on the practice field. We failed in our preparation. At times, we coaches put the wrong calls on the field and consequently we were unsuccessful in that game along with several others. It just became evident that we had not prepared well enough in virtually all areas—on the field, off the field, and that went for both coaches and players.

As with Jake Waters and Daniel Sams several years prior, we had a quarterback situation in which Alex and Skylar Thompson each carried the capacity to lead our team while each proved to possess his own unique set of qualities and talents. I was neither prepared to rely solely on a predominate passing quarterback or a run-only quarterback nor were we going to eliminate the quarterback run game because we knew more about that particular aspect of offense than anyone else in the country. Week by week or during the course of a game, we decided whose talents gave us the best chance for success against a particular defense.

This quarterback dynamic was nothing new to our program, but once again, it appeared that certain players favored one quarterback while other players favored the other one, and at times, our coaches weren't on the same page. Some of our meetings weren't particularly pleasant. We had the least productive scoring offense in 26 years in averaging 22.5 points per game and also ranked last in the Big 12 in both total offense and passing offense during the season.

A narrow loss at TCU (14–13) dropped our record to 3–6. Our track record suggested that we had the capacity to achieve positive results down the stretch in any given season. We felt the misery of losing, and I felt badly for our fans who stood by us. Our fans had long been accustomed to success, and we were moving in the opposite direction this particular season, which perhaps caused some of our fanbase to lose hope in our ability to respond to adversity in an appropriate manner.

In the closest Sunflower Showdown in 14 years, we needed a touchdown in the final three minutes to beat Kansas 21–17 and avoid our first home loss in the series since 1989. A 21–6 win against Texas Tech on our Senior Day the following week gave us back-to-back victories for the first time that season.

We had an abbreviated week of practice prior to the final game of the regular season at No. 25 Iowa State because we always allowed our players to leave and be with their families on Thanksgiving. I spent a portion of my time planning our annual team awards ceremony and decided that I would honor Robert Lipson with the Merit Award as an outstanding contributor to our program. Despite limited finances, Robert followed the Wildcats to every away game I can remember and was always the first one to greet us when we got off of the bus at the hotel. I became a believer when Robert met our bus in Japan.

Although we had beaten Iowa State in all nine meetings since we returned in 2009, single digits decided eight of those victories, including each of the last three games in Ames: 27–21, 32–28, and 31–26. All that we needed to do was win this game and we would qualify for a bowl game.

And it appeared that we were headed in that direction. We scored 17 straight points to take a 38–21 lead with 12 minutes, 27 seconds remaining in the fourth quarter. At that point in the game, ESPN gave us a 98.5 percent chance of victory. After a season full of difficulties and with our backs against the wall, our coaches and players had pulled together, and we were on the verge of keeping intact our trend of strong finishes toward the end of the season.

But little did we know that our sizable lead would evaporate. Little did we know that we were on the brink of suffering perhaps the worst fourth-quarter letdown in school history. We led Texas A&M by 15 points entering the fourth quarter in the 1998 Big 12 Championship Game. This time, we led Iowa State by 17 with less than 13 minutes to go.

Then we allowed a 77-yard touchdown drive. Then an Iowa State linebacker hit our quarterback, and the ball popped into the air, and a defensive player caught the ball and ran 21 yards for a touchdown. That play truly changed the game. It was a gift and it motivated Iowa State. Its Senior Day crowd of 54,430 people came alive, and we couldn't run out the clock or stop them. Late in the game, we allowed an 18-yard touchdown run. That was the final blow. Iowa State scored 21 straight points in less than six minutes. Suddenly, we trailed 42–38.

And then it was over.

I can't ever remember leaving a football field after a game like that. It still stands out in my mind. I walked off the field. I felt alone. I was alone. We weren't going to a bowl game. For the first time in my life, I had no idea what I would share with our players in the locker room. I felt so many different emotions at the same time. The season was in ruin. We had suffered painful games before. This was the most painful loss ever.

I had never felt so alone.

Over the next week, I sat and contemplated my future, the future of our coaches, and the future of the program if I was to step down. I tried to define how I could help our players and how we would be able to transition from finishing a season so poorly to remaining motivated for the 2019 season. I knew there would be some transition within our coaching staff. I just was uncertain of how much transition. I always kept a list of potential assistant coaches just in case. But first I had to define my future.

Media speculation regarding my future and the future of our program ran rampant throughout the week, and rumors were everywhere. In this age of social media, the alleged scoop among the experts changed by the minute. Everyone expected something to happen at any moment. And this went on day after day.

Shortly before 6:30 PM on Friday, November 30, I left the Vanier Family Football Complex, walked into the parking lot, and saw four TV camera people filming me as I climbed into my car. A reporter approached my vehicle. I said, "Everything is fine."

Then I closed my door and drove away. Another reporter, who was already in his vehicle, followed me as I left the parking lot and headed down Kimball Avenue. I drove around until I lost him. I wanted no one to know where I was headed. President Myers had asked me and Gene Taylor to meet him at his home.

Even though I had anticipated it, I had never before been in this position. I was uncomfortable because of the way that our season ended. The final loss of the season had been on my mind virtually nonstop throughout the week. It was crazy how I was fortunate to have a 215–117–1 record; how I was fortunate to be the 20th winningest coach in FBS history; and how I was fortunate to coach in 19 bowl games, enjoy seven 11-win seasons, and capture two Big 12 Championships—and all I could do was hang onto this season-ending loss.

During my drive to President Myers' home, I pondered everything and was uncertain what I was going to do. Since Day One, I said that I didn't want a contract. I always said that if for some reason I was no longer wanted, then I wouldn't be here, and a contract wouldn't make any difference. I felt it was time, but I also felt it was time after the 2005 season, and so I didn't know whether the feeling would wear off. And actually I didn't know if I wanted to give the feeling time to wear off. It was an emotional time. I just wanted my emotions to settle down.

I parked, went into the house, and President Myers, Gene, and I sat down.

I thought about the wonderful Kansas State people I met while walking around the campus prior to my hiring in November 1988 and I thought about those 13,000 fans in the stands during our first season. I thought about our original 68 members of The Foundation and our first ever win against North Texas State. I thought about our first ever bowl win (the 1993 Copper Bowl) and the three largest crowds in the history of college football ever to cross a state line to attend a football game. I thought about how we built our home in Manhattan, how all of our children graduated from Kansas State University, and how several of our grandchildren were now in the process of also doing so. I thought about Jack Vanier assuring us that he would do anything necessary to build our original facility and I thought about how I could see the top of our football stadium and the Powercat painted upon the indoor practice facility each morning from my bedroom window. I thought about the greatest turnaround in the history of college football and all of the wonderful Kansas State people through the years who played such an important part in helping our vision become a reality.

I thought about my loving mother, I thought about my supportive family, and I thought about our three decades with the Kansas State family. I thought about the loss of Matthew, Meredith's accident, whether I truly wanted to continue coaching, and what Sharon and the family would want me to do. I loved everyone so dearly.

I sat across from President Myers and Gene. Myers broke the silence. "Do you think it's time?" Myers asked.

I knew what he meant. We sat in silence for a few more seconds. "Yes," I said, finally. "It is time."

"Coach Snyder is one of the greatest coaches of all time. What he did in twice turning the program around—the first time was when they thought about shutting down the program; the second time he turned it around again—he never wavered from what he did. He didn't change. Obviously, he's in the College Football Hall of Fame and he's one of the greatest coaches, if not the greatest, because of what he did at Kansas State. Nobody thought it was possible."

—Jordy Nelson, Kansas State wide receiver, 2004–07

CHAPTER 26

THE SNYDER FAMILY

"Dad is so caring with his family and with people. Growing up and seeing his caring nature was unbelievable. That carried on through all of the years. He spent time with all of his children and is able to do so even more today. Family has always been very important to him. But it's important to not just talk about the impact that he's made in the lives of our family but the impact he's also made on so many young men throughout their lives and his push for us to be better people and better family men. It wasn't all football."

—Sean Snyder

Bill Snyder (Sharon—wife)

Son: Sean Scott Snyder (Wanda—wife)
Grandson: Tate (Nikki—wife)
Great-grandson: Pearce
Granddaughter: Katherine (Colton Stueve—husband)
Great-grandson: D.J.
Great-grandson: DeClan
Great-grandson: Murphy
Grandson: Matthew—deceased

Daughter: Shannon Renee Snyder (James Walters—husband)
Granddaughter: Sydney Lucero Snyder (Jake Vang—husband)
Great-granddaughter: Sawyer
Great-grandson-to-be

Daughter: Meredith Nicole Oakes (Bryan Oakes—husband)
Grandson: Gavin
Grandson: Kadin
Grandson: Tylin

Son: Ross Snyder
Granddaughter: Alexis (Damion Rogers—husband)

Daughter: Ryann Whitney Hydeman (Micah Hydeman—husband)
Granddaughter: Lou Ann
Grandson-to-be: Dean Edward

Judy Snyder—mother of Sean, Shannon, and Meredith

I've been blessed to have so many special people around me, but none have been more prominent than my mother, my wives, my children, grandchildren, and great-grandchildren. No one could be more proud of their children. Their mothers were fantastic because I was away far more than other fathers due to my profession. So much of our children's development was due to the excellent guidance from their mothers.

Football consumed many years of my life. Later in my career, I altered my schedule in order to spend more time with my family. I wanted to become a better husband and father and find ways to connect with all of my family. Many years ago, I began calling Sean, Shannon, Meredith, Ross, and Whitney every day and I frequently speak with our grandchildren. All of our children and grandchildren of college age have either graduated or are presently enrolled at Kansas State.

There was a time when all of our children lived in Manhattan. Walking each of my daughters down the aisle was very special. When a father gives away his daughter, it's a special moment in his life, and their spouses have become a major part of our family. Our family is expected to reach 30 members in 2022. Before our family grew quite large, we usually had everybody at our home for Thanksgiving and Easter and we either spent

Christmas at home or celebrated together in a hotel on bowl trips. Slowly the children and their families moved away. Sean and Wanda moved to the West Coast when Sean became special teams coordinator at USC in 2020. Then Whitney, Micah, and Lou Ann moved to Kansas City. Micah served as captain of the Manhattan Fire Department and joined the Kansas City Kansas Fire Department in 2021.

That means Sharon and I are now totally empty nesters in Manhattan.

I have so many fond memories with our children. I still remember Sean, Shannon, and Meredith racing down the hallways of our football facility when they came to visit me when I was on the coaching staff at the University of Iowa. I remember taking them on bowl trips. They knew more about hotel living than most 40-year-old people. I still remember taking our entire family on a weeklong vacation at the Lake of the Ozarks following my first retirement and how much we enjoyed boating, playing board games, and barbecuing on a back porch that overlooked the lake. Sharon and I look forward to making more memories with our family.

No one could have a more wonderful family—collectively caring, loving, hard-working, service-minded individuals who are great parents and who love to help and serve others. I am so very proud of each of them.

Sharon, in additional to all of the chores that mothers do, served her communities as a teacher and elementary school principal (in Des Moines, Iowa). She has served as president of many Kansas State organizations (the Beach Museum of Art, Kansas State libraries, Kansas State Gardens, as well as a member of others). She is a member of the Philanthropic Education Organization and she prepares and serves meals for the needy through our church. She loves gardening and has surrounded our home with an amazing landscape.

Sean, the oldest, is a truly caring father, grandfather, and son who possesses all of those 16 intrinsic values that have been a part of our program. His football career has taken him from Greenville (Texas) High School to the University of Iowa to All-American status at Kansas State and then into the NFL before spending the next quarter of a century as our director of operations, assistant head coach, and special teams coordinator. He then had offers from Nebraska and the University of Southern California, choosing the latter as special teams coordinator. Sean was named National Special Teams Coach of the Year on two occasions at Kansas State, and during his first year at USC, his special teams units were collectively ranked No. 1 in the country by Pro Football Focus. But above all he has become a model parent and grandparent.

Wanda attended high school with Sean. Courageous and strong, Wanda fought through some very difficult family issues in her youth. Her strength and discipline helped hold her family together. She remains a caring, loving, and helpful mother and grandmother. Sean and Wanda's first son, Tate, played football at Manhattan High School and at Kansas State. His career has taken him into the surgical instrument field, which positions him to view firsthand a variety of types of surgical procedures. He and his wife, Nikki, also are talented interior designers and great parents. Katherine, their daughter, is a great mother to her three boys and a great wife to Colton, who manages thousands of acres of farm/ranch land in southern Kansas where they live. Katherine was also a Manhattan High and Kansas State graduate. Matthew, the youngest son to Sean and Wanda, was a great young man who was seeking his direction just before his death at a very young age. Matthew was a gentle, kind, and caring young man. It's often been said that he probably has our Lord laughing daily.

Shannon is a caring and loving mother, grandmother, and daughter. As a young girl (five to seven years old), she was a strong competitive swimmer, as were Sean and her sister Meredith. Shannon was on her high school dance squad and attended and graduated from Kansas State University as did each of her brothers and sisters. After moving to Manhattan, she was employed at a local bank and eventually was promoted to a vice president position. Having recently married a special young man (James), she moved just outside of Dallas and she still does occasional work for the bank. An extremely hard worker, Shannon continually initiates new projects. I always remember the pleasure I had teaching competitive swimming (all four strokes) to her, Sean, and Meredith, and watching them compete. Sydney, Shannon's daughter, worked with us at the football office while she finished her degree at Kansas State. She was popular with her co-workers and proved to be a productive worker. She presently owns a photography business and is half owner of an online clothing business. She learned her photography skills from her aunt Meredith. Sydney and her husband, Jake, a defensive assistant coach at Michigan State, have their second child on the way. Jake also helped us at Kansas State.

Meredith, our middle daughter, has proven to be one of the most courageous individuals I've ever known. Her fight through the difficulties created by her automobile accident has been remarkable and indicative of her strength, toughness, and work ethic. Raising three boys, owning and operating three separate businesses, and managing 80-plus acres, along with housewife chores has continually amazed me. Meredith was active in her youth in school activities and competitive swimming. She, too, is a caring and loving wife, daughter, and mother. Still today she runs her photography business called Especially Newborn Photography in Emory, Texas, with professionalism and passion. I love the photos she takes of babies and young mothers. Following her accident, Meredith graduated from Greenville High School and Kansas State. Bryan, Meredith's husband, has served as an athletic director, a head football coach, and an assistant coach at several high schools in Texas. Bryan is a great husband to Meredith and a great, caring father for their three sons—Gavin, Kadin, and Tylin. All three boys play multiple high school sports, and Gavin is a member of the National Honor Society. They are all very polite ("yes, sir" and "no, sir"), disciplined, and hard workers.

Ross, our youngest son, also played for us at Kansas State as a running back after he participated in football, soccer, baseball, and track at Manhattan High School. He also played the piano as a youth and over the years became a very popular young man through his friendliness and passionate concern for others. As are all of the others, he is a loving and caring father and who would do anything for his daughter. Ross had been employed in Kansas City for several years before returning to Manhattan a few years ago to serve as project specialist with a local communications company. Ross's daughter, Alexis, is an honor roll student and is majoring in psychology at Kansas State. She is a very bright young lady. Her husband, Damion is a captain in the military.

Whitney, our youngest, was an equestrian competitor from age nine through her college years. After competing at South Dakota State and then Baylor University, she returned home to ride for Kansas State when it started its equestrian program at my request. She became captain of the team and an All-Conference rider along with placing in the national championships. After graduation, she taught equestrian riding for several years. She majored in education and taught in elementary school for four years before retiring to start her family. She is always a hard worker and a caring, passionate mother who plays with her two-year-old 24/7. Whitney and Micah's oldest daughter, Lou Ann, plays every waking moment of every day with a smile on her face the entire time. They will present us with another grandson, Dean Edward, about the time of this book's publication.

Our 27 (soon to be 29) family members all embrace the fond memories of Matthew (also so very special).

Life with Bill

Bill and I were introduced by our good friends, Tom and Gay Ross. Tom, a former football player for the University of Iowa, met Bill when he served as offensive coordinator and quarterbacks coach under Hayden Fry. Gay and I grew up in Des Moines, Iowa. We were teachers and then elementary school principals. However, Tom was the real matchmaker. During our first meeting, Tom casually asked me what I thought about Chuck Long, knowing full well my response. I said, "Who's Chuck Long?" In Kansas, that would be like asking, "Who's Michael Bishop?" or "Who's Collin Klein?" Those people more gifted in football trivia knew that Chuck was the star quarterback at Iowa and later became the Heisman Trophy runner-up to Bo Jackson. Needless to say, the sports section of *The Des Moines Register* was the first thing I threw away on Sunday mornings. I was not a football fan.

A period of courtship—or recruitment, as I viewed it, ensued between me and Bill. One evening, Bill asked me what I thought about getting married. I asked, "To whom?" I learned that I needed to be very specific during our conversations. Although I don't recall my exact initial response, I determined that Bill was talking about us. I must've answered, "Yes." We ultimately blended our two families and never looked back.

That doesn't mean that we haven't thrown a yellow flag or two. For instance, the time that Bill asked if I would mind if he put a sofa/bed in his office for those nights that he worked late—I did mind. Or the time when three-year-old Whitney pointed to the Kansas State football complex as we drove past and asked if that was where Daddy lived. From the mouths of babes…However, ultimately, life with Bill was a touchdown.

When we were first introduced, I had no idea what life as a football coach entailed, even during the months when there were no games. Over the next 40 years, I learned how much time is involved and truly gained a great appreciation for the dedication that it takes in order to become a highly-respected, Hall of Fame coach. I am now a football fan and, especially, a fan of Bill.

—Sharon Snyder

Memories from the Snyder Children

We were young, wild, wandering kids when we visited dad at the University of Iowa. We ran around the football facility and at times probably irritated Dad when he was trying to work in his office. However, my activities changed one day when dad introduced me to Iowa punter and long-range field-goal kicker Reggie Roby. Reggie played at Iowa from 1979 to 1982 and set an NCAA record by averaging 49.8 yards per punt during the 1981 season. Reggie went on to become a three-time Pro Bowl selection as a member of the Miami Dolphins and Washington Redskins. Reggie inspired me to become a punter and a kicker. He taught me skills and proper technique, and I shagged footballs for him on the practice field at Iowa. Reggie really made a positive impact, and I was grateful that he took the time to work with me.

I always enjoyed when we piled into Dad's car and drove to visit Grandpa Owens and Grandma Snyder in St. Joseph, Missouri. Dad enjoyed showing us where he grew up and showed us the parks and swimming pools, and it was always fun to hear about Dad's childhood. When Grandpa Owens broke his hip, we sat in his room and shared stories. He had such a sharp mind and told us about the Pony Express. Grandpa lived to be 101 years old. I admired how dad always took the time to visit Grandpa Owens and Grandma Snyder.

It was probably one of the first times in my childhood that I witnessed Dad's caring nature, and I admired that trait in him. I saw a side of him that wasn't all about football.

I really grew as a person during my college years. I went to Iowa to play under Dad. Then when he became head coach at Kansas State, I transferred to play under Dad again. From a young age and on through college, Dad always emphasized the importance of me earning my way, so I had to prove that I was worthy of a scholarship. Dad instilled into me the competitive edge and resiliency to overcome any obstacle or challenge in life. He really thrived in trying to reach perfection, so he always encouraged us to find one thing to improve upon each day and become better at it, which continues to be a great philosophy for all aspects of life. His persistence, consistency, and desire to help his players become better family members, better students, and better athletes impacted so many young men in our program. My playing years at Kansas State made a huge impact upon my life.

After Dad retired, we began meeting for coffee several times a week. Although we were around each other virtually every day year after year, this was a different dynamic. We finally had a chance to sit down for one or two hours and have great talks about ourselves, our family, grandkids, great-grandkids, and our conversations weren't just about football. It was so much fun that we now had a chance to talk about things other than the daily operation of our football program. Obviously, we knew each other, but this was an opportunity for us to really get to know each other again on a different level. We had so many great talks after Dad retired, and those conversations continue on a regular basis over the phone, as I continue my coaching career as special teams coordinator at the University of Southern California. It's been really good to just talk with dad about life.

—Sean Snyder

Some of my fondest childhood memories were when Dad was at the University of Iowa. We spent a lot of time running around the football office while Dad worked, but when he was home, he always made sure we spent quality time together as a family. I was around 11 years old when

Dad introduced us to what still remains my favorite card game, *Kings in the Corner*, while we listened to Dolly Parton and Kenny Rogers on the record player in his home. The white carpet we played on always had a perfect pattern etched upon it, as Dad vacuumed the house almost daily. As we traveled to and from his office, Dad allowed us to sit on his lap and he taught us to drive in empty parking lots. During this time in our lives, Dad began taking us to watch the fireworks on the Fourth of July, which has remained an annual family tradition.

My favorite moment with my dad was our father-daughter dance at my wedding. Dad chose the song "My Way" by Frank Sinatra. I wasn't an easy child and always seemed to do things the hard way. As we danced, Dad and I laughed at the irony of it all. He said that although I didn't always take the easy or expected path, I kept going, I succeeded, I did it my way, and he was proud of me. It was one of the most special moments of my life.

I have so many wonderful memories with my father, but perhaps the lessons that I learned from him over the years stand out the most. Some of those lessons entailed stern, lengthy conversations, but he taught many of those lessons through his day-to-day actions. First and foremost, family is everything, and we must never take that (or anything else) for granted. For years, my father has called me virtually every day. Although there isn't much news to share some days, the fact that he takes five or 10 minutes out of his day to call and chat means the world to me.

—Shannon Snyder

Traveling back and forth from Mom and Dad's was always hard. I loved being at both but hated when it was time to leave. Summers were spent on the football field playing with players and footballs, spending time in the office, and playing with what seemed like all of the pens and pads of paper in the world. I loved it. We spent evenings playing cards at Dad's home. *Kings in the Corner* and *Spoons* were favorites. I always remember singing and dancing to Dad's favorite song, "Eye of the Tiger."

My all-time favorite memory, which most people don't understand, was spending Christmas on the road. I don't think anything really beats Christmas in a hotel room. It was always special, and we always had a tree. We loved running around the hotel, playing in the players' game room, enjoying an endless supply of drinks and snacks, and getting to visit and experience so many different places. I'm so thankful my husband and kids were able to experience Christmas in hotels. Although our Christmases in hotels ended just a few years ago, I miss our family tradition so much.

Although I grew up while living with my mother in Texas, Dad always did everything possible to remain a part of my life through my childhood and adult years. He calls every day to check on us to see how things are going and to ask if he can do anything to help in any way. He always checks up on my boys' academics and their sporting events. Dad is a great resource for them, enjoys helping them, and enjoys giving them football tips. Everyone always talks about Dad's handwritten letters, and yes, we always receive the most meaningful cards and notes on birthdays and holidays. I have saved and cherish each and every one of them.

During my high school senior year in 1992, I was involved in a terrible car crash near Dallas. Dad, Sharon, Sean, and Shannon drove through the night to be with me in the hospital. I suffered a broken neck and I remain a quadriplegic. I believe the experience helped Dad and I to create an even stronger bond and I knew that he would do anything for me. I definitely know that my stubbornness comes from him. Dad has sent me to several rehabilitation facilities and is relentless in researching and speaking with professionals about the latest procedures for spinal cord injuries. It's difficult to put into words what Dad means to me, but I know that he believes in me and that I can accomplish anything that I set my mind to. Dad gives me strength and sets my mind at ease when times are tough. I've always been so thankful for his constant love and support even during the busiest football seasons.

—Meredith Oakes

When we were at the University of Iowa, I always enjoyed going to the office and getting the latest football poster. I always enjoyed running down the hallway and down the stairs so I could pay my respects to Floyd the Pig— the Iowa–Minnesota rivalry trophy that was almost always in our football building—on my way to the new field inside the pressurized practice bubble.

Sometimes, Sean taught me how to kick field goals and punt. Those were great memories.

I was 13 years old the first time we pulled up to the Kansas State football complex, which was a limestone building wrapped in barb wire on a flimsy chain-link fence. I thought to myself, *This is your office?* It was great to watch the renovations over the years, but it was sad to see the Vanier Football Complex go when the new building took its place.

Even though Dad didn't like fishing, I enjoyed going fishing with him behind our house on Father's Day. I enjoyed our boating excursions on the lake during the summer and family vacations over the Fourth of July. I enjoyed going with my parents to watch my niece and nephews' sporting events and sitting in the back to stay discreet.

I remember Dad calling me on the first play of the game in the 1999 season opener against Temple. At the time, I was staying in Rochester, Minnesota, and receiving chemotherapy and radiation treatments for colon cancer following surgery at the Mayo Clinic. The first play of the season was a five-yard sweep to the right by David Allen. We beat Temple 40–0.

—Ross Snyder

Getting to sleep was difficult the night before my first horse show when I was nine years old. Dad and I were in a hotel, and we were both so anxious and nervous for the show. Mom was going to meet us at the event that morning. Dad and I woke up at 4:30 AM and headed to the show grounds to meet with my trainer and the other riders and so I could ride my pony before the show. However, when we arrived at the show grounds, nobody was there. Then we discovered that we were an hour early. It turned out that nobody had ever adjusted the clock by the nightstand in our hotel room after Daylight Savings Time.

Dad was unable to attend many of my horse shows due to football, but I always felt like he was still there because he made a tremendous effort to support me whether in person or in spirit. One particular Saturday, Dad even called me from the locker room during halftime of the spring football game just to get a quick update on my horse show.

We have family videos of me and Dad playing tennis against older kids on the courts two blocks from our home in Iowa. I was a two year old in diapers and ran around the tennis court picking up the tennis balls. When I was three or four years old, Mom and I would sometimes meet Dad at the Cico Park playground in Manhattan over the lunch hour. Although I don't recall every detail because I was so young, I still think about those times whenever I pass by that playground.

When I was a child, I visited Dad's office so often that I made an office in Dad's office closet and gave myself the title of personal assistant to the football coach. I fetched his mail and office supplies, organized everything, and ran errands around the building, but my favorite thing to do was design football plays for him. Using all of the different-colored markers, I drew the X's and O's and used solid lines for running plays and dotted lines for throwing plays. I was rather proud of my ingenuity and attention to detail. When I was eight years old, I designed one play in particular that I felt very strongly about and it was pretty basic—the quarterback threw the ball to the wide receiver, and the receiver ran all of the way to the end zone. I handed Dad that play and told him that he should probably use it in a game. During the 1993 Copper Bowl, I was shocked and cheered so loud because Dad used my play, and it resulted in a 50-yard gain. After the game, I told Dad how excited I was that he used my play. He said that they called it the "Whitney Play." I still have my original drawing of the Whitney Play. Dad kept it on a shelf in his office until he retired.

I walked across the stage in four different graduation ceremonies at Bramlage Coliseum. Dad was able to attend three of them. He spoke at one of my graduation ceremonies and he walked me across the stage and handed me my master's diploma in another one. He missed the graduation ceremony when I received my second undergraduate degree, but I totally understood his absence because he was in New York City with Collin Klein, who was a finalist for the Heisman Trophy. A lady waited for me when I walked across the stage. She handed me a huge bouquet of flowers. I knew exactly who had bought them for me. The waterworks began. Dad was always there—maybe not physically—but he was always there.

—Whitney Hydeman

APPENDIX

CAREER AND PERSONAL ACHIEVEMENTS

(made possible through the sacrifices, dedication, and hard work of our coaches, players, support staff, and my family)

1990 Big 8 Coach of the Year
1991 ESPN National Coach of the Year
1991 Big 8 Coach of the Year
1993 Kodak District Coach of the Year
1993 AFCA District Coach of the Year
1993 Big 8 Coach of the Year
1993 Copper Bowl champions
1994 CNN National Coach of the Year
1994 Aloha Bowl participants
1995 Holiday Bowl champions
1995 Manhattan Citizen of the Year
1996 No. 32 jersey retired at Lafayette High School
1997 Cotton Bowl participants
1997 Fiesta Bowl champions
1998 Bobby Dodd National Coach of the Year
1998 Bear Bryant National Coach of the Year
1998 Walter Camp National Coach of the Year
1998 Associated Press National Coach of the Year
1998 *Playboy* National Coach of the Year

1998 Downtown Athletic Club National College Coach of the Year
1998 Schutt Division I-A National Coach of the Year
1998 AFCA District Coach of the Year
1998 Big 12 Coach of the Year
1998 Alamo Bowl participants
1999 AFCA District Coach of the Year
1999 Holiday Bowl champions
2001 Cotton Bowl champions
2001 Insight.com Bowl participants
2002 Big 12 Coach of the Year
2002 Holiday Bowl champions
2003 ESPN Big 12 Coach of the Year
2003 Big 12 champions
2004 Fiesta Bowl participants
2005 Namesake "Bill Snyder Family Stadium"
2006 Kansas Community Service Award
2006 Kansan of the Year Award
2006 Kansas City Sports Commission Lifetime Achievement Award
2006 Meritorious Leadership Award by Delta Chi Fraternity
2006 Missouri Sports Hall of Fame inductee
2007 Holiday Bowl Hall of Fame inductee
2007 Austin College Athletics Hall of Fame inductee
2007 Joe Spencer Award for Meritorious Service and Lifetime Achievement
2008 Kansas Sports Hall of Fame inductee
2008 Big 12 Legends inductee
2008 Kansas State Athletics Hall of Fame inductee
2008 State Farm Distinguished Speaker Award
2010 Pinstripe Bowl participants
2011 Woody Hayes National Coach of the Year
2011 CBS Sports National Coach of the Year
2011 *Sporting News* National Coach of the Year
2011 Touchdown Club of Columbus National Coach of the Year
2011 Liberty Mutual National Coach of the Year finalist
2011 FWAA Eddie Robinson National Coach of the Year finalist

2011 Big 12 Coach of the Year

2012 Bobby Dodd National Coach of the Year

2012 Bear Bryant National Coach of the Year finalist

2012 Bobby Bowden National Coach of the Year finalist

2012 Liberty Mutual National Coach of the Year finalist

2012 FWAA Eddie Robinson National Coach of the Year finalist

2012 Maxwell National Coach of the Year semifinalist

2012 Big 12 Coach of the Year

2012 Kansas State Athletics Powercat Choice Awards Coach of the Year

2012 Big 12 champions

2012 Cotton Bowl participants

2013 Kansas City Sports Commission Coach of the Year

2013 Honorary Mayor of St. Joseph, Missouri

2013 Fiesta Bowl participants

2013 Buffalo Wild Wings Bowl champions

2014 Maxwell National Coach of the Year semifinalist

2014 Missouri Western Alumni Award

2014 Namesake of the Inaugural Bill Snyder Highway Half Marathon and 5K

2015 Namesake "Snyder Leadership Legacy Fellows"

2015 Touchdown Club of Memphis Coach of the Year

2015 College Football Hall of Fame inductee

2015 National Excellence in Mentoring Award by MENTOR

2015 Alamo Bowl participants

2016 Liberty Bowl participants

2016 Texas Bowl champions

2017 Cactus Bowl champions

2018 Namesake for Bill Snyder Pavilion at Missouri Western State University

2020 Bear Bryant Lifetime Achievement Award

2020 Namesake of the National Football Foundation Kansas Chapter "Bill Snyder Family Chapter"

2020 Cotton Bowl Hall of Fame inductee

2020 Flinchbaugh Family Kansas State Alumni Association Wildcat Pride Award

2020 Kindest Kansas Citian Award

2020 Board of Trustees—William Jewell College
2021 Tom Osborne Legacy Award
2021 St. Joseph Area Sports Hall of Fame
William Jewell College Hall of Fame inductee
Lafayette High School Hall of Fame inductee
Outstanding Career by Jewish Community Center of Greater Kansas City
Chairperson of YMCA in St. Joseph, Missouri
Alpha Tau Omega Outstanding Campus Leader Award
Kiwanis International Tablet of Honor Award
Via Christi Hospitals "Be The Difference" Certificate of Recognition
Department of Veterans Affairs Certificate of Appreciation
Kansas State Student Government Commendation for the Snyder Family
NAIA Champion of Character Award
Appreciation Award by the 28th Infantry Black Lions of Fort Riley
215–117–1 overall record in 27 years at Kansas State
One of six coaches in history to win 200 career games and only coach at one
     school
School-record 11 wins in 1997, 1998, 1999, 2000, 2002, 2003, 2012
One of two schools in college football history to win 11 games in six of seven
     years
Finalist for ESPN Coach of the Decade for the 1990s
Eight consensus All-American honors
216 All-American honors, including 81 first-team All-American honors
284 All-Conference honors since 1993, including a school-record 20 in 2012
15 Academic All-American honors
10 CFA national scholar-athletes
Six National Football Foundation postgraduate scholars
313 Academic All-Conference honors
47-year member of the American Football Coaches Association

ACKNOWLEDGMENTS

As you have read in the book, my mother, Marionetta Snyder was—and remains—the most loved and significant person in my life. Her passion for raising, guiding, and providing for her only child in such a meaningful, loving, caring, and disciplined way will forever be embraced.

This book is for her and my maternal grandparents, George and Marie Owens, who were always there for me and my mother and who guided us toward faith-based lives. They, too, were special, caring, and loving people.

I have been truly blessed to have an amazingly wonderful family, which continually grows in a beautiful way—28 members going on 30. We are so very proud of each of the five children, who are each special in their own way, and nine grandchildren, who are also so very special. One of those grandchildren, Matt, we lost. Matt was a very gracious, friendly, and caring young man who will never be forgotten and will always be remembered with deep heartfelt love and appreciation, as are each of the other children, grandchildren, and great-grandchildren.

As most people know, each of the children—Sean, Shannon, Meredith, Ross, and Whitney—attended and graduated from Kansas State University. Three of them participated in varsity athletics at Kansas State. Sean was a consensus All-American punter, a record holder, and is in the football stadium Ring of Honor and Kansas State Athletics Hall of Fame. Ross also was a member of our football program after playing at Manhattan High School, where he also competed in the wrestling program. Whitney was an All-American equestrian rider at Kansas State. All of our college-aged grandchildren—Tate, Katherine, and Sydney—graduated from Kansas State, and another granddaughter, Alexis, is presently attending school there. Our other grandchildren—Gavin, Kadin, and Tylin—have expressed their desire to follow their cousins. And two-year-old Lou Ann is somewhat uncertain, as are our great-grandchildren—D.J., DeClan, Pearce, Sawyer, and Murphy.

Thirdly, I want to thank those special people who contributed dearly to my career and my life at each stop along the way. My gratitude goes to so many players, coaches, staff members, fans, high school and university/college teachers, administrators, and students who formed our "football family" at each coaching stop throughout my life. And a heartfelt recognition for the two administrative assistants who guided me during my 27 years at Kansas State—Joan Friederich and Teresa Williams along with two special office aids at the University of Iowa—Rita Foley and Debbie Abbott. In fact, we could fill this book with only names of the special people who provided assistance, guidance, care, and love throughout my life.

And my appreciation to the cowriter of this book, Scott Fritchen, who also authored *Expect to Win: Stories about Kansas State Football Coach Bill Snyder, His Program and His Players*. Scott is a bright young author who has penned thousands upon thousands of words addressing athletics and has done so in a very unique, caring, creative, and passionate manner.

—Bill Snyder

"I'm going to write stories about that man someday!"

I was a 16 year old experiencing my first Kansas State football game. I spotted Kansas State head football coach Bill Snyder standing on the sideline in the final seconds of a last-minute, come-from-behind 16–12 victory against Kansas in Manhattan on October 12, 1991. Students tore down the south goal posts to celebrate Coach Snyder's first of many wins against the in-state rival in the Sunflower Showdown.

I stood with my parents, Dave and Kay Fritchen, and my younger brother, Steve, in the west side stands of the stadium and soaked it all in. It already felt like home. My parents, natives of nearby Council Grove, are proud Kansas State alums. So were my grandparents, who lived near Wichita and purchased the tickets so we all could enjoy the game. We flew in from

Washington, D.C. My father, a naval officer, was stationed at the Pentagon. Over the years, we had visited Manhattan when we visited family in the summer. But, man, this was something else. It was like a dream.

At birth, I wanted to attend Kansas State University, and at age 10, I wanted to be a sportswriter. What I didn't know was that my passion for sportswriting and Kansas State would evolve into a 27-year labor of love. And I absolutely didn't know that exactly 30 years after I spoke my future into existence by proclaiming that I would write stories about Bill Snyder and that I would be blessed with the profound gift of helping tell the life story of the man who engineered the greatest turnaround in the history of college football. He brought excitement to Kansas State and Manhattan. He taught young men about appropriate values that would prepare them for success in all facets of their lives. He was king of the 18-hour workday, an offensive innovator, a willing volunteer for statewide leadership initiatives who wrote handwritten notes for every occasion and never went a day without calling his five children.

It is an incredible journey, and I hope you enjoy it.

I want to recognize Kansas State sports information, Iowa sports information, *Sports Illustrated*, ESPN, Sporting News, the Associated Press, CBS Sports, NBC Sports, Athlon Sports, *The Kansas City Star*, *The Topeka Capital-Journal*, *The Manhattan Mercury*, *The Dallas Morning News*, *The Oklahoman*, *Lincoln Journal Star*, *The Desert Sun*, *St. Joseph News-Press,* and Powercat Illustrated/GoPowercat.com for providing some particular details involving Bill Snyder, Kansas State, or Iowa football and/or statistical data related to Bill Snyder, Kansas State, or Iowa football that were used in researching this book. Chapter-opening quotes came from the Kansas State Sports Information Department, Kansas State football media guides, and my interviews over the years.

Thank you, God, for restoring, establishing, strengthening, and confirming me and for opening this door so that I might share this wonderful experience with Coach. Thank you, Coach, for the immeasurable ways that you continue to impact my life, the lives of my family, and the lives of countless others across the country in so many special ways.

Thank you, Mom, Dad, and Steve, for your limitless support throughout my life. Thank you, Kaylee, as the joy of my life truly is the blessing of being your father. Words fail to describe how much I love each of you.

—D. Scott Fritchen